THE SIEGE OF LONDONDERRY

The Siege of Londonderry

PIERS WAUCHOPE

FOUR COURTS PRESS

Set in 10.5 pt on 12.5 pt Ehrhardt MT for
FOUR COURTS PRESS LTD
7 Malpas Street, Dublin 8, Ireland
www.fourcourtspress.ie
and in North America for
FOUR COURTS PRESS
c/o IPG, 814 N Franklin St, Chicago, IL 60610

A catalogue record for this title is available
from the British Library.

ISBN 978-1-80151-062-2

Printed in England
by CPI Antony Rowe, Chippenham, Wilts.

Contents

Preface

IN THE SEVENTY YEARS since Cecil Davis Milligan wrote, after painstaking research, his *Siege of Londonderry* in 1951, there have been four other books devoted to this subject. There are nevertheless two good reasons for writing yet another. Milligan recognized the first of these. At the time of his death in 1956, he was working on a second book on the siege. His obituary, in the newspaper he edited, reads: 'He was fortunate, about five years ago, to be able to secure from the French military archives copies of the despatches sent from the French armies aiding King James in his attack on Derry, and he had made good progress in drafting what would have been his greatest book.'[1] This book is an attempt to carry out the project that Milligan was prevented from completing, a task that has been made immeasurably easier now that the despatches referred to in his obituary have been published by the Irish Manuscripts Commission.

There is also much material that has been overlooked in collections outside Ireland, notably in the British Library (which holds Michelburne's writings on the siege) and the National Records of Scotland (which has Lundie's account). This material collectively allows a fresh analysis based on sources that have not before been used in any of the histories.

The second reason for writing this book is as important. The two earliest printed histories of the siege, George Walker's *A true account of the siege of London-Derry* (1689) and John Mackenzie's *Narrative of the siege of London-Derry* (1690) have never satisfactorily been evaluated for what they are: wartime accounts published in London for a wartime readership. These two accounts have been adopted as the primary sources and the arguments as to their accuracy have by and large been confined to the question of party bias displayed by these writers. The chief complaints against Walker have been made by Presbyterians; the chief complaints against Mackenzie have been made by Church of Ireland men.

In my view, this is the wrong approach. It does not lay any, or at least sufficient, emphasis on the readership for whom the two accounts were written, and gives wholly improper emphasis and validity to Walker's *Account* as a history of the siege. It also then ignores Mackenzie's stated aim, to write a narrative, albeit for a wartime readership, 'to Rectifie the Mistakes, and supply the Omissions of Mr. *Walker*'s Account'. Mackenzie's intention 'to Rectifie' is important. These primary sources are not two contemporary accounts each independent of the other on which one may write a composite history by compounding them. One is corrective of the other.

The purpose of the corrections is also important. Mackenzie found particular fault with both the part that Walker gave himself in the siege, and with Walker's failure to acknowledge the contribution of the Presbyterians who made up the majority of the defenders. He did not set out to correct Walker's *Account* where it referred to the enemy, except in cases where Walker represented facts that were considered utterly risible at the time. In writing his *Narrative*, Mackenzie adopted much of what Walker wrote, including daily lists of rationing and the garrison's declining strength throughout the siege, but rather than challenge what he considered to be the many inaccuracies in Walker's *Account,* he simply excluded them.

To take a prime example, Walker described Irish miners getting under the walls. Mackenzie is simply silent on this. He made no mention of Irish miners because he knew there were no miners, Irish or otherwise, and the geography of the city prevented there being any. Mackenzie did not refer to Walker's claim so that he could contradict it, he simply ignored it.

In the same way, Mackenzie passed over the inaccuracies to be found in the many false and imaginative accounts that had by then appeared in London newssheets and pamphlets. His position was simply that if an event was not mentioned in his *Narrative*, it did not happen, and if it was not described as he described it, it was wrong. Mackenzie later corrected some of Walker's inventions in the pamphlet war that followed, but confined his criticisms to those passages in the *Account* where Mackenzie felt that Walker had falsely depicted himself as a heroic figure. Mackenzie read all that Walker wrote, and left out much for a reason. It was because Walker was untruthful.

The many falsehoods in Walker's *Account* prevent him from being used as a credible or trustworthy witness. Everything he wrote needs to be approached with considerable caution, but Mackenzie's own *Narrative* is also greatly debased both by his own inaccuracies, and by his ill-judged, exaggerated and bitter personal attacks on Walker. Most writers have since recognized (and often condemned) the vindictive flaws in Mackenzie's *Narrative*, but have used them to ignore the far greater flaws in Walker's *Account*.

This book aims to analyse and evaluate these accounts alongside the other sources that have since come to light.

I owe a great debt of gratitude to Professor James McGuire of the Royal Irish Academy and to Dr Harman Murtagh of the Military History Society of Ireland for their help and encouragement over the years, to Dr Helen Glanville in all matters concerning the French language of the seventeenth century, to Sam Tranum, my editor at Four Courts Press, and to Sarah Sherrington for providing the maps. No book on this subject would be worth writing without the work of the late Dr Sheila Mulloy, the transcriber and editor of the *Franco-Irish correspondence.* Labouring for years, upstairs in her home in Mayo with a film projector to display the microfilmed text on a bedroom wall, she copied out for publication the often nearly illegible handwritten despatches, and received as her only financial reward a modest sum for preparing an index.

I have used, throughout, seventeenth-century place-names (such as Newtown Limavady for Limavady, Dawson's Bridge for Castledawson and so on), but I am conscious that this may be a sensitive area to some. I have chosen the title because in the seventeenth century the city of London built a great stronghold in Ireland and called it Londonderry, and that is what was sieged. I am indebted to Professor McGuire for his guidance on this and I have followed the example of the earliest siege writers by referring to the city both as Londonderry and Derry, as is illustrated by the use of the city's two names in the title used by Walker: *A true account of the siege of London-Derry by the Reverend Mr. George Walker, rector of Donoghmore in the county of Tyrone and late governor of Derry in Ireland.*

Throughout, I have referred to the Williamites as the rebels simply because, at the start of this history, they certainly were rebels against their undisputed lawful king (albeit, in some quarters, an unpopular one) and his government in Dublin. I have also referred to the governor before the siege as Robert Lundie as, although his contemporaries often spelt his name as Lundy, that was his family name and that is how he signed himself.

As is the practice in all the siege histories, I have adopted the Old Style calendar for the dates, starting the year on 1 January, and have adjusted the New Style calendar dates (which in 1689 were ten days in advance) given in the French correspondence.

Piers Wauchope
On the 333rd anniversary of the siege

Illustrations

MAPS

PLATES APPEAR BETWEEN PAGES 160 AND 161.

Dramatis personae

Aickin, Joseph. Not present in the siege, author of the epic poem *Londerias* in 1699.

Ash, Thomas. Militia captain, author of *A circumstantial journal* of the siege.

Baker, Henry. Soldier and joint governor (with Walker) during the siege.

Bennett, Joseph. Captain, author of the *True and impartial account.*

Blayney, Henry Vincent, baron. Colonel of Monaghan volunteers.

Buchan, Thomas. Scottish brigadier in King James' army.

Cairnes, David. Lawyer and courier to and from London.

Cunningham, John. Colonel and commander of first relief expedition.

d'Astier, Paul-François de Lozières. French engineer in King James' army.

d'Avaux, Jean-Antoine de Mesmes, comte. King Louis' ambassador to King James.

Fumeron, Jean-Francois. King James' paymaster.

Hamilton, Gustavus. Governor of Coleraine, Lundie's major and later lieutenant colonel.

Hamilton, Gustavus. Governor of Enniskillen.

Hamilton, Richard. King James' lieutenant general in Ireland.

Holmes, George. Militia captain.

Irwin, William. The boy messenger.

James II. King of England, Scotland and Ireland from 1685.

Kirke, Percy. Major general and commander of second relief expedition.

Louis XIV. King of France.

Louvois, François-Michel le Tellier, marquis de. King Louis' minister of war.

Lundie, Robert. Colonel and governor before the siege.

Mackenzie, John. Presbyterian minister and author of the *Narrative*.

Massé, Jean-François, sieur de. French engineer.

Maumont, Jaques de Fontanges, marquis de. Lieutenant general in King James' army.

Michelburne, John. Lieutenant, later colonel and (with Walker) joint governor.

Mount-Alexander, Hugh Montgomery, earl of. Commander of the Northern Association.

Mountjoy, Sir William Stewart, Viscount. Colonel of regiment of foot.

Murray, Adam. Farmer, militia colonel.

Plunkett, Nicholas. Author of the *Jacobite narrative*.

Pointis, Jean-Bernard de Saint-Jean, baron de. Architect of the boom.

Pusignan Jean le Camus, marquis de. Major general in King James' army.

Richards, Jacob. Colonel, Kirke's artillery officer.

Richards, Solomon. Colonel of regiment in Cunningham's relief expedition.

Ramsay, Robert. Brigadier in King James' army.

Rawdon, Sir Arthur. Colonel of dragoons.

Roche, James. 'The swimmer', messenger from Kirke to the city.

Rosen, Conrad de. The marshal or general of King James' army in Ireland.

Tollymore, James Hamilton of. Conspirator.

Tyrconnell, Richard Talbot, duke of. King James' viceroy of Ireland.

Walker, George. Clergyman, joint governor of Derry, and author of the *Account*.

Wauchope, John. Colonel in King James' army.

William III. Prince of Orange and (with Queen Mary) king of England from 1689.

Prologue

On 9 August 1689, George Walker, a middle-aged Church of England clergyman, sailed down Lough Foyle on a merchant ship on his way to Scotland. He had survived a 105-day siege, which had devasted Londonderry. Behind him he left a city in ruins and some ten thousand Protestant corpses, mostly women and children. Some had met violent deaths, but most had died from starvation or the 'pestilential fever' that had raged through the city. The countryside, as viewed from the lough, was barren. All the villages, the houses and outbuildings had been burnt down, and the cattle and sheep had disappeared.

It had been the most eventful year of Walker's life. For decades, he had been the rector of a quiet rural parish some fifteen miles from Armagh. When the Irish army had marched north to flatten the Protestant rebellion in March of that year, he fled to Derry and was there when the Irish invested the city. He had proved himself cleverer and more subtle than the military men he had been forced to deal with, and had pushed himself to the front. Throughout the siege he had been a joint governor, or the civil governor, or, as he put it, 'The Governor', and now his was the best-known name in the three kingdoms. He left Londonderry in triumph, and was now going to deliver a 'humble address' to the king. His reception was certain. He had saved the nation.

His arrival in Scotland was one great fête. He was made a burgess and guild brother of the corporation of Glasgow. He continued to Edinburgh where the lord provost made him a burgess and guild brother of that city as well. One of his travelling companions, Captain Archibald MacCullough, as if to demonstrate the horrors they had suffered together, brought the illness with him and was too sick to travel any further. Walker went on without him. From Edinburgh he travelled in a coach to Chester, where he was welcomed by the mayor and was mobbed by admirers. 'When he walks abroad the people accompany him, gather in knots around him, surround him and follow him in crowds. Admitting him as if he had dropped from heaven, they gaze and stare intently at him; his words they drink into their eager and greedy ears.' They threw a feast in his honour, where 'he was handsomely entertained with dessert and wine', and 'he told a number of amusing and authentic anecdotes'. They loved his amusing anecdotes. 'Strange tales he told.' And he loved telling them. 'He gives many and wondrous narratives of victories rescued from defeats, of the fortunes of the war, of the destitution, and the deliverance, of the deeds and the sufferings, of the valour and the exertions of the townspeople.'

From Chester he travelled south. He was 'highly Complemented and Caressed by all sorts of People on the Road'. It was the progress of a hero. 'His company is very Acceptable to all who are well wishers to the Protestant interest.' When he reached Barnet, he was collected by a private coach and made a quiet entry into London to avoid the crowds that were waiting to welcome him. In his first week in London, he travelled to Hampton Court where he met the king and presented his 'humble address' from the officers, clergy and gentlemen of Londonderry. Everyone loved him. The king gave him £5,000, then a life-changing figure, and 'assured him of his further kindness, and that he would also have a care of the other officers and gentlemen in Derry'. He was fêted everywhere. 'Mr. Walker is caressed by all sorts of people', noted Narcissus Luttrell, 'and entertained at dinner'.

In London, he took lodgings on Fetter Lane just off Fleet Street. He set about publishing his account of the sufferings and sacrifices of the city that had held out against tyranny. The first of many editions of his *True account of the siege of London-Derry* appeared on the booksellers' stalls three weeks after his arrival.

Perhaps he simply shut himself away and wrote rapidly from his notes and his memory. But in the midst of all the excitement and the feasting and the mobs of happy admirers, this is highly unlikely. What almost certainly happened is that he fell into the hands of what we would now call publicists: journalists and booksellers who wanted to get the message out. Walker had never published anything before and, with proper handling, there was a lot of money to be made.

His tale was a simple narrative of misery and triumph, but it needed more. For the first time in a generation, England was at war, and the country needed a heartening tale of English bravery. The book men took his jottings and improved them greatly. They questioned him and added the things that he had been too modest to mention. Or, indeed, added things that had not happened. They wanted to know more not so much about the siege, which was but a backdrop to his adventures, but more about what he did in the siege. Was he the governor of the city? Yes, he was. Was he a witness to this particular incident? Yes, he was. They got him to leave it to them. They would make sure it was alright. They could work out what he did in the siege. Other participants were not important to the account that needed to be given. Walker's role, wherever it was peripheral, was placed at the centre of events.

All this happened in London. Walker, flattered by the hospitality and admiration of others, lost control of the publication. Those with a better idea of what would sell wrote it for him. The book became about him. In some cases, instances of sheer improbability were added. He may well have objected to certain passages. He may have been overruled. Other passages were no doubt added amid thigh-slapping laughter at the audacious nature of the claims. By the time the book reached the printer, it drew a sketch of the siege of Londonderry that Walker would barely have recognized, and a picture of him that no one recognized.

What made his *Account* so very special was that the siege was brought alive by his presence. It was the history of how George Walker saved the city. No Englishman could read Walker's *Account* without feeling a glow of pride in what a fellow countryman had done. It described the trials and tribulations of a country clergyman with a small living in a village in Co. Tyrone. It was a tale of an ordinary, good man, albeit an ingenious one, showing leadership against great odds, fighting off the jealousies of others inside Londonderry, and fighting off a savage enemy outside the walls. He had inspired not only his flock, but the whole city. He had won over the faint hearts and brought everyone together. He had directed the military strategy, led by example and exposed himself to great danger. He had done so for the king and queen, for the Protestant religion and for his country. His tale was an inspiration to the whole English nation.

The siege of Londonderry was to become the most iconic event in Ulster's history. It epitomized the hard-fought struggle of a beleaguered people enduring the worst of hardships while standing up against tyranny and superstition. And for centuries to come, Walker's *Account* was to be taken by commentators and historians as the solid foundation on which rests the history of the siege.

A true account of the siege of London-Derry by the Reverend Mr George Walker, rector of Donoghmore in the county of Tyrone and late governor of Derry in Ireland was inspired, as we would now say, by a true story. It was the publishing sensation of the year, and was unmatched for many years to come. *Robinson Crusoe,* inspired by the adventures of Alexander Selkirk, was published in 1719, and the author, Daniel Defoe, was hailed as the first English novelist. With the assistance of the London booksellers, Walker had beaten him to it by thirty years.

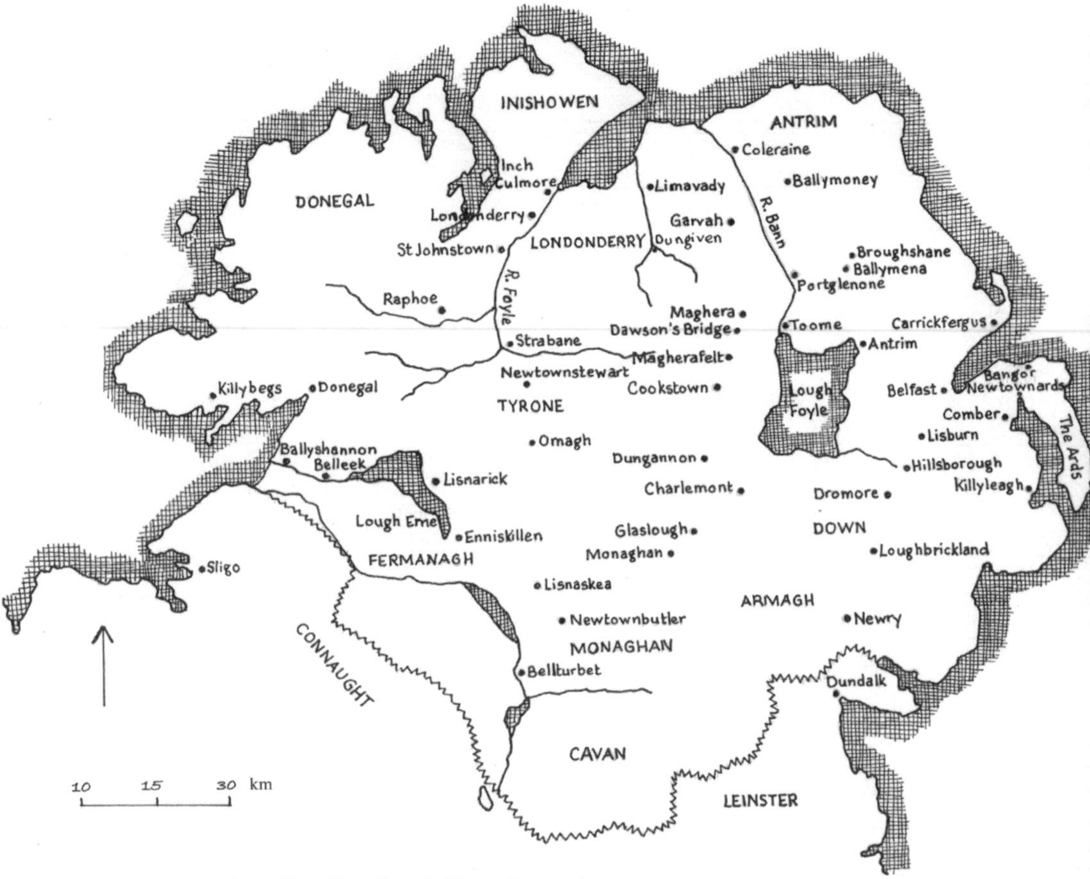

1 Ulster in 1689. (By Sarah Sherrington)

Introduction

THE MIDDLE YEARS of the seventeenth century were disrupted by civil war. Overwhelmingly in these islands the war was fought by Protestants against Protestants. Scottish and English armies fought the Irish and each other in Ireland. The Scots and English fought each other in England and Scotland, and the English and the Scots fought among themselves at home.

In Ireland, the war began at the end of 1641 when the Gaels, especially the Ulster Gaels, rose up in rebellion with the aim of driving out the English once and for all. The violence against the settlers was so unexpected that it took the government forces by surprise. They held what they could from the rebels, but reinforcements were not quick in coming. While the worst of the massacres were being committed in Ireland, England descended into civil war.

The massacres of 1641 and early 1642 became engrained in the Protestant consciousness. It became widely (and absurdly) believed that a hundred thousand Protestants – men, women and children – had been butchered in the most terrible circumstances. The reaction, when it came, was fearful. Massacres were followed by counter-massacres of such violence that modern scholarship is of the opinion that 'it is far from clear on which side the balance of cruelty rests'.[1] But two generations later, in 1689, the Protestants who fled to Londonderry had no doubt that civil war included the real threat of widespread massacre. That fear explains why, of the thirty thousand people crammed behind the walls in the spring of 1689, twenty thousand of them, rather than go home when promised the king's protection, elected to stay in the city in the face of a besieging army and put themselves and their families at risk to the dangers by which half of them perished.

When the 1641 rebellion broke out, Londonderry served both as a refuge and a base for the settlers, and was held first by the royalists and then the parliamentarians. In March 1649 it was attacked by a royalist army, known as 'the Laggan army' or 'the Lagganeers', formed of Scots settlers from the Laggan area around Raphoe. The Laggan army enjoyed a successful war against the Irish, but in April 1649, the English garrison troops under Charles Coote sallied out, defeated the Lagganeers and captured their commander. It was the first time since the beginning of the civil war that Protestant settlers had killed fellow Protestant settlers on the battlefield, and was the first defeat suffered by the Laggan army. Joined by a larger army of Ulster Scots in May 1649, the Lagganeers besieged Derry throughout the summer. Relief came only after Monck, the parliamentarian general in Dundalk, made a three-month truce with Owen Roe O'Neill the former 'lord general' of the Irish

Confederate forces. In August 1649, O'Neill reached Ballykelly at the head of an army of Ulster Gaels, and the Lagganeers were forced to abandon the siege. 'Upon the arrival of O'Neill at Derry, he encamped on the opposite side of the river, where Coote went to compliment him and his officers, and afterwards entertained them most splendidly.'[2]

It must be that some of the Irish who besieged the city in 1689 were the sons or grandsons of those of those who had relieved the city in 1649. Some of those besieged inside the city in 1689 were the sons or grandsons of the Lagganeers and Scots who attacked it in 1649. Some of the older inhabitants of Derry in 1689 would have lived through the first siege when the Lagganeers attacked them until they were rescued by the Irish.

Peace in Ireland was brought about by the Cromwellian conquest, which pitched parliamentarian Protestant against royalist Protestant. 'Between the siege [of Londonderry in 1649] and the end of 1650, a period of little more than one year, more Ulster settlers were killed by the parliamentary forces (in which fellow settlers were well represented) than had been killed by the rebels since 1641.'[3] The Cromwellian land settlement dispossessed the royalists, which included most of the Catholic landowners. A longer-lasting peace came to the three kingdoms by way of the restoration of the monarchy. In Ireland a Protestant parliament was called in 1661 and it passed the Act of Settlement to rectify the division of land made by the Cromwellians in the previous decade.

Population growth in Ulster after the Restoration was greatly fed by Scots immigration. Most were driven by poverty, but a substantial number were driven by the state of unrest, especially in south-western Scotland, brought about by the bloody struggle by the Covenanters for Presbyterian control of church and state. Many of the newly arrived Presbyterians in Ulster saw themselves as the victims of state persecution. The Scottish state saw them as a threat to the peace. When King James came to the throne in 1685, Ulster was quiet, but the greater part of the Protestant population was Scots, brought up on a hatred of Catholicism, a mistrustful acceptance of the English, and a dread of the Irish.

The war in Ireland of 1689–91 would not have been fought had it not been for the extraordinary influence that Richard Talbot had over James, duke of York. When the duke of York became King James II, succeeding his brother in 1685, he ennobled Talbot as the earl of Tyrconnell and sent him to Ireland to reform the Irish army, which then was made up entirely of Protestants. Commissions were cancelled and new commissions issued. Men were dismissed and replaced by new, Catholic levies. Tyrconnell, as he then was (and will be referred to from now on), had at all times one great plan in mind. He wanted to break the Act of Settlement and restore to the Catholic owners the lands they had before the 1641 rebellion. His interest was not in the Gaels, but those who in Irish terms were the 'Old English' or the 'Anglo-Irish', the Catholic landowners who had lost everything during the Cromwellian settlement and had gained far too little under the Act of Settlement.

King James promoted Tyrconnell to lieutenant general and in 1687 made him the lord deputy of Ireland. Tyrconnell then turned his attention to the judiciary and local government as a prelude to reforming parliament in order to carry out his principal aim, the repeal of the Act of Settlement. It was an enormous task, and carried out by a consummate politician. While Tyrconnell forced through the changes, everything was denied while it was plainly happening, and everyone could see what Tyrconnell planned. The Catholics were expectant of the great changes that the restoration of estates and power would bring. The Protestants were fearful.

2

The Comber letter

THE CITY OF LONDONDERRY was new in that it had been built at the beginning of the seventeenth century by the Society of the Governor and Assistants of London of the New Plantation in Ulster ('the Irish Society') on what had been a vacant site alongside the ruins of the old monastery of St Colmcille. The English had arrived in 1565 and chased away the monastic community, but, following a fire in 1566 that resulted in the destruction of the old church, the English garrison left. In 1600 Sir Henry Dowcra reoccupied the site, which had been uninhabited for three decades. All that remained were 'the ruins of an old abbey, of a bishop's house, of two churches, and at one of the ends of it an old castle'.

Dowcra built two forts and some houses on the site, and left a garrison that in 1608 was overrun by Sir Cahir O'Doherty. The governor was killed and the settlement was 'wholly spoiled, ransacked and fired'. The English returned to the ruins later that year and began rebuilding. In 1609, the decision was taken for a permanent colony or plantation of Londoners, and in 1613 the Irish Society was incorporated in the City of London to provide the finance to build and fortify the town. In that year King James I granted 'the city, fort and town of Derry, and the whole island of Derry' to the society, and renamed the town 'the city of Londonderry'.[1]

The new city was built alongside the river Foyle on a low hill that itself was almost an island. On the east side was the river, and the whole extent of the western boundary of the island was a 'wet bog' or slob, over which the tide flowed freely, so that the two roads into the city from the south and the west were over causeways. 'The circumference of the hill or island is of an oval form; the hill ascends to the height of 119 feet above the level of the Foyle, and contains 199 acres.'[2] Completed in 1619, and just under a mile in circumference, the walls extend down the north-eastern slope of Derry Hill from the crest at Bishop's Gate and the cathedral to Shipquay Gate on the riverside, overlooking steep slopes down to the bog on one side and the river on the other. Captain Joseph Bennett, who wrote an account of the beginning of the siege, described the defences as they appeared in 1689:

> The outward Wall being about 21 or 22 Foot high, and of a great thickness, and the inward Wall rising as high or near the heighth of a Man of the outward Wall, and between these two, Earth filled up in the middle, whereon eight or ten men may walk in Breast, so that no Gun can batter it to make a Breach.

There were four gates, nine bastions mounted with cannon, and 'a dry Ditch round the Town, over which there are two Draw-bridges, one at Bishopsgate, and the other at Ferry-Key-Gate; but in some places this Ditch is filled up, not being kept clean for a long time'.[3]

Although then only the sixth largest town in Ireland, as a walled market borough, a port, a garrison town and a bishopric, Derry was 'the most considerable City in the Province of Ulster'. Nevertheless, fewer than two thousand people lived within Derry's walls in 1688. The seventeenth-, and even the late eighteenth-century maps show there were fewer than two hundred houses built in rows along the streets, and that the area within the walls was mostly occupied by gardens.[4]

In 1688 Tyrconnell carried out his local government reforms. Protestant corporations of towns such as Londonderry were set aside, and new charters were issued wherein all corporation members had to be approved by Dublin. When Londonderry refused to comply, the government issued a writ of *Quo warranto* ('By what authority') that was upheld by the court. On 13 August 1688 a new corporation was appointed, with its members selected by the Dublin government. Although at least sixteen of the Protestant aldermen and burgesses stayed on, as did the two sheriffs, two-thirds of the members were Catholics. The new mayor chosen was Cormack O'Neill, one of Tyrconnell's new colonels, a substantial landowner in Antrim and, nominally, at least for the time being, a Protestant. He had no connection with Derry, and no real intention of forming one. The idea was to have the corporation run as before, but with a reserve of Catholic members from across Ulster who could be called upon to attend should their votes be needed, in particular when the time came to select a member of parliament.

O'Neill came to the city to be sworn in, appointed Alderman John Buchanan, a Protestant merchant, to stand in as his deputy, and then left for good, as did all the Catholic members. Buchanan's willingness to collaborate with the new regime by taking up the mayor's duties made him from that time on, something of a pariah.[5]

The Protestant population in the northern counties looked to England for relief. By the end of September 1688, unsettling rumours abounded that the prince of Orange was planning to invade England. The feeling in the north became more frantic, but, for the majority of Protestants, this was not a time to take any action. If the government in England changed, then Tyrconnell would fall. In the meantime, it would be better to remain quiet and watch. But there were those who felt that the time for action had come.

The year 1688 proved to be one of great change. On 10 June, the queen, who had been married to King James for fifteen years, gave birth to a son, James Edward Stewart, the new prince of Wales. There was now a Catholic successor to the throne. In England, feeling against James was heightened by his Declaration of Indulgence, which sought to dispense with those laws enacted by Parliament concerning the established church and the employment of those who are not members of the church. He ordered his declaration to be read out in all the churches. Seven of his bishops refused and were indicted for seditious libel. Their trial sharpened both anti-Catholic feeling and the national hostility towards the king, and their acquittal on 30 June 1688 was met with great rejoicing throughout the country.

On that same day, a letter was signed by seven peers of the realm inviting the prince of Orange to invade England. Referring to the royal child, the letter affirmed that 'not one in a thousand here believes [him] to be the Queen's'. Throughout the kingdom 'nineteen parts of twenty of the people' wanted change. The army is 'very much divided', officers were discontented and 'very many' of the soldiers would desert in the face of an invasion. Of the seamen, 'not one in ten' would serve to stop a Dutch fleet.

James had at first taken reports of Dutch invasion preparations less than seriously, but William was a desperate man and had been planning the invasion of England since the year before. While his ally the Holy Roman emperor devoted his resources to beating the Turks, William was facing the full might of Louis XIV who had taken territory after territory on France's eastern border. English neutrality was not enough for William. He needed England to be committed to war against the French. Now that he had been invited to invade by men at the highest level, and had been assured that he would be welcomed, the time was right. The great question became not whether the Dutch would invade, but who would win when they did. James needed as many troops as he could get. He ordered Tyrconnell to ship over from Ireland a battalion of guards and three regiments 'with all diligence and speed possible'.

By 10 October 1688, the Dutch invasion fleet was ready, and Prince William issued a five-thousand-word declaration. His reasons for coming to England, were to preserve the Protestant religion and to restore 'the laws and liberties of England, Scotland, and Ireland'. King James' 'evil counsellors' (a phrase he used twenty times in the text) had subverted the state, and had published that the queen has had a son while 'not only we ourselves, but all the good subjects of these Kingdoms, do vehemently suspect that the pretended Prince of Wales was not born by the Queen'. He would rid King James of the evil counsellors by calling a parliament. He separately assured the emperor that he had 'not the least intention … to make an attempt upon the crown, nor wish to appropriate it for myself'. The new 'pretended' royal baby aside, his wife was next in line to the throne of the three kingdoms, and so he and she were duty bound to intervene.

The prince of Orange sailed for England with fifteen thousand men and set foot on English soil at Torbay on 5 November 1688. Gathering his army on Salisbury Plain, King James sent an order to Tyrconnell to ship to England another Irish regiment 'with all diligence and speed possible'. William waited three weeks in the West Country. The longer he waited, the stronger he became, and the strain on the English army began to tell. The business of the loyal officers became one of preventing troops from joining the invaders. On 20 November the king sent fresh orders to Tyrconnell for troops. His secretary of state added a rider: 'We shall stand in need of all the assistance you can give us.'

The urgent demands from England for soldiers meant that the regiments in Ireland were marched to the ports to find transport. Newly raised regiments, all of them Catholic, were ordered to take their places as garrisons. Lord Mountjoy's regiment, which had been the Londonderry garrison for the past three years under the command of Lieutenant Colonel Robert Lundie, was ordered to march for Dublin by 23 November. They were to be relieved by Lord Antrim's newly raised regiment, but Antrim's regiment had not yet finished recruiting, was unarmed, had no uniforms and the deadline did not give it enough time to get to Derry. The desperate state of affairs in England did not allow for any delay, and the result was that Londonderry was left ungarrisoned until Antrim's regiment could get there. It left open a window of opportunity.

On 23 November, the same day that Lundie marched his men out of Londonderry, King James called a council of war at the camp on Salisbury Plain. His troops could not be relied on to fight, and it was unanimously decided to withdraw towards London. The next day, the army began to crumble. Lieutenant General Lord Churchill and the king's nephew, the duke of Grafton, deserted. They were followed by the dukes of Ormonde and Northumberland, and by Prince George of Denmark, King James' son-in-law.

In Ireland, the Protestants hoped that the country would return fairly painlessly to the happy days enjoyed under Charles II. The land question would be finally buried, and the violence promised by the worst of the Catholics and the worst of the Protestants could be avoided. But Tyrconnell was determined to re-establish the pre-civil war balance of power by overturning the Restoration settlement in favour of those Catholics who held land in the reign of Charles I. That would never be acceptable to an English parliament, and would inevitably lead to war. There were also Protestants who favoured a new Cromwellian-style settlement under which lands that had been restored to the Irish at the Restoration would be seized. That also could not be achieved without war.

One man, now long forgotten and generally overlooked by history, but of great influence at the time, was James Hamilton of Tollymore,[A] Co. Down.[6] Greatly encouraged by most of the army being ordered to England, Tollymore began gathering together those who would resist Tyrconnell by force if necessary.[7] He got an easy audience from those who had just been stripped of their positions in the army, including the two dynamic, young, titled Ulstermen Sir Arthur Rawdon (of Monea, Co. Down) and Lord Blayney (of Castleblayney, Co. Monaghan), and those who lived in fear of losing their estates should Tyrconnell repeal the Acts of Settlement.

Under Tollymore's direction, the Northern Association, or 'the Association' as it became known, began to gather support. Protestants pledged themselves to join the Association's forces in preparation for war. In Down and Antrim, they

[A] There are so many Hamiltons and, indeed, James Hamiltons in the coming narrative, that from now on in the text he is referred to (in the Scots fashion) with reference to his estate.

appointed officers and mustered volunteer troops. The Association needed a general. None of the northern nobility would join (other than Lord Blayney, who was too inconsequential to count). The two leading titled Protestants of the north were the lords Mountjoy and Mount-Alexander, both still in their thirties, both of Scots extraction, and both men of great local influence. Mountjoy at the time was the colonel of a regiment of foot, a brigadier, the master general of the ordnance and a member of the privy council of Ireland. He was very much part of the establishment, wholly loyal to the crown, and had every confidence that he could hold Tyrconnell back and steer the country away from trouble. To Tollymore and the conspirators, he was unapproachable.

Tollymore and his people concentrated instead on the senior Protestant peer in Ulster, 38-year-old Hugh Montgomery, the earl of Mount-Alexander. Like Mountjoy, he was a privy councillor, but success had otherwise eluded him. A decent, unambitious man, Mount-Alexander was a peripheral name in Irish politics, with an interest in horse breeding. He was also 'deaf to all arguments' put forward by the conspirators, but they needed to win him over and to achieve that, they would stop at nothing. James Hamilton of Tollymore lit the match that ignited the fuse that started the Irish war. He and his conspirators were dedicated to precipitating all Protestants into action in a way that would personally include Mount-Alexander. They, perhaps Tollymore himself, produced a forged document that incited a three-year war that would cost over a hundred thousand lives in Ireland.

On 3 December 1689, a letter was found lying in the street of Comber, Co. Down. The letter was addressed to Mount-Alexander, who owned the village. It purported to be written by a friendly but anonymous Irishman who wanted to warn Mount-Alexander that the 1641 massacres were to be repeated. The letter asserted that 'all our Irishmen throughout Ireland' were sworn to 'kill and murder' all the Protestants, 'man wife and child' in six days' time on the 9 December.

The 'Comber letter' was without any doubt a hoax, written by those who hoped to force the issue in Ireland. There was no plan for a massacre of the Protestants and in all the years since there has not been a shred of evidence found to suggest otherwise. Nevertheless, in those febrile times, the letter struck home. Similar letters were received in Lisburn and Hillsborough. Copies were ready even before the original had been dropped in the road in Comber. The text was distributed across the country. To ensure that the warning was received in time, four of the northern gentlemen sent an express galloping off to Dublin to warn the Protestants there. The contents of the letter were widely accepted. The effect was electric. In Dublin, some five thousand Protestants appeared in arms that very night and there was over the next few days a rush for shipping to get their families out of the country. Tyrconnell was forced to issue a proclamation to say that it was all untrue, and that there was to be no massacre. England soon had an influx of refugees. Importantly for the conspirators, Mount-Alexander himself was taken in: 'I am convinced' he wrote, 'that a massacre was intended … which made self-defence necessary'. The Association now had a general.[8]

3

The apprentice boys

ON THURSDAY, 6 DECEMBER 1688, a day after the Comber letter arrived in Derry, and three days before the date of the purported general massacre, Lord Antrim's rag-tag regiment of un-uniformed and variously armed recruits marched into Limavady on its way to Derry. Instead of the expected six or eight companies to replace Mountjoy's men, there were at least double the number and they were accompanied by 'great numbers of women and boys, which the Ultoghs[A] always bring along with them when they expect spoil'.[1] Those soldiers without muskets had armed themselves with 'skeans,[B] clubs and other such weapons'. The very sight of them prompted the Protestants to expect the worst.

As the MacDonnells' hereditary interests lay on both sides of the sea, the regiment differed from the other new Irish regiments as it was 'composed of *Highlanders* and *Ulster* Papists'. No part of society was considered as low as that of the highlanders, seen as people ungoverned by the rules of civil behaviour. Their dress was then simply a plaid worn as a cloak over a long shirt, without breeches or stockings. The common mocking term for a Scottish highlander was a 'redshank', a man whose legs were raw and red from exposure to the elements, and the regiment was sneeringly referred to as 'Antrim's redshanks'.

Copies of the Comber letter were received by Alexander Tomkins, one of the Londonderry aldermen, and the landowner George Phillips, who, although not quite yet sixty now lived a quiet life at Newtown Limavady, some seventeen miles away, a martyr to gout.[2] On the following morning, on 7 December, Alderman Tomkins spread the news of the massacre to take place in two days' time. While he was doing this, a message arrived from George Phillips to warn Alderman Samuel Norman not only of the intended massacre but also that Antrim's regiment would arrive that very day. They could expect danger from 'so ill a crew', and should 'take care of their own safety' by causing 'the gates of the city to be shut'. Phillips was no fanatic. This was the assessment of an educated man. His messenger had passed Lord Antrim's recruits on the road, and the leading companies were only two miles from the ferry. The effect was immediate. Phillips' message to Norman served to corroborate the message received by Tomkins. There was to be a massacre, and the instrument of that massacre in Derry was to be Antrim's redshanks.

Here was a dilemma. There was a regiment marching towards them. If that regiment meant them harm, they could lock the gates and keep it out. To do so

[A] An Ultogh is a native of Ulster, an Ulster Gael.

[B] A skean is a long-bladed knife.

they would have to use or threaten armed violence. Any man that did that would be committing an open act of rebellion against the crown. The punishment for rebellion was death. There was no easy choice. Resistance could either prevent a massacre or incite one.

Alderman Tomkins turned to James Gordon, the charismatic but occasional Presbyterian minister of Glendermot, who was busying himself in writing to neighbouring parishes to alert them to the massacre. Gordon was a complete rogue and, in Scotland, a notorious reprobate. He had been excommunicated by the synod of Moray in 1667 for 'rapt'.[B] [3] He fled to Ireland, and on his return to Scotland, on a plea that the young woman had been 'rapt' of her own free will, he was ordered to undergo public humiliation by appearing in sackcloth in kirks throughout Strathbogie, and was barred from holding office or 'the holy ministry' in Moray. He switched to a different synod and took a new ministry in Aberdeenshire, where he was in 1671 again deposed for adultery and for 'swearing, drinking, striking, denying his own subscription, and lying'. He returned to Morayshire and managed to become the minister of Cabrach, but in 1681 was again excommunicated, this time for performing irregular marriages and for fornication with his domestic servant. He ran back to Ireland, where he preached around Derry, was 'turned out' from the Presbytery of Coleraine, and then in 1682 tried to get a Church of Ireland benefice from Bishop Ezekiel Hopkins by informing on Presbyterian plotters. Although Bishop Hopkins paid for the information, he did not believe it. Gordon, in his view, was 'infamous among his own party', 'unfit to be owned of any', and 'to handle such a tool would only smut the hand that toucheth it'.[4]

Like Phillips, Gordon suggested that they shut the gates, and Aldermen Tomkins and Norman consulted the bishop. The bishop was very much against any such action. The dangers were manifest, and it was wholly unrealistic to think that the king would, through his lord deputy, order a sudden massacre of his Protestant subjects, but the mood was against him. Whatever the bishop said, there was a genuine fear that a massacre was intended, and the question became how to keep Antrim's men out without being implicated in the crime. The matter was solved, perhaps Gordon played a part in this, by the city youths being encouraged to shut the gates. In essence a rebellion was incited by the city elders so that they could, if need be, say at a later date that they took no part and could not control these young men whose names they could say they did not know.

In the late morning, three companies of Antrim's men appeared on the other side of the river and waited while two officers were rowed over to present their orders to the deputy mayor, John Buchanan, and discuss the men's quarters. It was the business of the city's sheriffs to arrange quarters, and one of them, Horace Kennedy, let the youths know that he intended to quarter the troops that night on

[B] 'Rapt or ravishing, is that crime, which is committed in the violent carrying away a woman from one place to another, for satisfying the ravisher's lust'. George Mackenzie, *Laws & customs of Scotland* (1678).

the other side of the river. Any action needed to be taken soon. While Buchanan was engaged with the two officers, the first detachment of soldiers landed on the quay, and made their way towards the Ferry Gate. It was here that the citizens got their first sight of them. They were 'a pack of ruffians'.[5]

A group of a dozen or more young men, 'the apprentice boys', armed themselves with swords and raced to the main guard where the city's keys were kept. They threatened the guards, snatched the keys and ran back to the Ferry Gate, where they hauled up the drawbridge and locked the gate, with the Irish troops now only sixty yards away.

Mackenzie named nine 'of the youth' involved: Henry Campsie, William Crookshanks, Robert Sherrard, Daniel Sherrard, Alexander Irwin, James Steward, Robert Morrison, Alexander Cunningham and Samuel Hunt. That number then increased to at least thirteen, as they were 'soon joined' by 'several others' who he did not specify as youths: James Spike, John Cunningham, William Cairns and Samuel Harvey.

It is not clear when the term 'apprentice boys' was first coined. The original sources used terms such as 'the younger sort', 'youths' and 'the boys'; but others referred to 'the townsmen', 'the protestants' or 'the rabble'. Maybe most of them were apprentices, but that does not exclude the possibility of servants or labourers being among their number, or of some of them being well past apprentice age. Alexander Irwin, for instance, could not have been an apprentice as he had an 11-year-old son, who was later to play a crucial part in the siege. In the introduction to his journal of the siege (first printed in 1792), Ash referred to 'a few resolute Apprentice Boys', but we do not know whether he wrote that months, years or decades after the event, or even whether he wrote the introduction himself.[C] [6]

Having secured the Ferry Gate, the youths were joined by a crowd and they ran round the city locking the other three gates. John Buchanan made his way to the marketplace with the two sheriffs, the two officers from Antrim's regiment and a group of worried citizens. The bishop did what he could to calm things, and Buchanan tried to get the youths to hand over the keys. They were shouted down.[7]

In the middle of this muddle there was a musket shot. Henry Campsie, a son of the recently deposed mayor, led a party to the city magazine to seize arms and ammunition. While struggling with the sentry, Campsie was shot in the shoulder. It was not a fatal wound, but the fact that blood had been spilt served to inflame the situation. The magazine was stormed and the sentry was hauled off to gaol under the cuffs and jeers of the crowd.[D] [8] The Irish troops standing outside Ferry Gate were subjected by the townspeople to a harangue from the walls. One of them, James Morrison, shouted out orders to a body of imaginary troops behind him: 'Bring about that great gun here!' The soldiers took the ferry back across the river.

[C] At the time the gates were locked, Ash has it that the two officers had crossed the river while only part of the regiment 'was then near the Waterside'.

[D] Mackenzie named the sentry as Linegar, 'a reputed Papist'.

Although relieved that the Irish troops had been denied entrance, no one wanted to take responsibility. Samuel Norman and John Campsie, the last Protestant mayor, drafted a letter to Lord Mountjoy in whom they had great faith as a decent man and a Protestant. He moved in the highest circles in Dublin, and if anyone could intervene on their behalf with an irate lord deputy, it would be Mountjoy. The rabble had shut the gates. 'We could not refrain them.' They had 'since' learnt of the intended general massacre in Ulster. Friars and priests were gathering great numbers of horses and arms. Terrible threats had been made by the soldiers. Antrim's men had broken into houses and robbed the owners, and one of them had 'without any provocation cut the ferryman almost to the loss of his hand'. But all was now well. The stolen arms had been returned to the magazine. It was a 'most wonderful Providence of God to stir up the mobile[E] for our safety, and preservation of the peace of the kingdom against such bloody attempts as these northern people had formed against us'. They assured Mountjoy of their loyalty to King James, 'to whom we resolve always to bear true faith and allegiance against all disturbers of his government whatsoever', and begged him to intercede with Tyrconnell on their behalf.[9]

In the afternoon, David Cairnes rode into town. Well known to them all, a lawyer and a city burgess, he was as close to being an establishment figure as the Presbyterians had. He assured the excited mob of his support, walked round the walls to encourage the new sentries, and did what he could to win over the nervous citizens. He showed leadership at a time when there was none. That night he called a meeting of the burgesses and aldermen and persuaded them to help him in writing letters to people of influence. Their greatest deficiency was in numbers. Of those able to bear arms, aged from sixteen to sixty, there were only three hundred men in the city, and maybe the same number again in the suburbs. They checked the magazine to find they had powder, match and lead bullets, but only a hundred and fifty serviceable matchlock muskets.[10]

The next day, Saturday 8 December 1688, the day before the massacre was supposed to happen, the city's population began to swell as people from the surrounding country brought their families in.[11] There was a fresh rumour that those few Catholics left in the city intended to set fire to the place that very night. They were chased out. The bishop also rode out of the city, not wanting any part in the rebellion, and went to the bishop's palace in Raphoe to collect his family and flee to London. Alderman Tomkins got the Reverend Gordon to use his influence to get his people to join the city's defenders. Cairnes was in charge, but not in control.

History has nothing bad to record of Alexander MacDonnell, the third earl of Antrim. Although his two grandfathers, Sorley Boy MacDonnell and Hugh O'Neill had been, to the Protestants, the bogeymen of the sixteenth century, he was a cultivated man, then aged seventy-three. After a childless marriage, he remarried late in life and had two children. Having regained his 3,500-acre estate at Glenarm after

[E] 'Mobile', from the Latin, a word now always used in its short form: the 'mob'.

the Restoration, he was the only Catholic magnate in Ulster. When Tyrconnell came to building the new Irish army, Antrim could not be ignored, but he was not involved. He saw the regiment as a means of employment for his illegitimate son, Colonel Daniel MacDonnell.

Lord Antrim followed on behind his men in his coach with his wife and their two young children. News reached him of his regiment's reception in Derry and, rather than press on, he paid a call on George Phillips at Newtown Limavady in the evening. Politeness determined that Phillips invited Lord and Lady Antrim to dine with him and stay the night. If Phillips believed the contents of the Comber letter, he would also have believed that Antrim was planning to have his throat cut sometime after midnight, but the presence of Lady Antrim, their daughter and 8-year-old son was reassuring. It would be unusual for a man to bring his young family along with him if he intended to butcher his host.[F]

On Sunday, 9 December 1688, the city was in a state of excitement. A post boat arrived with the news from England that the king's son in law, the prince of Denmark, together with the duke of Ormonde, had deserted King James and had gone over to the prince of Orange. That same morning, the day of the great massacre, George Phillips and Lord Antrim rose early and made their way along the Londonderry road in Antrim's coach.

According to Mackenzie, eager to emphasize the Presbyterian contribution to the rebellion, the Reverend Mr Gordon proved himself a useful man and 'sent a considerable number' of recruits into the city. They were put under the command of Alderman Tomkins' son, John Tomkins, who now styled himself 'Captain'. All eyes now were on Antrim's men, who were across the river on the Waterside. To unnerve them, and in celebration of the good news from England, two of the cannons were discharged across the water. Youths mimicked military preparations by marching along the shore by the ferry. Thirty or forty horsemen from the city mounted up and galloped down to the ford at Lifford and back up the east bank onto a hill overlooking Antrim's men. It was all bluff, but Antrim's men feared the worst. There was cavalry on their side of the water, and there was infantry waiting to cross over to their side. They were ordered back along the Limavady road. It was, wrote Mackenzie, 'so hasty a flight that many of their officers left their boots, and soldiers their coats, behind them'.[12]

About a mile along the road, they met Lord Antrim's coach. Antrim and George Phillips were regaled with fearful tales of rebel troops preparing to launch an attack. Phillips volunteered to go on ahead to find out what was happening. He crossed by the ferry and was refused entry into the city. They trusted no one. Phillips was eventually brought before Cairnes who asked him to stay in Derry and to help with its defence. Phillips was not a military man, although he had once served once as a cornet of horse, but since the days of the militia, had been

[F] This 8-year-old boy, Randal MacDonnell, succeeded his father as earl of Antrim and married Clotworthy Skeffington's daughter. Among their many descendants was Winston Churchill.

styled 'colonel' and he had also recently been a caretaker governor of the city and of Culmore Fort.[13] Importantly, he was the only member of the landowning class to stand with the rebels. Tempted, but fearful of the consequences, Phillips agreed to stay and help only if it was made clear to everyone that he was doing so under duress. Cairnes obliged, and Phillips wrote a letter to Antrim to say that he had been detained against his will and it would be unwise for the old earl to follow him. The fiction of Phillips' arrest spread. He had been sent to Derry as Lord Antrim's ambassador and had been seized. Inside the walls, so long as he was publicly threatened by Cairnes, Phillips even agreed to take over as governor.

When he received the news, there was nothing Antrim could do other than go back to the comfort of Newtown Limavady. The next morning, he set off for Coleraine with his family, and then took the road south, back to Antrim.

4

Rebellion

By MONDAY, 10 DECEMBER 1688, word had got out that Londonderry was in rebellion, and people rallied to the city to show their support. Hundreds of men came in from Donegal for a show of strength, after which most went home again. No one could doubt but that there would be volunteers aplenty to fight for the Protestant cause. The problem was that, given the state of the city's armoury, there would be nothing to fight with.

David Cairnes was chosen to travel to London to the Irish Society to beg for help. He carried a letter signed by Phillips, who was then too deep into the rebellion to hide behind any pretence of being coerced. 'We heartily beseech you as you are men of bowels and charity',[A] he wrote. 'Just as the Soldiers were approaching the gates, the youthhood by a strange impulse ran in one body and shut the gates.'[1] No one was to blame, and they 'blessed God' for this unforeseen event, which had saved them. Now, it was all or nothing. Phillips helped supervise the organization of the townsmen into six companies and left for Limavady the following morning to gather his tenantry. When he returned a few days later, he brought with him 'about 3 or 400 horse'.[2]

Similar things were happening in Enniskillen, then a village 'of eighty dwellers' resting in the shadow of a small castle hastily built at the beginning of the century.[3] Rumours of the intended great massacre had reached there at the beginning of December and, as in Derry, the news was almost immediately followed by what was considered corroboration in the form of a letter announcing that two companies of soldiers were to be quartered on them. On 16 December, hearing that troops were marching towards them, the town turned out everyone it could muster, then 'not two hundred foot, and they not near half armed, our horse about 150 such as they were'. The plan was to attack the column, but the news of the activity in the town spread ahead of them and, rather than risk a confrontation, the Irish troops were marched away. There was a sense of triumph in the town. As in Derry, there had been a successful rebellion by an anonymous, leaderless mob. No shots had been fired, no blood had been spilt, and no one need be named.

The problem the Enniskillen rebels faced is that they had no one to lead them. The only one to have held a commission in the army was Gustavus Hamilton, who had spent a year or two as a cornet of horse. Nevertheless, he was the only officer

[A] Bowels were considered the seat of the tender emotions.

they had, and he was willing, and so they elected him governor.[4] Hamilton moved into the castle and sent two messengers off to Derry.[B]

News of the Londonderry and Enniskillen garrisons being refused entry reached Dublin within days. When Colonel Lundie and Mountjoy's regiment arrived at Dublin after a 150-mile march from Derry in 'the depth of winter', Tyrconnell allowed them three days' rest and ordered them to march back again.[5] This time their colonel was sent with them. Mountjoy was to speak some sense to the fools who were begging the government to send an army to knock them on the head.

Sir William Stewart, Lord Mountjoy, had inherited large tracts of Tyrone and Donegal, and from 1678, as the chief magistrate of Donegal, was active in enforcing the laws against Protestant dissenters and in suppressing banditry.[6] He had been a soldier for eleven years, and a colonel for four, and was elevated to the peerage in 1683. Having been made the master general of the Ordnance of Ireland, he in 1686 travelled across Europe and joined the international army of the Holy Roman emperor. He took part (and was wounded) in the siege of Buda, which threw the Turks out of Hungary. On his return, to reassure the Protestants, Tyrconnell promoted him to brigadier. Mountjoy was a reasonable, trusting man, perhaps to the point of naivety, and had convinced himself that whatever changes needed to be made in Ireland, the king would look after all his subjects. So long as there was proper law and order in the country, there was nothing to fear.

The mood in Londonderry varied between one of defiance and fear. Mountjoy knew that the place had been seized by a rabble, but had no idea who, if anyone, had taken charge. On 18 December, when he got to Omagh, he sent a message on ahead requesting that a delegation of two or three should meet him at Raphoe. Alderman Samuel Norman, now calling himself 'Captain' Norman, rode out to Raphoe with John Mogridge, one of the burgesses, to discuss terms.

They met the next day. Mountjoy was civil and told them he was empowered to negotiate on behalf of the crown and, so long as the city was surrendered to him immediately, he would 'procure a free and general pardon' for what had already happened. The implicit threat was that should the city not be surrendered to him, it would face the usual rewards for rebellion. Norman and Mogridge rode back to Derry. Mountjoy's easy authority had impressed them, and once inside the walls a meeting was called, and they urged everyone to accept the offer. They were shouted down. A messenger was sent to Mountjoy to tell him that his terms were rejected. He sent the messenger back with the demand that they should select someone who had power to treat with him, and meet him at Mongavlin Castle in St Johnstown, seven miles outside the city.

[B] His first name is explained by his father and uncle having served in Sweden under the great Gustavus Adolphus in the 1630s. His mother was Swedish. He is not to be confused with the other Gustavus Hamilton (of whom more below), who was to be governor of Coleraine in the months to come.

The city was willing to admit a Protestant garrison but not a Catholic one. Most importantly, before any garrison was admitted, they needed protection from prosecution by way of a general and free pardon, not from Mountjoy, but stamped and sealed by the king or his deputy. It was decided to send a delegation of five men: George Phillips, the newly and illegally appointed governor; Horace Kennedy, the sheriff, who had given the nod and wink to the apprentices; and Alderman Tomkins, now calling himself 'Captain'. The ungovernable youth of the city were represented by 'lieutenants' James Lennox and William Crookshanks, the last of whom was one of the young men who had shut the gates at sword point. They bound themselves to hold to their list of demands, and set out for St Johnstown.

They met Mountjoy on 20 December. His position had not changed. If his regiment was reinstalled as the garrison immediately, he would take no action over what had happened since the beginning of the month. Phillips and the others were not in any way able to negotiate. They had been given their instructions. They needed pardons before the garrison was admitted. Mountjoy told them that he could not agree any such terms, although he would use his influence to secure pardons after the garrison was admitted. Exasperated that he had again been sent a group of go-betweens, he told the delegation that he would come to the city in the morning. Phillips' delegation returned to the city.

First thing in the morning, Mountjoy and Lundie mounted up and rode to Londonderry. They arrived at the Bishop's Gate and Mountjoy asked to be let in. He then waited while the mob argued it out inside. Many did not want him in. They were in open rebellion and he was the king's representative. But the older ones prevailed. He was, after all, Lord Mountjoy. He was a Protestant, he was sympathetic, his sons were in the town, and he could not do anything by himself in any event. On top of that, it was a gross discourtesy to keep him outside.

Eventually, Mountjoy was brought before a special committee headed again by 'Governor' Phillips and Sheriff Kennedy, but now also including a greater number of aldermen posing as captains and youths posing as lieutenants. They were still uncompromising, but Mountjoy was determined to stop them from starting a war. They drew up articles, which he signed.

The important clause, to Mountjoy, was that two companies – commanded by Lieutenant Colonel Lundie and Captain William Stewart – were to be allowed into the city. Lundie, a somewhat inflexible Scotsman, was a career soldier, a veteran of the siege of Tangier,[c] and had been Mountjoy's lieutenant colonel since the regiment was founded. The 20-year-old William Stewart, who had been a captain for five months, was Mountjoy's eldest son.[7] Importantly to the

[c] Tangier was acquired by England from Portugal on the marriage of Charles II to Catherine of Braganza in 1662. Frequently attacked by the Moors, the expense of maintaining the garrison was such that the English abandoned Tangier in 1683. Apart from the naval wars with the Dutch, which ended in 1674, Charles II's England had been at peace in Europe and retained only a small standing army. Consequently, the only battle-hardened officers were those who had either been in foreign service or in the Tangier garrison.

committee of citizens, both Lundie and Stewart were Protestants, as were the men in their companies. Mountjoy agreed a clause that 'the Inhabitants of the said City shall not be disturbed in keeping their Guards and Watches', but the two companies were to enter the city before any pardons arrived from Dublin. To smooth things along, in his capacity as master of ordnance in Ireland, he immediately pardoned William Hemsworth, the clerk of stores who had handed out the muskets in his care to the new rebel companies, and Alexander Watson, the gunner. For the rest, he agreed to return to Dublin to secure what pardons he could for everyone so far involved. Until that pardon arrived, he agreed that the only troops in the city would be the two companies commanded by Lundie and Stewart, and that no other companies would be allowed into the city until March unless they were at least half Protestant. He also agreed that two of his younger sons, who were being tutored in the city, would remain there 'as pledges for the full and final performance of these articles'. The articles ended with a declaration of loyalty to King James:

> The inhabitants of the said city nowise doubting or mistrusting, that since their undertaking and late actions took their rise from self-preservation, and to avoid imminent danger, they shall be absolved before God and the world from all tincture of rebellion, perverseness and wilful disobedience to the King's authority, and the established laws of the land.[8]

Mountjoy ordered Lundie to ride back to Strabane, collect the two all-Protestant companies and march them to Derry. The remaining four companies, each of which was approximately mixed half and half, were to go into quarters in Strabane, Newtownstewart and Raphoe 'till thoroughly reformed' along religious lines.

On the next day, Saturday 22 December 1688, Colonel Robert Lundie marched his two companies of redcoats into the city and took possession of it. The emergency was over. The king's garrison had returned. Mountjoy remained in Newtownstewart with one of the as yet unreformed companies. While there, he received two delegates from Enniskillen. They outlined the town's fears of the intended massacre. Mountjoy told them that they must admit a garrison, promised to go to Enniskillen on Wednesday and 'intreated that we might be cautious of falling into blood, which we promised and so departed'.[9]

Tyrconnell, meanwhile, had run out of patience. King James had surrounded himself with Protestant army officers, and they had betrayed him. They often had done so after giving him every reason to trust them. Now Mountjoy, this mischievous man as Tyrconnell saw him, had left a Protestant town in revolt with an all-Protestant garrison. Tyrconnell became gripped with the suspicion that Mountjoy was behind everything that was going on, and ordered him to return to Dublin. Mountjoy sent a message back to the effect that he was unwell and so could not travel. The delay rang alarm bells in Dublin. Tyrconnell had to get rid of him.

The news from London had not reached Derry at the time Mountjoy was negotiating to install Lundie and his two companies. The political situation had changed quickly over the preceding fortnight. On 11 December 1688, King James fled from Whitehall and tried to take a boat to France. He was seized by a mob in Kent and sent back to London as a prisoner. London itself had grown dangerous. There were anti-Catholic riots, and a general apprehension of a planned massacre by King James' vengeful Irish troops. On 17 December, the first occupying Dutch troops marched into the capital. William was in a quandary about what to do with James, who was sent back to Rochester to await his fate. He had to be released, and on 23 December, the day after Lundie marched into Derry in his name, King James took a boat with the duke of Berwick, and left England for the last time.

Mountjoy was determined to do his duty, and after having caused three days of fretting in the capital, he sent his apologies to the rebels in Enniskillen and took the long road south. In Dublin, he was rewarded with a grand performance of Tyrconnell's theatre. Tyrconnell told Mountjoy that he did not know what to do. He was bound to obey orders from the king, but the king was in France and there was no contact between them. He was going to send Sir Stephen Rice to France to get instructions and to find out what the king wanted. Tyrconnell was fed up. He 'swore most solemnly that he was in earnest'. Tyrconnell's view was that the French care for 'nothing but their own Interest, and they would not care if Ireland were sunk to the pit of hell'. All they wanted was to 'give the Prince of Orange but three months' diversion'. If King James does not see that, he told Mountjoy, 'he is neither so merciful nor so wise as I believe him to be'. King James could 'never expect to conquer England by Ireland' and such an attempt would ruin Ireland. It was imperative that Mountjoy go to France to let the deluded king know what state the country's affairs are in.

This was Tyrconnell at his persuasive best. Mountjoy had been told not to trust him, 'that this was all sham and trick', and that Tyrconnell's purpose was simply to get Mountjoy out of the way. Mountjoy was not so sure. His own father had been killed in the last civil war, and he knew that everything must be done to avoid another. There was a chance, perhaps only a slim chance now that James was in French hands, that Mountjoy could make a difference. And he knew that no one else could do it. He agreed to go to France, but only if Tyrconnell gave him four assurances. The assurances were that Tyrconnell would stop issuing commissions and levying new troops, no troops would be garrisoned in any private houses, no one would be prosecuted for what had happened in recent months and, most of all, Tyrconnell was absolutely not to send any more troops to Ulster. Tyrconnell, with all the appearance of being thoroughly disheartened and beaten, agreed to everything 'on his Word and Honour'.

Before leaving Dublin, Mountjoy wrote a circular letter to the north on 10 January 1689. He set out why he was going, the assurances that had been given by Tyrconnell, and the dangers of what would happen if he failed.

> I am morally assured, that this [agreement with Tyrconnell] must do our work without blood, or the misery of the kingdom … I do therefore conjure you to give your friends and mine this account, and, for the love of God, keep them from any disorder or mischief (if any had such design, which I hope they had not;) and I am fully satisfied, every man will have his own heart's desire.[10]

Mountjoy set off exhibiting great confidence. The alternatives were too terrible to contemplate. 'All will end', he said, 'in a can of mild beer'. He travelled with Sir Stephen Rice, who carried a private letter from Tyrconnell to say that Ireland was awaiting the king's arrival and preparations were in hand for founding a great army to enable the king to get his thrones back. Rice was also to tell King James that Mountjoy was one of the prince of Orange's agents, and that Tyrconnell 'feared his power and suspected his fidelity'. They arrived at St Germain, King James' residence in exile, on 1 February. By 11 February, Mountjoy was safely locked up in the Bastille, and James was making urgent preparations to go to Ireland.[11]

In London, the suddenness of the success of the revolution had prevented any planning for an Irish solution. The demands on the new administration were many. Ireland needed a speedy remedy, but nothing could be done in the immediate days or weeks ahead. The enormous expenditure aside, it would take months before an expedition could be mounted. It was hoped to find someone to treat with Tyrconnell. Colonel Richard Hamilton, whose regiment had been disarmed and moved out of harm's way to the Isle of Wight, was an urbane man and well connected with Tyrconnell. He let it be known that his influence was such that 'he might prevail with the Lord *Tyrconnell* to deliver up the Kingdom'. Hamilton agreed to offer Tyrconnell terms to avoid a war. All Tyrconnell need do was to accept King Charles' settlement, which they had lived under peacefully for over two decades, and accept the new order in London. The Irish could keep all they had and a line would be drawn under what had happened in recent years. Hamilton was released on parole and allowed to travel to Dublin on his undertaking, to return within three weeks with an answer. To show the new administration's goodwill, he was allowed passports for a company of Irish soldiers who had been stranded in England. If only Tyrconnell could see what everyone in London could see, he would take what terms he could and simply give up. There would be no war.

Richard Hamilton was a man with important connections: he was a grandson of the duke of Ormonde, and Tyrconnell was married to his brother's widow. Now aged about forty, Hamilton had spent much of his early life in France, where he had commanded a French regiment for over six years. He had been popular at the French court, and in 1681 danced before Louis XIV in a ballet. On leaving France in 1685, he was made a colonel in Ireland and in 1686 was promoted to brigadier, making him the third most senior member of the Irish army. In 1687, he was given the colonelcy of an English cavalry regiment, and at the revolution King James promoted him to major general.

Hamilton arrived in Dublin shortly after Mountjoy had left for France. He was described celebrating his arrival in a Ringsend tavern: 'The Colonel [Hamilton] broke out into loud laughter, saying he could not forbear it, thinking how finely he had shammed the Prince of Orange.' According to Sir Oliver St George, 'The Papists in Dublin made bonfires when Dick Hamilton came over, saying he was worth 10,000 men.' The archbishop of Dublin agreed: 'The Irish were very low then, but from his coming they took heart ... This was the crisis, the fatal hour of Ireland.' Lord Longford warned that 'vigorous preparations are making here for war ... It will (besides the miseries which will inevitably fall upon this kingdom) cost England much blood and treasure before it be reduced out of popish hands.'[12]

5

On the brink

LUNDIE HAD BEEN A career soldier under Charles II. He had been seriously wounded in the great victory over the Moors at Tangier in 1680 (for which he received a pension), and had been the commanding officer of Mountjoy's regiment for three years. In Ireland, Tyrconnell's government had brought swift changes, and now the news from England was unsettling for everyone. Protestants had been dismissed from their posts in the government and the army, and Lundie now found himself, as a lieutenant colonel, the fourth most senior Protestant officer in the country. Loyal soldiers all over England had changed their allegiance and the prospect of war loomed large in Ireland. Everyone faced stark choices. Quietly at first, and cautiously, Lundie threw in his lot with the rebels at an early stage.

On arriving back in Londonderry on 22 December, he settled his men into their quarters. As he had been the garrison commander for the last three years, he knew the city well. He had lived there with his family, and his daughter had been baptised in the cathedral, but garrison duty in peace time was no real preparation for what he now had to guard against. If a few hundred Irish raiders had made an attempt on the city, they would not have had the means to get in. No one had cannon in the country except the Dublin government, and there was now a possibility that he may have to defend the city against that government. The city was not tenable in its present state. The magazine contained no more than four barrels of powder, together with five hundred musket barrels that needed new stocks. The wooden carriages for the guns on the walls were rotten and broken. In places, the walls themselves needed repairing and platforms needed to be built. And the two large dunghills outside the walls had grown to be almost as high as the walls themselves.

He called a meeting of the leading citizens on Christmas Eve. If he was to defend the city, he needed to put the defences into a state of repair, and in order to do that, he needed money. Without a functioning city corporation, he had to call for donations. A hundred pounds was raised by subscription, a sum that Lundie 'modestly employed for new mounting the guns, making of platforms, repairing the gates and walls, removing the two dunghills and new stocking of 500 old musket barrels'. The re-stocked muskets were issued to those living outside the walls so as to form another five companies of men to add to the six that had been mustered in the city.[1]

On the 2 January, the remaining city burgesses and aldermen decided to act as if King James' charter was invalid, and called a council meeting. Those who were aldermen and burgesses under the old charter returned themselves as aldermen and burgesses. Those who had been newly appointed to the council under the charter were not invited. John Buchanan, the lawful deputy mayor, who had been a burgess before the new charter, was not welcome and did not attend. It was a show of bravado. The reinstated council members did nothing other than reinstate the mayor who had been deposed by the new charter, John Campsie, and record their attendance in a new minute book. If anything went wrong, they could throw the minutes away and no one would be any the wiser, but they now had their Protestant mayor back.

Lundie made Alderman Norman the lieutenant colonel of the new regiment of volunteers, and promoted one of his own men as their major. Lundie was scornful of the rude democratic attempts of the Londonderry men to regiment themselves. He could not rely upon an undisciplined mob led by teenaged captains. He neither needed nor trusted them. He discharged them from keeping guards, which they objected to in the impossible belief that they could run their own guard rosters at the same time or in place of the garrison. Besides, they argued, it was one of the conditions that Mountjoy had signed. As the conditions said nothing about ammunition, Lundie refused to let them have any. He then compromised by allowing them to join in the guard duties, but only so that they were at all times greatly outnumbered by his own men. In every field of duty, he put the volunteers under his own officers and allowed only one volunteer officer as a guard commander. 'These things', wrote the Presbyterian champion, John Mackenzie, 'disgusted the city'.

Away from the buzz of Dublin, Ireland was quiet. Everyone waited for news from England. The Association's numbers grew, but they needed arms, and a plan was devised to disarm the troops in Belfast, Lisburn and Armagh. Leading the Belfast attempt was Sir Arthur Rawdon, a very active 26-year-old of great authority and charisma, 'generally then known by the name of *The Cock of the North,* because of his boldness and great forwardness'. His father, an able Yorkshireman, had been a member of the Dublin Parliament before and after the Restoration, and was made a baronet by Charles II.

In each case, Protestant officers were to disarm their men on the evening of 4 January. Lord Blayney managed to disarm a troop of dragoons in Armagh, but the successful attempt at Lisburn was abandoned when it was found that the Belfast conspirators had failed. Fearing reprisals, the immediate result was a general flight of the Protestant officers and troops, and several of the leading conspirators fled to England. Isolated in Belfast, the Irish troops were ordered to march 'quick and thick' to Newry, which was then, with Carrickfergus and Charlemont, one of the three remaining Irish garrisons in Ulster.[2]

Thwarted but determined, Tollymore sent out another round of letters to all those he felt may help in an insurrection. He invited them to a meeting at Comber on the 13 January. Only sixteen attended, but they elected a 'junto'[A]

[A] Junto, the favoured seventeenth-century anglicization of the Spanish word *junta,* a council.

of five to direct the business of the Association in Down. The first act of the new junto was, at the suggestion of Tollymore, to elect Mount-Alexander as their commander-in-chief 'who being wholly ignorant of all military discipline, and not much prepared for so great a command, resigned himself sometimes to the directions of Mr. Hamilton of Tollymore, a person less qualified than his lordship'.[3]

They then agreed to send Captain Baldwin Leighton to London to ask for financial and military help and to issue commissions for the regiments they hoped to raise. Juntos were established in Antrim and Armagh, and a supreme council, 'the Consult', was formed in Hillsborough under the presidency of Mount-Alexander. The proceedings of the Consult proved difficult. 'Our Councils were betrayed, and nothing was a secret', wrote Mount-Alexander. 'A faction was made, and my opinion was but single and over-ruled. The gentlemen of the country were divided, and opposed each other, and many petty factions were made'. Raising troops was the priority. No one seemed sure how many people were involved. There was no question of pay, and there was a temptation to inflate the numbers. Small groups of men were called companies. Small groups of companies were called regiments. Those who had prior military experience or who could raise men on their own account gave themselves ranks. 'Their best subsistence was upon the Irish plunder, open acts of hostility being now common to both parties, insomuch as the frontier towns were quite wasted.'

'Sir Arthur Rawdon was hot and forward', wrote Mount-Alexander, 'and spoke greatly of the numbers they had raised, but I could never see a roll of them, and when it came to the test, not above 300 appeared where 1000 was expected; all art was used to conceal this from me, and from what is past I may conclude that my countenance was all [that was] aimed at, and few cared how I was exposed to share the folly as well as fate of my country'. That was the reality. Tollymore and Rawdon needed Mount-Alexander for his 'countenance', but did not want him to interfere. If things went wrong, Mount-Alexander was there to take the blame.

In Dublin Tyrconnell was also preparing for war. He issued commissions to raise forty new regiments. One of these was sent to Cormack O'Neill, one of the great Irish landowners of Antrim. He appointed Felix O'Neill as his lieutenant colonel, and gave him the task of raising recruits in Down and Antrim, and marching them to Carrickfergus to join Lord Antrim's men. The town's garrison swelled to nineteen companies, the best part of two thousand men, mostly without uniforms and armed with nothing more than the clubs and skeans they had brought with them. Now that both sides were plundering each other, much of the Irish population of Antrim had also flocked to Carrickfergus for safety. Carrickfergus had a castle and was the only walled town in the counties of Down and Antrim. Just as Derry was about to become a haven for the Protestants, Carrickfergus was 'the only Popish asylum in those parts'. It was in effect blockaded and all provisions had to come by sea.

Archibald Edmonstone of Dunteath, a 51-year-old Scot of uncompromising views with a history of involvement with the Presbyterian cause, had raised a company of men in Scotland. Styling himself 'Colonel' Edmonstone, he came to Ireland to 'defend the Protestant interest'. He persuaded the Consult to allow him to seize a boat laden with provisions for Carrickfergus, which he did and took to Bangor. Antrim's response was to threaten to burn down both the town of Bangor and Edmonstone's house at Redhill outside Carrickfergus. Now that they were under threat of a military expedition by Antrim's men, the Consult resolved to attack Carrickfergus.

Antrim demanded a parley and rode out to Belfast. Once he discovered that the main cause of anxiety was the sheer numbers crowded into Carrickfergus, he offered to disband the new levies who had been sent to him by the O'Neills, in return for passes for them to return home unmolested. It appeared to many of the Protestants to be a happy compromise, and it certainly helped Antrim as the men were no good to him until they were armed, and if they were sent home he would not have to pay or feed them until they were recalled to the colours. Antrim was secure in the knowledge that so long as he kept the castle, the situation was unlikely to deteriorate, and everything would be resolved by the Dublin government. Mount-Alexander, or more probably Tollymore by Mount-Alexander's side, formed the impression that if Antrim was prepared to negotiate, it was because Antrim was weak, and if Antrim was weak, there was no point in negotiating. Antrim rode back to Carrickfergus to prepare for the worst. The Association made plans to attack Carrickfergus on 22 February.

The earliest recorded military clash was on 11 February 1689. Cormack O'Neil ordered a troop of dragoons raised on the west side of the Bann to join him in Carrickfergus. As they tried crossing into Antrim by the ferry at Toome they were attacked by some Association troops who 'pursued them, killed some, and having given them a total Defeat, dispersed that Troop of *O Neil*'s'. The Association troops were led by John Michelburne, who had deserted the Irish army in Dublin at the beginning of the year as a lieutenant, and had been given a commission in a new volunteer battalion raised by Clotworthy Skeffington, the thirty-year-old son of Lord Massereene. The action was later described in a grossly exaggerated fashion by Michelburne, but he did command the troops that spilt the first blood of the war. The Association fired first.

Michelburne's men went on to pillage Cormack O'Neill's house at Broughshane, outside Ballymena, leaving O'Neill's wife 'half dead with fear'. This low-level, often petty violence and theft was now endemic, particularly in areas far from any effective authority. Protestants were robbed and their cattle stolen. Catholics were robbed and their cattle stolen. The political situation had given both sides the excuse to act in ways they would have regarded as unthinkable a few months before. People took measures to protect themselves and their property, or moved to where they would be safer. Both sides saw danger and opportunity all around.[4] Illustrating the confusion of the times, Mackenzie wrote of another incident in February in Tyrone:

> A considerable party of the [Irish] forces of Charlemont, joined with other Irish of the country near Benburb. A party of our men both foot and horse, beat them off, and took a prey of cattle from them.[5]

Given the improbability of the Irish attacking with their cattle, this may have been as easily written: 'The Irish had a herd. Our men beat the Irish and took their cattle.'

In the days that followed the Toome incident, three thousand Association volunteers gathered in Belfast to march on Carrickfergus. The Association relied upon Henry Davies, a wine merchant in the town, to give Antrim's officers 'such a hearty welcome as might drown all sense of their duty; and make them incapable of opposing the protestant onset'. Late on 21 February 1689, while Davies plied the garrison with drink, the Protestant volunteers led by Colonel George Bermingham and Major Henry Baker marched out of Belfast through a rainy winter's night. It took them until daybreak to cover the ten miles to Carrickfergus where they waited outside for Mount-Alexander and Rawdon and their five hundred horsemen.

They waited too long. The thin morning light exposed them to the sentries, and Antrim's officers were given 'time enough to sleep themselves sober'. The alarm was raised for a rapid stand-to-arms. Although 'they had neither cannon to batter, nor ladders to scale, nor any other provision fit for such an attempt', Bermingham divided his men into battalions and under fire from the town cannon marched up to the walls 'which they would have undoubtedly taken if scythes and pikes could have prevailed, but having spent their ammunition and experienced the impossibility of the attempt', they retreated out of range.

There was a parley. 'They consulted how to come off with Honour, and entered into Articles, not to Surrender the Town, but to Raise the Siege.' They were offered the same terms Lord Antrim gave them the day before: that O'Neill's recruits be disbanded and allowed safe passage to go home. That is what happened. Articles were drawn up, the first of which provided for the disbanding of O'Neill's regiment 'by Monday next'. Having forced Lord Antrim to disband a whole regiment, albeit an unarmed one, Bermingham and Baker led their three thousand men away in triumph.

They also managed to get Antrim to agree to a letter being sent to Tyrconnell that would be signed by both Antrim and the Consult. The man chosen to deliver the letter was a Friar O'Haggerty, who gave Tyrconnell 'the following (too true) account of the condition of the North, viz. that they were untrained, and had few experienced officers: That the most part were without arms, and such as had 'em, their arms were unfixed and unfit for service. They were very much scattered, and their number not near what had been written.'[6]

The Association had shown its hand, and a pretty limp hand it was. By going on the attack, they encouraged the Irish to behave in a like manner. 'The Dragoons of the *Newry*, who never before durst quit their Garrison, ventured themselves abroad, and having intelligence of the advance of a Protestant Party under the Command of Capt. *Poe,* which had been detached from Loughbrickland for Forage, they laid an Ambuscade, and by a Surprize killed the Captain and Eight of his men.'[B] [7]

Although everyone now knew that King James had fled from England and that the prince of Orange was soon to be crowned, the future was far from certain. To an outsider, the Dublin government showed every sign of confidence. Rumours flew around as to what was happening overseas. King Louis had freed up his forces by making a peace with the emperor. The English could not afford to send troops to Ireland because they faced an invasion. 'There are fifty thousand French a-shipping at Brest in France.' King James was coming to Ireland with the French. The states of Holland were demanding the return of all Dutch troops from England to face an imminent French threat to the Netherlands. The reason Tyconnell had not sent any forces to Ulster was because he had been held back by 'some designing headpieces of the north' who wanted the Protestants to rebel so 'that they might have the fairer hit at their estates'.[8]

In Londonderry, Lundie had turned his mind to securing outside help. He sent two ships to Strangford to recover powder that had been stranded there, which resulted in another fourteen barrels being added to the magazine. On 15 January he called a meeting of the city council. There was, he said, no ammunition in the country, and they needed to buy some urgently. The council raised £400 and secured a vessel to go to Scotland. Lundie wrote to his relation, Major George Arnott, the governor of Dumbarton Castle, asking him to let the privy council in Scotland know their desperate plight. The privy council agreed to order and pay for another forty-two barrels of powder and five hundred matchlock muskets from Stirling Castle. Lundie also wrote letters to everyone he knew who may have had any influence on the prince of Orange to say that 'without a speedy supply of men, money, arms and ammunition, they were all lost'.

Mount-Alexander's Consult called the landowners of the counties of Londonderry, Tyrone and Donegal to a meeting on 16 January. They were urged to follow Down and Antrim by setting up their own associations for 'defence of the Protestant religion'. Lundie advised them against it. They should concentrate on 'putting themselves in as good a condition for defence of themselves as was possible, but', he warned, 'with little noise for fear of bringing an army amongst them before they were ready'. His advice was taken, although it was also agreed to hold weekly informal meetings in the three counties. At the first meeting in Co. Londonderry, it was resolved to raise three regiments of foot and one of dragoons in addition to Lundie's garrison, and to bestow on Lundie the new post of 'county governor'. Similar meetings in Tyrone and Donegal resolved to raise six regiments between them.

[B] Daniel Poe from Dromgoolestown, near Ardee, in Louth, was the first named fatality of the war.

As there was no cadre of experienced officers around which the new regiments could be formed, Lundie took the lead. There had been a general flight of Protestant soldiery from Dublin, although not all made it. In January, forty men from Mountjoy's regiment marched off in a body in uniform with their colours and muskets. Utterly exhausted, they were overhauled in Navan by the brisk Colonel Nugent and taken back as prisoners. In that same month some eighteen Protestant officers resigned their commissions. Many made their way to Derry.[9] Protestant soldiers in the mixed companies deserted and followed their officers northwards. Lundie allocated them to the new regiments yet to be formed. There was no way back.

Outside Ulster, the Protestant Association of Sligo was established on 4 January 1689 under the leadership of Lord Kingston and Chidley Coote. Tyrconnell had not troubled to send a garrison there, but they feared the possibility. The Sligo Association now boasted some six hundred horsemen and twelve hundred foot soldiers. It all made encouraging reading to the Protestants of Dublin. 'Lord Kingston is in arms in Sligo with 2,000 men. The last general muster at Enniskillen was 4,000 … Derry is in posture.' A strong conclusion was drawn from the fact that Tyrconnell, with his supposedly massive army, was doing nothing about it. The government was all bluster.

The defence of the north was now down to two men. In the north-east, Lord Mount-Alexander was braced with his Consult to receive the first blow. In the north-west, everything lay in the hands of Lundie. At the beginning of February, Mount-Alexander wrote to Lundie suggesting they join forces. Lundie should march his men to the east and face the Irish advance. Lundie refused. He could not leave Londonderry undefended and needed to unify his forces, not spread them. He instead gave Mountjoy's son, Captain William Stewart, the local rank of colonel so as to outrank the militia leaders, and sent him to Dungannon with three troops of dragoons, a hundred redcoats, six volunteer companies and two field pieces to 'keep the garrison of Charlemont in awe'. There were no more men to spare.

Tyrconnell made one last attempt to draw Lundie into his net. As the commander of the Irish army, he ordered Lundie to Dublin. Lundie refused, in the politest way. He could not come, he wrote, because to do so would breach the articles Mountjoy had made with the people of Londonderry.[10]

6

Uprising

On 13 February 1689, while the Association troops were plundering Broughshane, King William and Queen Mary were crowned king and queen of England, Scotland and Ireland. Parliament ruled that King James' desertion had been an abdication, and his only legitimate son, the infant James Francis Edward, was ruled illegitimate. News reached Dublin within days, but did not get through to the north until the end of the month and, even then, was treated as rumour.

Dublin had also been waiting for good news. Tyrconnell promoted Richard Hamilton to lieutenant general, and concentrated on organizing the army in anticipation of King James' arrival. On paper the Irish army had some forty thousand men, but arms were scarce and much depended on what the French might send. In preparation for the king's arrival, the northern rebellion needed to be crushed and, in the absence of a large army, Mount-Alexander's rebels would be flattened by a solid brigade of experienced troops.

Tyrconnell issued a proclamation on 7 March 'to prevent the effusion of blood'. It read: 'We, the Lord Deputy, have caused a party of His Majesty's army, under the command of Lieutenant General *Rich. Hamilton,* to march into the province of Ulster to reduce the rebels there by force of arms.' The army would not harm anyone who submitted. There would be no violence towards 'women, children, aged or decrepit men, labourers, ploughmen, tillers of the ground, or to any other who in these commotions demean themselves inoffensively'. Eight people, 'persons not deserving his Majesty's mercy or favour', were excluded from the proclamation: Lords Mount-Alexander, Massereene and Kingston, Clotworthy Skeffington, Sir Robert Colvill, Sir Arthur Rawdon, Robert Sanderson and Francis Hamilton.

On the next day, 8 March 1689, Hamilton led his army out of Dublin. The Association's only plan was to meet the Irish head-on in the field, but the preparation was pitiful. There were some ten thousand Association volunteers, albeit 'indifferently armed' and mostly untrained, but they were not drawn together. Nothing was done to block the Irish advance, not even at Hillsborough where they 'neither suffered the trenches to be scoured, nor commanded any other thing for the defence of it'.

On 9 March, Captain Baldwin Leighton, who had spent the last month travelling to London and back for the Association, returned to Hillsborough with the first official confirmation of William and Mary's coronation. He carried a letter addressed to Mount-Alexander from King William which read: 'We are resolved to employ the most speedy and effective means in our power for rescuing you from the oppressions and terrors you lie under', and assured him that 'speedy relief' was on its way from England. 'Some of the cannon and ammunition were shipped, and 15,000 men were ready at the waterside.' It was not true, and even if it was, it was not encouraging. The English could not get to them in time. The Association would have to face the Irish army alone.

Leighton also brought over commissions for the thirteen colonels who had raised or were raising regiments, and blank commissions for the officers yet to be chosen. Mount-Alexander and Blayney were now colonels of horse; Sir Arthur Rawdon and Clotworthy Skeffington colonels of dragoons; Sir William Franklyn, Sir John Magill, Francis Hamilton, James Hamilton of Newcastle, James Hamilton of Tollymore, Arthur Upton, Hugh Montgomery, Baldwin Leighton and William Leslie colonels of foot. All the commissions were dated 5 February and signed by William as prince of Orange. Everything was now done in a rush. The blank commissions were hurriedly allocated, 'but they came there so late that we had no great benefit from them'.[A] [1]

On the same day, Alexander Osborn arrived in Hillsborough. A Scots Presbyterian minister, Osborn had been given a pass from Tyrconnell to rush to the north with the proclamation. Osborn wrote letters to Mount-Alexander, Massereene and Rawdon demanding an audience. In the letters he set out Tyrconnell's message to the North: bloodshed could only be avoided by accepting protection from Hamilton and immediately delivering up their arms and serviceable horses. General Richard Hamilton's army would to 'be at Newry on Monday the 11th. instant, which will from thence march to Belfast, and from thence to Coleraine and Londonderry'. He ended his letter with this warning:

> The Country Irish, not of the Army, Man, Woman and Boy, now all armed with Half Pikes and Baggonets, in the counties of Cavan, Monaghan, Tyrone and Londonderry, &c., will, on the Approach of the said part of the Army, and Resistance thereunto made, immediately enter into a Massacre of the British of the said Counties.[2]

Claiming that 'the real design of his coming was to prevent their being surprised with the descent of the Irish Army', Osborn addressed a meeting of the Association. Mount-Alexander scribbled a dispatch to Lundie. 'We most earnestly entreat you', he wrote, 'to march up towards Newry'. It was far too late, and the main consequence of Osborn's arrival was panic. His letter was an encouragement for men 'to lay down their arms' and for 'their leaders to shift for themselves', which they did, 'and left all their plate and jewels and sweet meats behind, and took nothing of value but their race horses'.[3]

[A] All the colonels left the country before the siege of Londonderry, except Montgomery, who fled to Enniskillen, Edmonstone, who died, and Leslie, who took protection.

As Osborn had predicted, Hamilton reached Newry on 11 March, to the great relief of the Irish garrison. His army was small in that it was made up of only two and a half thousand men, but they were an impressive sight. They were all in uniform, they marched in companies, they were fully armed, and they were accompanied by cavalry and dragoons, and followed by a horse drawn train of supplies. They were a professional army with professional officers.

The Association command was a mess. Mount-Alexander had a colonel's commission, and the Consult had made him commander-in-chief, but Rawdon would not be held back by his orders. Mount-Alexander needed all his men to be brought together, and ordered everyone to join him, hoping to amass some four thousand volunteers in Hillsborough, a town that had the benefit of a small fort. Sir Arthur Rawdon, he wrote, 'burnt the order' and instead based himself at Loughbrickland, twelve miles from Newry. Rawdon then demanded reinforcements, but was told that no one was ready. Mount-Alexander ordered him back. Rawdon told the inhabitants of Loughbrickland to pack their things and leave, and pulled out with his men. Rawdon then, without any authority other than his own, decided that the Irish could and should be stopped at Dromore, five miles south of Hillsborough on the Newry Road. He got Hugh Magill to ride to Dromore from Newtownards with eighty dragoons, and the following night Henry Baker marched in with three half-armed companies of foot soldiers. The numbers were inadequate. Rawdon had, said Mount-Alexander, 'exposed 300 men in an open village' where the Irish army 'could surround them as they pleased'. Rawdon then sent urgent requests to Hillsborough for more men, arms, powder and ammunition. The reinforcements had not yet arrived in Hillsborough, and were only expected to get to Lisburn that night, another five miles beyond Hillsborough. It was hopeless.

Mount-Alexander was in no position to stop Hamilton's army. Not only were his troops for the most part untrained and disorganized, but the forces he had gathered were disintegrating before his eyes. 'A night or two before, 3 troops of my regiment deserted; Sir John Magill's regiment [were] totally gone. The men in Belfast and Lisburn would not move thence, nor obey their officers. Sir William Franklin and the most considerable in Belfast fled into England, and I was informed both these towns intended to capitulate. The inhabitants of the towns everywhere as well as of the counties fled daily with what goods and provisions they could carry.'[4]

On 13 March, Richard Hamilton's army marched into Loughbrickland without any opposition, and the next morning, 14 March, they made for Dromore. Surprised by the speed of the determined Irish advance, the first Rawdon knew of their approach was when they were almost upon him. A scout rode back to tell him that 'two troops' of Irish horse were on the road. Rawdon then made a terrible mistake. He decided to give Hamilton's advance party a bloody nose. He mounted up and led his horsemen

> to within view of the enemy, who he discovered to be very numerous and advancing in great haste but in excellent order, which made Sir Arthur halt, and consulting his officers what was fit to be done, he found his right wing

> surrounded, and concluding the enemy designed to hem in his party, they all agreed upon a retreat, and the only doubt that remained was, who should be foremost.[5]

That was the 'break' of Dromore.[B] There was no hesitation by the Irish cavalry. Led by the very able Dominic Sheldon, they saw Rawdon's dragoons and went for them. Some of the rebels were caught, some fought, but overwhelmingly they turned around and raced away. The rebel infantry was left in Dromore. They waited until the Irish were almost within musket range, 'but seeing themselves at the point of being overwhelmed by the cavalry' they did the only sensible thing and ran.[6] It was all over in minutes. Tradition has it that 'a woman went out to see the fight when it commenced, leaving bread at the fire, and on her return after the affray had ended, the bread was not burned'.[7] Such fighting as there was, probably by those who had been cut off and had to fight their way out, perhaps left no more than twenty dead, while Rawdon's horsemen 'hasted full gallop to Hillsborough'.[8]

Apart from Sheldon's horsemen at the head of the column, Richard Hamilton's army was not involved. Nor was the Association army. 'The first news I heard', wrote Mount-Alexander, 'was of our being beaten, [and] pursued to within half a mile of Hillsborough, where I was, upon which I mounted with about sixty horse and in the fort about 100 foot. Before I could march, the enemy was near the town, and our men flying in crowds down the street. I stopped what I could, and made shift to draw up about 100 horse in the town, but as I went to give orders … the men slipped away, and the officers told me it was in vain to expect they would stand a charge, for there appeared seven troops of the enemy's horse.'[9]

Panic raced ahead of the Irish army. Hillsborough was abandoned, together with all the supplies that had been gathered there. All the papers of the Consult were left behind. As soon as the volunteers at Lisburn heard the enemy had taken Hillsborough, they 'shrunk and stole away'. It was the end of the war for Mount-Alexander. 'The matter being thus, it was now time to shift for myself, having neither men nor money to carry with me to Derry.' Everyone fled, and everyone with the means fled straight out of the country. Mount-Alexander raced home, took what he could, including his young son and £10 in cash, and tried to find a boat at Donaghadee, but was too late. Tollymore had got there before him, taken the last boat and set off for Portpatrick. Mount-Alexander rode off to Portaferry where he found another boat, and sailed 'in a great storm' to the Isle of Man. He did not return to Ireland for over eighteen months. Everything had been an outright failure. Against his better instincts, he had been used to assist those who had provoked Dublin into sending an army into the north, and they had now lost everything.

[B] This meaning of the word 'break' has been overlooked by both the *Oxford English dictionary* and the *Dictionary of the Scots language*. It is described in the *Montgomery Manuscripts* (at p. 282) as 'a word common among the Irish Scots for a Rout'.

In the weeks before Hamilton marched out of Newry, there had been sporadic fighting in the north. News came to the Association of rebel successes 'in small skirmishes in Armagh and Monaghan'.[10] The successes were small, if they were successes, and were always followed by retreat. Claims that 'we' killed a hundred and forty of the enemy here, or a hundred and eighty of the enemy there (in incidents usually unnoticed by anyone other than the person giving the report) did not alter the fact that the Irish were gaining, town by town, the disputed counties.

Lord Blayney's account, which Mackenzie included in his *Narrative,* follows this pattern. Having been chosen by the Association to command all the forces in Armagh and Monaghan, Blayney called a general rendezvous and found he had about eighteen hundred men 'indifferently well armed'. There were 'several skirmishes' with the Irish troops from Charlemont, he wrote, in which 'considerable numbers' of the enemy were killed 'every day', whereas he only lost one man. On 13 March, the day before the break of Dromore, he learnt that his own house at Monaghan had been taken by the enemy. Most of the Monaghan forces and civilians had fled and had got as far as Glaslough on the Tyrone border. Blayney sent orders for them to march to Coleraine.

Mackenzie included an anonymous report of the fighting at Glaslough.

> They were about five to one in number, and yet there were (as Mr. Anthony who stayed in the country told us) 180 of 'em killed, among whom was Colonel Mackennah, 4 Captains, 6 Lieutenants, and 6 Ensigns: We only lost that brave Man Capt. Ancktall, who after the Enemy was routed, was unfortunately shot by a fellow that lay in a bush. More of the enemy had been cut off, if they had not had a bog to retreat to: But after this encounter, we had only so much ammunition left us, as served to charge our arms on our march.[11]

This account of an obscure and long forgotten incident is illustrative of many of the confused reports of these times, and it is the only incident in Co. Monaghan that we know happened. A further description appears in Walter Harris' *Life and reign of William-Henry.* The Irish were led by 'John McKenna, an Irish major', and the party from Glaslough were led by Matthew Anketill, 'a gentleman of clear courage'. 'Eighty nine of the Irish were slain, and McKenna and his son taken prisoners; the former of which was put to death by the brutish rabble, who followed Mr Anketill, in revenge for their leader'.[12]

The 'brutish rabble' was all that either side had. There were few soldiers in any of these actions, and very few or no uniforms, just mobs of ill-disciplined countrymen, some on horseback, but mostly on foot, and mostly without firearms, noisily shouting out their presence as they skirmished in the gloom of sodden woods. In this incident, later elevated to the dignity of the battle of Drumbanagher, the good behaviour of each side was overseen by a member of the gentry. A band of

Irishmen under the direction of John McKenna, one of the sheriffs of Monaghan, attempted to eject a band of armed rebels who had gathered from all over the county and illegally occupied Glaslough. Matthew Anketill gathered his two or three hundred men together and chased McKenna's men off. It was not a massacre, because McKenna surrendered and Anketill's men captured both him and two of his sons. 'A rogue lay behind a bush', wrote Bennett, 'and shot Mr Anketill dead'. Once Anketill was no longer able to supervise matters, the prisoner, McKenna, was killed by his captors. The rebels fled from Glaslough to catch up with Blayney on his march towards Coleraine, and if anyone asked, they had defeated many, or six hundred, or a thousand Irish and killed many of them, or eighty-nine, or a hundred and eighty, or two hundred.[c]

We do not know what happened, other than that which is set out in the last paragraph. It may well be that no one was killed other than Anketill and McKenna. The point, which will be illustrated often below, is that the reading public in London was eager for reports of the war in Ireland. Whoever had access to the printers in London managed to secure his version, true or false, in black and white forever. To feed the press, the writers would eagerly record any ale-house boasts by those who claimed to know what was going on. There was then nothing like the London press anywhere else in the world, and almost all the printed accounts of the war came from London presses. A few leaflets and newsletters were printed in Dublin, but by a factor of fifty to one, London led the way. Dublin could not even begin to compete.

By way of illustration only, a pamphlet appeared in Dublin later in the year, *A relation of what passed in Connaught*. It described the capture by the Irish of Boyle, Jamestown and Sligo. It is a mirror image of the London publications in its careless use of numbers of the parties involved, the casualty figures and accounts of bravery (in this case by the Irish commanded by Henry Luttrell and Patrick Sarsfield) in driving out of Connaught the Enniskillen troops (commanded by Robert 'Laird' Weir, Thomas Lloyd and Theodore Russell). First, two hundred rebel horse were 'put to flight', and pursued for fourteen miles. In another action, the enemy are made to 'run back in full speed'. Weir tried to escape, but was killed with fifteen of his men. The Enniskilleners counter-attacked, but were 'two several times beaten back with loss'. Later, they 'were forced like hard hunted deer to … swim three rivers in which there were 80 drowned and several killed'. Out of '400 horse and dragoons' not 'ten got home together'. Attacked by two bodies of rebel horsemen, Luttrell 'broke both the parties, killing fifty upon the place, the rest he pursued in sight of Sligo'. When the Irish attacked Sligo, 'all the horse and foot that were

[c] The incident at Drumbanagher has been described as the first battle of the war, a claim founded on it having taken place a day before the break of Dromore, which itself is often cited as the first battle, although both took place after the attack on a troop of O'Neill's dragoons at Toome (on 11 February), the attempt on Carrickfergus (on 22 February) and the ambush of Captain Poe outside Loughbrickland a few days later.

in the town ran away with Lloyd and Russell'. No mention was made of any Irish losses, just repeated, bravely won victories. The London publications covering the same events could not hide the fact that Sligo had fallen to the Irish, but mention neither the casualty figures nor the headlong flights. They simply recorded that the Enniskillen 'losses were not great', that they ran short of ammunition and that the Irish outnumbered them by 'at least ten to one'.

In wartime, victories are always glorious and crushing. Defeats are always slight.

7

King James

On 12 March 1689, escorted by a French fleet, King James arrived in Kinsale. With him were Lord Melfort, his principal secretary of state; the comte d'Avaux, the special French ambassador; and over a hundred officers, including many who would serve before Derry: Rosen, Maumont, Pusignan, Pointis, Léry-Girardin, Wauchope, Vaudrey, Sir Neil O'Neill, John Hamilton and James' two teenaged sons, the duke of Berwick and Henry FitzJames. The country was in rapture. Tyrconnell met the king in Cork and was rewarded for his good work with a dukedom.

The general commanding all King James' forces was the tall, lean and fit 60-year-old Conrad de Rosen. The von Rosen-Kleinröb family were Baltic Germans long established in Livonia, then a Swedish dominion encompassing modern-day Latvia and Estonia.[1] Rosen was twenty-three before he first set foot in France, a fact illustrated by his dispatches being written in idiosyncratic French with an excessive use of negatives and missing conjunctions.

Rosen's early career is remarkable. He ran away from school in Riga to join the prince of Saxony's army. He then served three years as a cadet in the queen of Sweden's guards, but fled Stockholm after killing another youth in a duel. Penniless in Frankfurt, but 'tall and well built', he joined a French cavalry regiment and was brought in 1651 to France, where he served for three years as a trooper. Having lost his horse, he and some other soldiers were caught 'raiding' and were made to draw lots to determine who should be hanged. At this point Rosen broke cover and told his colonel that he was related to the great General Reinold de Rosen. 'As the Colonel liked the general, he gave the marquis a cornetcy in his regiment in 1654.'[2]

This began a distinguished career in which Rosen served in thirty battles and sieges. To fit in with his new masters, he renounced the Lutheran church to become a Catholic, and, following the peace in 1679, was engaged in King Louis' often brutal internal policy of suppressing the Protestants in France. He spent two years in Languedoc, where that policy was applied with vigour, and left on being promoted to lieutenant general in August 1688. Within months he was chosen to lead the expedition to Ireland.[3]

The break of Dromore took place while King James was in Kinsale, and in the days that followed, Richard Hamilton occupied Lisburn and then Belfast. Leaderless, the Association collapsed as a fighting force. Most of the men deserted and took protection, but several thousand made their way to Coleraine, the only rebel stronghold east of the Bann. Only two of the colonels, Sir Arthur Rawdon and Archibald Edmonstone, went with them. The garrison commander at Coleraine was Lundie's major, Gustavus Hamilton. Lundie now commanded all the rebel forces in Ulster, and the remnants of the Association placed themselves under his direction.

Although Hamilton's army was making for Coleraine, Lundie feared a supportive move by the Irish troops from Charlemont, which is why he had sent William Stewart to Dungannon to guard the southern approach to Derry. In Dungannon, Stewart found a body of local volunteers, and it is with these volunteers that the Reverend George Walker enters the narrative.

Walker was then in his mid-forties,[4] and had been for the previous fourteen years the rector of Donaghmore, three miles north of Dungannon. Walker's father had also been a country clergyman in the north of Ireland, but had left the country during the civil war, and during this exile George Walker was born in Yorkshire.[5] When the family returned to Ireland after the Restoration, Walker matriculated at Trinity College, Dublin in 1662 and, after a few years at Lissan, Co. Londonderry, he was installed at Donaghmore in 1674. There he led a quiet, unexceptional life in an area where the conformists were greatly outnumbered by Presbyterians resentful at having to pay him church tithes. The village had been devasted in the civil war, and he built (or rebuilt) both a mill and a rectory for his family of eight children.

George Walker was a remarkable man: intelligent, determined and very assertive while at the same time well able to present himself as charming, modest and self-effacing. His *True account of the siege of London-Derry* shows him also to have been a man of great imagination, often unfettered by the truth when he came to describe instances of his own bravery or ingenuity, but his lively mind, his drive and his education set him apart from the country people he led. He gave them both motivation and direction. He was a great organizer, an inspiring leader and, above all else, a natural politician.

In his *Account*, he introduced himself with these words: 'Mr. Walker saw it not only excusable, but necessary to concern himself and raise Men out of which he formed a Regiment', always referring to himself in the third person, 'and to apply what interest he could make towards the preservation of that town [Dungannon]'. This short passage is an early example of the exaggerated manner in which he portrayed himself. He did not raise just a company, he raised a whole regiment. The impression given is that he did it himself, but we know that the commanding officer of this body of men was Richard Swan, a young man who had a few months before been commissioned as an ensign.[6] During the siege when Walker was in Derry, Swan's evidence to the House of Commons Committee on Irish Affairs was 'that he and Mr. *Walker*, and others, persuaded Captain *Williams* [William Stewart] to keep the Fort at *Dungannon*, where they raised a Foot Company, and Two Troops of Horse'. Mackenzie also referred to 'Mr. *Walker* and his *Company*'.[7] By dint of commanding a band of militia, Ensign Swan now styled himself 'Lieutenant Colonel Swan'. Others were also involved. The Reverend Peter Maurice, then the rector of Drumglass immediately outside Dungannon 'maintained 50 men at his own charge, in defence of the Protestants, and … was put to great charges in defending the Castle of Dungannon'.[8] The officer elected to be the commander of a company would have taken the title 'captain', as would the commander of each of the troops of horsemen. Three units would entitle them to have three captains and, by being the senior captain, Swan felt entitled to call himself a colonel of this modest body of civilians, some armed with muskets, but most with pikes, scythes and swords. To assist the colonel, Walker appointed himself 'the major', a man who in this case had no military experience and no company of his own. It was as a major that Walker presented himself to Londonderry.

Had Swan, with or without Walker, raised a regiment as Walker claimed, Swan would have said so with great pride, but Swan's claim was limited to a single company (at a time when a regiment was expected to have thirteen companies) and two troops of horsemen. They probably had about fifty volunteers nominally under their command. Walker at no point mentioned Swan or Maurice in his *Account*. Without Walker, is the pervading message, nothing would have been done.

Walker then wrote that 'in order to settle a correspondence with Londonderry, Mr Walker rides to that town and consults Colonel Lundie'. Walker could not train or drill the volunteers but he could make the hundred-mile round trip to Derry. It was Walker's opportunity to meet the man in charge. He wanted Lundie to agree to defend Dungannon and told Lundie of his plans for the town. 'He [Lundie] Approves and Encourages the Design, sends two Files of his Disciplin'd Men to *Dungannon,* and afterwards two Troops of *Dragoons*.' Neither Lundie nor anyone else made any mention of Walker's visit or his advice, but according to Walker it was thanks to this visit that Lundie acted.

Walker next related an anecdote concerning his time in Dungannon. The volunteers complained they did not have enough gunpowder. He saw to it that 'a bag of mustard seed was laid upon the carriages, which by its resemblance, easily obtained the credit of a bag of powder, and immediately gave motion to the soldiers'. Whether this really took place, or whether Walker had heard the story somewhere else and adopted it for his *Account*, we will never know. These are the first three references to Walker in his *Account*. One of them was untrue (Walker raising a regiment) and the second is unlikely (Walker directing Lundie's military strategy), and the third may be no more than a pleasing fiction to illustrate Walker's cunning. None are supported by any other evidence. They all have one thing in common: they are about Walker and, like every other reference to Walker in his *Account*, they are entirely to Walker's credit.

Once the threat to Coleraine became imminent, Dungannon's importance to the defence of Londonderry faded. As soon as he heard of the defeat at Dromore, Lundie sent orders to Captain Stewart to march to Coleraine with all the soldiers under his command. One officer was to stay behind in Dungannon with the fifty volunteers to guard the castle. At the same time, Lord Blayney with his party arrived in Dungannon with news that Armagh and Glaslough had been taken by the Irish. Of Blayney's men, Lundie noted, 'not one man would stay at Dungannon' and 'for the most part dispersed of themselves to their several homes'. Stewart did as he was ordered and set off for Coleraine with his redcoats, but the volunteers were reluctant to go with him. According to Walker, 'some, considering the advantageous situation of the place [Dungannon], and the great quantity of provisions already laid in, and the consequence of leaving both, to give strength to their enemies, showed some unwillingness to comply with commands so different from the measures they had hitherto pursued'. They had amassed, Swan later told the House of Commons, 'two thousand pounds worth of oatmeal and other Grain'. Dungannon was abandoned. According to Walker, once Stewart had left, he and his men 'at last, agreed to march to Coleraine or Derry according to Colonel Lundie's orders'. Or, more accurately, they set off for Derry in disregard of Lundie's orders.

Mackenzie, who, as will be seen, was never slow to correct Walker's *Account* when he could point out any failings on Walker's part, also recorded the reluctance of the volunteers to go with Stewart. 'That great quantity of provisions which the country about had sent in' to Dungannon, he recorded, 'fell into the enemy's hands.'[9] It was clearly possible to move the stores. The Reverend Peter Maurice, who was also there, was said to have 'conveyed all his parishioners, with their provisions, to the stores at Londonderry'.[10] While Lundie was scrambling around to get supplies for the city, the Dungannon stores were neither removed nor destroyed. According to Swan, the Irish troops based at Charlemont were 'at that very time ready to starve, and could not have held their own garrisons much longer for want of provisions'. Nevertheless, he and Walker did nothing. 'All the provisions' were left behind and were seized by the Irish garrison from Charlemont.

Blayney, his force now much depleted through desertion, set off 'with all the speed he could' to the north. It was a perilous trip. He reported that he was attacked at Ardtrea Bridge on the road to Moneymore. This time it was by a force of 'a thousand' or 'twelve hundred' Irishmen, with another 'five hundred' in the rear. He fired at them and they ran away. He killed 'a hundred and forty', or 'about hundred and fifty-five' of them 'besides several that were drowned'. Blayney's was not the only group fleeing northwards. 'The gentlemen in the country in other parts were very active, particularly Sir Francis Hamilton, and Captain Robert Sanderson, in the county of Cavan', but now Sir Francis rode north, 'escaping several imminent dangers'. All the talk was of retreat and surviving Irish attacks. It was not that the Irish army was after them, as the Irish army was nowhere near, it was bodies of irregulars. The country was armed against them. Inflated reports of these skirmishes, and of the great numbers killed by the rebels, did not disguise the reality. The Irish were too strong to face up to, and the ever-victorious rebels were for the most part surrendering in exchange for protections, or else running for the safety of the north.

Londonderry's first line of defence was the river Bann. The Lower Bann flows for forty miles from Lough Neagh to the sea, and was not fordable at any point. The only two bridges were at Portglenone and Coleraine, and widespread flooding was an annual event. As soon as Lundie heard that the Irish were making for Belfast, he detached Captain Richard Gorges to break down the bridge at Portglenone. Hamilton's only way of getting to Derry would be through Coleraine.

'I writ to Sir Arthur Rawdon that I would be with him next day', recorded Lundie, 'and was sorry for his misfortune and the cowardice of his men'. He then called a meeting of all the leading men in the city. 'It was time to look to ourselves and lay down ways how to get in provisions of all kinds into our stores.' Although they had been told that £3,000 was on its way from England, they had no money. In anticipation of the funds arriving, he appointed four trusted men as storekeepers, and started gathering together a store for a siege 'by beat of drum through the town and afterward marched up on the pillar of the town house praying and desiring all people to bring in of all kinds, and they should have public faith for it to be paid out of the first money that came over'.

He also insisted that the buildings outside the walls be pulled down, as otherwise 'the enemy might roam at leisure and lodge themselves in comfort within ten yards of the walls', and that a ravelin, a great earth bank, be thrown up outside Bishop's Gate, which he saw as the weakest part of the town's defences. The gate faced the higher dry ground on Windmill Hill, the only place where cannons could be got close to the walls which were otherwise bounded by low lying ground, bog or the river. His plans were agreed. On the next morning he marked out the ground where the ravelin should be built, and ordered his men to start pulling down the houses.

Having promoted his second in command, Major Gustavus Hamilton, to colonel, Lundie rode with him to Coleraine. He found there the depleted remnants of the nine volunteer regiments from Down and Antrim. He did what he could to encourage them at a council of war: 'I told them I was very sorry for their disaster' and insisted that they consolidate their forces. The volunteer regiments of Londonderry, Donegal and Tyrone were already marching to join them, as was Lord Blayney, with his Monaghan men. 'We would make a considerable body of men', he said. 'Coleraine was a good post and easy to be kept.' Once the town was properly garrisoned, the rest of the army should cross over the bridge onto the Londonderry side and quarter themselves along the river from where they could both reinforce Coleraine if needed, and prevent the enemy from crossing in boats.

Lundie was the leader they needed. Unlike the commanders of the now evaporated Association, he knew what he was doing. 'They pressed me to stay to command. I told them I could not, but would give them all the assistance I could but Colonel [Gustavus] Hamilton would return in two days to command, which pacified them.' But having already been deserted by their entire leadership, some were far from pacified. If Coleraine was the best place to stop the Irish army, then Lundie ought to be there to defend it.

> Some subaltern officers and almost all their men began to be very troubled, some saying that they were betrayed by their officers and in their madness

> drew up their drawbridge against me and presented their arms at me. I went to them and desired them to recover their arms and desired to know why they had done so but could get no satisfactory answer, only the bridge was let down. I was forced to stay all that day to get them pacified for I never saw such disorder and distraction for everybody was running up and down like mad men. Next day I had them all under arms but still mutinous. I was forced at last to desire Sir Arthur Rawdon to put a guard of his men to the bridge that I might not be stopped as they intended which he did and the first night with great difficulty I got from them and rode all night and got to Derry.

That was the last Coleraine saw of Lundie. The redcoats, the regular soldiers from Mountjoy's regiment and the detachments and deserters from other Irish regiments were not to him the problem, but they were in a minority. Overwhelming the forces at Lundie's disposal were volunteers. Mackenzie, in writing what was the most detailed account of siege, acted as their voice: 'The commonalty at Coleraine suspected Colonel Lundie', he wrote, 'and they imagined he was going away, and drew up the bridge, and the guard presented their muskets and pikes at him'. At no time did Mackenzie give Lundie credit for doing anything. 'It was concluded that, because there was much to do at Derry, to fortify and provide it with stores, that Colonel Lundie should remain in Derry, and Colonel Gustavus Hamilton manage the field'. To read Mackenzie is to be left thinking that there was a democratic vote as to who should command or whether Lundie should return to Londonderry. Mackenzie went on: 'it was ordered by the Committee of Derry, that a ravelin should be built to defend the Bishop's Gate', as if the committee had come up with the idea of the best means of defending the town while Lundie stood by, perhaps amazed at their collective wisdom.

Lundie got back to a Londonderry more packed with people than it had ever been. He did not need any more refugees, and on learning that the Tyrone militia, who had now restyled themselves 'Lord Charlemont's Regiment' after the great landlord in south Tyrone, led by Swan and a clergyman called Walker, had reached Strabane, Lundie ordered them back. They were to retrace their steps and block the road at Omagh with several troops and companies from across Tyrone, Londonderry and Donegal. It is not clear what happened to Swan, but he took protection before the siege, spent time in the Irish camp and Dublin, and was in London in the summer, where he gave evidence before committees of both Houses of Parliament.[A] [11] Walker claimed then to be in command of five companies, which he took to the Rash just north of Omagh, while another five under the command of the newly styled lieutenant colonel Henry Mervyn occupied Omagh itself.

[A] In 1691, Captain Richard Swan commanded the artillery train at Sligo, and was appointed master gunner to Dublin Castle at the end of the war.

On 15 March 1689, Lundie held another of his great committee meetings, with 'all the noblemen, gentlemen and townsmen'. If Coleraine fell, he told them, the Irish army would be at the gates in four days. Their safety depended on Coleraine holding out. 'I desired them to think of a way to raise a sum of money to be sent to Coleraine for finishing their ramparts and subsisting the men, for nothing could be expected from them without pay, as they told me, for they would not venture their lives to preserve their landlords' estates for nothing.' He raised ('with much difficulty') £400 from the meeting, £300 of which he gave to Gustavus Hamilton, who rode straight back to Coleraine to get started. 'In a short while', wrote Lundie, Colonel Hamilton 'put the men on a good footing for they began to obey, they being under pay'. In Derry, notwithstanding Lundie's requests for provisions, stronger measures were needed. He requisitioned and moved to the stores all the salmon, butter and cheese from the city merchants, and wrote 'to the gentlemen of the country to oblige their tenants to send in all the grain that they could on the public faith otherwise they would lose it, for if our own men or the enemy came amongst them, they would take it for nothing'.

On Thursday 21 March, the *Jersey* frigate, commanded by Captain John Beverley, arrived accompanied by the *Deliverance*, a Chester merchantman with a cargo of gunpowder, arms and ammunition. In overall command of the supplies was the 28-year-old Captain James Hamilton, a (Protestant) nephew of Richard Hamilton, but a remarkably well connected young man. He was a great nephew of the duke of Ormonde, formerly a groom of the bedchamber to Charles II, a privy counsellor to Charles II and then James II, and he was yet to inherit his cousin's title as Lord Abercorn. He had the best of connections with the new king and queen, his mother having been a maid of honour to Queen Mary and, at a time when trust was more important than experience, he was given the important mission of supplying arms and commissions to Londonderry.

Once Lundie had boarded the frigate with his officers, Captain Hamilton got down to the formal business. Everyone was to leave the cabin except himself, Lundie, William Stewart, Henry Mervyn and Captain James Corry. The rest, including Arthur Rawdon and the ship's captain, were left on deck to wait in the rain. James Hamilton's instructions were to give Lundie his orders, a colonel's commission as the city's governor, £1,000 in gold and a freight of arms and stores 'for the use and defence of the Protestants against the Papists'. Hamilton's instructions were explicit: 'You [shall] first cause him to take the oaths herewith sent, on board the ship wherein you shall arrive there, in the presence of the mayor, or chief civil magistrate of Londonderry.'[B]

Lundie informed Hamilton that there was no mayor, and there was no chief magistrate. The lawful mayor was Cormack O'Neill, who was now a colonel in King James' army. Notwithstanding any fiction that was being perpetrated by (Lundie

[B] Only Protestants who swore allegiance to William and Mary were to be trusted. The oaths were those of Allegiance and Supremacy as set out in the Bill of Rights (12 Feb. 1689).

might think) a group of self-important former aldermen and burgesses whose authority had long since been taken away, the old corporation did not exist. The only person who could lawfully carry out the mayor's duties, was John Buchanan, the deputy mayor appointed by Cormack O'Neill, but Buchanan was 'suspected for a Papist'. Therefore, Lundie took the oaths, which were administered by James Hamilton in the cabin of the *Jersey* in the presence of Henry Mervyn, the militia colonel from Omagh, and Captain James Corry from Enniskillen. No one has ever suggested that James Hamilton was in anyway untrustworthy. He would not have given anything to Lundie had Lundie not taken the oaths. The only concession he made was to dispense with the need for a mayor. After it was all over, Hamilton told the others waiting outside that Lundie had taken the oaths.

When the arms and ammunition were landed, Lundie was disappointed. There were only sixteen hundred muskets, of which six hundred, over a third, were defective. Most of the muskets were the older matchlock models ('and the match was very pitiful stuff') rather than up-to-date flintlocks. 'This supply did much more hurt than good for they were in great expectation of having much more', wrote Lundie. He had also expected £3,000 but, although Hamilton's orders were to take £1,000 in gold, all that could be scraped together in Chester was a total of 'five hundred ninety-five pounds, sixteen shillings and eight-pence'.[12]

Lundie also had to deal with the damaging talk in the city concerning the defenders of Coleraine. There was a rumour that the Association men were going to run or take protections if the Irish got anywhere near them. He called a meeting of the officers, gentry and councilmen that same day and had them all make a reassuring 'declaration of union' to be posted in the town. The rumour was 'false, scandalous, and malicious'. Lundie, the committee and people of Londonderry were united with the Association men. They were 'absolutely resolved to oppose the Irish Enemy with their utmost Force'. Should they 'be forced to retire into this city for shelter, (which God forbid) the said Lord Blayney, Sir Arthur Rawdon, and their Forces, and all other Protestant friends, shall be readily received into this City'. It was signed by the senior officers present, the aldermen, burgesses and sheriffs.[c] [13]

On the following day, the oaths were administered to all the civil and military officers in the town. The formalities were conducted by both Lundie and John Campsie, the *de facto* mayor. Lundie, having ensured the garrison took the oaths, and having proclaimed King William and Queen Mary, was urged to take the oaths publicly. He looked upon the request as an impertinence. He had already taken the oaths in front of witnesses, as James Hamilton had told them (and as James Hamilton would later tell the House of Commons committee), and was not now going to go through the charade of repeating the process again. A year after the event, when Lundie was suspected of having been a traitor, Rawdon said that 'most' people were dissatisfied. 'It was much wondered at', wrote Mackenzie, 'that when

[c] Of the thirty-six signatories, only four were present during the siege.

the committee of Derry, and the officers, the next day desired that Lundy might take the oaths before them all, for their greater satisfaction, he absolutely refused it on pretence of having taken 'em on board the day before'. George Phillips, always a sensible man, tried to talk Lundie around on this, but Lundie was a man with no political sense, and would not do it. In many ways it did not matter, but it would have been an easy concession to make, and would have cost Lundie nothing. Instead, he fed feelings what would later turn to distrust, and would later still be used against him.[14]

None of that worried Lundie. What concerned him was the lack of firearms. He wrote a letter to the secretary of state, Lord Shrewsbury, setting out his disappointment, and sent it off with George Phillips on 23 March. The meagre supply of weapons had 'bred a great deal of bad blood and made a great many leave the kingdom that had no thoughts of it before'. Without arms and experienced officers, the city 'must inevitably fall a prey into the Irish hands'. He needed money because 'the men were negligent and would do nothing, neither could we punish them having no money to make them subsist', and above all he needed provisions for 'the great numbers of people that flood from all parts to Derry being chased there by the Irish'.

The most important part of the shipment had been the invaluable gunpowder. It was more than enough for the city's magazine. Lundie sent twenty barrels to Coleraine, and allocated five barrels to Enniskillen, three to Sligo and one for Ballyshannon. The last allocations were done with some reluctance because he needed to consolidate forces. Only a week before, he had sent an urgent request to Lord Kingston in to Sligo to 'hasten' to Derry with his men. Well aware of their isolation, the Sligo Association voted to abandon the town. They evacuated Sligo on 21 March. Every Protestant left. They burnt the stores they could not take, disabled the larger guns, and took everything else with them. Four days later, after great hardships, harried by the weather and the Irish, they made it to Ballyshannon and its sturdy fort surrounded by two thick outer walls and a deep moat. Sligo's allocation of gunpowder from the *Jersey* also went to Ballyshannon, where Kingston got a further letter from Lundie ordering him and his men to stay there with the garrison to prevent the Irish from invading Ulster from Connaught. Kingston was furious. To him, after all the work fortifying Sligo, abandoning it was a betrayal and, when the time came, motivated him to give bitter evidence against Lundie.[15]

King James arrived in Dublin on Palm Sunday, 24 March. He was greeted by joyous crowds, lines of soldiers, bells ringing, cannons roaring, music and dancing. When he heard the pipers playing 'When the king enjoys his own again', he wept. On the next day he issued a proclamation promising freedom of religion and announced that he would be calling an Irish parliament to sit on 7 May.

8

Coleraine

COLERAINE WAS THEN half the size of Derry, and had recently increased in importance since the building of a large timber bridge over the Bann. The town was now crammed not only with Gustavus Hamilton's garrison, but with the remains of the Association army, still several thousand strong. Defended by stone-fronted earthen ramparts 'of a considerable height' and a series of small bastions, the only ways in were across the bridge on the Bann, or through the two gate houses, each with a drawbridge over a wet ditch. The south-facing gatehouse through which the road ran from Belfast, was called (for reasons that are now obscure) the Blind Gate.

On the morning of 27 March, Lundie's supply train of twenty barrels of powder entered Coleraine. No sooner had it arrived, than Richard Hamilton's army marched into view. Little care had been taken to clear the area outside the defences and, under shelter of hedges and ditches, the Irish got up to within fifty yards of the ramparts and, by occupying a mill, within forty yards of one of the bastions. They quickly set up their five small field guns in two batteries and opened fire, randomly it seems, all over the town 'battering down a few chimneys, and making a few breaches in the church roof'. The bombardment went on for six hours, but as the afternoon wore on, Hamilton saw that he was getting nowhere. He did not have the means to break down the defences, it was bitterly cold, his men needed shelter, and there was a heavy fall of snow, 'which covered the ground in an instant'. Once it was clear to Hamilton that he had failed to overawe the defenders, and could not entice them out into the open, he ordered his men to withdraw. As the light failed, his army marched off into the gloom of the snowstorm.[1]

There was no organized pursuit and no attack on the main body of the enemy. The dangers of facing the Irish army in the open, and especially the Irish cavalry, had already been demonstrated at Dromore. The weak explanation for the Association forces not issuing out was that the Blind Gate had been blocked up 'with timber, earth, and rubbish, which was not to be removed suddenly', although some jumped down from the ramparts to chase the stragglers and even managed to take a few prisoners. 'We lost but three men, which is very little, considering the continual firing of the enemy. What they lost is uncertain, because they carried off their dead.'[2]

The French, who were not there, were unimpressed. The gunners were so poor that they could not even hit the houses. Hamilton's planning was abysmal. He had staked everything on the rebels surrendering as soon as he appeared and so had only brought enough provisions for a day. After a useless attack, he withdrew for six miles. The rebels' performance was even more pitiful, as they had not risked a single sortie even though they outnumbered the Irish. A single French battalion, wrote d'Avaux, would have finished the job. And Derry as well.[3]

The defence of Coleraine was reported as a great victory in London. The Irish army had laid a formal siege, and the Protestants made two successful sallies. Then:

> The Third Sally is made, and further than before, where pretending to run they made towards the Garrison; the deluded Foe, with much Fury, pursues to the Gates, where the Protestants, opening to the Right, and Left upon the Signal given, they Fired six Pieces of Conceal'd Cannon, which made such Slaughter amongst the Poor Irish, that it Stopt their Career for that time, the Rest being blown up in a Mine to the Number of 2 or 3,000.[4]

Of course, there were no sallies. There was no feigned retreat. There were no concealed cannon. There was no mine. And there were certainly not three thousand Irish soldiers to kill. London had already seen a report that month of the Irish being defeated in battle at Hillsborough with the loss of six thousand men. As will be seen below, wartime publications reporting events in Londonderry were going to be no less imaginative.[5]

Hamilton's army had had a long, wet march, and returned to Ballymoney and beyond to rest and dry out. Hamilton knew he was not going to take Coleraine with the small army he had with him. While he paused, he looked at other options. He investigated the new bridge twenty miles upriver at Portglenone, described at the time as being one of the best timber bridges in the three kingdoms: 'there are seats upon it to rest and view the pleasures of the Bann water, and a draw-bridge'.[6] Hamilton sent his scouts off to inspect it. They were too late. Lundie's men had burnt the bridge, although not perhaps beyond repair.

The more difficult route to Coleraine was on the west side of Lough Neagh. The absence of proper roads and the great bogs made for slow progress but, should Hamilton fail to cross the Lower Bann, he would have no choice. Assured of four thousand new troops who were being marched up from Dublin, he ordered them to assemble at Dungannon.

It was from Dungannon that an Irish scouting party reached Moneymore, fifteen miles away. Rumours reached Coleraine that there were two thousand of them, and Gustavus Hamilton responded quickly. He held back three thousand men in the town and sent the rest of his forces out to block the threat from the south and to cover every crossing along the forty miles of the Lower Bann. It was an ambitious plan. Arthur Rawdon was sent ahead with the horsemen, and a regiment of foot followed to occupy Moneymore and Magherafelt. Two other regiments were sent to guard the river around Kilrea, to block the road at Dawson's Bridge, and to cover the two crossing points on the Bann above Portglenone at Toome and Newferry. It was miserable work. The Bann was flooded, as was the countryside around it. Opposite Toome, the floods were so bad that 'they could seldom get to their posts, or relieve their guards'. Orders were issued to destroy all the boats and cots.[A] [7]

Edmonstone's volunteers were given two small field guns and the task of stopping the Irish from fixing the wooden bridge at Portglenone. The weather was grim and, as the village of Portglenone lay on the opposite bank, they had no shelter. They dug trenches from where they could shoot down any attempt to lay beams across the gap, but there was nothing they could do to stop the flooding, and the men were forced to stand, sodden with rain, up to their knees in cold water.[8] It was clear from the start that stopping a crossing was not going to be easy. There were hundreds of boats and cots on the Bann and its tributaries, and on loughs Beg and Neagh, and the Irish were probing. Reports came in of attempts to cross at Agivey, eight miles upriver from Coleraine, and at Newferry, downstream from Lough Beg, and a whole Irish regiment appeared at Portglenone and exchanged fire across the river with the men in Edmonstone's trenches.

Arthur Rawdon and his dragoons rode the seventeen miles to Moneymore on 2 April to find the place deserted, so he occupied himself in scouring the country for provisions. While he was there, Edmonstone sent an urgent message to say that his men were almost starved at Portglenone bridge and needed provisioning quickly. Leaving a small garrison at Moneymore, Rawdon brought his men back to join Edmonstone on the evening of 5 April to find 'continued firing on both sides'. On the next day, according to Mackenzie, 'We killed near twenty of the enemy, and with hot iron bullets fired the town where they lay, and drove them all out of it'.[9] But the position was far from secure. At two on the morning on 7 April, Rawdon got the urgent news that an Irish army of four thousand men, a larger body than Hamilton commanded, had arrived at Dungannon, and intended to attack Moneymore. Deciding to divide his forces, he mounted up and, with Major Henry Baker, Captain Hugh Magill, Captain Philip Dunbar and all the horsemen, made off to meet the new threat. Edmonstone and his men were left to guard the bridge alone.

Of the six senior French officers King James had brought with him from France, the first into the field was the brigadier of infantry, Jean de Camus, the marquis de Pusignan, for the past eight years the colonel of the Languedoc regiment. His instructions were to go to Dungannon to rendezvous with the troops there and to use them as directed by Richard Hamilton to take Coleraine. Pusignan's intention from the beginning was to support Hamilton's attack on Portglenone by making for the bridge from the opposite bank. He anticipated Coleraine would be abandoned if the Irish army advanced on both sides of the river. If not, once the armies

[A] 'They call in Ireland Cots things like Boats, but very unshapely, being nothing but square pieces of timber made hollow'. G. Boate, *Ireland's natural history* (1652), viii, p. 64.

had joined forces, they could take Coleraine from both sides, which would 'completely disconcert' the rebels in Derry.[10]

Pusignan arrived in Dungannon on 6 April. 'Nobody has kept their word about anything that was promised me', he wrote, 'not even the setting up of post horses that I have so often requested'. Instead of the four thousand infantry and six hundred horsemen he had been led to expect, he found only about two thousand men, and they did not have a sword between them. There were not enough muskets to go round and, as many of those were in no fit state to fire, most of the infantry were equipped with pikes. Although Tyrconnell had given Pusignan a French-speaking officer with instructions 'never to leave my side', he had only seen him for two hours. 'You can well imagine the state I am in with no knowledge of the language.'

He had understood there were nine cannons at Charlemont, but was now told that there were no gun-carriages. He instructed the carpenters he had brought with him from Dublin to build two, 'but they ask for twelve days and even then I do not know if they will do it well, as I cannot be there to supervise'. At Charlemont, there were only twenty balls for a fourteen- or fifteen-pounder, and six balls for the smaller guns. It simply was not worth the trouble of taking them. 'It would give me the greatest pleasure in the world', he wrote, 'if you sent M. de Pointis' people with some ready-made gun carriages'. There were only thirty-seven barrels of powder at Charlemont, and part of that was ruined, and half as many musket balls needed for the quantity of powder, and he now learnt that everything he needed was seventy miles away at Drogheda.

The rebels, he heard, had made off with two thousand cattle and entrenched themselves at Dawson's Bridge on the road to Portglenone. When he arrived at Dungannon, three companies of his cavalry and dragoons were out looking for forage, and so he sent Lieutenant Colonel Francis Carroll with his remaining sixty horsemen to find them. The answer came back that his foragers had found some of Rawdon's dragoons, killed seven of them, brought back some prisoners and had since set off after another group. The prisoners knew nothing of what the other troops were doing because they had all been dispersed to take back to Coleraine all the forage they could find which, wrote Pusignan, 'means that there will be nothing left for me'. He let the prisoners go. 'They would be an embarrassment if I kept them, and are not worth the trouble, I thought it better to let them loose to publish the fact that I am here, and to frighten the others'. When Carroll returned, it was with the news that he had chased Rawdon's men to Moneymore, fifteen miles away. The enemy were in a blind panic. It was time to get moving before they could organize themselves or pillage anything else.

While Edmonstone's men had been blazing away at Portglenone, the commander of the Irish regiment facing him, Colonel William Nugent,[11] made other plans. His men seized 'five or six great boats' upstream, packed them with thirty or forty grenadiers, and set off down the river in the dark. Half a mile above the bridge, the grenadiers jumped out and the boats pulled away to the opposite shore to ferry the rest of the regiment across. Edmonstone, wholly fixated on preventing the bridge from being repaired, had left his flanks undefended. As the Irish came at him, he ordered half of his men to line a ditch along the side of the bog, where 'two or three companies of the grenadiers' were wading towards them. There was fierce firing between the sides, before the Irish, now too numerous to deal with, stormed out onto the dry ground, swept Edmonstone's men aside and rushed the trenches. The defenders fled into the night.

Rawdon's party had barely left when the shooting started. Leaving his men, Rawdon raced back with Captain Dunbar. He was too late. As they galloped to the bridge, they were greeted with a volley of shot. A hundred Irish redcoats ran behind them to line the hedges to block their escape. One of the Association officers, Lieutenant Colonel Whitney rushed his five companies along the road to help, but when he saw what had happened, he changed his mind and ordered them to pull back. Captain James Magill, went on ('ashamed', wrote Mackenzie, 'of so base a retreat'). At the same time Sir Arthur Rawdon and Captain Dunbar made a dash for safety, while 'the shot poured in upon them from the hedges'. Magill was shot off his horse. 'A captain of the grenadiers came up and run his sword several times through him, and another of them dashed out his brains with a musket'.[12]

Mackenzie, who played down the losses on his own side (as, we shall see, he was prone to do), wrote: 'Besides Captain James Magill and several common soldiers who were lost, one Captain Henly was wounded and taken prisoner.' His vagueness as to numbers is juxtaposed with his confident assertion of the day before that Edmonstone's men had 'killed near twenty of the enemy' on the far side of an impassable river. The most detailed Irish account, the *Poema de Hibernia*, claimed great losses were inflicted on the 'Scots army'. The Irish, having crossed 'on silent oars', crept up on the defences and launched a surprise attack, catching the officers together. It was a great victory. 'Oh, what a mighty slaughter could a band so small upon so many thousand wreak!'[13] Like Aickin's poem *Londerias*, the *Poema* is written in flamboyant terms. It describes Nugent himself striking off the head of an officer named Craig. Eleven other rebel officers are named as having been killed, but whether these men had Association officer ranks (or whether they even existed) we will never know, and the one officer known to have died, Magill, is not mentioned. A more humane image of William Nugent was given by Joseph Bennett:

> The business being over, on viewing the body of Capt. Henly, being strangely mangled, Col. Nugent observed him to move, and asking whether he was not dead, Capt. Henly said, he was not, and therefore desired honourable quarters, which [he] was given, and he [was] sent to the hospital near Coleraine, and well recovered of his wounds by the particular directions of Col. Nugent.[14]

There followed, on that miserable morning on the road outside Clady, an impromptu council of war. The senior Association officers decided to act on their own initiative. They had lost the bridge of Portglenone, and another Irish force was advancing on Moneymore. Edmonstone and Whitney headed off for Coleraine. Rawdon, exhausted, with his dragoons, and the rest of the infantry, set off for Derry.

On the day of the Portglenone crossing, Pusignan mounted up all the horse he could muster, sixty cavalrymen and eighty dragoons, and rode north. 'We were in no state to frighten anyone except militia', he wrote, but there was no opposition because the rebels 'were so overcome with terror'. He wrote back to d'Avaux: 'Those I sent to fight can exclaim like Caesar "*veni, vidi, vici*": Moneymore, Magherafelt, and Dawson's Bridge which were castles, and a bridge at the latter where the enemy had dug in, have been abandoned'. The rebel collapse was complete. Apart from a few captains who took protection, the enemy had 'fled over the mountains'.[15]

Lundie was furious, especially at Rawdon's actions, or lack of action. The rebels had as many men as the Irish.

> About 700 of the enemy passed the river a little above by boats and came down and attacked our 700 that was entrenched, killed two of their captains and put the rest to flight out of their trenches, the sight of which put the rest of their men in such consternation that without more consideration they of shamefulness instead of going to force back that party ran straight to the walls of Derry.[16]

Isolated in Coleraine, Gustavus Hamilton gave up. He abandoned the town, cut and set fire to the bridge, ordered his men to Derry and told the officers, according to Michelburne, 'Everyone shift for themselves'.[17] He then took a boat and left the country, 'so rebuked', wrote Lundie, 'with the cowardice of the men that he would stay no longer. A great many followed his example and went off'. Rawdon blamed Gustavus Hamilton: 'I was sent by Col. Gustavus Hamilton out when Coleraine was quitted. The Colonel seemed dissatisfied at our taking arms so soon, and said we should not see the Kingdom quiet again. He seemed dissatisfied with the proceedings in England, and with our taking arms.'[18] Pusignan wrote to d'Avaux: 'Half our task has been accomplished. Coleraine belongs to the king.' There was now not a single defended post held by the rebels between the river Bann and Derry.

9

Preparations

'IF MY TROUBLES WAS GREAT BEFORE', wrote Lundie, 'it was much more now for all the British of Ulster, apart from only a few at Enniskillen, was got to Derry and in such consternation that they looked like people bereaved of their senses. In spite of all my endeavours the town was full of them.' He pulled in his outlying garrisons and allotted them quarters in the Laggan, the lowlands around St Johnstown. He sent another letter to London. His condition was desperate. 'The men were downright mutinous and would do nothing but what they pleased.' Unless the king sent a general with an army and provisions, it would be too late.

He needed to calculate the state of the supplies in the city, and sent for the storekeepers. Two of the four he had appointed had simply disappeared with their boat. He took Colonel James Hamilton to the stores to carry out an inspection. 'To my great surprise', wrote Lundie, the quantity of meal he had expected to find was not there. His plans were thrown out. He ordered searches of private houses the inhabitants had left behind, and had all the foodstuffs brought into the stores. He issued a proclamation offering ready money for all hay brought in from the country.

Nothing was now going to be fast enough. On the following day he made use of the horsemen who had come from Coleraine and Portglenone, and sent out them out to scour the country as far as Letterkenny for all the meal, oats and hay they could find. Farmers were only to be left with 'a competency for the use of their families'. 'This', wrote Lundie, 'so incensed the country against me that they said I was worse than the enemy could be and from that minute buried their grain underground.' Nor did he make himself popular in setting his men to work on 'levelling all the suburbs', but he was not going to let the Irish get as close to the city as they had at Coleraine. He requisitioned the sixty tons of salmon stored in Lord Massereene's fish house. Anticipating that the Irish would first concentrate their efforts on Culmore, he took a decision that almost certainly saved Londonderry: he had the six big guns at Culmore Fort brought up into the city to prevent them falling into Irish hands. There was also frenetic activity in getting the ravelin finished, not assisted by the shortage of spades and shovels. He wrote again to London, adding tools to the list.

Protestants from all over Ulster fled from the Irish advance. Michelburne described 'poor country people', men women and children, clutching their belongings as they drove their cattle, going 'they knew not whither'.[1] Crowds of people of all sorts arrived in the city each day. Some were Association men gathering to fight for the last Protestant refuge in Ireland, but most were families looking for refuge or shipping to Scotland. It was not always a happy union. The newcomers from eastern Ulster were almost all Presbyterian Scots and quickly swamped the local population, most of whom sought ways to leave. Arthur Bushe, a Revenue man who had fled from Athlone, wrote: 'I arrived at Derry the beginning of March and intended [to travel] no further till by the dissentions between the Protestants and Presbyterians in those parts (which appeared upon the approach of Tyrconnell's forces) it was apparent I was not safe there.' Another correspondent wrote: 'The factions were great but are something abated, scarce a pedlar would take a commission less than a captain's and the Presbytery would allow no officers but of their disciples. The covetousness, ambition and factions will ruin the Protestant cause there. But besides religion, nation puts in and the Scots' covetousness to have Ireland to themselves made them divide from the English till the defeat of the Down and Antrim forces showed them their own weakness and folly.'[2]

Among the throng were deeply suspicious characters. Off the ships with James Hamilton was Captain Nicholas Darcy, a man with a thousand-acre estate in Meath. One of Tyrconnell's new intake of captains in 1686, Darcy had been sent to England to stop the Dutch invasion, and had then fled to Scotland to make his way home.[3] Lundie had him arrested. He also arrested William Blacker of Castleblacker, Co. Armagh, who had fled north after being captured with his family by the Irish in Tyrone, and old George Twynyhoe, once a sergeant in Cromwell's army, but now commissioned in Mountjoy's regiment. They were improbable King James loyalists but, according to Mackenzie, they had been sent from Charlemont by King James himself 'as was reported, and confirmed by an intercepted letter' with instructions to get the garrison to surrender with 'accounts of the clemency of the King on the one hand, and the formidable strength of his army on the other'.[4]

On 9 April, 'the body of our army came to the ferry', wrote Mackenzie. 'It was no small trouble to see so many brave and resolute men, both horse and foot, without a general.' They were exhausted and many were in a bad condition. While the infantry and others were ferried across to the city, Lundie ordered the horsemen to ride down to Lifford and Strabane and wait there. Edmonstone and his infantry were sent to Culmore, where Edmonstone, having 'contracted those distempers in the trenches at Portglenone', died on 14 April.[5] Sir Arthur Rawdon was also ill, and took to his bed.

On the following day, 10 April, David Cairnes returned to the city from his mission to London to beg for help defending the city. He brought with him a letter from King William's principal secretary of state, addressed to Lundie. 'There are two regiments already at the sea side ready to embark, in order to their transportation into the province, with which will be sent a good quantity of arms and ammunition … They will be speedily followed by so considerable a body as (by the blessing of God) may be able to rescue the whole kingdom.' The king was relying on Lundie, who was to demand of everyone 'more than ordinary vigour, to keep out that deluge of Popery and slavery which so nearly threatens them'. The letter ended: 'You will always find the King graciously disposed to own and reward the services you shall do him in such a time of trial.'

Lundie called a council of war of all the senior officers then in the city. Buoyed up by the king's letter, they were determined to hold out. Their principal concern was discipline. Lundie calculated that he had provisions for a thousand extra men to join the garrison. They would be formed into companies and put under officers. Everyone 'not of this garrison' was to stay outside the city. Only the garrison troops would be entitled to provisions from the magazine: 'eight quarts of meal, four pound of fish, and three pounds of flesh' a week, and 'a quart of small beer per diem'. The garrison troops were to be assigned posts 'to which they shall repair upon any sudden alarm' and 'upon beating of the retreat every night, shall repair to their several quarters and lodgings'. The thousand new members of the garrison would be put to work by having all 'the old houses about the walls and ditches without the gates divided among them, to be levelled with all possible speed'.

The articles of war were to be read out at the head of all the troops, and 'a pair of gallows shall be erected in one of the bastions upon the south-west of the city, whereupon all mutinous or treacherous persons of this garrison shall be executed, who shall be condemned thereunto by a court-martial'. The troops and officers were to defend the city as a disciplined body under Lundie's governorship. A declaration was issued:

> We the Officers hereunto subscribing, pursuant to a Resolution taken, and agreed upon at a Council of War at *London-Derry* held this day; do hereby mutually promise and engage, to stand by each other with our Forces against the common Enemy, and will not leave the Kingdom, nor desert the public Service, until our affairs are in a settled and secure Posture. And if any of us shall do the Contrary, the person so leaving the Kingdom, or deserting the Service, without consent of a Council of War, is to be deemed a Coward, and disaffected to their Majesties Service, and the Protestant Interest.[6]

'This Resolution', wrote Mackenzie, 'was read next morning at the head of every battalion, at which the soldiers expressed their great satisfaction with loud acclamations and huzzas'.

All of the above point to one thing. Lundie and those with him saw Londonderry as a fortress that could be defended so long as it was populated by a defined number of soldiers. None of them saw it as being a place of general refuge. The 'mutual agreement' applied only to the garrison and the forces outside. It did not apply generally. It did not extend to those who were not in arms, nor to the women and children. Lundie granted passes to those who wanted to leave the country.

The attitude of those who stayed to those who left was generally one of acceptance. Thousands had already taken protections and gone home.[A] Others thought it better to get out of the way of the advancing Irish army, and had fled not only to Derry, but to Enniskillen and the villages of Donegal and, where they could, Scotland. Lundie needed to make room for the new men who were to join the garrison. There were so many volunteers waiting to join, that the city would only be strengthened by 'unuseful mouths' leaving. Everyone could see that difficult decisions had to be made. People had to weigh up the dangers and expense of getting to Scotland, against the dangers and uncertainties of staying in Ireland. Captain Thomas Ash stayed throughout the siege. He offered no criticism of those who got on the boats to Scotland. He wrote with particular affection of his younger brother, James Ash ('much respected by everyone that met him'), a lieutenant in Mountjoy's regiment, who went to Scotland with his brother Henry. Ash's stepmother, since re-married, left with her husband and Ash's four youngest siblings. They all survived the siege by getting out. Ash's sisters, Mary and Sarah, stayed in the city and their children died. It was a time of hard choices. If a man could save his family, he should go.[7]

On the afternoon of Saturday, 13 April 1689, the Irish at last put in an appearance. 'Three squadrons of the enemy's horse appeared on the other side of the river and sent some horse near the town, I suppose to view it', wrote Lundie. 'I had a gun fired at them and they immediately retired.' The cannon shot from 'the bastion next Ferry-gate … did no execution.'[8] Soon, 'a considerable part of King James' army' came into view on its victorious march from Coleraine, 'horse and dragoons near three miles in length all in scarlet and blue'.[9] The Irish set up camp for the night across the water in Ballyoan. No army could march without its baggage, and the fifteen miles of road to Lifford was bad and boggy. If they marched in the morning, they would be in sight of the fords at Lifford by the end of the following day and would attempt a crossing on Monday.

Lundie called his officers together. 'I laid our condition before them telling how we were all driven into a little place where certainly we must all perish by famine if all stayed there, their numbers was so great.' However, the Irish would have to cross the Finn and 'we ought to venture all rather than suffer them to pass'. He would lead them and force a battle. 'This was approved of by all.' He already had the fords covered by troops and defences thrown up. 'All that had or could carry arms should rendezvous on Monday the 15 of April by ten in the clock in the morning between Long Causey and Lifford.' Everyone not already at the fords would join his great mobile force, ready to give support wherever the Irish attempted to cross.

[A] Protections were granted 'to all such as will submit themselves, and lay down their Arms, and peaceably live in their own Dwellings'. They were generally written in these terms: 'I Richard Hamilton, Lieutenant General of His Majesty's Forces in Ulster, do receive into His Majesty's Protection, the Body and Goods of [name] and promise and oblige myself, That none of the Army shall molest, or hurt him, or take anything from him.' Anon., *An apology for the Protestants of Ireland* (1689), pp 32–3.

The call to arms was proclaimed by beat of drum and pinned up around the city. Everyone would know that the leadership was united in the plan to stop the Irish in battle. Every man aged from sixteen to sixty was to go.[10] He sent riders off to Enniskillen and Ballyshannon, demanding mounted reinforcements for the coming battle and, in preparation for the worst, he had the few remaining houses outside the city burnt.

That same evening, the twenty-four members of the city council met to put themselves in order. The mayor they had reappointed in January, old John Campsie, had died. They elected Gervais Squire.[11]

The river Foyle is formed of the confluence of the rivers Mourne and Finn. The Finn runs from west to east and had to be crossed if Hamilton's army was to reach Derry. From Strabane the quickest route in good weather and at low tide was over the ford at Lifford, overlooked by a small plantation fort. The next crossing point was four miles upriver at Clady, where there was a bridge built over the old ford. Two miles beyond Clady was another ford at Castlefinn, and beyond that the road led to the crossing points upstream through the bogs to Killygordon and Stranorlar.

The countryside in the spring of 1689 was not as it is today after several hundred years of man-made improvements to the land. The Irish landscape was then notoriously 'extremely overgrown with woods, bushes, briars, and other cumbersome things. The rivers, for want of keeping up the Banks, or cleansing, overflow upon every small rain … whilst the bogs lye as low; and … they are extreme large, mirey, and dangerous to pass'.[12] There was little drainage and the Finn was not confined within its current banks, but spread over a muddy estuary, and the area around Clady was for the most part bog. The water level was higher, and the weather was then wetter and colder, in a period now referred to as the 'Little Ice Age'.[B] After months of rainfall, the Finn was so deep and fast-flowing as to be considered uncrossable except at the three crossing points, and the narrows at Clady were two hundred and fifty paces wide.

The problem was that whereas the enemy could concentrate on any one of the crossing points, the defending force had to cover all of them. Lundie's solution was to position his main force, that great body of eager volunteers, at the Long Causey ('Long Causeway') and Ballindrait a couple of miles from Lifford. Defences were thrown up at Lifford and Castlefinn, and the bridge at Clady was broken down.[C] [13] If the Irish formed up to cross at Lifford, the rebel army could race to the ford to

[B] The term 'The Little Ice Age' is applied roughly to the years 1300 to 1850 where temperatures in northern Europe were generally some 2°C lower than they are now. The coldest period of the Little Ice Age was 'the Maunder Minimum' between 1645 and 1715. Records of the weather in Ireland during this period are sparse, but there had been ice on the Thames at London in 1689, which had already frozen over some ten times that century.

[C] Clady bridge was broken on 9 April. Like the bridges at Portglenone and Coleraine, it was almost certainly made of timber.

face them. If the Irish moved upstream, his main force could shadow them to Clady or Castlefinn. Wherever the Irish chose to cross, they would be blocked. Morale was high. The preparations appeared formidable, and there was in the back of everyone's mind an expectation of reinforcements being brought by Lord Kingston.

Lundie posted one of his regular officers at each of the crossings. At Lifford, Richard Crofton (now temporarily promoted to major) commanded a company of redcoats supported by a company of volunteers gathered together by a local landowner and magistrate, Captain Hugh Hamill. A trench was dug across the road leading from the ford, and defences were built to house the field guns covering the crossing. The position could not be outflanked because the river was too wide below the ford and Lifford was shielded by a large bog to the west. Hamilton's men would have to wade through the river straight into the heavily defended breastworks. At Clady, William Stewart (now made a colonel by Lundie) had barricaded the end of the broken bridge behind which he posted another company of redcoats. The rest of the regular troops were sent to Castlefinn, where Major (again, one of Lundie's new ranks) John Michelburne, commanded another company, supported by a troop of volunteer horsemen.

Of all Lundie's officers, the Sussex-born Michelburne was the most solid. His grandfather, Sir Richard, had been a man of some substance and a high sheriff, but Michelburne was the son of a youngest son and had had a hard life. His mother died giving birth to him, the family estate had been mortgaged to a London brewer and repossessed, and his father had then settled in Wicklow. Michelburne had spent his entire life in the army, starting as a boy soldier at the Restoration. He was a sergeant in France, returning home after seven years 'with wounds and scars, the badge of a soldier's honour', and then (probably only after the Wicklow property was sold on his stepmother's death) bought a commission and served as a lieutenant in Tangier, and more recently under Lundie in Ireland. Now aged forty-one, he was a rough, tough, angry man.[14]

At Castlefinn, waiting for relief or reinforcements or the Irish, Michelburne described himself as spending three nights by 'an old demolished castle by the river side'. His position was strong behind 'the great fresh in the river'. The ford was covered by field guns, and he had supervised the fortification of the riverbank and for trenches to be dug across the road. His men were in good spirits. Everyone had great confidence in Lundie, who was judged 'a man of greater experience and conduct and accounted, no jot inferior to General Hamilton his self'. Let the Irish come: 'Their great heroes will do as they did at Dromore', he wrote, 'Bring their dogs to bark at us'.[15]

King James' chief advisor, Lord Melfort, was firmly of the view that if the rebels could only see that the king was in Ireland, and be assured that he meant them no harm, the rebellion would collapse without any further bloodshed. With that in mind, James was determined to get to Derry before there was any more fighting. Rather than follow in the wake of Hamilton's army through Down and Antrim, he set off to Charlemont. The senior French officers – Rosen, Maumont and Léry-Giradin – accompanied him, as did d'Avaux, unwilling to leave the king alone in Melfort's hands. Orders were sent to Pusignan to join them from Dungannon.

The king was taking a great risk. It is thirty miles from Charlemont to Omagh, and Omagh is less than thirty miles from Enniskillen. As he rode north, he would have no one on his left to protect him. Everything to the west was bandit country. There were no Irish troops between him and the rebel hordes in Sligo, Enniskillen and Ballyshannon, no cavalry patrols, no strongholds of his own, and the few men he was bringing with him were spread out along the route. They were new troops and, noted d'Avaux, were hopelessly equipped. There were not four in a company who had swords, and most of them were marching without powder, match or musket balls, and the muskets they carried would be for the most part useless in the constant rain. D'Avaux's advice to King James was to go no further than Charlemont. Nothing was to be gained by going on. If the rebels were going to collapse, they would collapse whether he was there or not. The trip was uncomfortable and dangerous, and he should leave it to the generals.

On the morning of 14 April, King James, d'Avaux and Melfort set out from Charlemont to ride to Derry, escorted by Rosen and three squadrons of cavalry. The weather was atrocious and the roads little more than muddy tracks. They rode through cold, driving rain mixed with hail, and the gale blew with enough force to bring the horses to a standstill. 'We passed ten or a dozen torrential rivers, [and] on the whole journey did not pass more than three miserable cabins; all we saw was mountains and precipices.' There was nowhere to buy hay or oats. 'This country is a complete desert.' The foot soldiers had to wade through waist-high water. 'Only men from this country are capable of such endurance.' The horses were worn out with the effort. They found that Omagh had been left by the rebels only the day before. 'They left', wrote d'Avaux, 'neither wine, nor beer, nor forage, and even took the locks off the doors and smashed all the windows and chimneys ... they left nothing for us or our horses'. Few supplies had been brought with them and the men were exhausted. Some of them fainted on arrival. All they had to eat was a small amount of flour mixed with water into a paste, and made into thin biscuits over a fire.

On the next morning, 15 April, a dispatch arrived from Richard Hamilton to say that thirteen ships had been seen off the coast. This changed everything for James. D'Avaux described the anxious king, half-dressed, telling d'Avaux that they must go straight back to Charlemont. D'Avaux fought the temptation to tell him that if he had listened to his advice in the first place, they would be there now, 'but I contented myself by replying that I approved the resolution that he had taken'. The king agreed to send Rosen on ahead with two of the three troops of his cavalry escort. Each troop only had fifteen men, so Rosen gathered six cavalrymen of his own and with the two most senior French generals, Maumont and Léry-Girardin, made off to Strabane as fast as he could. After they had gone, the king had another change of mind and told d'Avaux that rather than go back immediately, they would rest for a day and leave in the morning. The baggage train was to follow Rosen but, before it left, another dispatch arrived at Omagh from Hamilton. This time it was better news. The rebels had abandoned Strabane. King James after some debate, again changed the plans. The supply wagons were to wait until it was known that Strabane was safe.

Shortly afterwards, an officer of dragoons, who had been escorting some ammunition carts, raced into Omagh to warn the king that the enemy were coming. There were three or four thousand of them and there had already been some skirmishing as they advanced. The alarm was sounded, everybody seized their weapons. D'Avaux wanted some infantry posted on the bridge just outside the town, and with some difficulty got a cavalry detachment sent back along the road to get news. 'Sire', he wrote to King Louis, 'we had not a single officer capable of giving an order'. He then saw that the king's boots had been brought to him so that he could mount up. 'I begged him to wait for the return of the cavalrymen that we had just sent out, but he wanted nothing of this, so I quickly left to put on my own boots to follow him.' The King mounted up, and they set off onto some high ground to see what was happening. 'We were no more than twenty mounted men in this fine expedition', wrote d'Avaux, exposed to enemy attack in the middle of nowhere.[16]

There was no attack. A few Irish soldiers, 'who by chance had a little powder', had lagged behind the main body of their regiment and loosed off a few shots. The escort had imagined the worst and raised the alarm. 'This caused a great deal of agitation and worry to the King of England. Most of his servants were openly cursing Lord Melfort for exposing His Britannic Majesty to such danger.' 'It was very disagreeable', wrote d'Avaux, although he clearly took some pleasure in witnessing Lord Melfort, who had pressed the king to go to Derry in the first place, having to make his groveling apologies. Melfort then changed his position and now did all that he could to make James go back to Dublin. He added an extra reason. A letter had been intercepted suggesting that once the king had gone north and Tyrconnell had gone south, the prince of Orange should make straight for Dublin. 'Your Majesty can judge the manner of service that the king of England enjoys', d'Avaux wrote to King Louis on the afternoon of 15 April. 'Lord Melfort had not told him anything about that letter until that moment.' They were now going to leave in the morning for Charlemont, 'so long as nothing occurs to make him [King James] change his mind'.[17]

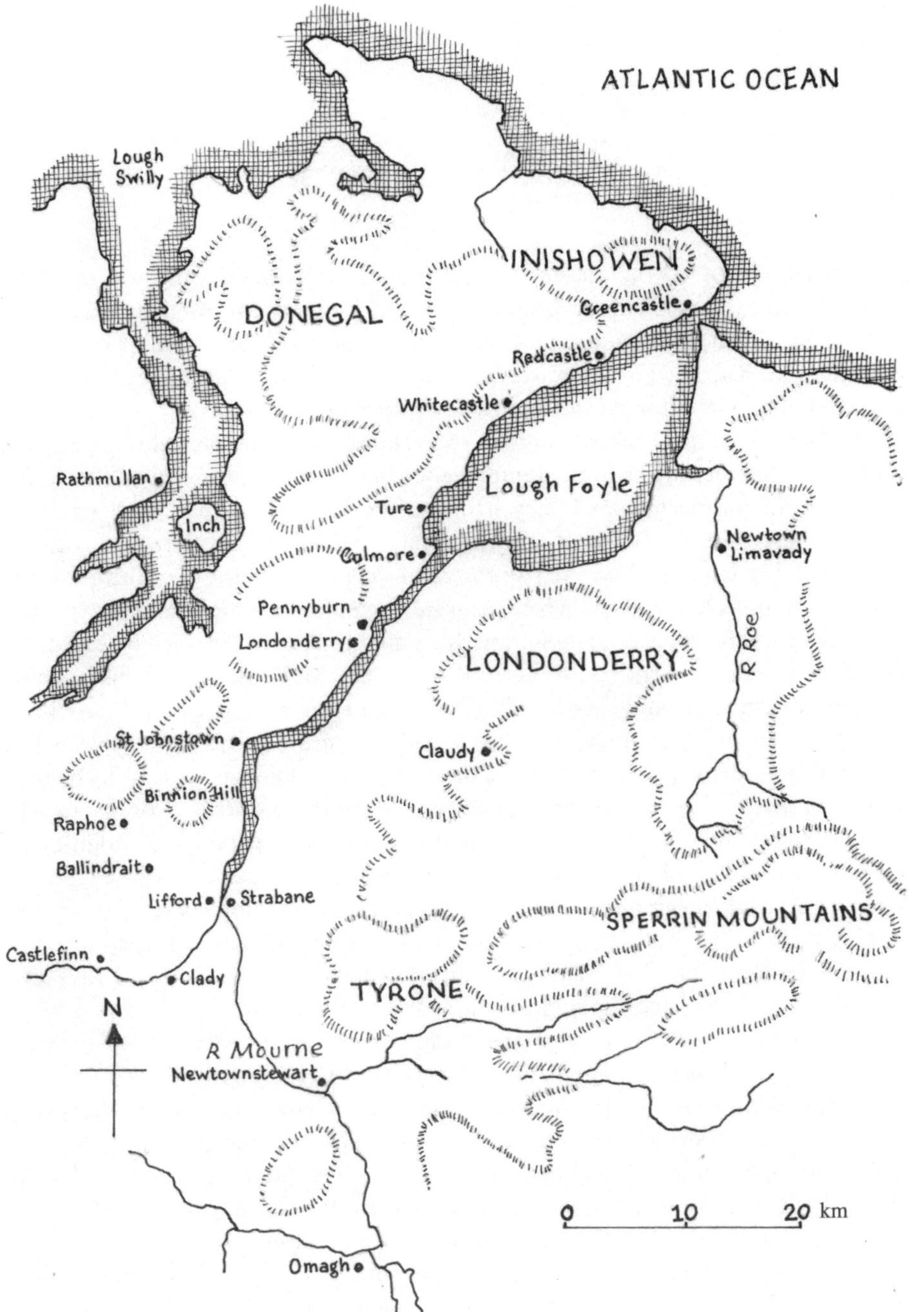

2 Londonderry area. (By Sarah Sherrington)

10

The bridge at Clady

'I HAD INTELLIGENCE BROUGHT ME that the enemy's whole army was on their march to Strabane', wrote Lundie. Ash and Bennett also used the term 'the whole army'. That is what everyone believed but they were all wrong. The 'whole army' marching up the Foyle towards Strabane was only that part of the Irish army commanded by Hamilton fresh from their capture of Coleraine.

Although there had been rumours of two thousand or more men at Dungannon, no one had seen them. The limited intelligence they had was provided by Rawdon's scattered foraging parties, and they had seen nothing other than Irish scouting parties. There were no means of knowing that even before Hamilton had reached Coleraine King James had ordered all the reinforcements for the north to gather at Charlemont and Dungannon. While Hamilton marched his men along the northern route through Limavady, another, perhaps slightly larger, army led by Pusignan was on its march from the south on the Newtownstewart road. It was made up of two thousand infantry and four hundred horse, and now racing up separately were generals Rosen and Maumont, with two squadrons of the king's cavalry escort.

Hamilton ordered a detachment of a thousand foot soldiers to march fast behind him, and rode on ahead with three squadrons of cavalry and two of dragoons. He got to Strabane on the afternoon of Sunday 14 April, expecting his infantry to arrive by ten on the following morning. There was great urgency because thirteen ships had arrived far out on Lough Foyle, suggesting that Lundie's reinforcements were at hand. That Sunday afternoon, Hamilton's small advance guard tested Lifford's defences. Having drawn great fire from the rebel cannon and muskets, they pulled back to spend the night in Strabane and await the army's arrival, leaving a detachment by the river to stop any raids from Lifford. On news of the first exchange of fire, Lundie 'immediately' sent Stewart to reinforce Lifford.

George Walker, the major of the Dungannon volunteers, was at the Long Causey in anticipation of the general rendezvous. Hearing that the Irish army was on the march, he mounted his horse and raced to Derry to break the news that, as it turned out, everyone knew. Lundie was unperturbed. He already had the three crossing points on the Finn guarded in force and everyone, as Walker knew, was going to gather at the Long Causey in the morning. Everything was going to plan, and Lundie's army of ten thousand would be assembled by the time the Irish were ready to make any attempt. Lundie did not want his men lying out all night in the open fields and ending up in the same deplorable condition as the troops who had joined them from Portglenone. Such was the excitement in Walker's mind that he rode back to the Long Causey, saw that nothing was happening there, left his men for a second time and raced on to join Richard Crofton at Lifford, where the two sides had started firing. It was the first time Walker had heard shooting in earnest. 'All night long the enemy and we fired at each other', he wrote, which is a way of saying that the Irish had no intention of crossing in the dark, but kept everyone's nerves on edge by firing across the water, while Crofton allowed his gunners to fire back 'with great and small shot'. There was nothing to fire at. Each side kept to its own side of the river, no one could see anything, and no one was going to do anything.

Pusignan's orders were to join Hamilton at Strabane, but as he rode north from Newtownstewart he had a better idea. Reasoning that the more places he and Hamilton tested on the Finn, the more difficult it would be to defend against them, he rushed straight for Clady, hoping he could get to the bridge before the rebels could destroy it. He got there at nine in the morning on Monday, 15 April, four days too late. One of the spans was down and a breastwork had been thrown across the far end. Behind it was the company of about sixty redcoats left by Stewart.[1] Although his infantry had got no further than Omagh, Pusginan saw no reason to hold back, but was stopped by a message from Hamilton, who was in Strabane. He was to wait as Hamilton's cavalry had just crossed the Mourne with the first of the infantry, some three hundred foot soldiers. With increasing frustration, Pusignan did as he was told. Two hours went by, and by eleven o'clock the rebels over the bridge had been joined by five hundred horsemen, and then a whole battalion of volunteers took up a position behind them.

While waiting for Hamilton to get to him, Pusignan detached some of his horsemen to reconnoitre the crossing at Castlefinn, two miles upriver. They reached the ford sometime before midday. It appeared passable but deep, but it was also clear that the north bank was bristling with muskets. Having crammed the castle ruins at Castlefinn with as many musketeers as he could, and lined an orchard with his men, Michelburne took up a position in the centre to direct them. Further along, but in full view of the south bank, were four or five troops of volunteer horsemen. Pusignan's scouts advanced to the ford to get as good an idea of the rebel strength as they could. Michelburne began bellowing out orders: 'Fire from the castle! Fire from the breastwork! ... Advance whole battalion! Right hand shot fire!' The Irish scouts turned and raced away from the river to great cheers from the rebels. Michelburne was delighted. He seized his officers in turn: 'You are my brave boys!' he said, as he planted large kisses on their faces. It was a great victory.[2]

In the meantime, and unknown to any of those standing on either bank of the Finn, Rosen was on his way. He covered the twenty miles from Omagh and reached Strabane at noon to discover that Hamilton had gone to find Pusignan at Clady. While Rosen waited for his two troops of cavalry to catch up, he reconnoitred the ford to Lifford as Hamilton had already done. It was difficult, but not impassible. He could see the fort, and could see the fortifications that had been thrown up across the road on the far side, and that the rebels had cannon. 'The enemy were advantageously dug in', he noted and, to make matters worse, 'the rain had swollen the river and there was a high tide', but there was no point in waiting on the bank outside Strabane. He took another snap decision. As soon as they arrived, he ordered the two cavalry troops to cross the Mourne and make for Clady along the south bank of the Finn to join up with Hamilton and Pusignan. He then ordered the newly arrived infantry, now 'about six or seven hundred men', who had been sitting around in Strabane for the past two hours, to follow him under cover so that they would not be seen from the north bank.

Meanwhile, the Irish scouting party galloped back to report to Pusignan. Castlefinn, was not, they felt, likely to be the best option. Hamilton then made a suggestion. He should divide his forces, sending Pusignan and his men beyond Castlefinn to look for another crossing upstream and, when or if they found one, they could attack the rebels in the flank, and Hamilton would then make a simultaneous attack across the river. That, he felt, would be the prudent option and, in any event, Hamilton said, the men were tired after their march, it was getting late, and the attack should be on the following day.

Pusignan exploded. 'Hamilton', as d'Avaux reported, 'was stuck to the road and unwilling to try anything', whereas Pusignan urged an immediate attack. 'With troops like the ones they had, it was better not to give them time to prepare.' His plan was simple, and could be abandoned at any time in its execution without any great risk. If enough men were advanced to within easy range of the breastwork on the other side of the bridge, the rebels would be beaten back under the concentrated fire of a few hundred muskets. Once the rebels were beaten back, the horse could try and make their way across the ford, and if they reached the other side in sufficient numbers to hold the enemy back, the engineers could patch up the broken bridge and the infantry could then cross over and meet the enemy on equal terms in the open.

We may picture the angry scene of the two men arguing in French, while the Irish officers and troops waited for the outcome, not understanding a word. Pusignan was the more forceful, and Hamilton let him have his way. Two battalions marched straight to the water's edge and poured volley after volley into the detachment at the end of the bridge and at the troops waiting behind them. It was sudden and deadly. The defenders on the bridge pulled back to where the infantry battalion stood behind them. As they retreated, two troops of cavalry surged through the Finn on either side of the broken bridge 'dragging the foot by tail and mane after them'.[3] The water was so deep that for twenty yards in midstream the horses had to swim. Major Robert Nangle[A] and two troopers were swept away and drowned in the flood, but the rest scrambled up the bank on the far side. In the meantime,

[A] Usually referred to as 'the son of Tory Nangle'. The Nangles were Protestant landowners whose lands were lost in the Cromwellian settlement. As the Nangles had rebelled against the king as well as parliament, the lands were not returned under Charles II's Act of Settlement. Edward 'Tory' Nangle led a rebellion and was shot dead raiding Longford in 1666.

Pusignan ordered forward the regiment of guards who had been stripping planks and timbers from every habitation they could find to repair the broken span on the bridge. With a great roar, they ran through the smoke of the heavy covering fire and made straight for the bridge clutching thick boards before them as protection. They flung the timbers across, laid the boards and the whole body of Irish infantry surged on over onto the north bank.

While Pusignan was preparing his attack, Lundie was forming up his infantry at the Long Causey in readiness to march on Lifford. As soon as he received the news that the Irish were gathering to cross at Clady, he raced on ahead with Lord Blayney and Captain Coote to investigate. He wrote:

> As we came to within a mile of the place we heard great shooting which made us ride the faster. In half a mile further we came opposite to most of the Irish army, then we heard a halloo and saw them beat their kettles. When we gone a little further, then we plainly saw that our men were run away from the bridge and the [Irish] regiment of guards posted on the end of it firing very hard, and about 700 carrying of deal boards thinking to reach that part of it which was cut. At the same time, I saw two troops of horse also take the river which was so deep that they all swam.[4]

The battle of Clady had been lost before Lundie arrived. It was not lost to the army from Coleraine, which Lundie had taken such pains to track over the last two days, and which for the most part was yet to reach Strabane, but lost to Pusignan's advanced troops who had within the space of half an hour smashed their way across the river and chased the defenders away. The easiest crossing on the Finn, the bridge, was now in enemy hands. According to Lundie:

> Our men was so scattered before we could overtake them, that there was not four together and all the fields covered with them and no possibility of rallying of them. Then I sent an officer to Ballindrait Bridge to stop them at least so long as to make the retreat of the foot good, but all in vain. When I saw this, I immediately sent an express to Derry to shut the gates and not suffer a man to enter.

Before Rosen could reach Pusignan, the attack on the bridge had begun, and from there on things got very confused. Rosen could hear the gunfire at Clady, but as he made his way there he could also hear the sound of the enemy horse racing back towards Lifford. Determined to get across, he led his horsemen straight into the swollen river and swam them across to the other undefended shore. Away from any ford, it took some time to make it over, but once he had, he formed the opinion that as there seemed to be a general flight of the enemy back towards Lifford there was probably little he could do to assist Pusignan. If the rebels were fleeing from the attack on Clady, it was time to press home the advantage and strike at Lifford. He led his riders back into the river a second time, crossed back to the Tyrone bank and galloped back up to the ford. The infantry were told to advance and Rosen spurred his horse back into the river for a third time and ordered his cavalry to the other side. On giving the order he was also somewhat surprised to see, rather than a junior officer leading by example, his own major general, Maumont, plunging his horse headlong into the river (which was, wrote Rosen, 'a little rash').[5]

The crossing was not easy, as the ford was 'more than 250 paces across', but it was a ford over which the horses could make quick progress. The impression made on the defenders was great. Already terrified at the news that the Irish had crossed over at Clady, they fired one volley and ran for it. Nevertheless, Rosen could not cross directly over the ford because the defences were still in place on the Donegal bank, and the bogs alongside the road forced him to make something of a detour around the town. By the time he broke into Lifford, the enemy had all but disappeared: there were only forty of them left. The infantry waded through the ford behind him and took possession of the village, together with all the rebels' abandoned munitions, supplies and baggage.

Most of the rebels made their way back by the most direct route, along the road through Ballindrait and to the rendezvous at Long Causey where Lundie had left Colonel Sir Francis Hamilton, with the main body of his army. The 32-year-old Sir Francis was one of the few experienced professional officers Lundie had to rely on, having been a cavalry captain for over a decade. He had succeeded to the baronetcy earlier that year, and was a man with connections, being Mountjoy's first cousin and Mount-Alexander's brother-in-law. Sir Francis had his men drawn up on the slopes of Binnion Hill overlooking the causeway, which stood, half of a mile long, over the rain-swollen bog through which the Swilly Burn made its slow way into the Foyle. It was the best defensive position between Strabane and Derry. To get to them, the Irish horse would have to ride two abreast into their guns. Lundie ordered Sir Francis to gather in the men retreating from the fords. John Chichester, an experienced infantry officer who Lundie had recently promoted to colonel, told Lundie to 'tarry, and give some orders, or all would be lost'. Lundie replied that 'Londonderry was his post'. Sir Francis was in charge and Lundie needed to secure the city.[6]

The fighting was getting nearer: Rosen, drenched to the skin at the head of his two cavalry squadrons, dug his spurs in again and galloped after the rebels running away from Lifford. 'I chased them for three long miles', he wrote, 'killing them and taking prisoners'. A messenger raced after him to say that two more companies of Irish dragoons from Hamilton's Coleraine army had reached Strabane. He sent Léry-Girardin back to collect them and to lead them straight to him. At the Long Causey, Rosen paused at the sight of Sir Francis Hamilton's men. 'On a height in front of me were at least five hundred horse and dragoons and three battalions.' He was now rather exposed, stuck on the edge of a boggy country with no infantry support and vulnerable to a counter-attack. He held back and waited until Léry-Girardin arrived with the two companies of dragoons. 'The enemy who had abandoned Clady and those that had gone to help them rallied on my left', wrote Rosen. 'I was between two enemy columns. I decided to put a brave face on it and wait for the night before pushing them back, having already got the drums I had mounted on horseback to make the enemy believe that the troops were over.'[7]

What prevented him taking any more aggressive action was the arrival of Colonel Nugent (the hero of Portglenone) from Clady with a garbled message about Hamilton facing twenty enemy squadrons. The fact that Rosen had not yet seen any of Hamilton's men seemed to corroborate the message, and so he drew back and made for Clady. He found that Hamilton and Pusignan had been entirely successful, but had been chasing the enemy on the left rather than pursuing the enemy back towards Lifford into Rosen's path. Nugent, who had perhaps at best an imperfect grasp of French, had delivered his message to Rosen, who had no English. It was, wrote Pusignan, 'a misunderstanding that prevented their total defeat'.

> This halt gave opportunity to the rebels to get safe into Londonderry, and hindered the loyal cavalry and dragoons to be in with them pell mell, besides their slaughtering of the runaways in the road and taking of prisoners, which is looked upon to be the first imprudent management of the northern enterprise.[8]

Pusignan had chased the enemy horsemen on the road to Raphoe, where the confusion was complete. 'The troops that we were chasing absolutely scattered the infantry into the bogs which are very common in this country, and the cavalry we chased for nearly four leagues[B] ran away in groups. The loss was amongst those who were the most poorly mounted.'[9] Losses were not high. The infantry waded their way through bogs and were safe from attack because the Irish cavalry could not follow them and after their river crossing had 'scarce a dry shot between them'. Berwick heard the rebels had lost four hundred men, but he was not there, whereas Rosen and Pusignan, who were there, made no claims of significant slaughter, and Plunkett (who was not there) said that the Irish chased the rebels for three miles 'yet without execution'. Bennett says a hundred were killed, but appears to only refer to the men from Lifford who were attacked by Rosen. Those who made it back to the city feared the worst. Thomas Ash, who may not have been there but who knew men who were, wrote that 'many were killed in the pursuit'. Mackenzie recorded that the Irish did 'great execution' on Hugh Montgomery's regiment of foot soldiers as they ran away along the Raphoe road, but many just disappeared, as did Montgomery himself. Some made their way to Raphoe and turned right for Londonderry. Montgomery turned left and headed for Donegal and then down to Enniskillen, and many may well have taken the same route, scattered perhaps, but not dead.

[B] A French league, a somewhat flexible measurement, is usually said to be four kilometres.

Sir Francis stayed put, but as the evening approached, a sense of unease affected the troops. Rosen's horsemen had withdrawn. All was quiet, but they had no way of knowing what the Irish were doing, and the fear grew that they had made straight for Raphoe. If they had, they would bypass the Long Causey and march unopposed to Derry, cutting off the entire rebel force while it waited twelve miles away. Walker wrote that 'The regiment at the Long-Cawsy was in some danger, having staid too long, expecting orders, but got off under the shelter of some horse and followed the army, which was 10,000 strong, and make good their retreat to Derry.'[10] Demoralized not by the sight of the advancing Irish, but by the fear of an invisible army moving behind them, the rebel force melted back to Derry. All Francis Hamilton could do was to go with them.

At Castlefinn, Michelburne was soon aware that something substantial was happening downstream. He was joined by the three troops of horse commanded by old Major Stroud,[11] who had pulled back from Clady. There was a general retreat and Michelburne's detachment was the furthest from the city, and was now cut off from it. Everyone had given way. He ordered his own men back, but once the Irish cavalry was let loose along the road to Raphoe, he could use neither the road nor the high ground. His own account is that he was forced to march his regiment, 'with flying colours and drums beating a march', into a bog where he could not be charged down while Major Joseph Stroud and his hundred horsemen raced off as best they could. As half of Michelburne's men were pikemen, the Irish cavalry were able to do no more than watch them wade their way to safety. They got back to Londonderry with the loss of one man, an ensign who lost his nerve and deserted the regiment in the hope of getting back on his own.[12]

The recriminations started immediately. History was written by those who had not been there, but who had listened to the excuses of those who were. The bridge had not been properly defended because the main body of rebels were not there, and it was Lundie's fault. Captain Ash wrote in his diary:

> The enemy came over at Clady ford without much opposition, although there were five to one against them, which caused suspicion that Colonel Lundy was a traitor to our cause; for had he marched the army on Sunday the fourteenth, the enemy had not all probably so easily have gotten over. It was noon before he left Derry, and many were killed in the pursuit.

The anger at the defeat, and the immediate search for a scapegoat, led to another legend. A forged letter, purporting to come from Walker, was published in London while the siege was still taking place. 'As soon as ever Colonel Sheldon [the commander of Hamilton's cavalry] with his horse advanced, he [Lundie] gave him a sign to come over, and ran away, swearing a great oath and saying, 'Gentlemen, I see you will not fight', though at the same time they were in all appearance very zealous and willing to engage.' Leading the attack on Lundie after the siege,

Bennett (who was not at the fords) adopted this allegation. He placed Lundie at Lifford: 'Col Lundy fled, crying out, "You are all cut off, shift for yourselves"', and somewhat slyly slipped in: 'The enemies … broke in at Clady-ford, (whether upon a Sign from Col. Lundy or not, I cannot positively say)'. It was not an allegation that Walker made in his *Account*, no one else repeated the story, and it was clearly so ridiculous that Lundie was not questioned about it by the House of Commons committee.[13]

Mackenzie pointedly left out the allegations of Lundie saying 'shift for yourselves' or making a signal, but set out the main criticisms:

> So inexcusable was the conduct of the general, both in abandoning so many passes and those so easily defensible by a few men, if they had been either supplied with ammunition or constantly relieved, and in never so much as attempting to draw the forces into a body when there were in the field above 10,000 men who, whatever he pretended to the contrary wanted more care and resolution in their leader than courage in themselves.[14]

Together with the main part of Lundie's army, the resupply of ammunition was either at or on its way to Long Causey. There was no shortage of powder in the city, no suggestion that the stores had withheld supplies, nor any suggestion that any of the officers had warned or begged Lundie to give them more powder or ammunition before going out. Nor was there a shortage at Lifford, where the rebels had been shooting at the enemy all night, and only stopped when they heard that the Irish had crossed at Clady. At Castlefinn, Michelburne wrote that he had not been sent any additional ammunition, but then described himself giving the order: 'Fire as hard as you can!' Pusignan's attack had been so unexpected, and its success so immediate, that neither reinforcements nor supplies could reach the troops at the river in time.

Afterwards, scrambling around for another charge against Lundie, Walker criticized him for not taking action on three suggestions made by Major Stroud: Raphoe Castle should have been defended or demolished; harrows should have been thrown into the ford at Clady; and some of the companies and troops of horse should have been amalgamated. None of these suggestions, had they been followed, would have made the slightest difference to the outcome. Had Raphoe Castle been defended, it would have been isolated and forced to surrender; no one could anticipate where horsemen may swim across a river; and the problems associated with an administrative reorganization on the day before a battle need not be commented upon.[15]

The failure at Clady was not brought about by the defenders having no ammunition. It certainly was not brought about by treachery. It was a failure to withstand a sudden and resolute attack by the unexpected arrival of a body of trained men directed by determined French officers. It was those drenched, sabre-wielding horsemen who made the difference. Lundie had expected the enemy to do what

Hamilton had in fact planned to do. The Irish army would wait until all their army had arrived, they would then form up in battle array, and then attempt to force a crossing in strength against the rebels, who, having found out where they planned to cross, would also have formed up in strength, reinforced and resupplied. The unexpected had happened. A small body of well-drilled horsemen, a few hundred strong, had simply appeared, so it seemed, out of nowhere. Lundie, riding out to defend Lifford, was suddenly diverted to Clady, and by the time he got there, Pusignan's attack, executed with both great suddenness and aggression, had scattered the defenders and punched a hole in the line.

Forgotten in all this, was the absence of reinforcements. On Thursday, 11 April, Lundie had sent expresses to Enniskillen and to Ballyshannon asking for urgent help. The Enniskilliners, as McCarmick put it, 'resolved not to stir'. Kingston, who had been asked specifically to come with Captain Coote and eighty horse (for which there would be accommodation and provision), did not want to split up his men 'till something should happen' and also declined to help. Once Lundie had made his plans, under the impression that they had either left in answer to his first summons, or were else on the verge of leaving, he sent a second set of urgent messages to Enniskillen and Ballyshannon, demanding help in the coming battle and giving them details of the rendezvous. Gustavus Hamilton in Enniskillen again did nothing, but Kingston, who only got the second message at ten at night on the day before the Long Causey rendezvous, instead called a council of war. It was decided that, as he was thirty miles away and could not get there on time, he should instead take 'ten or twelve horse' and ride to Londonderry 'to see how matters were'.

This is only of interest because Kingston has over the years been portrayed as one of Lundie's victims. Lundie had 'double crossed' Kingston by encouraging him to leave Sligo and then telling him to remain in Ballyshannon. On the day of the battle, Kingston and his small party got as far as Stranorlar, a hamlet ten miles from Clady, where he met some fugitives from the fighting. It must have been late in the day, because he was also told that the Irish had got to Raphoe, and so he could not get to Londonderry. The non-appearance of Kingston and his reinforcements caused great disappointment. It was widely believed that he was on his way with his entire force, and before the battle it was rumoured that 'My Lord Kingston is come to Raphoe with his forces between 2 and 3,000'. He and they were nowhere to be seen. Lundie was blamed.[16]

Rather than return to his men, Kingston sent instructions for them to split up and attach themselves to the garrisons at Enniskillen, Donegal, Ballyshannon 'and other places'. He then raced first to Donegal, and then on to Killybegs where he got on a boat. Like everyone else of his rank, he took the opportunity to go to London 'to report', and eagerly joined the queue to go before the House of Commons committee to say it was all Lundie's fault.

The House of Commons committee appears not to have asked the obvious question of why Lord Kingston, a former professional soldier and (with Coote) one of the two highest-ranking officers in both Sligo and Fermanagh, got the first boat he could find to take him to Scotland. Although Coote made it to the Long Causey, in his evidence, Kingston withheld the fact that he had received Lundie's urgent message on 11 April asking for him and Coote to come with two companies of horsemen. He said that he waited at Ballyshannon 'for further orders, but could get none, till the enemy got between that place and Londonderry, whereby all communication was intercepted'. Kingston was not a witness of truth, but the committee was not to know that, and found 'that by this means the Lord *Kingston*'s forces were dispersed, and the best regiment of horse the Protestants had, broken'.[17]

Mackenzie's judgment was:

> So unhappily were the designs of that Noble Lord, (who inherits the Courage as well as the Honour of his Father,) for the preservation of that part of the Country, which he prosecuted with extraordinary Zeal and Resolution, frustrated by the confused, but peremptory Orders which he received from Colonel *Lundy*.[18]

11

Relief

THE *SWALLOW* FRIGATE AND its convoy left Chester on 10 April, and made the mouth of the lough, some twenty-two miles away from Londonderry, on the morning of 15 April. The convoy was not carrying provisions for the city, it was purely a hastily assembled military expedition to reinforce Lundie with two regiments commanded by Colonel John Cunningham, who was in overall command, and the 70-year-old veteran of Cromwell's expedition to Ireland, Colonel Solomon Richards.

The men were by then in a bad way. The ships were crowded and there were no platforms below decks to lie down on. It was the bare decks or nothing. Matthew Anderton, the customs official responsible at Chester for all provisioning on behalf of the Navy Board, had felt that seven ships were enough to transport the fifteen hundred men in the expedition. The officers complained of being 'straitened', and Anderton at last, by way of a compromise, provided a further small ship to carry a hundred and fifty of the men. When the officers demanded another small ship to carry their horses, Anderton refused. 'For that', he told them, 'there was no order'.

Anderton was to supply the troops with ten days' provisions. Each man was to be given a daily allowance of a pound of biscuit, a pound of cheese and a gallon of beer.[1] The men had been on board for five of those days already, and the provisions supplied by Anderton were of the poorest quality. The brewers and bakers of Chester had queued up outside Anderton's premises to offer him the cheapest they had, and cheap it was because they could not get rid of their failed produce to anyone other than the navy. Several of the men and officers had died on the voyage, and others were suffering sickness 'occasioned by the badness of the bread and beer'. The beer was sold in casks often a foot or more empty. Some of it stank so badly that in their desperation 'the men chose rather to drink salt water or their own urine'. The biscuit was rotten and mouldy and most of it was inedible, and a rumour got around that it had been sitting in the castle since Monmouth's rebellion four years before.[A] [2]

Lundie arrived back at Londonderry in the early afternoon. The city's gates had already been secured, but he was by no means the first to get back. He ran a gauntlet of those who had been locked out. An enraged rabble, he wrote, 'swore

[A] Six of the officers gave evidence of the dire state of provisioning, and Matthew Anderton was summoned to answer the charges before the House of Commons committee. He did not attend ('a bruised leg'), but sent his son instead with certificates from all the Chester brewers and bakers to say the provisions were good and that he had 'paid the best rates, as appeared by their receipts'. No brewer or baker in Chester was going to cross Anderton.

they were betrayed and that I had sold them and the town to King James for 17,000 pound, and swore to kill me when I came myself'. With his entourage of officers, he managed to get in through a wicket-door in one of the closed gates.

On entering the lough at Greencastle, the relief ships had been met by a messenger sent by Lundie before he left that morning. He needed the men to land quickly as he was off to engage the enemy. Cunningham sent the rider back with his reply, which was now placed into Lundie's hands:

> Hearing you have taken the Field, in Order to Fight the Enemy, I have thought it necessary for His Majesty's Service, to let you know there are two well-disciplined Regiments here on Board, that may join you in two days at farthest, I am sure they will be of great Use in any Occasion, but especially for the Encouragement of Raw Men, as I judge most of yours are: Therefore it is my Opinion, that you only stop the Passage of the Enemy at the Fords of *Finn,* till I can join you, and afterwards, if giving Battle be necessary, you will be in a much better posture for it than before

Lundie scribbled a reply and sent the messenger galloping back past Culmore and along the shore to hail the ships out on the lough. He wrote:

> I am come back sooner than I expected when I went forth, for having numbers placed on Finn water as I went to a pass, where a few people might oppose a greater number than came to the place, I found them on the run before the enemy who pursued them with great vigour and, I fear, march on with their forces, so that I wish your men would march all night in good order lest they be surprised. Here they shall have all the accommodation the place will afford. In this hurry. Pardon me for this brevity.[3]

He added as an afterthought: 'If the Men be not landed, let 'em land and march immediately.'

By the time Cunningham received Lundie's urgent reply, the ships were off Redcastle, halfway down the lough. The request for immediate disembarkation included Lundie's description of his men 'on the run before the enemy'. This phrase changed matters for Cunningham. His written orders were: 'If it is unsafe to land, he is not to expose his troops to any extraordinary hazard.' He sent ashore his major, Zachariah Tiffin, to assess the level of hazard his men would face. Major Tiffin took with him Captain John Lyndon and the commander of the *Swallow*, Captain Wolfran Cornewall. They arrived some three hours after Lundie had sent his urgent message to Cunningham.

As old Tangier hands, Cornewall and Tiffin were well known to Lundie. Cornewall's career had been unusual in that he had served in the army, but had transferred to the navy briefly six years before, then returned to the army, and earlier that year had again taken a command in the navy. Tiffin was a career soldier and had served in Flanders as well as Tangier. He was the sort of man whose opinion Lundie valued. Tiffin began by looking rather sniffily at the city's walls and told him that he considered the city not 'to be so strong as a burg in Alsatia'. Such burgs, or walled towns, never held out against an army equipped with cannon. 'He was much surprised to find it no stronger, for in England it was said to be one of the strongest places in the world.' Lundie told him what had happened at the fords. His men 'would not look the enemy in the face'. Tiffin told him he was sorry for him. Lundie asked him if the fleet had brought the provisions and money he had asked for. Tiffin told him they had brought neither.

Despair swept over Lundie. He had hoped to defeat the Irish in the field, but after what he had seen at Clady, that hope had gone. He now faced having to withstand a siege without provisions. He hesitated. In that fateful moment, according to Lundie, Tiffin advised him to consult Cunningham before making any decision about disembarking the troops. He agreed, and sent another letter asking Cunningham to come to the city 'very early' in the morning:

> Major Tiffin is come here and I have given him my opinion fully which, I believe, when you hear, and see the place, you will both join with me, that without an immediate supply of money and provisions, this place must fall very soon into the enemy's hands. If you do not send your men here some time tomorrow, it will not be in your power to bring 'em at all.[4]

Tiffin and the others returned to the fleet. There followed a night of great anxiety, but the Irish made no appearance. Having issued orders that the gates be locked and no one should enter the city, Lundie awoke on the morning of 16 April to find that ropes had been let down over the walls and some five hundred 'of the rabble' had climbed in. It was less than a week since he had allowed the additional thousand volunteers to join the garrison, and this was their repayment. The gates were opened in the morning to let in more provisions, and a desperate crowd stormed forward. Five hundred of them managed to get in. That was another thousand hungry mouths since last night.

During the night, the ships moved up the lough and stood off Ture, a mile or so beyond Culmore. Early in the morning, colonels Cunningham and Richards rode into the city with Captain Cornewall and eight of their officers. Cunningham was able to impress with his local knowledge. He had been to school in the city and had visited it several times as an adult. His brother still lived there. 'He never looked upon it to be a place of any strength', he said. The gentry and officers gathered in the governor's house to meet him. While they were there, Richards said, 'Colonel Cunningham and the governor whispered together at the window.' He could not hear what they were saying, but we do know that Cunningham presented Lundie with the orders Lundie had been sent from Whitehall. They gave Lundie command of the two regiments, notified him that 'further succours of money, men, arms and provisions of war' were being sent, and stated: 'We do expect from your courage, prudence and conduct that in the meantime you make the best defence you can.' Lundie was also directed to receive into the town 'such Protestant officers and men able and fit to bear arms, as you may confide in'. He was also sent a caveat of what was blindingly obvious even from four hundred miles away. He was to take care 'that you do not take in more unuseful people, women and children into the said city than there shall be a provision sufficient to maintain besides the garrison'.

Cunningham's own orders were to place himself under Lundie's command in Londonderry and 'to make enquiry whether you may with safety put our said regiments into the same'. 'In case you shall find it unsafe to land the said regiments at or near Londonderry so as to put them into the town, which you are to endeavour by all reasonable and prudent means, you are not to expose them to extraordinary hazard in so doing, but to take care that they be carried in the same ships and under the same convoy' to Carrickfergus or Strangford or, failing that, back to Liverpool.

The issue that needed to be settled by the best military minds in the city was whether it was 'reasonable and prudent' to put the regiments into Londonderry, or whether such an action would 'expose them to extraordinary hazard'. Lundie had Cunningham and the officers sent round the walls to inspect the defences, and then held a meeting in the council committee room. It was not a public meeting. Lundie selected who should be there, and 'the gentry and officers' were not invited. There were sixteen people in the room. The only civilian was John Mogridge, one of the burgesses who had for years been the clerk to the city council. He was there to draft whatever needed drafting, but not, it appears, to take any minutes. Cunningham was there with four of his officers (including Tiffin), and Colonel Richards was there with four of his officers. The other five were Lundie; James Hamilton off the *Jersey* frigate, who had stayed behind as one of Lundie's colonels; Colonel Lord Blayney; Captain Chidley Coote, who had recently arrived from Sligo; and Wolfran Cornewall, the captain of the *Swallow*. Lundie presided as governor.

Both Walker and Mackenzie bitterly bemoaned the fact that there was no one from the city there (apart from old Mr Mogridge, whose opinion was not sought). Walker wrote that those there were 'unacquainted with the condition of the town, or the inclination and resolution of the people'. Mackenzie expanded on that: 'several of the principal officers (who had some suspicion of Col. Lundy's design) as Col. Francis Hamilton, Col. Chichester, Col. Crofton, Lieut. Col. Ponsonby, &c. desired to be admitted, they were absolutely refused, though at the same council he [Lundie] pretended he had sent for the two first, but said they could not be found, and for Sir Arthur Rawdon, who he said was a dying'.[5]

These criticisms miss the point. The meeting was a council of war. It was not a town council meeting. Lundie was not trying to elicit the feelings of a representative body. He was the governor, and the decision was his alone. He needed to decide what action he should take, and so invited those whose opinions he needed and respected. Some of the officers had experience of siege warfare on the Continent, and after the disappointment of the preceding day, he needed advice and reassurance. He did not need to hear from junior garrison officers and certainly not from self-appointed militiamen with sudden and unofficial ranks. Everyone had been promoted well beyond his usual experience. The example given of Colonel John Chichester is a good one. Chichester had been a captain in Ireland for twenty years. His service had taken him as far as Charlemont and Carrickfergus and, until he lost his commission in Tyrconnell's purge, he had been the senior captain in Mountjoy's regiment. Lundie had given him the rank of colonel, and after the siege he would revert to plain Lieutenant Chichester. Lundie did not need to hear from him on the subject of siege warfare, but he did need to hear from people like Tiffin, Cornewall and Chidley Coote, and he was especially interested in what James Hamilton, Cunningham and Richards might have to say on the likelihood and timing of a proper relief convoy carrying men and provisions, and on the condition of their troops.

The House of Commons committee sitting in the summer was misled into finding as a fact that 'Colonel Lundie did refuse to admit divers of the officers, who did use to come to former councils; particularly Colonel [Sir Francis] Hamilton, Colonel Chichester, Major Walker, and Major Baker.' Of that list, only Sir Francis had been invited to past councils of war. Walker was a volunteer rather than a professional soldier, and so would never have been allowed near a council of war. The committee also found 'that Colonel Chichester, and Major Walker, endeavouring to thrust into the room, Colonel Lundie ordered them to be kept out'. We may note both that Walker was thrusting himself into the room, and that Mackenzie failed to mention him doing so.[6]

Having heard evidence from five of those present at the council of war – Cunningham, Richards, James Hamilton, Blayney and Lundie – the House of Commons committee found:

> Colonel Lundie was the first man that spoke at this council of war; and made a proposition to quit the town, and send the two regiments back again; alleging, for his reason, that there was not above a week or ten days provision left in the town; and that the enemy was five-and-twenty thousand strong, and within four or five miles.

There were two assertions by Lundie (on provisions and enemy strength), and a proposition by him (to abandon the city). The proposition was Lundie's. It was the purpose of the council of war. He set out what he felt was the best option, and invited those present to tell him if he was wrong. Lundie informed the council of war that 'that there was not above a week or ten days provision left in the town', and the others took his word for it. Those others were not just the officers newly arrived off the ships (Cunningham, Richards, Tiffin), but also Colonel Lord Blayney, who was in a position of some authority in the defending forces, and James Hamilton, who had been shown around the stores in the magazine by

Lundie and seen the state of them. Neither Blayney nor James Hamilton, nor anyone else, challenged Lundie's assertion.

Evidence was heard that Lundie had said otherwise before the meeting. Cornet Charles Nicholson said that 'Lundie himself had told Lord Blayney that there was 'sufficient, at this time, for three months, for *three* thousand men'. Yet Blayney was at the council of war, and did not challenge Lundie on the 'week or ten days' estimate. Blayney was also at the House of Commons committee and did not repeat Nicholson's allegation that Lundie had claimed three months' supply. Rawdon told the House of Commons committee that Lundie had told him that 'there was then in the town three months provision for *six* thousand men'. That is, twice as much as Nicholson claimed that Lundie had told Blayney. Lundie denied saying any such thing.

In his *True and impartial account*, which was printed in London before the end of the siege, Bennett claimed that 'upon search, it plainly appear'd there was Provision for 12,000 men for ten or twelve weeks'. This bold estimate was well in excess of anything anyone else had said, and Bennett chose not to repeat it before the House of Commons committee. Mackenzie wrote that the provisions were sufficient for three months for 3,000 'after the rate of four pounds of fish, three pounds of flesh, and eight quarts of meal per week for each man'. If Mackenzie was right (and he may have been), to feed only the soldiers (using Walker's figures, adopted by Mackenzie, of 7,361 officers and men) that supply at that rate of rationing would last about five weeks, but makes no allowance for the non-combatants.

Confusingly for the parliamentary committee, Bennett and others then gave evidence that Lundie had failed to bring in supplies and argued that, in the alternative, if there really were insufficient provisions, then Lundie was to be blamed. Rawdon, who had been too ill to play any part, told the committee that he 'often' asked Lundie to order Rawdon's men to fetch in provisions but that Lundie gave no such order, and so there came a day in which his men 'brought in three hundred horse load of meal, without order'. Bennett, eager to give evidence on every aspect of the enquiry regardless of his state of knowledge, told the committee 'that there was a stack of hay, and one hundred and fifty, or two hundred barrels of salmon, belonging to the Lord Massereene within a quarter of a mile of Londonderry; which might have been had into the town for fetching, but the governor took no care about it'. This was clearly untrue. Lundie told the committee that it was brought in, and in this he was supported by Captain Nevill, who told the committee that 'Mr. Jemmit, the Governor of Culmore Fort, did get it in.' (And, after the war, Lord Massereene bitterly sought compensation for the salmon seized by Lundie.) Cornet Nicholson gave evidence that 'provisions came daily into the town in boats'. There clearly had been a long and obvious effort to build up the city's stores.

These conflicting arguments amounted to this: if the city starved, then Lundie had negligently failed to get in sufficient supplies. If the city held out, Lundie was a traitor.

Lundie's own written defence reads:

> If I am blamed for not having more in the store, I am sure it is none of my fault for I appeal even to my enemies themselves if ever man took more pains to get provisions, for I tried both fair means and foul and am sure I went far beyond my instructions to get what I had and, I think considering the circumstances I was under without money and authority, I wonder I got so much.

The House of Commons committee did not know what to believe. When they heard this evidence in the summer, the siege was still in progress. Were there plenty of provisions in the city or were there not? Had Lundie misled his own officers by telling them that there were insufficient provisions, or had he been misled into believing that the provisions were insufficient? Cornet Nicholson's evidence was that 'there was a great store of provisions in the town; *every house having great plenty'*. Much of the provision in the city had not found its way into the magazine, but had been stashed away by private owners. Although Lundie did not know that to be the case at the time, that was the explanation he later adopted. The people had fled to the city with provisions. The provisions had been hidden or stored in merchants' houses. After Clady there was a great exodus; People paid their money and piled into ships, not only to avoid the advancing Irish, but because of 'the disorder and insolency of the rabble that entered the town'. The first refugees and the townspeople were driven out by the new refugees. 'The merchants themselves lost their houses, shops and all their merchandise besides the provisions.'

Many accounts refer to people concealing provisions, and recount how during the siege extreme (and sometimes successful) measures were taken to search out hidden supplies. Reference has already been made to Lundie's discovery that two of his storekeepers had deserted with a boat, and that when he inspected the stores with James Hamilton, he found a shortfall. The suspicion must be that the missing storemen had been selling supplies which were then secreted within the walls.

The second assertion made by Lundie concerned the size of the Irish army. He put the strength of the Irish army at twenty-five thousand, which clearly did not describe the forces that Richard Hamilton had under his immediate command. It was however the figure on paper available to Tyrconnell across the whole country. If the city did hold out, the Irish would send reinforcements from that great pool of men. No one challenged the figure at the council of war. Lundie was simply stating the obvious and used a figure they were all familiar with. The Irish army was large and by comparison the Londonderry forces were small.

Lundie knew he could not beat the Irish in the field. Even with Cunningham's two regiments, he would have no proper cavalry, and he had seen how woefully inadequate the volunteer horsemen were at Clady, and how the volunteer infantry had behaved when faced by a small force of Irish horse. The only alternative was to use whatever troops he had to man the city's defences. If the Irish could mount a formal siege with siege guns, the walls would be shattered. If the Irish had no, or had insufficient, artillery, they would blockade the city. The only questions then would be how long the provisions would hold out, and how long it would be before supplies got to Londonderry.

Lundie's proposition, that they should abandon the city, concluded the House of Commons committee after hearing the evidence, 'was consented to by all present, without any contradiction'. Lundie wrote:

> I desired to know all their opinions which was unanimous: that considering the great number of people that was in the town and the small quantity of provisions that was in it, and that we were to expect none by Major General Kirk, nor an army to our relief before the latter end of June at soonest, and that the place was of no strength, all those things considered it was resolved and agreed upon that the place was not tenable against a well-appointed victorious army and a formal siege which we daily expected. Therefore, we judged it most convenient for his majesty's service that the two regiments should return for England with as many officers and soldiers as could be carried off besides, and that the townspeople should make their own terms. This I own was my opinion with all the rest of the officers that was at the council of war.

John Mogridge was then told to write out a declaration to record the council's decision. It read:

> Upon the question resolved, that 'tis not necessary nor convenient for his majesty's service to land the two regiments now on board under command of Colonel Cunningham and Colonel Richards into the City of London-Derry. That forasmuch as London-Derry is not sufficiently provided with provisions or otherwise tenable against a powerful well-appointed army, it is therefore advisable for the principal officers to withdraw themselves, that the town and soldiers may make the better terms for themselves by capitulation.

Apart from Mogridge, who simply acted as secretary, everyone present in the council of war was offered the document to sign to record his agreement. There were no dissenting voices. They all signed. In doing so, someone (Richards thought it was Tiffin, but Tiffin denied it) 'swore that he would be hanged for no man's pleasure', and 'another said he would go home, let who would be displeased'. No one took the decision with enthusiasm. Solomon Richards (according to Solomon Richards) said that 'quitting the town was quitting of a kingdom'. No one was happy.[7]

The next step was not easy. If the decision was announced, there would be a scramble for the shipping and they would all be trapped in the throng. According to Richards, Lundie wanted everyone present sworn to secrecy, but Richards refused. They agreed instead not to disclose the nature of the resolution they had made, which was in effect the same thing and would get them all safely to the ships. Enquirers were falsely told that the troops from the ships were to be landed. Only 'the persons of quality' were told that they were to leave and that the ships were waiting for them. To explain their movement down to the lough, it was put out variously that they were going to bring up the reinforcements or 'to see the men land'. Lundie, 'to make it the more credible', issued orders to the sheriffs to find quarters for the two regiments.[8] He knew he was going to be hated.

By the time of Lundie's council of war, and without any encouragement from him, many of the senior army men had already left the country. Not only had Mount-Alexander and Tollymore and the leading Association officers left, but since then Gustavus Hamilton and Richard Gorges had disappeared from Coleraine. The senior men in the room lined up for Lundie to sign passes for them to leave. Over the next days, the remaining senior officers and the senior militia men all sailed away: colonels Lord Blayney, Sir Francis Hamilton, Sir Arthur Rawdon, William Stewart, Arthur Upton, John Chichester, Chidley Coote, Sir Nicholas Atchison, William Shaw and William Ponsonby; majors John Hill, Paulet Phillips, John Barry and John Tubman; and captains John Forward, Hugh Magill and Richard Whaley. Of the twenty-four signatories who had, only six days before, signed a declaration that anyone who deserted was to 'be deemed a Coward, and disaffected to their Majesties Service, and the Protestant Interest', only five remained for the coming siege.

None of these men were traitors, many of them returned to fight in the war, and some of those who survived the war lived to become high-ranking officers. Blayney, who had played such an important part at the beginning of the war, died in England a few months afterwards. Sir Arthur Rawdon, whose departure perhaps was seen as the greatest loss, excused himself on the basis that he was too ill to stay, an explanation that was accepted without comment, although it is a curious illness that drives a man to exchange his sick bed for a vigorous five-day sea voyage on Mr Anderton's rations. Mackenzie wrote of Rawdon: 'by continual fatigue and want of rest [he] cast himself into a dangerous illness, which afterwards forced him to leave the kingdom – a gentleman who in all those affairs of the North of Ireland, showed himself a true lover and friend of his country'.

'There was', wrote Mackenzie, 'scarce a Man left of any considerable Reputation for Experience or Conduct in Military Affairs'.[9] Those who left, wrote Bennett, had been 'cheated and deluded by this blind council of war.[10] Lundie, writing for his life at the end of the year, wrote these stark sentences:

> There was not one gentleman of any note after the break of Clady bridge that would stay any longer in Ireland. They were so rebutted by the cowardice of the men therefore they all came to me for passes telling me that they could signify no more in the town than so many private men. They were in no commission and under no pay for I had no power over them, [I]

> gave them passes and then I was to be left with none but the officers of the 6 companies of Lord Mountjoy's Regiment

Lundie was no coward and was not inclined to desert with the others. He stayed behind to face down the angry crowds and to deal as best he could with the enemy. Neither of these things was for the faint-hearted. Having made a decision based on the facts as he understood them, and having been backed in that decision by everyone whose opinion he valued, he stayed on to implement it knowing that he was in great personal danger. He even, according to Lord Blayney, approved a plan to destroy the ammunition to prevent it falling into enemy hands.

At about four in the afternoon, Cunningham and his officers left the city and made their way back to the ships at Ture. As the gates closed on them, Lundie lost control.

12

Anarchy

IN THE EARLY EVENING, the ships weighed anchor and dropped down the lough to wait off Redcastle. Despair gripped the city. The thousands locked out clamoured to get in. Once they discovered the relief expedition was leaving, their desperation turned to violence. Among them was George Walker, who had spent the last night with his men under the skies. 'With much difficulty and some violence upon the sentry they got in', he wrote. According to Mackenzie, one of the volunteer captains fired at the sentry, and ordered the gate to be burned. The garrison troops were at the same time contending with the new troops Lundie had allowed in as reinforcements, as well as the thousand or more who had climbed or pushed their way in since. Lundie described 'the rabble' inside the city forcing the keys of the gates from Lieutenant James Ash, the guard commander who had earlier let out Cunningham's party. They 'shot the sentry through the body with two balls for opposing them', and opened the gate. 'Then', wrote Lundie, 'the whole rabble entered'.

The crowds flooded in. The city's population swelled to thirty thousand. To Lundie, that was the end. The discipline that he had hoped for at the council of war a week before, the articles of war, the gallows and the court martials were things of the past. The arguments and calculations over provisioning were overtaken by events. 'Their disorders was very great', he wrote. 'I did endeavour to appeal [to] them, but at last was advised to go out of the streets otherwise I might expect to be affronted at least.' The movement of the ships down the lough 'put the whole town in an uproar swearing they would hang me for keeping them out of the town and they were betrayed by me.'

There was also violence on the river. Many sought refuge on the ships, but shipping for these desperate refugees was not free. They were plundered by their rescuers, who would not let them on board unless they handed over 'great sums'. Wolfran Cornewall, the captain of the *Swallow*, charged his passengers £4 a head.[A] Or, failing the £4, swords, watches or clothing were taken in lieu, 'in a very barbarous manner'. Colonel John Chichester clambered on board without any cash and 'for his passage was obliged to give the officer of the frigate his watch and pistols'.

Of the regular officers and those with the means to leave, very few stayed behind, other than the officers from Mountjoy's regiment who were ordered by Lundie to

[A] One cannot accurately measure inflation over the centuries, but, by way of a rough estimate, the Bank of England's inflation calculator estimates the value of £4 in 1689 as being the equivalent of £1,040 today.

remain. Escape was, as Walker wrote, 'not without some hazard; for the soldiers were under great discontent ... and were not easily kept from expressing it with violence upon some persons'. At least one boat carrying officers to the ships was forced back by gunfire. Humphrey Bell, a captain in Mountjoy's regiment, was shot dead in the boat and another officer wounded. Among those trying to desert in the boat with Bell was Henry Baker. Although Baker's presence in Captain Bell's boat was no secret during the siege, Mackenzie took the editorial decision not to name him, and Walker took the decision not to mention the incident at all. Michelburne described an officer telling him that he had heard shots by the strand and had run to see what was happening. 'In a boat that lay on the side of the sea, who should I see but Captain Bell of your regiment, lying gasping and speechless, rolling in his blood, and several soldiers plundering the boat.' The soldiers claimed they had orders to fire and that Captain Bell, Henry Baker and one other officer 'had hired the boat and were deserting the garrison as other officers had done the tide before with the intent to go on shipboard for England or Scotland leaving their soldiers to be hanged by the Irish'.[1]

To those determined or forced to stay, something needed to be done to stop the ships leaving. The word got out that Lundie had refused to let the reinforcements in because there were no provisions. Captain Thomas Cole, who, as a former officer and victim of Tyrconnell's purge, could speak to Cunningham in more persuasive terms than most, was chosen for the task. He rode as fast as he could along the lough to Redcastle and managed to get on board. The garrison suspected Lundie's integrity, he said, and would offer Cunningham the governorship if he brought his men back. Never mind what Lundie had said, they had sufficient provisions in the city, and they had great numbers of men, all willing to fight. Cunningham could stay behind the walls with his new garrison while the rest would march out and take the field. It was a desperate speech, and Cunningham did not believe any of it. The only authority that Cole had was 'from the rabble', Cunningham said. Only Lundie had the authority to make such offers, and he had 'a good opinion of Colonel Lundie's loyalty'. Cole was told to go back and obey him.[2]

On the next day, the ships dropped down to Greencastle, and on 19 April left the lough and sailed for England, but the meeting with Cole preyed on Cunningham's mind. Three days later at sea he came across the *Bonadventure* frigate and enquired if she was escorting provision ships, because, if so, even if there was only enough for a fortnight, Cunningham had resolved to return. Alas, the *Bonadventure* was escorting ships carrying arms and ammunition but no provisions. It was an unhappy ending for both Cunningham and Richards. Warrants were issued for their arrest 'on suspicion of dangerous practices against the government'. Both gave evidence at the House of Commons Committee on Irish Affairs later that year, and both were cashiered.[3]

There was no rapid Irish advance. Once the fighting on the Finn was over, Hamilton crossed the entire army at Lifford, and gave them the rest they needed. On the next day, 16 April, that busy day when Cunningham and Richards left the city, he made his first attempt to sound out the garrison. From his new headquarters in St Johnstown, Hamilton sent a Church of Ireland minister, a Mr Whitlow, to make contact with Lundie. Not a local clergyman, Whitlow was in all probability a refugee picked up by the Irish. (There was a Church of Ireland clergyman named John Whitlow in Newry after the war.) He had been persuaded to enquire whether 'the city would surrender on honourable terms' so as 'to prevent the effusion of Christian blood'. Given what was then happening, Whitlow was told to come back on the following day. Before he left, he met an acquaintance of his, one of the Sligo men, Cornet Charles Nicholson, who asked him what he thought would happen. Embarrassed perhaps at being spotted as the Irish army's emissary, Whitlow 'seemed at first very shy towards him', but then went on to say that 'the town would be delivered before Saturday following; and that he was to receive his letters next morning from Colonel Lundie, and he advised Nicholson, as an old acquaintance, to shift for himself'.[4]

The purpose of Nicholson's evidence on this point was to explain why he deserted the city. He did so because he had special information (unlike the other deserters, who did not have this special information). Nicholson's exchange with Whitlow was seized upon by Mackenzie as evidence that Lundie's plans were somehow known to the enemy, or that he was in league with King James. It showed nothing of the sort. Whitlow had come from the Irish camp, where there was an optimistic hope that Derry would surrender now that the king was in Ireland. Secondly, he told Nicholson that he would 'receive his letters next morning from Colonel Lundie', but he emphatically did not get any such thing.

Whitlow gleaned one scrap of information from the conversation. King James' presence in Ireland was generally believed to be one of Tyrconnell's lies. The consequence of this was that Berwick, on that same day, sent an express to the king to let him know 'in the name of all the general officers' that the town would 'infallibly surrender' if the king were to appear in person.

When Whitlow returned on the following day, Wednesday 17 April, Lundie had a council of war ready for him. Everyone on the last council had left, and we do not know who sat on the new one. Mackenzie recorded knowingly: 'This Whitlow was present; and sat near the governor', but we do not know at what time of day this happened, whether Whitlow was there at the beginning or simply brought into say his piece, or how long the council went on for after Whitlow had gone. What we do know is that the council did not let Whitlow know any more than that they would send a delegation to King James to find out what was wanted from them and on what terms. Whitlow was then sent back to the Irish army.

Having decided not to use Mr Whitlow for any purpose, the council of war resolved instead to send out three people they could trust: James Hamilton, the 63-year-old archdeacon of Derry; Captain Charles Kinaston; and Captain Francis Nevill. These three emissaries arrived at the Irish camp at St Johnstown, where they were given a brief note signed by Richard Hamilton and Rosen that contained 'but one article; *viz.* to surrender the town, their serviceable horses, and arms; and they might live peaceably'. They also got an assurance from Richard Hamilton that the Irish army would not advance to within four miles of the city until they had sent a reply. It was a brief audience, and they were back by the evening. After some difficulty, both Kinaston and the archdeacon were let into the city, having been at first, says Mackenzie, 'refused entrance by the multitude'.[B] [5] Nevill was not so lucky. Colonel Whitney was in charge of the guard when Nevill demanded entrance, and 'pretended, from the walls, that he did not know him'. The unhappy Captain Nevill 'lay in a little hut all night' and was then captured by the Irish and took protection.[6]

At four o'clock in the morning on 16 April, a report reached Omagh that five thousand rebels had been routed by Rosen. James was delighted. He wanted, he said, to go to Londonderry, but d'Avaux was firm. They had to return to Dublin, and if the thirteen ships seen off the coast brought aid to the rebels, the king's troops may be prevented from securing the countryside around the city, let alone besieging it. Melfort backed d'Avaux, and the king gave in, 'but he could not stop himself saying that he would have to put up with the French getting all the glory for taking Derry'. Having got his way, d'Avaux rode with the king to Charlemont. They got there at six in the evening. Waiting for them was bad news from the south coast. Sixteen English ships were anchored off Kinsale. The king needed to get back to Dublin to take charge, but as they were all tired, and the horses had had no forage for four days, he decided to remain in Charlemont for a day.

During the night, or as dawn was breaking on 17 April, the king received the dispatch from the duke of Berwick, who was with Rosen and Hamilton and the French generals. They now did not believe that there were any English ships, but they were all confident that if the king appeared in front of Londonderry the rebels would open the gates. This to James changed everything. The rebels were not being reinforced, and so d'Avaux's main argument fell away. Now that the senior French military men, together with James' son Berwick and Hamilton, both of whom he trusted, were telling him that his very presence would stop both bloodshed and a siege, he must go. It was his duty. He did not call for d'Avaux, who might try and find some other arguments against him turning back, he called for Melfort. Seeing what the king wanted from him, Melfort again changed his position. The king must go to Londonderry immediately.

[B] In his *History of the siege of Londonderry*, C.D. Milligan quoted at length from the 'Kinaston letter' in the Armagh Cathedral archives, which he felt 'proves up to the hilt how Lundy was acting the traitor'. The contents of the Kinaston letter are utterly false. It is one of two alternate versions Kinaston hoped to use to get money for being a witness against Lundie in the event of a treason trial, the other version is in HMC, *Finch*. In the Armagh version, Kinaston claimed to have been sent alone to a secret meeting with King James, who told him that he was satisfied that Lundie 'had done him all the service that lay in his power' to surrender the city. In the Finch version, Kinaston expressly stated that he was not sent out (and so had no such conversation with James) and he instead concentrated on treasonous words supposedly spoken by Lundie to him alone. Kinaston received a secret service payment of £100 for his inventions.

King James then sent for d'Avaux and showed him the letter. Melfort criticized Rosen, as the senior officer, for not having told the king this himself, and instead having left it to chance that Berwick might write independently. D'Avaux bridled at this. Rosen's silence, he said, was a sure sign that Rosen did not share Berwick's opinion. In any event, Berwick clearly intended the letter to reach the king at Omagh, so it was not written to request that the king should ride all the way back from Charlemont. If the king went back now, he would look ridiculous. The king was needed in Dublin. The country's affairs needed to be put in order, and they had already lost three weeks. Either Londonderry would give in before he got there or it would defend itself and he would have to come back. The joy of being there to see the rebels surrender, said d'Avaux, would be dwarfed by the displeasure he would feel if they did not.

> I could not stop myself from telling the king that he should not flatter himself that the rebels would surrender to him through loyalty, nor would they do so through fear, as seeing the king with so few troops would boost their courage, while if they did not see them, they might believe that the besieging troops were only a fraction of the king's army, and that His Majesty was following with the main body.

All d'Avaux got was an assurance that if the city did not surrender, the king would return as quickly as he had got there. On that understanding, King James left, leaving behind his camp bed and all his servants (except one valet) and, as there were so few horses fit enough to make the return journey, set off in a dangerously small group of only seven or eight riders. D'Avaux was left to make his way back to Dublin. He wrote to King Louis:

> The Irish are beginning to be very discouraged by the king of England's behaviour, and no longer believe as they did at the beginning that he will set things right; the only hope they have left is that Your Majesty will give me orders to engage His Britannic Majesty to behave in a different fashion.[7]

On that day, 17 April, the king covered forty-three miles through Omagh and late at night made it to Newtownstewart. Exhausted, he allowed himself a short night's rest and at the break of another wet day, on 18 April, he mounted up and made for Derry. The whole Irish army was in motion and marching north in the rain. Three miles north of Lifford, James overtook Pusignan and Ramsay leading his infantry, and then rode on to join Rosen who had gone on ahead with the cavalry and dragoons. He caught up with him outside the city, where Rosen had formed up the horse on the south side of Derry Hill, behind the windmill and out of cannon range, so as to get a good view. The king did not go any closer, but waited, at Rosen's suggestion, for the infantry to catch up.

What James did not know was that Hamilton had agreed with the city's delegates not to advance to within four miles of the city. Hamilton had been happy to give the assurance because he did not want to advertise his lack of artillery. Rosen knew of Hamilton's agreement, but overruled him. A display was needed so that no one in the city could be in any doubt of the king's intentions.

As the rebel army was now behind the walls, there was no opposition to the Irish advance. However, a large body, on being refused entry after the battle at Clady, had carried on past the city and camped wherever they could in and around Culmore. Most of the horsemen had gone there, as had perhaps some fifteen hundred infantry. One of the most vocal of the horsemen was Adam Murray, the son of a tenant farmer from Ling, outside Claudy, some ten miles away. He had been elected a captain of a troop of volunteers, and (according to Mackenzie, who lionized Murray) as the Irish army came into view from the south, Murray led the horsemen from Culmore towards the north side of the city. As Murray's advance risked inflaming matters, Lundie's council sent an urgent dispatch ordering him to withdraw his men out of sight. This message was carried by a man also called Murray. Adam Murray's reaction was described by Mackenzie:

> He understood not the meaning of so strange an order; but the messenger, being his relation, explained the mystery to him, that the Governor and his council were about making terms with the enemy for surrendering the town; and added, that several of his friends advised him to hasten to town, if he designed to make any effectual opposition to the enemy.

Now sitting on another council of war with his remaining officers, Lundie's position had not changed. There was no point in even contemplating a defence, now that 'the whole rabble' had got into the city. As if to confirm that Lundie had not arrived at the decision alone, John Mogridge asked Lundie to produce the document that Mogridge had prepared at Lundie's dictation and which had been signed by all those at the meeting.

Mackenzie, always unreliable when describing meetings he did not attend, has it that Mogridge 'declared he would conceal no longer the Result of that Council' and 'desired Governour *Lundy* to produce the Order, which was a great surprize to this present Council, who (tho they generally agreed too well with Colonel *Lundy* about surrendering) yet deeply resented the concealing so material a thing from them'. But as the ships with the reinforcements and officers had long gone and the signed document simply confirmed that all those officers had agreed with Lundie, the intervention by Mogridge can only have been in the context of him urging Lundie to defend himself by showing the declaration that every single senior officer had signed two days before. It no longer mattered. Lundie resigned:[8]

> I told them I was very sensible of the affront they had put on me but was sorry that I was not in a condition to resent it since I had no command over

> them. But since they had taken such a groundless jealousy against me, I was resolved from that minute to be no more concerned with them. They could not say that I had betrayed them for I leave the town in a much better condition than I found it to them.

Although it was arguably the inevitable consequence of what had happened over the last day, Lundie's resignation came as a shock, it was not what the officers wanted to hear. They had experienced the disorders of the previous nights. It was not just a choice between Lundie and the Irish, it was a choice between him and anarchy. Lundie held King William's commission, and if he went, all legality went. The ungovernable rabble could get them all massacred.

> They desired me to take the government again. I told them I never would where I had nothing but the name, which indeed was all, for they were under no command. They pressed me again. I told them that if it were put to my choice to accept of the command or to be shot, I would choose the latter rather, and as for my proceedings at that minute I defied their malice to lay either neglect or malice to my charge.

Lundie was not going to be a mere figurehead. He was not going to be another Mount-Alexander.

> Now judge what I could do at the head of nine thousand rabble under no command and at that time had a jealousy of me. Notwithstanding of all this I was resolved to stay had it not been the opinion of Col Cunningham and all the English officers as well as the officers of Derry and mine that considering the weakness of the place and the little provisions in it, and the great number of ungovernable rabble that we had to deal with, we judged the place not tenable any time against a Royal victorious army which we expected to invest it next day. I appeal to any general officer or any engineer that ever saw it whether or not it be a place to keep out 14 days against a formal siege, and we expected no relief in 2 months.[9]

The timing was of the worst. The enemy were in view of the city, all the senior officers had deserted, and the commander had given up command. While Lundie spoke, the Irish infantry were arriving on the far end of Derry Hill beyond the windmill. It was raining heavily. Rosen, having waved aside Richard Hamilton's protests, insisted on having the men march down to the strand with colours flying, and posted them 'very near the town'. Noting that the defenders were 'in very great disorder', the king ordered a trumpeter to ride to the city and summon it to surrender. The messenger returned to say that they had shouted down from the walls that they would 'dispatch a messenger of their own with an answer in an hour's time'.

In the middle of this, while the whole garrison was peering over the walls at the spectacle of the Irish infantry below them on the strand, Lundie made his move.

> I took that opportunity to get back to my own house which was very fortunate for me for about five hundred had proven my death. I took in all my companies and a great many officers that would not be concerned with the rabble. I had ammunition and provisions brought in, and was resolved to sell my life as dear as I could for, besides my own strength, I had a good party in the town who were resolved to assist me if I was attacked. At this rate was I on my guard four days. All that time I was threatened with a hundred kinds of death.

Outside, in the pouring rain, the king waited for a reply. On the walls, orders had been given that everyone should stand to the defences, but there was to be no firing 'on severe penalties'. Officers were sent round to warn everyone to hold their fire. The town was being summoned. It was a parley. Nevertheless, while, or perhaps after, the king kept his faraway position on the heights, there was a general firing from the walls of both cannon and musketry. Colonel Thomas Whitney dashed around commanding them to stop, but, wrote Bennett happily, had Whitney 'not made soon off, he had certainly been thrown over the walls'.[10]

Walker excuses this on the ground that Richard Hamilton had said that the army would not come within four miles and so the men thought 'they were by some means or other betrayed'. Mackenzie excuses the firing because by that point they all feared betrayal by Lundie and his council, and so 'our men on the walls paid so little deference to either them or their orders, and so little regarded the secret treaties they were managing with the enemy, that when King James' forces were advancing towards them on the strand, they presently fired their great guns at them'. The duke of Berwick sympathized. Rosen 'knew and had approved Hamilton's agreement' with the delegates, 'thus, when they saw the rest of the army appearing before their town, the rebels imagined that a surprise was envisaged, and that Hamilton's promise was simply an expedient'. Rosen was in the wrong.[11]

The triumphant boasts of those who opened fire from the walls were adopted by the chroniclers. Walker wrote that 'a great many were killed' by the gunfire, but no one else repeated that claim. Ash wrote that the guns 'did some execution'. Bennett claimed that three of King James' horse [men] were killed by a cannon ball. And Mackenzie added that 'when King James' forces were advancing towards them on the strand, they presently fired their great guns at them, and, as was confidently reported, killed one Captain Troy, near the King's person'. Captain Troy, if he was even there, was not killed, and no shots were fired at the king, who was too far away to be shot at in any event. King James' own account was clear on this: Rosen posted troops 'within less than half cannon shot of the town 'while the king 'kept himself just out of cannon shot from the town, and then sent a trumpet to summon it'.[12] The only discomfort recorded by King James was that he had eaten nothing all day, and that he was forced to remain on horseback 'under heavy and incessant rain'. He was not on the strand. The shots were fired at that part of the army, the infantry, that was within range. The infantry pulled back to safety, and then marched off. As Berwick put it, 'as we had nothing ready for a siege, we drew back a little'. There was nothing else they could do at the time. Neither the French sources nor King James' own account refer to there being any casualties from the initial firing, although the shooting 'continued the rest of the day and there were some soldiers killed'.[13]

Two contemporary Irish writers, neither of whom were there and both writing years afterwards, adopted this narrative. Plunkett and O'Kelly wrote of the king being shot at, but Mackenzie's *Narrative* was the sole source. To them it was evidence of the savagery of the Protestants, who had disgracefully fired on their king during a parley. The otherwise obscure Captain Patrick Troy, or his name at least, would have been known to some of those in the city. He had been commissioned in Mountjoy's regiment only six months before to replace one of the Protestant officers, which may in itself have generated enough resentment to make his death a case of wishful thinking. We have no evidence to suggest that he was present outside Derry, nor do we know what he did during the Irish war, but he was certainly alive afterwards, as on 20 March 1692 he was commissioned by King James (then in exile) to command the French ship *Berwick*.[14]

Murray raced to the city at the head of four hundred horsemen. This was no quiet approach. To the Irish it appeared as a significant and aggressive cavalry manoeuvre. In his account Murray says that 'he forced his way through the enemy dragoons' shielded by 'our cannon and musketeers'. Some Irish dragoons who had already made their way to the north end of the city drew their carbines and fired. Murray and his horsemen got to Shipquay gate, on the far side of the city from the approaching Irish army, 'with the loss of eleven of his number'. The gate was locked and the guards would not let them in. Walker suggested lowering a rope to haul Murray up, but Murray needed his men with him. The captain of the guard was now James Morrison, one of those responsible for shooing away the redshanks in December. Against orders, he opened the gates.[15]

The loss of eleven of his men was cited after the war by Murray. Mackenzie noted that the enemy's dragoons had fired on Murray but reported no casualties. It is a feature of Mackenzie's *Narrative* that losses were often not mentioned or were minimized. Mackenzie also described Murray's entrance to the city, slyly adding the preposterous detail that Walker was 'sent from the council'. It is preposterous because Walker, then an unknown major in the Tyrone militia, was not on any of Lundie's councils (and we may be sure that Walker would have had much to say of his heroics in the council meeting had he been there). It is sly because Mackenzie intended with these words to link Walker with Lundie.

There are two versions of what happened next. The first is carefully, gleefully even, given by Mackenzie. Murray raised the masses. Those inside the city knew he was coming, and when he got inside the walls he was surrounded by crowds of supporters. They 'followed him through the streets with great expressions of their respect and affection', and together they worked themselves into a rage. 'He would stand by them in defence of their lives and the Protestant interest, and assist them immediately to suppress Lundie and his council, to prevent their design of surrendering the city.' All who supported him were to tie 'a white cloth on their left arm' and in their hundreds they marched on the council house.

Lundie was inside. He could not ignore them, and so allowed in a delegation. Murray and the others demanded that Lundie tell them what was going on. There was something of a shouting match. In Mackenzie's version, Murray was able to crowd in a list of complaints about Lundie. He had failed them at the fords. He had ridden away rather than command ten thousand men eager to fight. He had failed to send them ammunition. He had abandoned the easily defended pass at the Long Causey. He was a fool or a knave. Murray demanded that Lundie go out and lead the rebel army against the Irish immediately. They were waiting.

This is Mackenzie putting his hero dramatically in the centre of the narrative. No one else suggested that there was any such face-to-face confrontation. The suspicion must be that Mackenzie was simply reciting what he himself would have liked to say to Lundie had he ever got the chance. He was, in a sense, practising in front of a mirror. If that is right, Murray's speech and plea to Lundie to stand up and lead them against the Irish army was a fanciful insertion to let the London readership know that Murray and his followers were loyal, obedient men whose only wish was to follow into battle the one man who held King William's commission.

Lundie's version is rather different. It is perhaps notable that Lundie does not once mention Murray by name. It was merely 'the rabble'. Lundie and Murray never met, and were never in the same room together. The volunteer officers were self-appointed, or at least appointed by the volunteers themselves. To Lundie one troop of rough-riders was much like another. It was not his department. Any number of people had been abusive to him, and Murray may well have been one of them. Such shouting as there was happened in the street rather than in the council room. Lundie was shouted down. The theatre of Murray reciting accusations in the council chamber while a humiliated Lundie sat without answer did not happen. The council chamber had emptied when James' army came into sight. Lundie had left long before Murray could have got there. The only point at which the two accounts agree is that even at this late stage, even after sending Cunningham and the officers to the ships, Lundie was asked stay on to command the defence. Lundie has it that the council wanted him back. Mackenzie has it that Murray also wanted him back.[16]

Murray's own account, as presented in the two versions of his *Case*, is very short. He does not claim anything more than that he went 'with a strong guard of soldiers and officers to Colonel Lundie'. He does not say where Lundie was. Lundie 'told him they had signed to surrender upon honourable terms' and 'showed him the instrument they had signed'. If one has in mind Mackenzie's version, this was all done with Lundie sitting at a table receiving an angry delegation, but Murray does not say that. Murray's version fits just as well with what Lundie recorded. Murray's 'strong guard of soldiers and officers' would have been to Lundie a great mob of angry men that needed to be kept back at musket point by his own troops. Lundie's redcoats were necessarily there and their message was just as blunt: Lay a hand on the governor and we'll shoot.

No 'instrument' had been signed 'to surrender on honourable terms'. The only document that had been signed was that which Blayney, Cunningham and Richards had signed two days before.[17] Maybe that was waved around to show that all these senior people thought the city should negotiate. Maybe another piece of paper was waved around. Maybe nothing was waved. Maybe Lundie used the phrase 'honourable terms'. Maybe not. All this was against a barrage of shouted curses and insults. Debate was impossible. Lundie's men bundled him into his house and the mob was kept back by soldiers. Not able to get at Lundie, Murray and his people stormed off. They made for 'the main-guard and seized the keys of all the gates and stores', and those with Murray purported to appoint him as governor. It was mutiny.

After Lundie had left them, the council of war sent Archdeacon Hamilton back out 'to excuse themselves for what had passed, and lay all the blame of it on the ungovernableness of the people, whose violent humour, they said they could not restrain'. The archdeacon set off again while the king was still on Derry Hill. This time he took with him Captain Robert White, chosen because he was one of the few men in the city who knew what King James looked like. The old archdeacon may not have been able to tell the difference between the king and an Irishman in a *papier mâché* crown, but White had seen James in the flesh 'often' and would not be fooled. The necessity to send out Captain White shows the state of knowledge of those in the city. They did not believe that King James was there. The story of Captain Troy being killed at his side can only have originated afterwards. One look was enough for Captain White, and he was allowed to go back to the city with the bad news. The man they called the king was indeed King James. The archdeacon did not return. Having seen the king, he took protection.[c] [18]

The impression the king got from the archdeacon and, perhaps from others who left the city, was that the shooting from the walls 'only proceeded from the rabble, who being drunk had seized upon the cannon and fired without order from any people of authority in the town [and] that the better sort were generally resolved to surrender, and did all they could to persuade the common people to the same'.[19] The king sent back a further summons asking the garrison to send out a delegation of up to twenty men to hear the proposals being offered.

[c] According to Mackenzie, 'That summer he sickened and died.'

'With a singular and unwearied benignity and forbearance', King James remained on Derry Hill, 'waiting for the effects of the assurances which had been given him, and endeavouring to bring these unhappy rebels to a sense of their duty'. There was no reply to his summons, and, knowing that he was getting nowhere, he ordered the troops to march back to St Johnstown and Raphoe to get some shelter from the weather. They would have to wait for 'the arrival of the cannon and other things necessary for the forming of a siege or blockade'. He rode off to St Johnstown.[20]

Inside the walls, there followed another night of anarchy. Mogridge's disclosure that Lundie had, with colonels Cunningham and Richards, signed a declaration that the city should capitulate, became known. 'This discovery occasioned great uneasiness and disorder in the Town', said Walker. There was 'rage and violence' in the garrison. 'The whole town', wrote Lundie, was 'in an uproar, swearing they would hang me for keeping them out of the town and [that] they were betrayed by me. About seven at night after the gates were locked for the night and the word given out and the retreat beaten, they forced the keys of the gates from the town major, relieved all the guards, altered the word and beat their drums and every man was at his arms, and they beset my house.'

Michelburne came upon a group of volunteers loudly planning to hang Lundie over the walls in view of the Irish army. His perception of the rabble was the same as Lundie's. He gave them a good beating with his cane: 'You damned rogues!' he roared. 'Who will you hang over the walls?' When the drums beat yet another alarm, his cane was handy to subdue the drummers: 'We can't hear our own ears from morning till night for these damned drums!' As far as Michelburne could tell, the rabble was leaderless. He made no mention of Murray. The mob had no officers and if they had any leaders, they were indistinguishable from the men. 'Who do you belong to?' he bellowed at them. 'You sons of whores!'[21]

13

Mutiny

LONDONDERRY WAS A PROTESTANT CITY, but it had never been a Presbyterian city. The thousands of Presbyterians then within the walls were refugees grateful to be there, but did not have, nor did they expect to have, any stake in the running of the city. They just did not want it surrendered. Some of them were Association men, but many were not. They were not an organized body and would follow whoever showed leadership. Now that Lundie had resigned, in the face of both the external enemy and the angry masses inside the city, it was essential that someone provided that leadership. A new governor had to be chosen.

The only men with a say in choosing a leader were those who held a senior rank either in the militia or in the Association. They needed an experienced military leader, which meant someone who had been in the army, which disqualified all the Presbyterians. The electorate was a gathering of (says Mackenzie) fifteen officers, and included in their number, as if he was there to represent the whole body of Presbyterians in the city, was the militia captain Adam Murray. He had played an important part in the mutiny, but Murray may then only have been in his twenties. He was a young farmer with no military or administrative experience and not someone who the officers were likely to take orders from, regardless of his ability to please a crowd. No one else had a vote. Mackenzie bemoaned the fact that the electorate was not bigger, by which he meant that there were not enough Presbyterians to stop what happened next.

There was no obvious choice as to who should be the new governor. All the colonels had left. According to both Bennett and Walker 'the town unanimously chose' Walker and Baker as the governors. But that is too bald a statement. Mackenzie wrote of three candidates being considered: Henry Baker, John Michelburne and Lieutenant Colonel Richard Johnston. They were all outsiders none of whom had any authority over the others, but they were all Association men. Baker had led troops in the disasters at Carrickfergus and Dromore, Michelburne had led the attack on O'Neil's recruits at Toome, and Richard Johnston was the most senior of the Association officers, having sat on Mount-Alexander's Consult.

There was then a vote of the fifteen officers, not a vote of the 'the town', and Baker received more votes than anyone else. Then in his fifties, Baker was the oldest of the candidates. He had not experienced the roar of battle (other than in the fighting of the previous weeks), but he came from outside Dundalk and his experience as a professional soldier in the Irish army spanned over a quarter of a century. He was first commissioned as a lieutenant 1662, a rank he still held with the Association at the beginning of the year. To the other officers, he was trusted. He was 'one of us'.

There had clearly been manoeuvring beforehand. Michelburne denied being a candidate but recorded that Baker's leadership had been arranged in advance. Before the meeting, Baker took him aside to announce that 'a great part of the officers have desired that I would take charge of the garrison, and be governor, because I have lived all my days amongst them and have never been out of this kingdom'. Michelburne depicted himself as approving the choice, but having no part in making it.[1]

Behind the scenes the outcome of the election was arranged by Walker. Walker was not going to stand on the sidelines as just another clergyman, and in his mind there was no one better suited to be governor than George Walker, but he lacked any military experience and needed a soldier to be a joint governor with him. Although Baker's reputation had been somewhat damaged by having just been shot up in a boat while trying to desert, Walker saw him as the ideal man. He was an old soldier who had been involved from the start of the rebellion and, if Walker could arrange matters, Baker would be forever grateful and obedient. In referring to Baker, it was observed, ''Tis well known Mr W. Engaged him in the Service, and not the contrary, after Mr. B's coming out of the Boat, so little persuasion obtained his Assistance.'[2] Arranging outcomes favourable to himself was what, as will be seen, Walker was good at.

Mackenzie has Baker making a ludicrous speech: '*That the work they had now laid on him, was too much for him to discharge, and therefore desired they would allow him an Assistant for the Stores and Provisions.*' The officers 'readily agreed' to allow Baker to appoint Walker.[3] Baker did not need the council's permission to appoint an assistant to look after the stores. Such an appointment would be far down the agenda under 'other business'. If Baker did make such a speech, it was a device to appoint, or rather to get the officers to appoint, a joint governor. If Baker did say anything along the lines suggested by Mackenzie, it could only have been a guarded response to the question, 'Why do you need a joint governor?' Walker had struck a deal with Baker. As Baker was not as senior as Johnston in the Association army, nor as experienced a soldier as Michelburne, Walker used his considerable powers of persuasion to get Baker chosen. In return for his efforts, Baker would insist on him being the joint governor. Baker would be in charge of all military matters, and Walker took over everything else, which included responsibility for the provisions and the civil government. Walker would be the voice of the city. In his eyes, he was the governor, and Baker was in charge of the mechanics of defending the walls.

In the pamphlet war to come, Walker's use of the title 'the governor' following this imperfect, Presbyterian-free election, so infuriated Mackenzie that he wasted much of the venom of his attacks on Walker on this issue. Mackenzie's case was always weakened by attacking Walker on the one ground where Walker was secure, and so Mackenzie was beaten off without Walker having to answer the many accusations to which he had no defence. Mackenzie initiated the centuries-long but sterile debate as to whether Walker was a deputy governor, the governor's assistant or simply the commissioner of the stores, but there can be no doubt that Walker was referred to as 'governor' throughout the siege, and that he was overwhelming considered to be so. Michelburne was quite clear on this. Walker was 'in joint command', his duties being 'more conspicuous in the Eating part than the Fighting, and reason good, the Charge of the Stores, and Provision being committed to him alone, whilst his Brother Governor was only the Martial Colleague'.[4]

If there was a formal election by a show of hands as suggested by Mackenzie, Baker got the votes of Michelburne, Walker and Murray and the four others he appointed colonels, which would have got him eight of the fifteen votes present. Walker, Michelburne, Vernon Parker, Hugh Hamill, Thomas Whitney and Richard Crofton were all made colonels of the foot regiments. Baker then made himself a colonel and, in a political move that would never have occurred to Lundie, he made Adam Murray colonel of horse (of which there were now some three hundred) and (although only Bennett says so) 'general in the field'.

The colonels were selected for their experience. Michelburne, Parker and Whitney had all been regular army officers since Charles II's time. Earlier that year, before he deserted and joined Skeffington's volunteers, Michelburne had been a lieutenant of grenadiers in Mountjoy's regiment, as had Parker. Both were Tangier veterans. Thomas Whitney had been a captain until Tyrconnell's purge, and now that Sir Francis Hamilton had disappeared, he took over one of the of Association regiments. Richard Crofton, who was then about sixty, was a career soldier and had been in the Irish army from the Restoration until he was purged as a captain in 1686. That left three regiments with colonels possessing no military experience: George Walker, Adam Murray and Hugh Hamill, a landowner and magistrate, who had raised a company of men in Lifford.[A] [5]

The council needed to respond to King James' proposals, or to at least hear them, and selected a delegation to go to the Irish camp. The king had asked for twenty men to go to his army to hear what was being offered. Someone suggested that Murray should go along, but (says Mackenzie) he refused 'and went to the walls'. Lundie was told of the delegation and sent two of his own nominees to the council to make sure (said Mackenzie) that the right sort of person was included.

> The twenty are chosen and ready to go out. The multitude on the walls and at the gates hearing of it, are so enraged, that they threatened, that if a man of them offered to go out on that errand, they would treat them as betrayers of the town, the Protestant religion and King William's interest. Upon which none of them durst offer to go, and so a stop was put to that dangerous capitulation, notwithstanding the orders of the Governor and Council. So little did the soldiers regard any commands, that seemed to cross their resolutions of defending the city.[6]

[A] Hamill's brother intriguingly referred to him as having 'kept a diary of that siege, and therein (amongst other things) entered the day of the death of each officer, and who succeeded him.'

That was the state of the city when Baker took over. He was unable to arrange the simplest of matters in the face of a violent mob and there was nothing he could do about it. Thwarted in his attempt to negotiate, Baker instead concentrated on organizing the new regiments. Unallocated men were to form themselves into companies and elect captains, and the new captains would join one of the existing formations. The sizes of the regiments varied from twenty-five companies in Baker's regiment and seventeen in Michelburne's, to twelve and fifteen companies in Walker's, Hamill's, Parker's, Whitney's and Crofton's, with eight companies of horsemen in Murray's. 'In all', Walker wrote, '117 companies, each company consisting of 60 men. In all, 7,020 men, 341 officers', but these figures were rough calculations, arrived at by multiplying 117 by sixty for the men and 117 by three for the officers (which he should have made 351). As will be apparent, many of the companies were under half strength, and Murray's regiment never had the five hundred that eight companies of sixty men each plus their officers would give.[7]

George Holmes, a Cumberland man who had ended up in the city, described the elections: 'We proceeded and chose captains and completed regiments, made two governors. We had 116 companies in the city; all our officers fled away, so we made officers of those that did deserve to be officers. I was made captain.' Michelburne took a jaundiced view of these methods. He described a group of shabby volunteers in old clothes carrying short guns and, as they had no bandoliers or cartridge boxes, each with 'a little leather bag of powder tied to the codpiece'. A sergeant with a halberd introduced himself with the words: 'I'se a sergeant and I'll teach you how to charge your guns.' The reply was: 'By my saal, if you ken it weel, you's be our captain.'[8]

Lundie was now a great problem. He not only had the king's commission to be governor, but he was the only one of them to have a colonel's commission, and still commanded the officers and men in the six companies of Mountjoy's regiment. He was now barricaded in his house and protected by a strong guard of redcoats. Rather than defend the city against the Irish, the only body of trained soldiers in the city was defending their colonel from 'the rabble'. The situation could not be allowed to continue.

Knowing that Lundie was not a traitor and that he was the only man in the city who held lawful authority, the governors would only find legitimacy if he left them. The first thing that Walker and Baker did on the morning after their election was to go to Lundie's house. They waited outside while the locks were drawn and the barricades removed, and were ushered into Lundie's rooms. He met them; cold, red-eyed, worn-out and unforgiving, and surrounded by loaded muskets in the hands of suspicious soldiers. They detested, said the two new governors, the threats that had been made against him, and they would do everything they could to help him escape. Walker wrote: 'The commission he bore, as well as their respect for his person, made it a duty in them to contribute all they could to his safety'. Lundie did not need any persuading, he was as keen to go as they were to make him. The two new governors left feeling a certain relief.

In his *Account*, Walker reversed the order of his election and Lundie's escape (as did Bennett, probably on Walker's instructions). Once Lundie had resigned, there can be no moral difference, but Walker was anxious to show that new governors were chosen only after Lundie had left the city. He described Lundie's departure and wrote 'The garrison, seeing they were deserted and left without a governor ... unanimously resolved to choose Mr Walker and Major Baker to be their governors.' It was untrue, and that untruth was compounded by Walker's claim that he then wrote to Colonel Cunningham asking him to take over as governor, but that Cunningham declined, whereas Cunningham had left two days before Lundie.[9]

Lundie was convinced of one thing: the city would fall because there was no one able to control the undisciplined violence of those now behind its walls. If they went on the offensive, they would be a liability to the troops he could trust, and would be smashed by the Irish army. If they remained penned up in the city, the Irish would blast the walls down and massacre them. And if the Irish did not blast the walls down, those inside the walls would starve until they would be too weak to defend themselves. And then the Irish would massacre them. Far better, he reasoned, to leave the city and report to the king that Londonderry had fallen because of the shameful treachery of his Protestant subjects, who by their cowardly indiscipline and mutiny had lost him a kingdom.

The Irish were taking matters at their own pace. They had sent some men to guard the road to Culmore, and sent dragoons out over the Inishowen Peninsula, where they searched for those unfortunates still hoping for a boat to take them to Scotland. When they found them, they robbed them of anything worth having and left them destitute, but there were no massacres. In the belief that the garrison had no other sensible option, James still hoped that he would be able to persuade them to surrender. Richard Hamilton's cousin, the 29-year-old Claud Hamilton, Lord Abercorn (known locally as Lord Strabane), was sent to the city with a white flag in the hope that he could speak to the governor and put a stop to all this nonsense. Walker recorded that Abercorn 'came up to our Walls, making us many Proposals, and offering his King's Pardon, Protection and Favour, if we would surrender the Town'. According to Mackenzie, Abercorn was met by Adam Murray, who was polite enough to meet him outside the gate and engage him in a lengthy conversation. The negotiations led nowhere and, after Abercorn had returned, six of the guns on the walls were fired at the orchard. The Irish soldiers who had been hiding there 'ran out like swarmes of bees' back to their lines.[10]

Great numbers of men in the city wanted to attack the Irish. They had not suffered defeat. Very few had fought at Dromore or Portglenone or Clady. They had been forced to retreat because of what had taken place out of their sight and hearing, following ill fortune or the incompetence, cowardice or even teachery of others. To Baker and the other old army hands, storming out and forcing a battle was unthinkable. A pitched battle against the Irish redcoats by men without either officers or training was not going to end well. Nevertheless, in the early evening, encouraged perhaps by the Irish having to keep out of cannon shot, 'a party of our Horse and Foot, marched out with a design to attack the Enemy'. It is not suggested that the governors ordered them out, or that anyone ordered them back. They returned without fighting, wrote Mackenzie, because there was 'information of some design against them in the town'. If they, the most forward of the rebels, left the city, there were those inside who might betray them. Or Lundie might stage a coup. It was all untrue. There was no such design against them, and if any rumour was circulated, it was as likely to have come from Baker as anyone else, to keep the men together behind the walls.

While they were out, Walker went straight to Lundie. The best time to go, he told him, was when this expedition returned. The gates will be opened to let them in, and a few men, dressed as private soldiers, could easily walk through the gates in the opposite direction. The fort at Culmore was still in safe hands. Lundie had appointed William Adair as governor of the fort, and his brother Benjamin Adair had come up to the city to collect a supply of powder and match, the slow burning tape used on matchlock muskets. Lundie agreed to leave with him, called for four of his officers who he could rely on to protect him and told them to get ready. Lundie put on a soldier's coat over his clothes and completed his disguise by heaving a load of match onto his shoulder. Walker walked with them to the gate to make sure nothing went wrong, and Lundie and his four companions slipped out into the night. The gates were locked behind them.

That night Baker and Walker knew they were alone. They were in rebellion against King James, and they had finally shed King William's representative. They kept quiet about their part in helping Lundie to escape. Rumours abounded. Ash repeated what he had heard in the garrison, that 'Colonel Lundy deserted our garrison and went in disguise to Scotland.' Lundie had, like pretty well all the officers, left the country. A year later, at a time when everyone knew that Lundie was in the Tower, knowing it to be false, Mackenzie wrote: 'Lundy bribed a sentinel with whom he stole away, and going to Brook Hall which was then in the enemy's power.'[11]

Lundie had taken the precaution of having a small boat ready on the quayside, and the five fugitives rowed down the river. There were no ships on the lough, and they spent the night at Culmore, probably in the fort with the Adair brothers. In the morning, Lundie was given permission by William Adair to take a 'a flat open shell boat about 5 ton', as he put it, suggesting the size of a ship's longboat with six oars. They set off down the lough with 'neither seamen nor provisions', and were spotted by two troops of Irish dragoons who shot at them. They could not land anywhere until it was dark, by which time they had covered the seventeen miles to Greencastle. 'We durst not set to sea, but rowed into a creek and lay all night'. At daybreak they set about trying to find a pilot to get them to Scotland, but failed as everyone had gone. They were then spotted a second time, but managed to capture an Irishman, who told them that he had 'once been in Scotland', which qualified him, poor fellow, to be kidnapped, bundled into the boat and put in charge of navigation. There was nothing else for it, but to set off with what they had. 'By chance there was some dashboards and nails in the boat. We nailed a board quite round which saved our lives for the sea was very rough and we took in much water.'

They made it across to Islay, where, wrote Lundie, 'I met with ill-usage enough for they had got it there that I had betrayed Derry.' From Islay, he made it to the Clyde, where he was picked up by the *Pelican* frigate, which at that time made up one-half of the Scots navy. The captain of the *Pelican*, William Hamilton, had the whole party searched, confiscated their firearms and sent them ashore as prisoners. 'So my usage continued till I came to Dumbarton [where] Major Arnott, the governor thereof, my relation, dismissed the officer that was sent with me and said he would answer for me.'

News of Lundie's treachery raced across Scotland ahead of him. He was told to avoid Glasgow, as 'the women were resolved to tear me to pieces', and so went straight to the privy council in Edinburgh. Although 'everybody was incensed against me', the council was no doubt impressed that he had reported from Dumbarton. 'Upon his giving parole of honour to go straight to wait on His Majesty at Whitehall', he was issued with a pass and a warrant to ride to London by post horses. There he went straight to the privy council to report and to justify his actions. He was sent to the Tower.[12]

The return of Cunningham's relief expedition was seen in England as a disaster that needed an immediate remedy. On 30 April, the secretary of state wrote:

> The king last night signed an order for sending four regiments to London Derry ... though I fear 'twill be too late, and has ordered Major General Kirke to go with them and take care of that very important place if it still be in the Protestants' hands.[13]

14

Culmore and Pennyburn

KING JAMES STAYED THREE NIGHTS in St Johnstown. He ordered a day of rest as the army was exhausted after its march in the rain, and announced that he was returning to Dublin to speed reinforcements to Derry and to prepare an army in readiness for the expected English invasion.[1] He ordered Rosen and Léry-Girardin to go with him, and left lieutenant generals Maumont and Richard Hamilton to conduct the siege, with Maumont in charge. With them were the duke of Berwick and Pusignan, now appointed major generals, and brigadiers Sheldon, Ramsay and Lord Galmoy. The king ordered them to take Culmore Fort as a priority, and set off for Dublin on 20 April.

The next morning, Sunday 21 April, perhaps within an hour or so of Lundie's departure, generals Maumont and Pusignan arrived at Culmore to carry out the king's orders. The fort stood on a peninsula bordered on one side by the river and the other by what was then known as the Great Bog of Culmore. 'We did not find the affair so straightforward', wrote Pusignan. 'There were more than two hundred and fifty men inside, well-armed, and with sufficient gunpowder and ammunition to hold the walls which are not really impregnable against cannon, but which, being twenty foot high and flanked by four small bastions, could not be attacked.' The king had suggested a surprise attack, but it was a hopeless idea. Apart from having no cannon, they did not have any ladders to scale the walls, and no engineers to undermine them. Maumont decided to see if he could bluff his way in, or as he put it, 'dispense with the rules'. He sent a man to summon the castle to surrender.

The governor of the fort, William Adair, was with his brother, Benjamin Adair, who had just arrived back with supplies. They knew the relief force had been sent back, that Lundie had set off for Scotland and that the city was in turmoil. They also knew that the Irish were claiming that King James was with them, and that a large army was expected to attack the city, no doubt with an artillery train from Dublin. They did not know how much of this was bluff. All they knew for certain was that a regiment of Irish redcoats was waiting to make a move. William Adair did not know what to do. He insisted on sending someone to Derry for instructions. He chose for this mission the most senior officer in the fort, Lieutenant Colonel Richard Johnston, the would-be governor of Londonderry, who had fled the city and ended up in Culmore because he had failed to get on a ship. The Irish had no intention of letting Johnston take instructions from Derry. He was instead persuaded to go directly to King James, and under escort was galloped off to catch him at Strabane.

Rather than wait for Johnston's return, Maumont moved his men forward into positions under cover of the hedges and ditches around the fort. There was an exchange of musket fire that went on, said Pusignan, 'for a considerable length of time'. Other than to impress the garrison that the Irish were in earnest, it was quite pointless. It was also very dangerous for the unfortunate Irish troops who had been ordered to fire at the fort, because they had considerably less cover than the troops inside. Three of Maumont's officers and thirty of his men were wounded, having got nowhere, and could not withdraw without the risk of being shot. Maumont's plan turned into a rather embarrassing mistake. The men were stranded. Pusignan, saw a way out:

> We decided to pull back, but the problem was to do this honorably without losing any more men. I decided to send a drummer to ask if the governor (who had asked for just two hours to send to Londonderry) had received a reply, and what had he decided to do. This gave rise to discussions on both sides and to proposals for terms. However, in order to show our good intentions, we agreed to withdraw our troops.

Once the troops were safely out of musket range, there were further discussions. The Adairs were then told that Johnston had ridden off to see the king. They wanted to know, in the event of King James' presence being confirmed, what conditions they could expect. After all the shooting, they were not going to hand themselves over to be hanged over the walls. Nor were they happy about being set free to be robbed or murdered by the first gang of vengeful Irishmen to find them. There would have to be assurances before any surrender. There was no rush. They could see no ladders or tunnellers or cannon.

At the time that Johnston rode off to find the king, the Irish army was scattered in a twelve-mile line from St Johnstown to Culmore. Brook Hall, the only substantial house between Culmore and the city, was commandeered as Richard Hamilton's headquarters. Brigadier Ramsay, with much of the army, stayed on the higher ground to the west of the city, and some of the infantry camped in and around the hamlet of Pennyburn, then a few cottages and a mill, a mile from Derry on the Culmore road. Two battalions and some cavalry occupied Strong's Orchard on the other side of the river to build a battery from which to cannonade the city.[2] The cavalry and dragoons pitched camp in the Laggan at Carrigans and St Johnstown, where the horses were put out to grass. 'All our cavalry was out foraging, even though we had said that no more than a third could go', wrote Pusignan to Louvois a few days later, 'but it is the custom of these troops to do nothing they are ordered to do'.[3] It was Sunday, and the Irish army spent the day improving their new quarters.

All relief to Londonderry could be stopped by a good battery at Culmore Fort, which was now cut off from the city. Those men who looked to Murray as their 'general in the field' collectively saw this as something that needed to be dealt with. A great force needed to march down to Culmore and drive the Irish away. The feeling was such that Baker could not stop them going. If he tried to hold them back, he risked getting the same treatment as Lundie, but he clearly wanted nothing to do with it, nor did any of the other senior officers. None of them took part. They all stayed behind the walls. The expedition was to be made up of a crowd of fifteen hundred armed men, all of them volunteers, led by officers they had appointed themselves, under the overall command of Adam Murray, a man with no military experience. Murray collected together all the horsemen he could raise, three hundred men divided into three squadrons. 'Our new General Murray, had a very great desire to take a Breathing to blood his Soldiers', wrote Bennett. This Culmore expedition was a great opportunity to do to the Irish what Lundie through cowardice or negligence or treachery had failed to do at the Finn.

Before going to Culmore, Maumont had ordered Brigadier Ramsay to detach from the main camp a regiment to join the troops already there. Ramsay sent John ('Jack') Hamilton, Richard Hamilton's youngest brother, whose regiment had only about two hundred men in it. They marched off in full view of the city towards Pennyburn. This modest troop movement incited immediate action. The gates opened, and Murray led his army out.

The most coherent descriptions of what followed are given by the only eye witness accounts we have, and both are by those who were in the thick of it, Major General Pusignan and the duke of Berwick. Berwick was then only eighteen, and it was the first time he had been in action. Once Murray came out of the city with his small army, the alarm was raised and an urgent dispatch was sent for help. The Irish infantry, positioned in the hedges in front of Pennyburn, hastily formed up to receive the attack. When the message got through to Maumont in the Laggan, he mounted up and gathered together whoever he could. 'Unfortunately, our cavalry was out foraging, so we were only able to use a guard of forty troopers', wrote Berwick, 'with whom we went at full gallop towards Pennyburn'.[4]

Murray advanced with great caution, not, wrote Walker, 'in any commendable Order'. There was no dash. He rode along the strand with the cavalry, but would not advance without the cover of his foot soldiers. Led by their own volunteer captains, they edged slowly through the hedges and ditches and gardens that lay between the strand and the bog, lining one hedge, and then moving forward and lining the next to force the Irish skirmishers back. The Irish infantry, perhaps nowhere near a thousand strong, stood firm and waited. 'Finding them too many for him', wrote Bennett, Murray 'made a halt and ordered 500 firelocks more to march out'.[5]

Notwithstanding the determination of his men to force a battle, Murray's path to Culmore had been blocked. That should have been the end of the day's manoeuvring, but then, thundering along the road, came the cavalry. Maumont had with him an assortment of dragoons, cavalrymen and mounted officers who had been rapidly formed into two troops of about forty men each. This body of certainly no more than a hundred men included five generals. With Maumont were Richard Hamilton; brigadiers Pusignan and Sheldon; and both of King James' teenaged sons, the duke of Berwick and the 15-year-old Henry Fitzjames. Even in a time of emergency, it was utter folly to risk so much. Sheldon saw the danger and begged Maumont to hold back and not to expose himself but, as he had shown at Lifford, Maumont was a man determined to lead from the front.[6]

Unable to attack the rebel infantry, not only because he had too few men with him, but because the rebels were under cover of the hedges, ditches and orchards, Maumont set out instead to smash the rebel horse. That meant sweeping across the front of the fifteen hundred rebel infantrymen who were lining the hedges, and then going round them and down the strand to get at Murray. He raced his men into position, and, kneecap to kneecap, wheeled them to the right to face the enemy.

Maumont did not hesitate. He charged. No firing, just the words of command, 'Draw swords!' and 'Charge!'.[A] The commands were followed by the roar of the troopers and the thunder of hooves. The rebel infantry fired a great volley diagonally as the Irish horse surged forward. Some of them fell, but the charge was pressed home. Most of Murray's men did not wait for the impact. The rebel cavalry broke and raced away back to the city walls. The Irish were straight after them, 'pistoling and slashing'. It was over in seconds. The rebel infantry, seeing this rout, and the threat of being cut off, pulled back and scrambled back through the hedges, ditches and orchards and made for the city as quickly as they could.[7]

As the Irish horsemen approached the city, the defenders on the walls opened fire from the safety of the ramparts. The Irish cavalry pulled up and retraced their steps along the strand. The rebel infantry were now on their left in the orchards, and as the Irish galloped back, they were fired on by everyone who had a musket. 'Of our number', wrote Berwick, 'not one, either himself or his horse, escaped injury'. And some of them were killed. The Irish infantry had not been engaged in the fighting, but on seeing the rebel horse scattered and the rebel infantry in front of them pull back, they advanced to encourage the general movement. There was no opposition left. As the day came to an end, the orchards were as free of rebels as they had been at the beginning.

At the first volley from the rebel infantry, before the Irish horse reached Murray's cavalry, Maumont was shot dead.[8] His body was recovered by the Irish. The mood in the Irish camp was one of shock. Maumont was a great loss. Also killed in the skirmish, probably on the strand on the way back, was Maumont's aide-de-camp Major John Taaffe,[B] and seven troopers.[9] There was no sense of a

[A] 'When a squadron of horse is to charge another, it is better they do it with their swords drawn in their hands than either with pistols or carbines'. R.H., *English military discipline or the way of exercising horse and foot* (1681).

[B] Major John Taaffe was then approaching fifty. His eldest brother, Lord Carlingford, was killed at the Boyne in the following year. The next brother in line to the title was Francis Taaffe, who was allowed to succeed to the title because he was a field marshal in the service of the Holy Roman emperor, King William's principal ally against the French. On Francis' death, the title and the Irish estates passed to Major John Taaffe's son.

defeat. 'We beat them', wrote Pusignan, 'but [referring to Maumont] at a cost'.[10] The Irish horsemen had been outnumbered by three to one and had won. The rebel infantry had outnumbered the Irish infantry, and had run away. The news that reached France was of a victory over 'four thousand Protestant rebels' and spoke of hopes that 'this defeat will force the inhabitants of Londonderry to surrender'.[11] As Pusignan noted four days later, 'the enemy does not seem to want to make another sortie'. His frustration was that the victory could not be followed through because there were so few troops at hand. They had been obliged by King James' order to stretch themselves all the way down to Culmore, and the cavalry had not been ready to give urgent support when it was needed.[12]

The incident generated one of Walker's flights of fancy: 'Some of his Horse were beaten to the very Gates; so that Mr. Walker found it necessary to mount one of the Horses and make them rally, and to Relieve Col. Murry, whom he saw surrounded with the Enemy, and with great Courage laying about him.' Mackenzie answered with sarcasm: Walker's story was 'spoiled by the unhappy disputes that have arisen about the matter of fact. For some have started such cross questions about the armour of the rider as well as the colour of the horse, as I fear will go near to dismount the doctor in the next edition of that account, and leave Colonel Murray to get off as well as he can without him.'[13]

Just as there was no sense of defeat in the Irish camp (the loss of Maumont aside), there was no feeling of triumph in the city. No one knew that Maumont had died. There was nothing victorious in the flight of Murray's horsemen. Thomas Ash, one of the volunteer captains manning the city walls, wrote of a defeat. There had been 'a hot skirmish' in which 'several were killed and wounded on both sides'. 'Our men were compelled to retreat', and 'for this the cavalry were blamed'. He added rather gloomily: 'Many who were wounded died soon after, but none of note on our side fell'. Another of the new volunteer captains, George Holmes, wrote that of 'nine or ten of our men' were killed. It was, he said, 'the greatest loss that ever we lost in the field'. The city saw the action at Pennyburn as a dispiriting failure.[14]

But history has not seen it that way. Despite Bennett, Walker and Mackenzie recording that the rebel horse ran away, all the commentators to date have held this cavalry action to have been a victorious action by Murray. Bennett says that Murray's horsemen fled 'at the first fire' (that is, as soon as their own infantry fired, as no one appears to have fired on them until after the cavalry clash, when, said Berwick, 'we only worried them from afar with some musket shots'). When his men fled, Murray was left behind 'with Captain Bull and some others engaged' in fighting. Both Bennett and Mackenzie say that Murray did not retreat until the rest had left him. Bennett made a poor attempt of suggesting (but not asserting) that the whole thing was planned, as if Murray had told his men to desert him and leave him to fight his way back through the pursuing Irish cavalry. Walker also reported that the rebel horse was beaten back. All of them describe a defeat.

Murray's army had set out to sweep the Irish out of Pennyburn, but had turned back without even reaching the village. Then, by the lazy addition of improbable casualty figures, the printed accounts turned it into a victory. Bennett, Walker and Mackenzie, writing for those in England eager to read an invigorating account of the war in Ireland, had a simple message to impart: even though our men ran away, we killed masses of the Irish. However long one reflects on this, it is a message that cannot be supported by sensible analysis.

The Irish losses were slight. Berwick, who was in the charge, estimated 'our loss was not considerable', being six or seven troopers killed as well as Maumont and Taaffe. To Pusignan, the Irish losses were so trifling that in his otherwise full dispatch, he does not even mention them. The only loss of any military importance was Maumont. Mackenzie wrote: 'We could have no certain account of how many of the enemy were killed, they were said to be above 200'. By the phrase 'said to be', he was referring to Walker's claim that the garrison 'killed above 200 of the enemies'. Bennett estimated the Irish losses as being '60 private men, as well as Maumont, Major Taaffe, Captains Fitzgerald and Burke, and nine other officers'.

There is no suggestion by any of the rebel sources that the Irish infantry were involved. All the Irish casualties were horsemen. If Bennett was right, there could only have been a handful of them left. If they had been wiped out, neither Murray, his horsemen nor his infantry would have had to leave the field. If Mackenzie and Walker were right, the Irish horsemen were all killed twice over. Four years later, in drafting a map of the city, Samuel Hobson recorded the Irish losses as being '70 officers and 500 Horsemen'. A decade after the event, Joseph Aickin, the siege poet, published *Londerias*, a colourful, triumphant account of the siege in verse. He wrote: 'Two thousand slain the mighty shore had fill'd, with seventy-three commissioned officers kill'd'. That is the entire Irish army.[15]

Years later, Michelburne, taking his lead from the printed accounts and writing for the same audience, portrayed himself hugging and kissing Baker: 'A blessed Sunday's work! Behold their white carcasses by scores lying on the shores as also in the fields. Brave Boys!' He made much of the booty, as had Bennett and Mackenzie. The men came back into the city shouting out 'Here's plunder!' and carrying 'a pair of boots', 'a fine saddle', 'laced caps for a saddle' and 'a fine laced coat'. He described 'one of the rabble' trying without success to get a captured horse through the wicket gate: 'Hee's no gang in at ye Door, he's ore muckle.'[16]

To those there at the time such celebrations were limited. Stripping the corpses of Major Taaffe and a few troopers who had died near the walls, and parading around in their coats was one thing, but the greater task was not going to be easy. The balloon that they had blown up for themselves in expectation of what they would have done to the Irish at Clady had only Lundie not been a traitor or a coward or had at least turned up on time, was now rather deflated. With a great numerical advantage, they had faced the Irish redcoats head on, by themselves, and had failed.

King James was 'heartily sorry' to hear of Maumont's death. 'He had entirely gained our royal favour and esteem.' He instructed Richard Hamilton to 'let nothing be wanting to show the favour we had for him or befits his quality, especially you are to have his body embalmed and either sent with a fitting guard immediately to Dublin, or kept with you till affairs there be over that more of the general officers may come along with it.' Everyone was likely to suffer from Maumont's recklessness. 'We must put you in mind that it is not for you, that are our general officers, to expose yourselves on all occasions, a thing quite contrary to the welfare of our service. You are judges [of] when it is necessary, but you are expressly ordered not to do it in other occasions.'[17]

While the fighting was going on at Culmore, and then at Pennyburn, Richard Johnston was on the road to Strabane and back. His escort had managed to get him there in time to catch up with the king. King James' own account of the meeting noted:

> Having been assured by those who commanded in Derry that the King was not in Ireland, but being admitted into his majesty's presence and satisfied it was the King he promised to use his endeavors to persuade them to surrender.[18]

Johnston was taken straight back to Culmore, and told the Adairs that he had been in the king's presence. Terms were then agreed. By the king's most gracious free pardon 'of all offences whatsoever since their taking up of arms', they were all to enjoy their lives, religion and estates, goods and chattels, be allowed to go to their various homes with guards, to have passes to go overseas 'without imposition of oaths', the soldiers could all take their swords, and the officers each a horse, a pistol and a gun 'as becometh his majesty's loyal subjects', and take all their goods and chattels with them, and everyone on application was to have a written pardon 'without expense or charge'. The Irish added a clause to record that everyone in Derry would be allowed the same terms if they surrendered within three days.

Hamilton signed the surrender document on 23 April and had the document delivered to Adair, who then needed time to consider, perhaps in the hope that things would change. But nothing did. The fort was still isolated. There was no shipping on the lough, and Derry was surrounded by the Irish army. Another two days passed before the signatures of William Adair of Ballymena, Richard Johnston and Benjamin Adair were added. On 25 April, they opened the gates, handed over the keys and marched out.

The capture of Culmore significantly changed the Irish army's position. Without cannon or loss, they had taken a sturdy fort capable of preventing all river traffic reaching Londonderry. According to Walker, the city only learnt of the surrender a couple of weeks or more after the event, leaving them to speculate 'what conditions, and for how much money' the Irish had bought off William Adair. Ash is also vague about the date that the surrender became known, but recorded much later in his diary that

> Culmore was betrayed to Gen. Hamilton by two of the Adairs and Long Galbraith the attorney who, it is said, sold it to the enemy for a considerable sum of money. I have heard since, that one of the Adairs has lost his senses. I know not how true this may be, but certainly God Almighty will not let such treachery go unpunished.[c] [19]

Strangely, the surrender of Culmore may have been known in London before it was known in Londonderry. William Adair, under the terms of the conditions, left the country. An account of what had happened appeared in a London news-sheet in May,[20] attributing the surrender to 'the persuasion of a small spill of French gold'. To show how King James' promises meant nothing, an account was added of the reception of the Culmore men in Coleraine, where they were 'not only disarmed, but stripped to their shirts, their money all taken from them and themselves sent a begging'.

This was good copy for the London readers. The tale of the stripping and robbing of the Culmore officers was investigated by the Church of Ireland clergyman Charles Leslie later in the war. He made a point of seeking out those who had been there: 'I have spoken with some gentlemen who were in that fort on its surrender who say that it is absolutely false, for that they were used with humanity by K.J. and that he preserved the articles to that degree as to give the chief of them his pass to go for England when it was desired, pursuant to the articles.' To say that King James and his officers never kept their terms was 'wicked, as well as ignorant'.[21]

While the Irish command concentrated on Culmore, the engineer, Pointis, arrived 'on the other side of the river with a party of gunners and bombardiers whom he has brought from France'.[22] Two demi-culverins, weighty cannons usually with an eleven foot (3.4m) barrel, were positioned in Strong's Orchard on the east bank. Their range was somewhere in the region of a third of a mile, easily enough to reach the city. At least a cannonade of sorts could begin, and its effect was to terrify rather than achieve much else. Mackenzie estimated the cannon fired balls of ten pounds weight. 'They played so incessantly', he wrote, 'piercing the Garrets and Walls, that some were hurt, and few durst stay above stairs'.[23] The two mortars were too small to do any great damage, and fired bombs that were 'little bigger than hand granadoes'.[24] The gunners aimed at the market house, which they managed to hit a few times, and some houses were demolished on Pump Street. A screen was

[c] William Adair was not a traitor. He went to Coleraine, and on to Scotland where he fitted out a ship and got a warrant to take provisions to Derry. Richard Johnston took protection, went to Dublin and six months later made it to Dundalk, where he was arrested, but he was at liberty in London the following year. The Irish saw the lawyer Robert Galbraith as the brains behind the surrender.

set up on the wall to try to stop some of the balls getting through, and the gunners on the walls fired back. Walker describes at this time the fire from the bastions killing several Irish soldiers and 'two Friars in their Habits, to the great Grief of the Enemy, that the Blood of those Holy Men should be spilt by such an Heretical Rabble, as they call the besieged'. Mackenzie adopted the story by referring to the deaths of 'two lusty friars', but added the words 'as was reported'. It was a coded way of indicating that this was the gossip on the walls, but that he was sceptical.[25]

'The cannons played without ceasing on both sides', wrote Ash. 'They fired forty shots at least that day.' Bennett made special reference to the cannons that Lundie had brought into the city from Culmore. Two guns were mounted on 'the top of the Steeple of the Church',[D] which gave them greater range and 'exceedingly gall'd the Enemy in the Battery on the other side of the Water, insomuch that their Battery was several times broken, and at length, when they discovered a Gun to be fired from the Steeple, the Soldiers would either run out of the Works in great disorder, or fall flat on their Bellies to avoid the Shot'.[26]

Murray and his supporters were persuaded that the failure of his expedition to relieve Culmore was due to lack of numbers. He was now allowed to lead a second sortie with twice as many men. It was thought better to bypass Pennyburn, where the Irish had dug themselves in, and get to Culmore by a more inland route. The infantry would advance under cover of the orchards, and the cavalry would shadow them as best they could.

At nine in the morning, on 25 April, the same day that Culmore Fort was handed over to the duke of Berwick, Murray marched out of the city with an army of three thousand or more men.[27] As in the first expedition, none of the regular soldiers took part.[28] Progress was again slow, and it took all day to push back the Irish skirmishers from the hedges and ditches. Murray made for the old mill, a mile further inland from Pennyburn mill, and there the ditches and hedges came to an end.[E] As the forward troops advanced into the open country, 'a Party of the Enemies Horse coming suddenly about the end of the little Hill forc'd 'em to retire back to the rest of our Party, who observing the Enemies Horse to advance so quick towards them, took themselves to the Ditch by the way side, and fired so briskly and continually on them, that they were forc'd to flee'.[29] Having no answer to the Irish cavalry in open country, the rebel advance halted. With no other option, the direction of attack changed back towards Pennyburn itself, where the horse could not get to them. Although outnumbered, the Irish had been joined by the troops freed up from Culmore and were

[D] By 'steeple' Bennett referred in the old-fashioned sense (as I will below) to the cathedral tower, which at that time was flat roofed, although a spire and an extra storey were added in the eighteenth century.

[E] The old mill was a mile further up 'the Pennyburn Depression', then a strip of low boggy ground that marked the boundary of the Inishowen Peninsula. Another mile inland were (and are) the ruins of Elagh Castle. Aickin described the fighting without referring to Pennyburn at all. It was 'the battle near Elagh'.

more numerous than in the attack a few days before. They were also joined by the dragoons, who 'left their Horses, and came down to assist their Foot and some Horse who were in hazard at Penny-burn-mill'. The rebels made a determined attempt and, as the day wore on, the Irish position began to look precarious.

Although the cavalry could not get into the orchards, there were some mounted Irish troops in Pennyburn itself. They came under fire, and Pusignan made the same sort of mistake that Maumont had made. He allowed himself to get too close to the enemy musketry. He, the duke of Berwick and the chief engineer, the baron de Pointis, were all wounded, and Lord Abercorn's horse was killed under him, forcing him to run for it, 'leaving his scarlet cloak, saddle &c. for a prey to the besieged'. Berwick was quite candid about the rebel success: 'We were chased away from all the hedges, and driven back to the last houses in the village. We ran the risk of being completely beaten.'[30]

The result again turned on the Irish cavalry. As the afternoon turned to dusk, Irish reinforcements arrived. Ramsay had at last managed to get two of the horse regiments to join him from the cavalry camp. Behind the walls, it was clear to Baker that the Irish forces at Pennyburn were not their entire army. In order to prevent any Irish attempt to get between Murray and the city, he sent out Colonel Parker's regiment to cover their rear. Parker took up a defensive position on a small rise between the orchards and the main Irish camp. Approaching from the west, and supported by infantry to clear the orchards, Ramsay made an attempt to cut off Murray's retreat. All that stood between Ramsay and the orchards were Parker's five hundred men. Murray's men at Pennyburn were alerted to Ramsay's attack by the sound of heavy gunfire behind them. Berwick was quite clear that the Irish were facing defeat up to that point, but once Ramsay 'began attacking the Rebels from behind', Murray and his men retreated 'in a hurry'.[31]

Parker was heavily criticized for his part in this rearguard action.[32] Mackenzie, who witnessed the action from the walls, wrote: 'A party of men that went out late to be a rear guard to our men at the mill, were beat in by a party of horse that were despatched (with each a foot-man behind him) from the enemy's camp, but without loss … Parker was too slow and negligent in bringing off [the rearguard], according to his orders, whereby they were exposed to great dangers from the enemy.' Bennett gave greater detail:

> The 500 firelocks posted on top of the hill with the foot which lined the ditches, made their retreat towards the town (having an account of Lord Galmoy and Sir Maurice Eustace's two regiments of horse marching with all speed to get between them and home) and narrowly escaped, with the loss of 7 men and a lieutenant, and then the guns from the town forced the enemy's horse to retreat.[33]

The action had again resulted in an untidy rout. Parker had ordered his men to stand firm until it was time to make an orderly withdrawal, but his men scattered in the face of the Irish advance. Some of them were overtaken by the Irish horse and killed, 'being pressed by the enemy's horse, who charged us on all sides', Walker said. As a professional soldier, and the only army officer to engage in any action outside the city's defences during the entire siege, Vernon Parker followed his own judgment. He had been ordered to protect Murray's retreat and so he engaged the Irish. He now faced a court martial for exposing his men 'to great danger'. Rather than face such a humiliation, or disgusted at the behaviour of his men or the way the defence was being handled, or furious at the way he had been criticized, Parker deserted that same night.

The flight back to the city (and Parker's desertion) did not give the impression of a victory, and for the second time, they had failed to clear the Irish out of Pennyburn. However, as Murray's horsemen had been kept safe from the Irish cavalry, there had not been the humiliation of the first action. They had spent the whole day in battle, they had pushed the enemy back, and had suffered only light losses. It was an improvement on their first attempt. Ash wrote in his diary: 'Another skirmish. Our men beat the enemy, but with some loss'.

The complaint against Parker illustrates the fears the garrison then held. The swaggering bravado was reserved for the London newsletters, and the accounts written after the siege. The defenders had a great fear of being caught in the open by the Irish redcoats and especially by the Irish cavalry. After that first action at Pennyburn, Murray's cavalry never faced the Irish horse again, and the infantry in both sorties confined themselves to moving only where the cavalry could not reach them. Parker's regiment was the only body that ventured outside that safe area, and he was condemned for courting danger by not running back at the first sound of hooves.

Parker made it to London within the month and in June 1689 was given a fresh commission in Colonel Gustavus Hamilton's regiment of foot as captain of grenadiers. He joined Captain Kilner Brasier (promoted to major) and Lieutenant Miles Wildman, who had both fled from Londonderry in Lundie's boat. Gustavus Hamilton, the one-time governor of Coleraine and the future Lord Boyne, who had himself got out of Ireland once things looked hopeless, collected most of his officers in London from those who had deserted their Irish regiments. No one was in disgrace. The regiment served at the battle of the Boyne in the following year, and Major Parker took part in the Cadiz expedition of 1702. Brasier married Gustavus Hamilton's sister-in-law, was promoted to colonel and was successively the MP for Dundalk, St Johnstown and Kilmallock, and in 1719 was the high sheriff of Tipperary.

It is now impossible to assess the losses on either side. All the defenders' estimates are vague or wholly unbelievable, often having been written to deceive. Ash wrote of 'some loss' to the garrison. Walker put the garrison's losses as two dead, a figure adopted by Mackenzie. Bennett put the figure at eight dead, but that figure only referred to Parker's men. 'What number of the Enemy was kill'd', wrote Mackenzie, 'we could not learn'. Bennett wrote that apart from Pusignan, 'some others were killed and wounded, but their names I cannot particularly remember'. Berwick's memory was that 'we did not lose many men in this action'. Tyrconnell's own cavalry regiment was commanded by Colonel Dominic Sheldon. In a letter dated 3 May he wrote, praising the behaviour of his officers and men, that his losses in both the Pennyburn actions were '17 men and 36 horses besides abundance of each that are wounded and in so bad a condition that several of them will never recover'.[34] Only Aickin dissented from the general view. Of the Irish, he gushed, 'multitudes were slain', these being in addition to the two thousand Irish troops and seventy-three officers killed in the first action at Pennyburn.

Although the Irish had held on for the second time in a week, they had been stretched to the limit. Just as the first fight at Pennyburn had cost them their general, in the second fight they lost his successor. Pusignan had been shot in the belly and there no surgeon in the whole Irish army. He died two days later. The defenders of Londonderry had killed two French generals in a week.[F] [35] 'What a misfortune it is to see such great commanders die by the hands of the mechanic rascals', wrote Plunkett. 'I doubt', sighed the French engineer, Jean-François de Massé, 'that we can take this place'.[36]

[F] A plaque in the Galerie des Batailles at Versailles commemorates Pusignan as one of those illustrious generals killed in combat for France. ('*Jean* LE *CAMUS* , *marquis* de *PUSIGNAN* , tué au siége de Londonderry (Irlande) le jer mai 1689.') Curiously perhaps, there is no plaque for Maumont.

15

Settling in

FAR OUT ON THE LOUGH, the *Bonadventure* frigate dropped anchor as if to remind the city that it was not forgotten, but there was no way of making contact. London needed to be told that the city was determined to hold out, and would do so if England sent relief. The man chosen to take that message was Joseph Bennett who agreed to try to bluff his way past the Irish. 'We sent Mr. Bennet out of the Garrison, with Orders to go to England, and to give account of our Resolutions to defend the Town against the Enemy. Our men were ordered to fire after him, that the Enemy might think he had deserted us.' After spending some time in the Irish camp, Bennett made it to Edinburgh in early May where the privy council sent him to London to report to the king. He published, just before the end of the siege, an account of the siege as he had left it.[1]

There was great despondency in the Irish camp after the death of Pusignan. The army had marched to Derry not only without siege cannon, engineers or entrenching tools, but also without a single surgeon. Berwick's wound was not serious. A shot in the back of his armour had left him badly bruised over the spine and put him out of action for a few days. Pointis, the engineer, was shot in the thigh and had a nasty wound that proved almost fatal, and left him incapacitated for much of the siege. The sheer enormity of the task before them was daunting. 'There are 6,000 men in the place', wrote Pusignan on the morning he was shot, 'and we have barely 2,000 foot, and they, like the enemy, are newly levied'.[2]

No analysis of the siege can be based on the bare numbers of each side. In the first month of the siege, there is no doubt that the forces inside the city were more numerous than those outside, although that was to change. The defenders were behind the city's sturdy walls, and not only had an advantage in the number of firearms, but an overwhelming advantage in artillery. According to Walker, there were twenty-two cannons in the city: two on the cathedral and twenty on the walls and bastions which he detailed as describes as '8 *Sakers* and 12 *Demi-culverins*' (firing five-pound and eight-pound balls, respectively), yet Captain MacCullough's map shows twenty-six cannons, and Bennett gives figures, perhaps including the smaller guns ('drakes'), that amount to over forty.[3] The Irish were camping in the rain and were at all times divided between the two sides of the river, and in camps down to the Laggan and Strabane. Both Walker and Mackenzie estimated there were over seven thousand men defending the city, although Bennett made it more.[4] Whatever the numbers, those men inside the city were overwhelmingly armed civilians whereas those outside were soldiers. The rebels, however brave and determined, were confined by an aggressive army. The leadership within the walls aimed to frustrate the Irish in their attempts on the city. They saw their only hope as being relief from outside, not that they could beat the Irish off. After the failures to break through to Culmore, there is nothing to suggest that anyone thought otherwise, either then, or at any time during the entirety of the coming siege.

No one in King James' army had any real hopes that the few cannon they had would bring down the walls. The six cannons they could deploy were of too small a bore, and they did not have enough experienced gunners to fire them. As Pusignan wrote to Louvois: 'We will do our best', but with what they had, it was not going to be easy. 'The walls appear very solid and bastioned', he wrote, but 'this affair should be quickly resolved with a plentiful amount of artillery'.

The first two mortars, the smaller of the three that would be used, were in position. They fired their first three bombs on 24 April, to little effect, and three more bombs the next day. It was a new danger. The city's stock of gunpowder was taken out of the magazine and hidden away around the town in 'several places, as the Church, dry wells, cellars, &c'. On the 27 April, the mortars fired almost the entire supply of mortar bombs. The terror of these sudden explosions was great, but the effect was limited. As Ash wrote:

> The bombs played hotly all night. Eighteen were shot into the city. One fell on Mr Long's house and killed a gentlewoman of eighty years old, a Mrs. Susannah Holding, and hurt many others.

There was silence for a week, and six more bombs were fired, ineffectually, on 2 May. After that, there was no more ammunition, and the mortars fell silent for a month.

The following day, Captain Thomas Hopson made an attempt to get to the city with the *Bonadventure* and the supply ships carrying arms and ammunition. We know few details, other than that he came under fire at Culmore, and that William Bagshaw, a 'seaman on board the ship *Bonaventure*' was badly injured by a shot in the arm.[5] The Irish had built a 'half-moon', a curved earthwork, on the riverbank opposite the fort, next to Lord Massereene's fish house, so that they could fire from cover from both sides of the river mouth. Hopson judged it too dangerous to send any ships up river. He and his convoy dropped down the lough and waited for the wind to change to get them back to sea.

The senior military leadership in the city was now in the hands of the four old soldiers: Henry Baker, Thomas Whitney, Richard Crofton and John Michelburne. The first three had similar service backgrounds on the Irish establishment, but only Michelburne had seen active service overseas. They would all have agreed upon one thing: the men needed training and plenty of it. A soldier was not simply a man able to fire a musket, he needed to act in concert with others on the word of command. Training took place, but it was always in view of the enemy. Ash recorded two incidents on 1 May. In the first a body of men was marching up

Shipquay Street when a cannon ball from across the water injured two of them. Later a cannon was fired at men being drilled by Michelburne alongside the bog. The ball 'killed one man who stood up, whereas the rest fell down to save themselves. Presumption is neither religion nor courage.'[6]

At the end of April, three prisoners were released. Darcy, Blacker and Twynyhoe had been arrested in Lundie's time. Hamilton asked for their release. The Irish were not locking people up who favoured King William, and a man should not be held for favouring King James unless there were proper grounds. There were no proper grounds. 'There was a council held upon them', said Mackenzie, writing of Twynyhoe and Blacker, 'but after some time they were both dismissed', a decision that 'enraged' the garrison.[7]

The third man, Captain Nicholas Darcy, arrived in the city with James Hamilton's supplies. He was not a prisoner of war, but was arrested by Lundie pending an investigation that never happened. The new governors saw no point in keeping him in the city and gave him a pass to leave with his arms and a horse (or perhaps horses), which he had managed to buy in the city. That was the last they heard of him.[A][8]

The Darcy incident had serious consequences for Colonel Whitney, who was court martialled and locked up. It is difficult to understand exactly what happened. According to Thomas Ash, the complaint was one of 'selling flour to one Capt. Darcy, who was adjudged an enemy for holding correspondence with the enemy'. Mackenzie records that 'Whitney had sold Darcy some horses, which were said to be none of his own, upon which and other misdemeanours, Whitney was confined, and after tried by a council of war and found to be no friend to this garrison, for which he was under confinement during the time of the siege'. But Ash, who may well have sat on that court martial, goes on to say with precision that on 2 May Whitney was tried by a court martial under the 'tenth article of war, and found guilty'. The tenth article has nothing to do with theft. It reads: 'If any officer or soldier shall behave himself disrespectfully towards the general, lieutenant general or other chief commander of the army or speak words tending to his hurt or dishonour, he shall be punished.'[9]

If the flour allegation is true, it could only have amounted to Darcy being made to pay for whatever rations he was allowed. If it was a horse, everyone would know that Darcy had not arrived with one, but that he had the governors' pass to ride out 'with horse and arms'. No finding was made on these allegations. The court martial removed Whitney from his command for breaching the tenth article. It amounts to this: having heard of Baker's annoyance at whatever had happened, Whitney responded in terms tending to Baker's 'hurt or dishonour', thereby offending against that article.[B] The consequence was that Whitney was locked up

[A] Darcy's commission was waiting for him. He commanded the Irish defence of Killashandra Castle, Co. Cavan, in April 1690.

[B] Had it been a face-to-face argument with Baker, a charge would have been laid under Article 15.

for the rest of the siege and his regiment was given to a volunteer officer, Henry Monroe. Another volunteer, Thomas Lance, took over Parker's regiment.[10]

To put the adjudication (and Whitney's supposed disgrace) in context: Whitney was back in the army before the end of the war, and by 1694 was the major of Lord Charlemont's regiment, which was then commanded by Adam Murray. Under him were captains Richard Crofton (also one of the siege colonels) and William Campbell (one of the lieutenant colonels during the siege). The peace of 1697 ended the military careers of the others, but Whitney served on in Queen Anne's wars.[11]

On the next day, 3 May, the *Bonadventure* weighed anchor and sailed beyond the point. The lough was empty. After dark, a party of Irish soldiers opened fire on the sentinels on the wall. No harm was done on either side.

The conformists and the Presbyterians in the city were bound together by a great fear of what the Irish would do, but their relationship was not always easy. The leadership was necessarily in the hands of the experienced officers and every officer who had been in the army was a conformist, but the majority of the men were Scots Presbyterians from Ulster. Among them were those who would have been considered to be zealous Covenanters, who had over the years felt great hostility to the crown and to conformists generally. The siege took place less than a decade after the battle of Bothwell Brig, which ended the great Covenanter rebellion in western Scotland, and only four years after Argyll's rebellion. Many Covenanters fled to Ulster during the subsequent savage repression. When the Scottish Highlands rose up to fight for King James in 1689, thousands of Presbyterians from the west flocked to join King William's army. General Hugh Mackay, the commander of King William's forces in Scotland, would have nothing to do with them. He would, he wrote, accept help from anywhere rather 'than see the enemies of the gospel fortify themselves in this kingdom'. Yet many of them had fortified themselves in Londonderry.[12]

There was no Presbyterian meeting house in the city before the siege, and Mackenzie, reluctant to give any credit to Walker, wrote that Baker agreed that the cathedral would be shared. Each Sunday, the conformists would have their cathedral for half the day until noon, and the Presbyterians would have it for the rest of the day. They were also given exclusive use of the cathedral every Thursday and allowed to hear two sermons every afternoon, on top of their 'two or three other Meetings in other parts of the City'.[13] This was not Baker's department, and the only conformist clergyman with civil authority was Walker. Sharing the cathedral was Walker's concession. This was his diocese and his cathedral, and they were outsiders. Walker's was the third largest regiment in the city. He was said not to be 'unkind to the Dissenters',[14] and the Presbyterian captains had chosen to join, or at least remain in, his regiment rather than any other. He enjoined 'all parties to forget their distinctions, and to join as one man, in defence of the interest of K. William and Q. Mary, and the Protestant Religion, against the Enemies of both'.

He even appointed Mackenzie his regimental chaplain, 'the generality of his officers as well as soldiers being nonconformists', but even that generated a grievance. Mackenzie pointed out that the Presbyterian chaplains 'received no allowance out of the stores'. And in his *Account*, Walker caused something of a storm.

> There were Eighteen Clergy-men in the Town of the Communion of the Church, who in their turns, when they were not in Action, had Prayers and Sermon every day; the Seven Nonconforming Ministers were equally careful of their people, and kept them very obedient and quiet.

The uproar was loudest in the nineteenth century. 'This passage gave great offence in many quarters, as it was considered altogether disingenuous, … it spoke of them [the Presbyterians] as if they had been an inferior class, who were entitled to no higher praise than that of remaining 'obedient and quiet', wrote the Reverend Killen. The Reverend Witherow agreed: 'Perhaps no other passage could be produced from the whole range of English literature in which an equal amount of deliberate and stinging malice is conveyed under the garb of innocence and praise.'[15]

Walker also listed in his *Account* the names and parishes of the conformist ministers who had been in the city during the siege. He then noted that there had been seven nonconformist ministers 'whose names I cannot learn, four of which died in the Siege'. This also caused anger. His claim not to know their names was certainly untrue in at least some cases. Anticipating the storm, he published his *Vindication* to pre-empt the criticisms and apologized profusely. He was deeply hurt by any suggestion that he had been motivated by spite in leaving the Presbyterian ministers unnamed. He had tried to discover their names, but the nonconformists had been obstructive. They were 'still more ready to reproach him, than able to inform him better … He little expected to meet such usage and reflections anywhere, except it had been in the Irish camp'. The London readers felt his pain.[16]

He then printed a list of 'the seven Nonconformist Ministers, which Mr. Walker at the writing of his Book could not learn'. He gave seven names, two of which were misspelt, and one was wrong. One of those ministers had been William Gilchrist of Kilrea, who died during the siege. Walker spelt his name 'KilChrist' (with the capital C). His own regimental chaplain, John Mackenzie, who no doubt Walker knew was behind much of this hostility, he spelt 'Mr. Jo. Machiny'. Walker could not help himself, he was having a wonderful time. They were all men of no significance.[c] [17]

[c] 'Such a puerile attempt to annoy the Presbyterian ministers by tampering with their names was unworthy', wrote Dr Killen, still outraged in 1861. Not so, said the Rev. W.S. Kerr, attributing instead to Killen an 'unenviable pre-eminence for bitterness and rashness'. Mackenzie printed the correct list, which had eight names.

16

Attack on the Windmill

THE WALLS OF DERRY surrounded the city on the northern third of the island formed by Derry Hill between the bog and the river. The remaining southern two-thirds of the island were unfortified and extended over an area then known as Windmill Hill or 'the Windmill'. The ribbon of small houses either side of the road that led from Bishop's Gate along Windmill Hill and down to the old gallows and the road to Lifford had been burnt by Lundie, leaving only the surprisingly sturdy stone windmill in the centre of the hill.[A]

Those advising Richard Hamilton saw the importance of Windmill Hill. They had occupied it briefly when King James was there, but it was very close to the enemy, and they then had no means of securing it while they were yet to take Culmore. If the Windmill could be taken and properly entrenched, it would be the best possible position for the cannon being sent up from Dublin. The artillery would have a direct view of the city and could batter down the Bishop's Gate. Anticipating this, Lundie had screened the gate with a ravelin, but nothing had been done since his departure other than to post sixty musketeers at the windmill.[1] In the days after the second Pennyburn action, Hamilton approved a plan to rush the defences at night and, in the darkness, dig in deep and fast.

The officer chosen to command the assault was Brigadier Robert Ramsay, who had saved the day in the second attack on Pennyburn. A Scots Catholic, Ramsay had known Hamilton since the early 1670s, when they served together in France as captains in Monmouth's regiment. In the reign of King James, Colonel Ramsay became adjutant general to the army and took part in the suppression of the Monmouth rising in 1685. He fled to France at the revolution, and by the time a warrant for his arrest was issued in Whitehall in March 1689, he was a brigadier in Ireland. He was, wrote d'Avaux, 'a man of great valour'.

The night of 5 May was miserably wet.[2] At midnight, Ramsay launched his surprise attack with two battalions of foot soldiers. Seeing them coming, the defenders on the Windmill fled straight back to the city walls. Some of Ramsay's men ran forward to attack the ravelin, and three small brass field guns were wheeled into place

[A] It was sturdy because it is the stump of a medieval round tower. Early seventeenth-century maps of the city show the round tower standing outside the city walls. C.D. Milligan in his *Walls of Derry* (1948) made reference to it as being 'obviously what is known as the windmill tower, still in existence'. In 2013, carbon testing of some of the original mortar established that it was perhaps built as early as the 1200s.

to provide some cover against the cannon in the city.[B] [3] Either side of the Windmill, under direction of their officers on horseback, the rest of the troops were frantically digging a ditch from the bog on one side to the river on the other. The cannon on the walls and the steeple opened up, and the digging was done under continual bombardment. Ramsay gave every appearance of having managed matters quickly and efficiently. By daybreak on 6 May, in anticipation of the counter-attack from their front, his men had dug a trench across the island and thrown up a parapet of mud that was from the bottom of the ditch to the top some eight feet high.

Once the Windmill was overrun, everyone in the city was awake in anticipation of an immediate attack. The men were formed up in their regiments. Brandy was distributed. Baker and the senior officers initially planned to counter-attack with a body made up of the best-armed men by detaching ten men out of every company. But the situation required more than that. As the night gave way to a grey, drizzling dawn, 'the men were impatient, and ran out of their own accord, some at Bishop's Gate, others at Ferry-Quay gate'. Thousands flooded out after them. 'The whole town came out.'[4] They swarmed forward and beat back the skirmishers.

Michelburne's recollection was of the enemy's colours flying to the right of the windmill, and the Irish still hard at work with their picks and shovels in the gloom. Ramsay's two battalions threw their entrenching tools aside and faced the whole rebel army. 'Sir Maurice Eustace's Fusiliers stood stiffly to their business', noted Michelburne of the enemy. The rebels were stopped short of the hastily built ditch and breastwork by steady fire from the Irish. The new defences held up well. Michelburne wrote of women being wounded, having 'supplied our men with powder and balls and water to drink when the poor men were just fainting'. This stand-off 'continued hot for more than half an hour on both sides and might have continued much longer with no great loss on either side', wrote Captain Ash.

Unable to attack Ramsay head on, the rebels went round him. The weak spot was where his trench dipped down onto the strand and into the Foyle. 'Having begun his work too late, the nights being extremely short', Ramsay was attacked 'before he could put his work in a condition of defence', was the message relayed to the king. 'The strand was their confusion', wrote Michelburne. 'It was there we got our first advantage.'[5] There was no one to stop the rebels racing in great numbers along the water's edge, past the trench. They began to pour through the gap. As soon as they saw that they were outflanked and likely to be cut off, the Irish troops in the trench next to the river fell back. Their flight was immediately apparent to those men standing their ground in front of the windmill, and they also ran. This precipitated a rush by Baker's men, with whom they had been exchanging volleys.

[B] 'Our Walls', wrote Walker, who had no idea what the field guns were for, 'were too strong for the Guns they used'. He added some post-siege bravado for the London readers: 'Our Men were not afraid to advise them to save all that Labour and Expense; that they always kept the Gates open, and they might use that Passage if they pleas'd, which was wider than any Breach they could make in the Walls.'

Ramsay and his chief officers lost control: they stayed to fight but could not stem the tide and were themselves cut down or captured. The rebel officers also lost control and could not hold back their men, who raced over the trench, past the windmill and down the slope on the other side in pursuit of the Irish (and, according to Ash, who was there, chased them for a quarter of a mile). Michelburne described Sir Maurice Eustace's fusiliers as the last to run, and did so 'like stags over the ditches'. The rebels, like 'true bred beagles, scoured after them'.[6]

'There was smart execution done on the enemy', wrote Captain Ash in his diary. 'Fifty one of them were slain.' In the confusion, Ramsay was killed, as were five of his subalterns. Lord Netterville, Lieutenant Colonel William Talbot, Sir Garret Aylmer and Lieutenant Thomas Newcomen were captured. 'We took no prisoners', wrote Captain Holmes, 'except nine great officers and they were so wounded that most of them died'.[7]

The rebel pursuit came to an end once they had overrun their old position. There was no Irish second line to stop the retreat, no reserve to support Ramsay, and the bulk of Hamilton's army was held back. Mackenzie wrote that 'our men pursued them, beyond all the ditches, to the top of the hill'. But it was not as far as that. Ash, who was there, was clear that 'we pursued a quarter of a mile beyond the gallows'[c] before pulling back on seeing a great body of Irish troops 'on top of the hill above the strand'. There was no attempt to attack them as the rebels were themselves in disarray, although 'several went near the enemy and lined the hedges to prevent them coming down'. The fear was of a counter-attack. 'A troop of the enemy came near the strand, all clad in buff, but advanced no further, fearing the shot of those who had lined the hedge near them.' By late morning, it was clear that the Irish were not going to try again that day. Their troops marched off, and at about noon, the rebel troops went back to the city.[8]

This engagement generated one of the great comedic episodes of the pamphlet war. According to Walker's *Account*: 'Mr. Walker draws a Detachment out of each Company, of Ten men, and after putting them into the best Order their Impatience could allow, he Sallies out at the Head of them (with all imaginable Silence) at Ferry-Key Gate, at four of the Clock in the Morning.' Mackenzie responded: 'if he did so, it was not only with all imaginable silence, but with so wonderful secrecy too, as to be neither seen nor heard by any of those that are said to follow him'. Walker, he wrote, 'was a man of peace all the time and was guilty of shedding no other blood to stain his coat but the blood of the grape'.[9]

Lord Netterville, Tyrconnell's cousin, who had been taken prisoner, was in a bad way. Michelburne remembered him as 'a big fat man' with 'three of his fingers cut off his right hand and a cut in his face'. He was carried in by three soldiers and placed

[c] The gallows are clearly shown on Francis Nevill's map on what is now the junction of Bishop Street (Moore Walk) and the Foyle Road (see plate 6a). In a straight line from the city walls to the gallows, the windmill is half-way. Beyond the gallows was bog, beyond which rose the high ground (now crossed by the Southway) where the Irish 'were in a full body on top of the hill'.

in a chair while he damned himself for taking up arms at the age of seventy. His captors were awed by him: he was offered brandy (but demanded 'sack' – Spanish white wine – and was given a glass by Michelburne), while Baker promised him 'a good room and good quarters'. Colonel Talbot was in no better condition. He was brought in 'all bloody and carried on a hand barrow', and was likewise treated with awe because he was Tyrconnell's nephew. Ash noted that 'They were brought to the garrison and their wounds dressed. They were confined in Mr Thomas Moor's and a guard placed over them, but honourably treated as persons of distinction'.[10]

Netterville died a few weeks later in the city. His son took no part in the war, swore allegiance to King William, and kept the family estate at Douth, Co. Meath. William Talbot (nicknamed ironically 'Wicked Will', because he was such a charming man)[11] was fatally wounded. The others survived their captivity: Sir Garret Aylmer was released after the siege and went back to live quietly on his estate in Meath. Lieutenant Newcomen, one of the six sons of Sir Thomas Newcomen, Bt., was unhurt and survived. Also captured was Captain John Browne of the Neale, another baronet's son. He took no further part in the war and was pardoned in 1693. His great grandson became the first Lord Kilmaine of many.

The Irish losses were the highest they had suffered in a single battle by far. Walker used his usual figure of two hundred dead and also adds a further three hundred that later died of their wounds. Mackenzie (again) repeated Walker's figure of two hundred. Writing six months after the event, and perhaps muddling or even conflating this action with the later attack on the Windmill, Captain Holmes wrote: 'Their own accompt told us that that day they lost 500 men, but I assure you we saw 150 stript beside all that they carried away.' Aickin put the Irish losses at two and a half thousand. By the time the news reached London, it was even better: the besieged had 'killed some thousands' of Irish troops. 'So obstinate and bloody was the fight, and their loss so great, that they were forced to raise the siege and are retreated above 40 miles.'[12]

In the confusion of the night, the slaughter caused such shock in the Irish camp that many thought it was at least as high as Walker's estimate. The first dispatches received by d'Avaux quoted the figure of two hundred, which was repeated by Berwick writing years later. The French engineer, Massé, noted that the Irish were defeated with 'considerable loss'. Plunkett who was not there, and who wrote two decades later, gave the figure of a hundred and fifty. But the whole of Windmill Hill was captured by the rebels and they could count, and clearly did. Ash, who was there, was quite specific: 'Fifty one of them were slain and several of their officers.' By the time d'Avaux made a considered report a few days afterwards, he wrote to King Louis that the losses were 'sixty or eighty'.[13]

The Irish loss was exacerbated by so many officers having been killed at their posts, desperately trying to stop their men running. The death of Brigadier Robert Ramsay was especially felt, and he was the third officer of staff rank to be killed in a month. 'He was a very good officer, and one whom the King regretted extremely.'[14] Ash listed the names of four subaltern officers believed to have died that night, to which Walker and Mackenzie added three more. The Irish also lost everything they had taken to the Windmill: not only their arms and the three field guns, but the precious collection of spades, shovels and pickaxes ('five cart loads', wrote Michelburne) and 'two pairs of colours and five drums' (says Ash).[D] The bodies were stripped. Michelburne records soldiers returning to the city with 'rich saddles, housings, bridles, hats, wigs, scarlet coats, laced cravats, etc., crying "Good plunder! Who buys a beaver hat, a good wig, a scarlet coat?"' He bought 'Lord Netterfield's saddle and bridle for 6s'.[15]

The rebel losses were lower, and perhaps much lower. The sources variously record 'three men, and only twenty wounded' (Walker), 'three or four private men, and some wounded, particularly Lieutenant Douglas, who afterwards died' (Mackenzie) and 'none of our men were killed but one or two, but several were wounded' (Ash). Walker, in describing the dead Irish soldiers, noted that 'most of which were shot through the Breast or Head'. As if to explain what Walker meant, Mackenzie added the detail that 'many of them [were] shot in the face, forehead, and breast, over their own line, as they were firing', which makes it more puzzling that the Irish, in successfully fighting off the initial frontal assault on their positions, caused so little damage. The reality is that the Irish were in easy range of the cannon on the bastions and the ravelin, and many of their losses came in the rout. Ash added details of the routine deaths that day. Not only was the quartermaster shot on the walls, but a cannon ball from across the river killed both one of his men and a woman, and injured three others. If his evidence is to be accepted, more people from the city were killed by those two random shots than in the entire battle on Windmill Hill.[16]

What is clear is that the rebels had acted, as Berwick put it, 'with great bravery'. For the first time in the war, they had stormed a defended position. In the city there was a feeling of great triumph. Michelburne described the celebrations: all-night drinking, dancing and music, and a feast, although, it being a time of siege, a somewhat frugal one of 'two little rolls of bread, and a little cheese with half a neate's[E] tongue'.[17]

In the evening, Baker sent a drummer to the Irish camp requesting that the Irish send a burial party to bury their dead. An officer and fourteen men were sent the following day, to perform the task 'very negligently, scarce covering their bodies with earth' wrote Walker, 'after a very careless manner', confirmed Mackenzie. 'Brigadier Ramsay was interred at the Long Tower', wrote Ash, 'and much lamented by all who knew him, for he was reckoned the best soldier in the army next to Col. Richard Hamilton. Some of the common men were buried, and some thrown into ditches as they lay.'[F]

[D] The colours were hung as trophies in the cathedral. Francis Nevill described one as being yellow, with 'a phoenix in flame, with this motto DUM SPIRO SPERO' (usually rendered as 'While I breathe, I hope').

[E] A cow's tongue.

[F] Ramsay was buried on the site of the old cathedral on which St Columba's Catholic Church was built in the 1780s. The stones from the ruins of the old cathedral had been used to build the city walls.

Ramsay's attack had spelt out both the vulnerability and importance of Windmill Hill. Baker ordered the digging of a new line of trenches across the hill, as well as defences along the strand so that the Irish could not replicate the breakthrough on an undefended flank. He also had redoubts built in that vulnerable corner by the river and to provide cover for the troops against the cannon on the far bank.[18]

'The siege of Londonderry is dragging along, and things seem to be regressing rather than moving forward', wrote d'Avaux to King Louis. 'The besiegers have lost heart, finding themselves almost completely without arms, outnumbered and facing a very well armed, much stronger enemy.' What was needed was French engineers and officers, more troops, and cannon, but he did not think that Hamilton had 'the ability to lead such an important undertaking'.[19]

On the following day, 7 May 1689, William and Mary declared war on King Louis of France, 'the disturber of the peace and common enemy of the Christian world': he had attacked the Holy Roman empire, a state 'in amity with us'; the French had been fishing in Newfoundland waters without paying for licences; they had invaded the Chalibee Islands and English territories in New York and Hudson Bay; and they refused to let English merchants trade in France. Louis had disputed England's authority over the Narrow Seas and had persecuted English Protestants in France 'to the extent of prison and the galleys'.[G]

> And lastly, as he has for some years last past, endeavoured by insinuations and promises of assistance to overthrow the government of England, so now by open and violent methods, and the actual invasion of our kingdom of Ireland in support of our subjects in arms and in rebellion against us, he is promoting the utter extirpation of our good and loyal subjects in that our kingdom.[20]

[G] The Chalibee islands were the Windward and Leeward Islands in the Caribbean (the French had attacked the English half of St Kitts); the Narrow Seas were the Straits of Dover and the southern part of the North Sea.

17

Counter-attack

KING JAMES OPENED HIS Irish Parliament on 7 May. It was a popular move in Ireland, but left the king uneasy. James did not want the Restoration land settlement dismantled, but the new members were determined to return the land to the owners of 1641, and James was told that the Irish would abandon him if he dissolved parliament. To pay for the new settlement out of forfeited lands, parliament also passed an act of attainder, which outlawed some two thousand named people, mostly Protestants who had fled the country. Although King William's parliament had done much the same in February (and would do so on a larger scale in the following year), it greatly damaged James' cause outside Ireland.[1] Parliament also proved a costly distraction to the continuing war. Stevens described the 'the nobility and principal gentry', who had been 'raising or encouraging and exercising their men or upon actual service', flocking to Dublin while the parliament sat. 'Everyone quitted his command to enter upon his estate, to settle his house and improve his fortune. And the estated men … kept with them for their own use all the better sort of country people, so that none but the most rude and useless sort of mountaineers took to the army'.[2]

From Dublin, Rosen sent a dispatch to Louvois on 10 May[3] to set out the miserable state of affairs. '*Tout est desolé*', he began. Administratively, the country was in near-collapse. Most government positions had been occupied by Protestants, and Tyrconnell's accelerated purge of all things Protestant in the government had opened up gaps everywhere. Later in the month, d'Avaux reported: 'We have to install everywhere new people who have not been trained in anything: all of the artillery officers have fled; there is not a single man left in the admiralty; the king's revenue collectors are leaving one after the other.' The country needed strong financial administration and the army needed better organization, especially as 'most of the colonels have not even seen their regiments'.[4]

The new French administrators needed to know what funding was available and where it was going. The French paymaster, Jean-François Fumeron, and Rosen worked on new scales of pay and estimates of how many men could be supported but, said d'Avaux, it was all taking too long because neither King James nor his chief adviser, Lord Melfort, 'nor anyone in this country, has the slightest knowledge of the least thing concerning warfare', and Tyrconnell was unwell and had left Dublin for a change of air without leaving any instructions. If the prince of Orange knows of the state of affairs in Ireland, he will send a force of seven or eight thousand men with officers to put at the head of the fifty thousand Protestants here 'and we will be more than a little embarrassed'.

There were plenty of recruits, but they needed equipping, clothing and paying, and the king 'has not even enough to arm and pay the troops that he has', so he was forced to rely on captains forming companies at their own expense. 'Not having enough money to make regular payments, the king gave it to those who shouted the loudest, and the others without subsistence pillaged the countryside.' The only new troops they could muster and equip were the five new regiments that were guarding the port at Kinsale.

The good news was that the arms shipment had arrived at Cork along with the new French officers who had been promoted to local ranks, so that all the cadets became lieutenants in the Irish army, the lieutenants became captains, and so on. Ten were sent to Derry and the rest placed in the newly formed regiments in the camps at Cork and Dublin. At last, an engineer was on his way to Derry, although that raised a fresh problem. The chevalier de Tangis had been sent in place of Jean-François, sieur de Massé, the chief engineer, who had fallen ill in Cork and was recovering in Dublin. Massé told d'Avaux to have Tangis recalled and sent straight back to France on the grounds that he is both 'incompetent and a lunatic'.

Massé was not happy. He had, he said, been struck down with 'a fever and a sickness which strikes new arrivals in this country, which is supposedly caused by the water and the beer'. Once he was fit enough, he was hurried off to Charlemont and then Derry. There were only three thousand troops there, he reported, and another four thousand being marched up, 'half of whom are unarmed'. Intelligence had been received that King William was embarking four thousand men to attack Dublin. Consequently, the experienced troops were being kept back to protect the capital, while the newly raised men were being sent to Derry. The new troops were, Massé thought, 'fine specimens of men, easy to discipline, and seemingly willing, but they are people who have never fired a gun, and most of them have no knowledge of the use of gun-powder'. Rosen was less kind: 'A single cannon shot passing over them at the height of a clock tower throws the whole battalion to the ground, and they will not get up unless you ride horses over them.' Most of the officers, he wrote, were 'wretches without courage or honour'. All this greatly encouraged the Londonderry rebels to make frequent sorties. Hamilton needed to get a firm grip. 'You cannot seize such a place using only your fingertips.'[5]

The state of the men's equipment was dire. A month after reaching the city, 'most of the soldiers there do not even have a sword', and, said Fumeron, were only armed with 'pointed sticks without iron tips'. They were 'unarmed and naked', said Rosen. Although arrangements were in place for the supply of bread to the besieging troops and for the upkeep of the hospital at Strabane, the artillery was another matter. There were no gunners to fire the few cannon they had, nor the most basic equipment needed for a siege, such as spades, picks and shovels all of which had to be collected or purchased or manufactured and, no small problem, paid for. The siege of Derry 'really cannot get any worse', wrote d'Avaux. 'It would have been quite easy to become master of this place, if we had means with which to make a trench and to fire twenty cannon shots.'[6]

While in Dublin, Massé had been asked to see what equipment was there that could be used in the siege. 'There is none in either the arsenals or the warehouses.' After Ramsay's men were chased off Windmill Hill, the Irish at Derry had not a single piece of equipment with which to dig trenches. Two of the cannons were out of commission and there was nobody capable of lighting the fuses on the mortar bombs. Massé was arranging for a mortar to be taken to the siege without knowing if the shells were of the right calibre, and the new shipment of arms arrived at Bantry with all the packing broken and half of the arms unfit for use. 'Send us a few mining experts and two men for the gunpowder and as many bombardiers', Massé wrote to Louvois, 'as the ones in this country are, according to M. Rosen, ignoramuses'.[7]

Exasperated by the lack of organization in the new Irish army, Rosen was increasingly frustrated at the siege's lack of progress. Although he had only stayed a few days outside Derry in April, he had taken in the lie of the land and, since the deaths of Maumont and Pusignan, he felt no one there knew what he was doing. A siege must be conducted properly following the rules of war. The first step was that the city must be properly and closely invested. At present, the rebels have a 'disdain for our poorly armed army', and their sorties had to be stopped. The way to do that was to ambush the next body of rebels that ventured out and 'cut them to pieces'. His low opinion of Hamilton is illustrated by the lengthy set of instructions he drafted for the king to issue as an order. What would have been obvious to any of the French generals, Rosen felt, needed setting out in great detail for Richard Hamilton.[8]

Accordingly, sometime after 10 May, Hamilton received orders from King James. Hamilton was to reconnoitre the areas around the city so that he could conceal great numbers of troops behind the rises and in the hollows out of view of the city walls and the steeple. If he needed more men, three hundred of the best armed troops on the east bank should be brought across by boat to spend the night in position and then ferried back the next day. The plan needed cooperation between cavalry, dragoons and infantry. The horsemen must be got into position in great secrecy and concealed. The riders should dismount and lead their horses by their bridles into cover and kept out of view of the town.

A detachment of infantry should march toward the city as if they are going to attack, but their intention will be to lure the enemy out. When attacked, the detachment should retreat, but should not run away. The enemy's attack must be resisted, but weakly, and at all times a rearguard action must be fought as the detachment withdraws. The enemy must be kept advancing and occupied to draw them further from safety.

In preparation for this, Hamilton was to wait in a position where he had a good view, with a cannon that would act as the signal. Only once he is satisfied that the enemy are sufficiently far from their escape route, was he to give the signal and all the horse were to come racing out from cover to block the enemy's escape. The concealed infantry would then break cover, form up and march to the aid of the detachment. All the principal officers involved in the action must have an overall understanding of the plan and, most importantly, there should be the utmost secrecy so that the enemy are caught by complete surprise.

The level of instruction that Rosen felt necessary to give to Hamilton is staggering. He even felt that Hamilton had to be told how to get horses into a concealed position. He emphasized twice the necessity for Hamilton to place himself on a height, near to the signal gun so that he could have it fired at exactly the right moment. These were not instructions from one military man to another. They were instructions from a career soldier to an idiot.

In his *Account*, after Walker described Ramsay's attack on the Windmill, he wrote: 'After this performance, the enemy's want of courage, and our want of horse occasioned, that some weeks produced but little of action, except skirmishes; in which Captain Noble was very active and successful'.

> Our sallies many times began but with small parties; Capt. Noble, and sometimes other officers, when they saw the enemy make an approach, would run out with about ten or twelve men at their Heels, and skirmished a while with them. When the besieged saw them engaged, and in any danger, they issued out in greater numbers to their relief, and always came off with great execution on the enemy, and with very little loss to themselves.[9]

As will be seen, they were not always successful, but these small *ad hoc* sorties by a dozen men at a time were not what concerned Rosen. The Irish did exactly the same, as is so clear from Ash's diary. Life was dangerous on the city fringes, but it was all petty stuff. What Rosen set out to stop were the large-scale sorties as had been made towards Pennyburn at the beginning of the siege.

On 7 May, the day after the battle on the Windmill, Ash recorded another raid on Pennyburn. We are not told by how many, but to travel a mile from the city walls required large numbers. These expeditions never involved fewer than a thousand men. Ash described it as 'a slight skirmish', but 'skirmish' is the word he used for the first two Pennyburn expeditions. In the first of those, he wrote that 'several' were killed and wounded on both sides. In the second expedition, he wrote, 'Cornet Brown and three others were killed'. In neither of those does he give any detail of the action. He was not there. He no doubt was simply repeating what he had heard on the walls. He was not on the third expedition either, but he did detail the casualties. This time it was said to be 'three of our men fell, and seven or eight were wounded'. On the next day, two of the wounded died. That was five of the defenders dead, in an action that (according to what he understood) was more costly than either of the first two Pennyburn raids, and even more costly than the great battle on Windmill Hill. Neither Walker nor Mackenzie mentioned the third raid. It was not good copy.

Four days later, on 11 May, the rebels made their fourth attempt on Pennyburn. Walker makes no mention of this. Mackenzie describes the Irish building a small fort there on which they placed some of their cannon. A plan was hatched to either capture the guns or else nail them up.[A] Ash recorded that the expedition was made up of 'a thousand or more', but Mackenzie says that it numbered two or three thousand men. It was as big an expedition as they had yet mounted. Early in the morning, they marched from the Windmill towards Pennyburn, 'thinking to beat the enemy out of their tents before they were aware'. Before they could get into musket range of the Irish, the field guns were fired at them. The Irish were up and ready. The rebels saw their surprise attack was no longer going to be a surprise. To avoid a pitched battle, the one, two or three thousand men marched back again. Or, as Aickin put it: 'Into the City we retreat apace, for us most boldly they began to chase',[10] The risks involved in facing the enemy in the open were too great. The attempt on the Irish positions was abandoned, and the only casualty was a man who was shot in the leg.

Hamilton considered Rosen's plan. It was unsuitable to counter a raid on Pennyburn, because the orchards and hedges would get in the way. It needed open country where the cavalry could come in from both sides in a pincer movement. The cannons on the walls made it too risky to send a body of men out as if to attack the city, so a different bait was cast. The Irish made a great show of building a small fort with fascines (cylindrical bundles of twigs) in view of the walls on 'the Heathy Hill' (says Mackenzie) 'above the Creggan' (says Ash). Well beyond the range of cannon, it was a spot from where there was no direct route back to the city, as any attacking force would have to go around the bog to get to it, and expose itself to the danger of being cut off. The Irish then waited for the city to react.[B]

Thomas Ash wrote in his diary on 15 May: 'some sharp words happened between Gov. Baker and Col. Michelburne that rose to such a height that they drew on each other. Michelburne was foiled and wounded, and committed to his chamber where he lay ill for some time'. Walker made no mention of this. It would have confused his London readers to learn of any cracks in Protestant solidarity. Mackenzie, eager to add what gossip he could, did record the event, but played it down: 'Colonel Michelburne was suspected by Governor Baker and the garrison. The governor confined him to his chamber, betwixt whom there was some little scuffle when he was apprehended. He continued under the rules of confinement but was never

[A] Cannons were fired by lighting powder in the touch hole. To nail up or to spike a gun, a nail (preferably a barbed nail) was hammered into the touch hole and the head either broken off or hammered flat, which, given the technology of the day, would make it impossible for the gunners to remove, and the cannon would be useless.

[B] If we may rely on Francis Nevill's 1694 map, the dummy fort was as far away from the walls as Pennyburn, on the high ground above what is now the Derry City Cemetery.

tried by a council of war. What the grounds of suspicion were is too tedious to relate.'

The grounds were petty rather than tedious, but it was a serious incident that could have affected the outcome of the siege. It followed an argument over the tobacco ration, and Michelburne suffered a slashed leg. Michelburne had allowed the companies in Baker's regiment only half a roll of tobacco each because 'the strongest company does not exceed twenty-six men' and could not expect the full ration due to a company of sixty. Baker's men complained and Baker took their side. He confronted Michelburne and called him a 'rascal'. Michelburne responded with the stinging rebuke: 'I was not in a boat making my escape when the soldiers fired and killed Captain Bell!' Michelburne described the event in a series of theatrical directions: 'They advance, Michelburne draws, Baker draws, they make five or six passes and close. Michelburne's hat flies off, one of the mob runs off with it. They [the mob] beat down their swords and disarm Michelburne and lead him away. They give his hat to Baker.' Baker then shouted out: 'Go your ways to his house! Secure all his arms! Plunder his house! Leave him not so much as a knife!' Michelburne then added the detail 'Coll. Murray takes the opportunity by their falling out and goes with some of his men and breaks open Col. Michelburne's stable door and takes from him all his horses'.[11]

Putting aside Walker's quite shameless self-promotion after the siege, or that as a country clergyman in his mid-forties he was not performing heroics at the head of sorties, he was badly needed on occasions such as this. It is not clear for how long Michelburne was sent to his bedroom, but it was not for long. According to Michelburne, Walker arranged a reconciliation over tankards of ale. At Walker's insistence, they kissed. And with Michelburne back on the loose, the horses stolen by Murray were speedily snatched back.

On the 18 May, the garrison set out to destroy the new Irish fort. 'A large party of our soldiers went above the Creggan', wrote Ash. Mackenzie listed the officers as captains Cunningham, Noble and Sanderson, 'and some others', which must have included Murray. It was another big expedition, although Mackenzie, in view of what happened, made a point of saying that it was only a hundred men, and withheld Murray's name. He may be doubted on this. What happened next was played down by the three Williamite sources, but it was clearly a shocking defeat. While the rebels were engaged in taking the dummy fort, the Irish cavalry swept in behind them. 'A party of the enemy's horse came at full career betwixt our men and the town', wrote Mackenzie. According to Ash, 'they were almost surrounded before they were aware'. To escape back to the walls, the rebels had to go through the horsemen or try to get through the bog, and the result of doing either was devastating. While the horse held them, trapped on the hillside, the Irish infantry closed in. The rebels could not get away. The fighting went on until nightfall. 'Captain Noble and the rest came off being good footmen', wrote Mackenzie, by which he simply meant that those who ran the fastest got away.[12]

The reasons why Mackenzie may be doubted on the size of the expedition being only a hundred men are these: they could not have expected to do very much 'in the open fields' by rushing a fort with only a hundred men, nor would they have needed so many officers to lead them. Nor would the fighting have gone on until nightfall. They simply would not have risked a party so small so far from home, as was demonstrated by the numbers they invariably needed to mount attacks on Pennyburn. It was, as Ash recorded, 'a large party', the same term he used for Murray's expeditions to Pennyburn, and, although one need not use Aickin as an authority for this or anything written above (or below), it is at least of interest to note that he claimed that the attack was made by fifteen hundred men led by Murray.

The Williamite accounts all claim that Captain Cunningham surrendered and was then murdered after quarter had been given, which to them was the most important part of the story. The fact that Ash recorded it shows that it was the story that went around the walls. According to Walker, the Irish had the 'impudence to deny it by the addition of many bloody oaths and protestations, but it was too evident by the testimony of their own officers and soldiers who were afterwards our prisoners'. Maybe it was true, or maybe Cunningham asked for quarter and was not given it. After what had happened that month, there was much savagery on that soggy hillside. Witherow made the fair observation that Cunningham's murder 'is not stated on the evidence of any one who could personally have known the fact'. Those Irish officers captured on Windmill Hill had all looked like officers, and were worth something as bargaining counters, or even as ransom. No one can say how many of the other officers or men had asked for quarter, nor is there any suggestion that a single Irish soldier on Windmill Hill was given quarter. No common soldiers were taken prisoner on the Windmill, nor was there any medical treatment for wounded Irish soldiers. Captain George Holmes' phrase was: 'We might have taken them alive, but we gave them old quarter.' They were all killed.[13]

The attack on the Creggan fort sparked a long action spread over a large area. We know that Cunningham was not killed in the attack on the fort itself because his body was recovered the following morning. There could have been no burial detail able to go up there to get his body. He was killed in the desperate rout that followed, perhaps shot while he was crossing the bog, as his corpse was close enough to the city for it to be brought in and buried 'with all the honours of a soldier'. Apart from Cunningham, 'we lost none of any note', wrote Walker. 'We lost fifteen or sixteen men', wrote Mackenzie, which, although we may believe it to be a gross underestimate, is nevertheless the highest figure he put on any loss in any action during the whole duration of the siege. Ash noted somewhat vaguely that, as well as Cunningham, 'several men' were killed. He then added 'and many were wounded of whom several died soon after. It is not known how many of the enemy died.'[14] Aickin made no claims of Irish losses, but described the rebels taking the fort and then being surprised and beaten off by Lord Galmoy's horse, who 'slew above thirty men'.[15]

When he heard news of the Creggan action, Rosen reported back to France that Hamilton had followed his instructions and carried out the plan. He considered it to have been only partially successful because he had hoped the Irish would have seized the opportunity of chasing the survivors through the city gates. His is the only surviving account of the action from the Jacobite side. He wrote, with some satisfaction: 'Two hundred of the enemies were killed on the spot, and we did not lose more than four men.'[16]

This was to be last expedition that Baker allowed or that Murray attempted. Moving more than a short distance beyond the safety of the defences was too risky, and the consequences of being caught in the open by concealed cavalry were too great. The Irish would soon bring their cannon and mortars over from the far side of the river and place them some four hundred yards from the walls. Other than by cannon shots fired from the safety of the ramparts, no attempt would be made to attack them. From that day on, trench raids aside, the initiative was always with the Irish, and the defenders were left to react.

Neither Baker nor Walker had any external endorsement to legitimize their authority. They were appointed by the garrison and could be removed by the garrison. As things got worse, criticism of them grew. Baker had the confidence of the officers, as he was senior to most of them. Everyone had noted his swift action against Whitney and Michelburne, but Walker's position was different. He clearly possessed natural authority, but had no military knowledge or rank to fall back on, no relevant experience for the post he held and most of the soldiers and junior officers did not belong to his church. Mackenzie calculated that although about half the colonels and lieutenant colonels were conformists, the Presbyterians 'far exceeded' the subaltern officers in number, and (Presbyterian) estimates of the soldiers varied from five Presbyterians to one conformist, to Mackenzie's assertion that the conformists made up fewer than 'one in *15* of the common Soldiers'.[17]

Walker was in charge of the stores, and as supplies dwindled, discontent was inevitable. All control had been placed in the hands of one man and his appointees, and all grievances and jealousies were directed at Walker. The denominational politics that so gnawed at Mackenzie may only have been of marginal interest to most, but among the non-conformists were those open to the message that they were being kept hungry by a self-appointed, Anglican joint governor.

According to Mackenzie, in late May 'most of the officers', having had long held suspicions of Walker, 'drew up several articles against him'. When he wrote his *Narrative* in London, Mackenzie produced a list, not from a written document but 'from the memories of some of the officers then present'.[18] The articles were not a formal set of charges but simply a loose series of allegations that were for the most part utterly risible. Mackenzie's list was as follows: when King James was outside the city, Walker and 'a secret cabal' sent the king a message seeking proposals for surrender; Walker then accepted King James' offer to surrender the town for £500 (plus £700 a year); the (unnamed) person who carried this message to Walker was arrested, but Walker set him free and sent him to Culmore, 'which was soon after surrendered'; and when the men were fighting at Pennyburn, Walker held 'a consultation with some others' to shut the gates on them 'to facilitate a surrender'. There were also, said Mackenzie darkly, other complaints 'relating to personal vices I shall not mention'. At the heart of all this nonsense were the complaints that Walker had been 'selling or embezzling' provisions and 'abusing' the officers who went to the stores.

Those working to get rid of Walker pressured the others to sign the articles. 'It is strange what a faction and confederacy there is against Walker', noted Michelburne. 'No less than 4 colonels has been with me to turn him out. They produced 21 articles against him and you cannot think what endeavours are used with my officers to sign it. They have corrupted 3 or 4 score already of the officers of the garrison.'[19] Mackenzie put the figure higher, although he named only seven, including Murray.[20] He claimed 'above a hundred' officers 'subscribed a resolution to prosecute' Walker 'in order to the removing him from all trust either in the stores or in the army'. That was their singular aim. Walker had tried to sell them out for £500 plus a handsome pension, but rather than lock him up or execute him as a traitor, or take measures to curtail his unmentionable 'personal vices', all they wanted was to take away his authority over the stores. Those behind the articles knew full well that all the allegations concerning secret cabals, private consultations, King James' money and so on were ridiculous. And Mackenzie knew that when he set them out in his *Narrative*.

Walker survived. After his 'scuffle' with Michelburne, Baker knew very well how difficult it was to ensure fair distribution. There would always be resentment from those who wanted more, or those who wanted others to have less. Although well aware of the accusations, the senior officers had not lost faith in Walker. They established a 'council of fourteen' members (according to Mackenzie) to supervise Walker's running of the stores. This was no material change on what was already in place. Most of the officers on this council were the very men who had appointed both Walker and Baker in the first place, and, being officers, they had other work to do, such as defending the city. According to Aickin, the council was made up of thirteen: all the colonels, including Walker and Baker, together with two town representatives (aldermen Squire and Cocken), two country representatives (Gledstanes and Doctor Jennings, 'the Rector of *Artree*'[c]) and John Mogridge in his usual post as secretary.[21] The new council perhaps helped diffuse the situation and, possibly, although one may doubt this, Walker was in some mild way chastened in that there was to be some rudimentary scrutiny of the governors. But he stayed on in charge of the stores until the end of the siege.

[c] 'Doctor Jennings' can only have been Captain the Reverend Christopher Jenny of Mullaghbrack, Co. Armagh.

At the end of May, Hamilton moved the army closer to the city. The camp at St Johnstown was broken up and a new one pitched on Ballougry Hill overlooking the south of the city. There we are left with a vivid description of Hamilton wearing a red cloak and a black plume in his 'shining bright' white hat, riding a black steed along the ridge in view of the walls.[22] Across the bog from the gallows, the Irish army was set to work digging trenches and building parapets. The besieged decided to do something about it.

On 31 May there was another of those clashes about which we have scant details. Walker skirts over this period by saying that there were many sallies in which the besieged 'always came off with great execution on the enemy, and with very little loss to themselves'. Mackenzie does not support this, but instead leaves a gap in his *Narrative* between the death of Captain Cunningham and 4 June, missing out one of the bigger actions of the siege. The only person inside the walls to write of it in any detail was Thomas Ash:

> We had a skirmish at the windmill; the cannons on both sides played smartly; about ten o'clock a number of the enemy came running down the fields and possessed themselves of a height beyond the place from which they had forced our men to retreat; on which a party sallied out of the city to the windmill; we then went over to their camp at the top of the hill where there was a stout battle for some time, but they beat us off again. Both cannon and muskets played almost the whole day with much execution. A cannon near the magazine burst and hurt the gunner.[D] [23]

Neither of the two London-printed wartime accounts describes any defeats in which the defenders suffered 'much execution' but, according to Ash, this 'skirmish' was the perhaps longest action of the siege and, as the objective was to overrun the new Irish positions, it must have involved thousands of men from the city. On two occasions, the enemy either 'forced us to retreat' or 'beat us off' in a day of fighting in which there was 'much execution'. Ash's account is supported by Aickin, who in his *Londerias* wrote of the Irish digging trenches 'just over the bog'.[E] Murray led three thousand men and beat the enemy out of the trenches, but was himself beaten off by Irish reinforcements backed with cavalry. Aickin wrote: 'Thrice he their Trenches gain'd, they regain them, No reinforcement from the City came; *Waughop* against us came with fresh supplies, Our beaten Forces to the City flyes.'[F24]

[D] Ash's grammar is confusing. 'At the windmill', could only have meant 'beyond the windmill'. 'We went over to their camp', only makes sense if the word 'to' is interpreted as 'towards'.

[E] The Irish trenches were in what is now the Kildrum Gardens/Southway area.

[F] 'Waughop' was Colonel (later Major General) John Wauchope, who had until 1688 been a colonel in the Scots brigade in Holland, and then the colonel of a short-lived regiment in England. He joined James II in France at the revolution. The author is not a descendant, but is descended from Sir John Wauchope of Niddrie (d. 1682) of whom this Colonel Wauchope (d. 1693, at the battle of Marsaglia outside Turin) was a nephew.

The Jacobite sources do not add much detail, but are consistent. Once the army was consolidated on Ballougry Hill, Pointis wrote, the rebels attacked. They 'sallied out three times, but were each time repulsed with loss on their side'.[25] King James' memoirs, based on now lost dispatches from Hamilton contains this entry:

> The great guns and mortars arrived not at the camp, till the thirtieth of May, and till then little was done against the town, except beating them back when they ventured to sally, and firing with what guns we had upon them, which, however, did considerable execution.[26]

Meanwhile, things were happening out on the lough. On Saturday 1 June, three English ships, the *Greyhound* frigate and two ketches, rounded Magilligan Point. By the afternoon, they were off Redcastle, fifteen miles from the city, where they dropped anchor, unable to make any headway against the wind and the 'great storms of rain and hail'.

18

Buchan's attack

KING JAMES' CHIEF ARTILLERY OFFICER at Londonderry was a 43-year-old naval captain, Jean-Bernard de Saint-Jean, baron de Pointis, a veteran of the naval attacks on Tripoli, Algiers, Genoa and Tunis. His speciality was coastal bombardments from ships and bomb ketches.[1] From his sick bed, where he lay incapacitated by the wound in his thigh, he wrote to Dublin requesting three frigates to sail up the Foyle. His suggestion was met with ridicule. It was as if the English navy did not exist. Perhaps because he was a navy man, and perhaps because of his glittering career, Pointis did not get on with the other French officers. There came a time, said Rosen, when Pointis would not speak to any of them. He was 'too refined and delicate a gentleman', wrote Léry-Girardin, for work 'in which one must at times get one's elegant hands dirty and go into dark and damp underground places'.[2]

The only obstacle between the English navy and Londonderry was Culmore Fort, and Pointis knew better than anyone the limitations of shore batteries when pitched against warships. If he could not bombard the city from the water, he could at least block the river. Still on his sick bed, he drafted a second, more modest plan. The river should be blocked with a boom. Hamilton approved, and when Pointis was back on his feet, he started work at the end of May. The boom was made of 'beams, joined one to the other by [iron] bands; each end of a beam is attached to the end of the next by two iron hooks, and I have run a rope along the length of the boom, from five to six inches thick, which is attached to the beams by the iron hooks it passes through. Care has been taken to attach the rope to the beams underwater, so as to make it difficult to cut.'[3]

He was in no physical condition to do the work, but there was no one else to supervise. His health deteriorated. 'My illness has seized me again', he wrote. 'My exertions have caused the splints to become detached and I am no longer able to move except with extreme difficulty.'

In the meantime, Hamilton prepared another attack on the Windmill. Ramsay's attack had failed almost by oversight. Either he had not anticipated the fatal weakness of his open flank on the strand, or had not had time to remedy that weakness. Nevertheless, and notwithstanding the cannon fire from the walls, the men had until then stood up well and the rebels had not been able to break through. Since then, Hamilton had been encouraged by the failure of the rebel expeditions to Pennyburn and the Creggan, and by the arrival of Brigadier Thomas Buchan.

Buchan was a veteran and contemporary of Ramsay, and was also a Scotsman who had spent much of the 1670s in France. The difference was that Buchan had served in the Royal Scots serving Louis XIV, but had then changed sides, becoming the commanding officer of Mackay's regiment in the Dutch Scots Brigade. He returned to Scotland to command a foot regiment, was promoted to colonel in 1686, and then to brigadier just before the revolution.[A] [4] He arrived at Derry in May as a conquering hero, having just crushed Hunter's rebellion in Co. Down. Henry Hunter, a captain in the Association army, raised a force of perhaps three thousand men in and around Newtownards. Although almost wholly populated by Scots Presbyterians, the area was then peaceful in that it was policed by only one company of Irish soldiers. Hunter's army, made up of men who 'had all taken protections from King James', chased the Irish troops out of the Ards Peninsula and Downpatrick. On 30 April, Hunter was caught in the open by Buchan's dragoons and his men were scattered at what became known as the break of Killyleagh. Accounts of how many rebels were killed vary from the specific 'sixty-one' to 'six hundred'. The survivors melted away, Down and Antrim returned to a surly peace, and Buchan was ordered to join Richard Hamilton.

The break of Killyleagh further illustrated the vulnerability of untrained footmen when faced by mounted troops. Hunter's rebels had massively outnumbered the Irish, but all Buchan needed at Killyleagh was two troops, one of cavalry and one of dragoons. It was a massacre. That lesson was very much in Hamilton's mind. The rebels had no answer to well mounted, disciplined cavalry and, if only Hamilton could get his horsemen onto the Windmill, the rebel defences would crumble in minutes.

The difficulty was that Windmill Hill was now extensively fortified. Not only was it cut about with trenches, but three redoubts had been built, two of which were on the river to prevent an attack along the strand. A seven-foot-high breastwork had been thrown up all around the hill, behind which was a second row of defences. Nevertheless, it had to be possible, Buchan reasoned. His horsemen could get past or over the defences, and clear the hill while the infantry made a full-scale assault. They could then occupy the defences, dig in properly, and beat off any attacks that might be thrown at them.

By the beginning of June the new, 'grand' mortar had arrived, together with a consignment of bombs and, for the first time, two large siege guns able to fire 18- and 24-pound balls.[5] Still suffering from his injury, and irritated that he had received only 120 of the expected 500 bombs, this was what Pointis was at the siege for. He took over the battery of three mortars in Strong's Orchard. They were each of a different calibre: the grand mortar fired 14-inch diameter shells, the smaller mortars fired shells of 10 inches and 8 inches in diameter. In the early hours of 2 June, he fired four ranging shots: one from a small mortar, and then three from the newly arrived grand mortar. He then stopped.

On 3 June, after a day in which his artillerymen constructed new gun emplacements, the grand mortar was back in action. For the first time the city came under a bombardment that lasted all day.

[A] 'His obvious fault as a general was over-confidence'. *Oxford dictionary of national biography.*

> The enemy discharged thirteen bombs. The first killed one man and a woman, the second or third killed Mr James Boyd in his own house, and hurt Anne Heath, who died shortly after. The others hurt nobody, but tore up the streets, making great holes in the pavement and where they broke. One of them flew back into the lough at Shipquay, one of them fell into Mr Cunningham's back yard on a dung hill and did not break. It was 270lbs. The powder weighed 151lbs. A cannon ball from Tamneymore over the lough struck Major Graham in the belly as he was leaning over the wall at Shipquay Gate. He died next day. That night we had fifteen bombs which did much mischief, killed and wounded several people and broke down many houses. Seven were killed in Mr. Harper's house in Shipquay Street and numbers elsewhere. Those seven belonged to Colonel Lance's company.

The civilians were terrified.

> The thin paper buildings soon shivered into pieces, and dropped in upon the heads of the poor frightened inhabitants … nothing was to be seen over the whole place but fire, smoke, ruins, and horrid death, pain and anguish in a thousand different aspects, nor to be heard but dying groans, the sharp accented screeches of dread and pain, the falling of houses, and the cannons roaring for more prey and slaughter … and to heighten and exasperate their pain in all the several views of death and misery that lay around them, they then were forced to see a father, mother, son, wife, husband, a friend, or some other dear relation lying in their gore.[6]

Buchan's plan was for a general attack from the south side of Windmill Hill. His cavalry were to charge straight at the defences next to the river and get through to cause panic and mayhem. While they advanced, the cannons and mortars across the water would pelt the rebel lines. He divided his infantry into three divisions, two of which, under Brigadier Dorrington, were to attack from the same direction as the cavalry. At the same time, Colonel Nugent was to lead his third division of infantry across the bog, past the Double Bastion and attack the ravelin to cut the defenders off from the Windmill. Buchan and Dorrington were confident they would take the Windmill 'without losing twenty men'.

There was little secrecy in the planning on either side of the city walls. Michelburne claimed to have learnt Buchan's battle plan from a spy who had been wandering freely in the Irish camp, a pedlar 'in a red cap and a red coat with a brandy bottle about his neck'. Spirits in the city were high. Far out, off Redcastle, a dozen or more miles off, the English sails in the lough were clearly visible from the steeple. It was only a question of time. On the evening before the battle, Baker declared: 'Let's have the other glass and drink their Majesties' health and confound the other Hogshead of the Bishop's March beer. We cannot do it at a better time than to comfort our hearts against the morrow's service.'[7]

Michelburne was in charge of the Windmill defences. He had five thousand men on the outworks, 'besides a hundred posted behind each regiment for a reserve, not reckoning our scythe men and our roundhead men which are posted on the river to fall amongst their horse'. The scythes and the 'roundheads' were mounted on four-foot poles, the roundheads having 'a ball at the end, something bigger than a man's head, with twelve long iron spikes'.

> They [the Irish cavalry] must pass within fifty yards of me where I'll salute them with seven hundred shot. When they get by me, the scythe and club men will fall amongst them. They'll find it very hard to get with their horse over our stone ditches. You'll see how they'll break and swim the river.[8]

Michelburne arranged for a 'bloody flag' to be raised in mimicry of the red flag flown at sea to signify readiness for battle, 'to shew the Besieged, as well as the Besiegers, the heighth of Resolution'. Michelburne's flag was not made up for the occasion, but was an old ship's 'ancient' or ensign. Red ensigns at that time were eight-ninths red, with the red and white cross of St George in the upper canton next to the mast head. Michelburne described himself giving this order:

> Tomorrow for the fighting part! Fergus, go and get me the largest ship's ancient you can find in the town. Place it at the top pinnacle of the church. Let the bloody flag fly! 'Twill animate our men to fight and give new life and courage. England's standard, boys![B] [9]

On the morning of 4 June, the city was ready. Everyone was in position when the attack started. Ash was one of those behind the parapets on Windmill Hill. 'A great party of the enemy, horse and foot, came marching down the strand towards the windmill, about ten o'clock in the morning, to attack our trenches. When they came as far as the gallows, near Serjeant Burns' house, they stood and paused some time.' Plunkett says, it was earlier, 'between seven and nine of the clock in the morning', but makes the point, 'so that the rebels had time enough to put themselves in a posture of defence. This was giving them fair play.' At the signal, 'the discharge of three cannon and three mortars', the attack began.

> They came on with a most desperate onset, and giving a loud huzza, the horsemen who were arm[our]ed cap-a-pee,[C] rushed with great courage down the strand. About twenty five leaped over our works, leaning down over their horses necks, to avoid the shots which were fired at them, and

[B] Elsewhere, Michelburne wrote of 'his planting the Bloody Flag on the Royal Bastion'. It was moved to the steeple when he later erected a gallows on the Royal Bastion (see chapter 24 below). Neither Walker, Mackenzie nor Ash mention the flag.

[C] *Cap-à-pie*, 'head-to-foot' in old French.

> rode up close to our trenches. Our men were commanded not to fire until they came very near, which they carefully observed, and then they poured a salute of shot, which made them drop apace.[10]

It was almost impossible to get through. The horse made their way for the gap at the end of the defences:

> They came by the end of the line (it being low water) notwithstanding our firing constantly on them. Our men, viz., Captain James Gladstanes, Captain John Gladstanes, with others next to them, left their redoubts, and took the Strand with their muskets, pikes, and scythes, and fell on them with that vigour that soon spoiled the tune of their huzzas, for few of that party escaped; many of them were driven into the river.[11]

The new entrenchments along the strand were too high to jump, and were crowded with defenders, but 'the front of the horse was composed of gentlemen that had bound themselves by an oath, that they would mount our line':

> Lieutenant-colonel Edmund Butler, being extraordinarily well mounted, resolved to show the way, if possible. At which, clapping spurs to his charger, he flies over, but was immediately taken prisoner. Cornet Purcell, of Thurles in the county of Tipperary, followed, but his horse was killed, and he leaped back in his armour, and so saved himself. A private man and an old gentleman, Edward Butler, of Tinnahinch, in the county of Carlow attempted and gained the ditch, but he and his horse were both slain.[12]

For those that did get through, there was no way out and, for the horsemen behind them, it was immediately clear that to go on would be suicide:

> The rear of the enemy, seeing the reception their fellows met, retreated in confusion; those in front, perceiving the rear to run, especially the horse which came within the line, wheeled about and endeavored to get off, but many of their horses were killed under them; for observing the shot made little impression on the men, on account of their arms [armour], our men shot at their horses with good success.[13]

At the same time, Brigadier Dorrington advanced with the Irish foot:

> A detachment out of all the grenadiers of the army marched a little before under the leading of captain John Plunkett, the youngest son of Mr. Nicholas Plunkett, of Dunsoghly, in the county of Dublin. After them came the line of colonels, with their pikes in hand, at the head of the infantry … In their march they were exposed to the cannon of the windmill; but by

> the time they advanced upon the place of taking their career, they received anticipately a shower of ball from the entrenchment in long *fowling pieces*, without seeing an enemy; at which discharge several of the king's men were killed. The aforesaid captain John Plunkett received at the first fire his mortal wound, and being carried off to his tent, he died within an hour after.[14]

Dorrington's men did not reach the defences, and within minutes Dorrington himself was shot three times.[D] Walker described some of the Irish infantry shielding themselves from the musketry with faggots of wood. 'They and the Horse began with a loud Huzza, which was seconded from all parts of their Camp with most dreadful shrieks and howlings of a numerous Rabble that attended the Enemy in the camp.'[15]

> They went on boldly, and attempted to mount the entrenchment; but their endeavours proved all in vain, by reason the work was so high that they had need of ladders to carry it suddenly. Otherwise a small delay would slaughter them all, by reason that the rebels were very numerous within, and, being wholly covered, could not be lessened by the fire of the assailants; for what harm could the assailants do when they could not lay sight on their foes?[16]

The attack outside the Double Bastion fared no better. 'The other party of foot, being grenadiers, attack our forts by the bog side, and came on fiercely.' It was, said Ash, 'near the double bastion, and beat our men thence, all but a little boy who, when they were climbing the trenches, stood stoutly upon the trench and threw stones at them'. The Irish were 'vigorously repulsed', overwhelmed not by musket shots, said Pointis, but by the hail of stones. 'Our men, then being reinforced from the city', wrote Ash, 'came down with spirit, and beat them quite over the meadows, making a terrible slaughter of them in their flight'. Mackenzie made special reference to Captain Michael Cunningham, who 'was at the bog side with his company, kept our men to their posts, and opposed the grenadiers with great, courage. He narrowly escaped with his life, a cannon bullet tearing up the ground about him.'

Throughout all this, the guns on the steeple, on the Double Bastion and from either side of the Bishop's Gate, were firing at the Irish. Over the river, the Irish guns had been moved from Strong's Orchard to Tamneymore to fire straight along the Windmill Hill defences. 'Their cannon from the opposite side of the water flanked our men and killed several of them, and struck off an arm of Capt. Maxwell (one of our regiment) of which wound he died.'[17]

Walker added this detail: 'We wondered the Foot did not (according to Custom) run faster, till we took notice that in their Retreat they took the Dead on their

[D] Although he survived, served for the rest of the war and later rose to the rank of lieutenant general in the French army.

backs, and so preserved their own Bodies from the remainder of our Shot, which was more Service than they did when alive.' This myth was not invented by Walker, it was one of those stories that went round the walls. Captain Holmes wrote of this Irish 'trick' to explain the comparatively low number of corpses found after the first Windmill battle: 'They carried away on their backs, which was a trick they had still when they ran, to take a dead man on their back, it was good harness.' It was an amusing jibe, but is of the greatest improbability. Wounded men were certainly carried off under fire, but the mindset of a man in full flight over boggy ground does not allow him to stop and haul a corpse onto his back as a makeshift shield.[E] [18]

Walker and Mackenzie both made a telling observation about their success: 'Our Men place themselves within our Line in three Ranks, so advantageously that one Rank was always ready to march up and relieve the other, and discharge successively upon the Enemy, which (though 'tis strange how they could think otherwise) was great surprize and astonishment to them; for they it seems expected we should make but one single Volley, and then they could fall in upon us' (Walker). 'In each redoubt there were four, and in some five reliefs, so that they were in a posture of firing continually … They imagined our men would fire all together, finding that they fired successively, they soon wheeled about, and drew off' (Mackenzie).[19]

Walker was right in that it would have been very strange if the Irish had thought that there would be only one volley. The military discipline of the day ensured that there would be a continual fire. Infantrymen were formed up in ranks, and each rank fired a volley in succession. The drill book gave the following directions for use by six ranks of men (with the words of command in italics):

> *The first five ranks. Kneel. The rear rank. Present. Fire. Fifth rank stand up. Present. Fire. Fourth rank stand up. Present. Fire.* And so of the rest. And as they have fired they are to charge again and be in readiness against the first word of command. This way of firing may be performed either by two ranks at a time or three ranks. The first kneeling and the second stooping, or the first two stooping.[20]

That was the way the army trained. All the professional soldiers would have been training their men, endlessly it would have seemed to them, to do just that. This rather invites the question as to why Walker and Mackenzie thought that the Irish expected them to behave otherwise. If they were right, there can only be one explanation: in the earlier engagements the defenders had not done that. They had all blasted off together and left themselves undefended while they reloaded, which

[E] 'Was there ever a funnier *ruse de guerre* than that practised by the retreating Irish according to Walker? Some might suppose the beaten soldiers to have done bravely in carrying off the dead. In our day the Victoria Cross peculiarly glories the achievement. By no means. It was simply to save their own hides! Such is history written on the spot, passion guiding the pen, and prejudice clotting the ink.' Charles Townsend Wilson, *King James and the duke of Berwick* (1876).

may in part explain why the actions at Clady and Pennyburn had ended so unsatisfactorily. It very much suggests that since then the professional soldiers, from Baker and Michelburne downwards, had been repeatedly drilling the men. There had been an improvement.

As the lines were not breached, the defenders' losses were small. 'We lost 5 or 6 private men', wrote Mackenzie, 'and one Captain Maxwell'. Ash put the figures as being higher: 'The enemy when they got the line near the double bulwark, killed Thomas Maxwell, a youth of the city. We lost ten or twelve men that day, mostly by cannon'. Colonel Hugh Hamill, who was directing part of the defensive line, was shot in the face, 'a hurt on the cheek with a small Bullet'.

As the Irish had been in the open, and were fired upon by men under cover, their losses were higher than in any other engagement. Plunkett gives the Irish loss as being 'at least two hundred men killed, without doing any damage to the defenders'. Ash puts the figure lower as being 'about sixty were killed, as near as could be computed', but he may have been only referring to the attack on the bog side, where Pointis recorded the losses to Nugent's regiment: forty officers and sixty soldiers killed or wounded, the lieutenant colonel killed and Colonel Nugent 'dangerously wounded'. Walker's estimate for the London public was naturally higher, '400 of their Fighting Men, most of their Officers were killed'. But not even Mackenzie would go along with Walker on that, and simply wrote that 'The enemy lost a considerable number of men. Most of their officers were either killed or taken prisoners.' Captain Holmes said that the Irish 'came again very boldly but in half an hour's time returned with greater loss then before'.[21]

Buchan had grossly underestimated Michelburne's preparations, and his failure deeply affected Irish morale. Three hundred men deserted, said Pointis, mostly from Nugent's regiment where the men had shown unwavering attachment to their colonel. Massé, wrote that 'We lost many brave officers, and many men killed or wounded.' 'Even more officers', according to Berwick, than in Ramsay's attack, 'and at least a hundred men'. Massé, reported that the troops were 'greatly disgusted' with Richard Hamilton and were questioning his competence. The officers felt the same. 'I immediately warned the ambassador', wrote Massé, 'and sent a message to M. Rosen to advance with all speed so as to reassure the soldiers who are deserting in batches'. Plunkett wrote, 'You see here, as you have seen all along, that the tradesmen of Londonderry have more skill in their defence than the great officers of the Irish army in their attacks.'

The king was told that the defeat had been due to 'the rebels having drawn out almost their whole garrison for the defence' (which, if one may state the obvious, they were bound to do) 'and some of the foot not going so heartily on as was expected'. His faith in Hamilton was undiminished. 'We cannot but be extremely sorry for so many good officers that have been killed or wounded upon this late occasion, but you must do what you can to hinder our people from losing heart, such accidents being natural to the employment you are about.' He promised Hamilton more troops. 'We have dispatched away a considerable number of officers of our own subjects as well as French who we hope will be useful to you. We are resolved to send the rest of Butler's regiment tomorrow and the day after Grace's and Bophin's.'[22]

Whatever the actual body count, it was not a general defeat. The Irish had been prevented from capturing an area outside the walls. However, despite their sense of triumph or relief, the besieged were still hemmed in behind their defences, unable to pursue the retreating Irish, and still wholly incapable of mounting any counter-attack. The situation remained as it was. Neither side was able to dislodge the other.

At night, the mortar restarted its bombardment. Thomas Ash ended his diary for the day with these words: 'That night they shot thirty-six bombs against the city, by which many lost their lives. One fell on Counsellor Cairnes' house; it made down to the cellar where some of my men lay sick, it killed two and wounded several. Some of Major Campsie's and Mr Sherrard's men were killed by them. Another fell on the Diamond House, went through it and dropped within two yards of forty-seven barrels of gunpowder which was hid in a dry well. So much for Thursday the fourth of June, one thousand six hundred and eighty-nine!'

19

Reconnaissance

IN THE LULL AFTER THE BATTLE, over the following three days, the grand mortar fired seventy-six bombs. The city was lucky on the first two days. Ash recorded that in Major Campsie's house a bomb damaged two hogsheads of wine in the cellar, another in Captain Cairn's house 'broke all the bottles and furniture', a third broke Captain Abrams' chin and smeared his house 'all over with syrup of cloves'. Three further bombs wrecked the market house and the clock. The city was hit by eleven more bombs on 7 June, and by then the bombardment was having its effect. In Walker's words:

> They ploughed up our Streets, and broke down our Houses, so that there was no passing the Streets nor staying within Doors, but all flock to the Walls, and the Remotest parts of the Town, where we continued very safe, while many of our sick were killed being not able to leave their Houses: They plied the Besieged so close with great Guns in the Day time, and Bombs in the Night, and sometimes in the Day, that they could not enjoy their rest, but were hurry'd from place to place, and tired into faintness and diseases, which destroy'd many of the Garrison.

Early on, precautions had been taken. 'On the advice of an experienced old soldier', people had 'uncovered the tops of their houses and taken up the pavements of the streets, the one to hinder the blast of the bomb to fire their houses, and the other to let the bomb bury itself in the removed earth which in the splitting of the bomb does not kill or wound them as the stones formerly did'.[1] The dread of the bombs, wrote Ash, 'forced our people to lie about the walls all night, and to go to the places remotest from houses, some out of Ferry-Quay gate, some to the Ravelin, and others to the Wind-Mill hill; and the cold which the men – especially the women and children – contracted hereby, added to their want of rest and food, occasioned diseases in the garrison, as fevers, flux, &c., of which great numbers died.[2]

Tales of the horror of the shattered remains of people in the city were matched by tales of close escapes from death. According to Captain Holmes:

> At this time they played abundance of bums [bombs], the weight of many of them was near 300 weight which killed many people. One bum slew 17 persons. I was in the next room one night at my supper – which was but

> mean – and seven men were thrown out of the third room next to that we were in, all killed, and some of them in pieces. Into this city they played 596 bums which destroyed many of our people and demolished many of our houses. Cannon bullets flew as fast as you could count them, and as soon as we took up their bullets, we sent them back again post paid.

Mackenzie gave these details:

> One of these bombs fell into the house of Captain James Boyd, and broke down the side of it, killing himself; but several officers who were then at dinner escaped the danger, though it fell near the room where they dined. Another bomb killed Mr. Alexander Lindsay, the surgeon, who was very useful to the sick and wounded soldiers; and one Major Graham was killed with a cannon ball; another bomb killed Mr. Henry Thompson, a burgess of this city, who showed great zeal for the defence of it; another killed fourteen men, and fired one or two barrels of powder in a back house; another killed seven, another killed three of our men.[A]

Some bombs failed to explode, through the fuses falling out or being extinguished in flight. Not only had Pointis not been sent enough mortar bombs, he complained, but the fuses were all too slender and had to be wrapped in leather sheathes to make them stay in.[B] [3] The path of an incoming bomb could be seen at night by the sparks from the fuse, which gave hope to an observer that evasive action could be taken. In daytime it was more difficult. There was, both Walker and Mackenzie agreed, one benefit of being bombed. The houses that were knocked down were used for firewood, a commodity that no one had collected in, and which they had no other way of finding.

Having positioned and tested the mortars, and supervised the beginning of the bombardment, Pointis had been busy completing his boom on the river. By 6 June, he had finished what was, in his opinion, a very fine boom which would withstand any attempt to ram it. It was placed halfway between the city and Culmore, where the river was about two hundred yards across, and Pointis had gun emplacements and shelters built at each end. The boom stretched from Charlesfort, a remnant of the 1649 siege, across to Grangefort, and a new emplacement downstream was named Newfort.[C] [4]

[A] Dr Alexander Lindsay, the surgeon to Walker's regiment, was one of only four medical men we know of in the city. Charles Ellingworth, who died in the siege, was 'chaplain and physician to Col. Monroe's regiment', and Aickin wrote of Murray recovering from a gunshot wound through 'the mighty Skill, of Dr. *Aickin* and *Herman*'.

[B] I have drawn heavily on, cannot add to, and do not attempt to compete with, Brian Scott's masterly article on 'The deployment of mortars in Ireland', in the *Ulster Journal of Archaeology*, 73 (2015–16), pp 204–18.

[C] The boom stretched under (or perhaps a few yards downstream of) the modern Foyle Bridge.

> I shall not be happy until the English are foolish enough to attempt this undertaking, for then I shall have the pleasure of defeating them for, as they must come when the wind is behind them or nearly so, when they reach the boom, return will be impossible, and they must remain under fire, for their force will not be strong enough for them to attempt to land, and they will perish.[5]

He recognized that others might not share his absolute confidence, so 'to put everyone at ease, I have to make another boom a little above this first, where I shall observe the same means, and I hope it will be made shortly; with that, all will admit that we are in safety.'

Even before Colonel Cunningham had set sail with two regiments to relieve Lundie, preparations were underway for a further two regiments to be sent to Ireland. Once Cunningham returned, Major General Percy Kirke was ordered on 28 April to rush to Liverpool, take command of all four regiments, and to sail for Londonderry. There then followed a delay while Kirke assembled a fleet of twenty-four merchantmen to carry the men and their provisions, with a convoy of three frigates.

Among the specialists ordered to Ireland was Colonel Jacob Richards, a man of great experience in fortification, and a compulsive diary writer. Four years earlier he had been present through the siege of Buda and he had then joined the Venetian service. He was appointed the army's third engineer on his return to England in 1688, and given the tasks of inspecting coastal defences and organizing the artillery train in preparation for the Dutch invasion. At the revolution, he transferred his allegiance to the prince of Orange, and was sent to join Kirke's relief force. Travelling with four French Huguenot officers, he arrived in Liverpool in early May, where the force was being assembled. Kirke gave him a special mission. He was to go on ahead to Londonderry with his party of Frenchmen and 'the gunners and the miners' to announce the approach of Kirke's force, and offer them such advice as he could.

Richards sailed from Hoylake on 13 May in the sixteen-gun, 93-foot, 180-ton *Greyhound* frigate, which was in the classification of the day a sixth-rate ship. He was escorted by the 48-gun, 125½-foot, 636-ton *Portland* frigate and two ketches, the four-gun *Kingfisher* and the *Edward and James* of Liverpool, an unarmed merchantman carrying a lieutenant, an ensign and forty soldiers 'till such time as I shall judge it necessary for them to be on board the *Greyhound*'. His orders from Kirke were to take no risks. He was 'to go no further than within cannon shot of Culmore Fort' to gather intelligence about what state the city was in, whether any batteries had been erected on the river, and 'whether any other means are made use of, as the choking the channel or chaining it over'. He was not to endanger the ship by passing Culmore if there was 'evident danger', but was to wait in safety on Lough Foyle or on the coast, and send the *Kingfisher* back to report.

The small convoy arrived in Lough Foyle in 'rainy weather' on 1 June. The wind was wrong for the ships and progress after that was slow. It took six days of dragging on her anchors, kedging and warping, for the *Greyhound* to get up the lough. On 7 June, she eventually stood about three miles out from Culmore. They took some people on board, all eager to give news of the situation on shore. The Irish had just placed a boom across the river, but the details were sketchy. Some said it was simply a chain, others that it was timber connected by cables, and others that it combined all three. More than one of them spoke of boats being sunk in the channel.

While they sat on the lough, Richards studied Culmore from the mast through his telescope. The Irish were pulling down a house near the fort, and loading the rubble into a large boat, which helped build the suspicion that they were sinking vessels in the river. Two more people were picked up off the shore and both said that the Irish had deserted Culmore. Richards doubted that, but he needed to investigate. After a conference with his four French officers, he told the captain that at the first fair wind, the *Greyhound* was to be taken up to Culmore.

The next morning, 8 June, 'the wind blew a handsome gale at N.W. – a very fit wind for our enterprise'. The captain of the *Greyhound*, Thomas Gwillam, had the ship cleared for action. The seamen's hammocks were taken down to barricade the quarter deck against musket shots, all the trunks and chests were stowed in the hold, 'the yards were slung and the guns all cleared'. The ship weighed anchor at eight in the morning, and set off with the *Kingfisher* and the *Edward and James* until they stood off at the mouth of the river within cannon shot of Culmore Fort, and dropped anchor. Nothing happened. It seemed at first that the Irish really had gone, but Richards could see through his telescope that 'they were thick behind their walls' manning a great gun. By careful inspection, only two guns could be seen in the fort. Gwillam gave the order to open fire with a broadside. The Irish fired back 'and by what we could observe one of their guns split'.

Of the *Greyhound*'s sixteen guns, only half were in a position to fire at the fort, but even those few guns were as many as the entire Irish army had at Londonderry. The return fire from the fort was pitiful and inaccurate, and Richards had on board some of the army's seasoned gunners. 'We lay pelting them for above three quarters of an hour', he wrote happily. All being safe, Richards climbed back up the maintop to find out what could be seen of the way ahead. Straining through his telescope, a little above Brook Hall,

> I perceived something that extended from side to side, and several boats at a small distance from one another lay just by it, as if they buoyed it up. At the same time I saw some horse on the inner side of the fort drawing some great weight, as I judged by the slowness of their pace, but I could not see what, by reason of the rising ground that hid all but the horses' heads and a little of their backs. I guessed it to be the cannon they were bringing into battery against us.

It was a perfect reconnaissance. He had established the existence of a boom, the weakness of Culmore Fort, and that the Irish could move cannon to defend their weak points. There was 'evident danger', and the *Greyhound* and the *Kingfisher* by themselves 'were not of a sufficient force to attempt the breaking or the cutting of this boom'. He climbed down, and told Captain Gwillam to weigh anchor and rejoin the *Portland* out on the open water.

Then things went very wrong. 'The wind shifted and shrunk two points to the northward'. There was not room to turn in the narrow channel they were in. Turning to head into the lough, the *Greyhound* struck the bottom and stuck fast in the mud on the far side of the river mouth from Culmore. The sailors scrambled to free her by throwing out anchors to warp her off, 'but the tide fell so quick from us, that all hopes were laid aside till the next tide'. They were helpless. By noon, the Irish had hauled heavy guns to a battery position just upriver from the fort. Other guns were raced down on the opposite back. 'The whole number we computed to be about eleven, some whereof were twenty-four pounders, eight pounders and three pounders.' The Irish gunners started firing. Stuck fast and tilting into the lough as the tide went out, the *Greyhound* was 'laid almost dry, and heeling so much on our starboard side that we could not make use of any one great gun'. Irish infantry came running along the riverbank. Fearing that they would be stormed, Richards ordered the forty musketeers to be rowed over from the *Edward and James*.

The Irish did not attempt an attack, but kept up a steady fire from the shore. The hundred and fifty muskets on the *Greyhound*'s tilting deck kept them back. Although well protected from the small shot, two were killed. Captain Gwillam 'was wounded in several places and about fourteen men more, some with splinters some with small shot from the south shore'. The real danger was from the cannons, but the gunnery was poor. The French engineer, Pointis, rushed down to the river to supervise. 'Our fire took no effect till the French gunners arrived', he wrote. 'We then sent nine of the 14 shot fired, into the vessel', which, said Richards, 'did very great damage to our ship, so that in eight hours they shot seventeen shot under water and above fifty in her upper works, masts and rigging'.

By seven in the evening, on a rising tide, the *Greyhound* was flooding. There was five feet of water in her hold, and she would not lift off the mud. To help float her off, they had already unloaded into the boats most of her provisions and guns and transferred them to the ketches, but the ship would not budge. On hearing that Gwillam was injured, the captain of the *Kingfisher*, Edward Boyce, came on board and got 'shot in the belly', but not badly enough to stop him taking over. He called the warrant officers together to ask them whether the ship could be got off. They told him it was impossible. Boyce ordered everyone who did not belong to the ship, together with the wounded, including Gwillam, into the boats so that he could set the ship on fire. The evacuation got under way. But, said Richards 'before we had gotten a quarter of a mile from the ship, the wind shifted and blew off the south shore at S.S.E., which those on board seeing, immediately they loosed all their sails and the ship righted'

The crew heaved at the capstan to drag on the anchor, the ship got under sail and pulled away from the shore. It was touch-and-go, and they were in danger of sinking. Boyce headed for the shore away from the guns and in half an hour he had the *Greyhound* run ashore to avoid her going under in deep water. The ship was saved and, importantly, the Irish did not capture the sixteen 6-pounder cannons she had on board.

Out of danger, Richards transferred to the *Portland* and waited to see if the *Greyhound* would float. 'In two tides all her shot holes were mended, her masts catted and rigging spliced'. But she was leaking badly and, as Richards had completed his mission, it was felt best to get her over to Scotland for repair.[6]

There were important consequences of Richards' reconnaissance. He was of the view that the river was blocked and that it would be too dangerous to try to get up, or at least too dangerous while the boom remained. A ground force would be needed to destroy the boom so that the ships could get through. The Irish thought the same. Richards' presence was seen not as a reconnaissance, but as an attempt to get through to the city. If the English could not get up the river, they would have to come overland. 'Hamilton no longer believes that the enemy's plan is to attempt to enter the river', wrote Pointis. 'He directs all his attention to the other side on which he believes the English will land and where they will be joined by the country people.' There was no need, Hamilton told Pointis, for a second boom. They would 'trust wholly to the first'.

Hamilton had accurately assessed the conclusions drawn by the English, but others were not so sure. Fumeron wrote that the boom had 'no chance' of holding because it was too long, being about two hundred yards from one mooring to the other. A dam was needed, built out from both sides of the river at low-tide, to shorten and make it more rigid. 'But', he sighed, 'I was not listened to'.[7] Whether Pointis' confidence in his boom was in any way shaken by the day's events, we do not know. He had seen the poor marksmanship of Hamilton's gunners, and had also seen a rather ordinary ship, a sixth-rate vessel, being pounded by artillery for several hours, and yet still managing to sail off. We may suspect that he gave it little thought. His wound flared up again and his condition worsened after a poor attempt at surgery. There were fears for his life, and he was only saved by the efforts of a French surgeon sent up from Dublin. He took no further part in the war and, after several months' convalescence, returned to France at the end of the year.[D] [8]

The significance of the *Greyhound* action was lost on the city. Mackenzie referred to three ships firing at the fort and one of them running aground and being 'much endangered' by cannon fire. 'The enemy called to us from their lines, to send down carpenters to mend her, but we soon had the satisfaction of seeing

[D] Pointis led the expedition that captured Cartagena (now in Colombia) in 1697, which made him very rich. His career came to a sudden end when he lost five ships during the siege of Gibraltar. He died in 1707.

her get off again.' Ash made no mention of the *Greyhound*. The day had passed like many other.

> June 8: The bombs began again. They shot 35 which spoiled several houses, killed some people, and hurt many more by shattering their legs and arms to pieces. One of them fell on Mr Moor's house, drove a stone out of it, which killed a man at the Shipquay bastion below the magazine.

On 10 June, after the *Greyhound* had set off for Greenock, Richards sailed with the *Portland* to look for Kirke and his relief force off Carrickfergus, Richards wrote: 'We got in under the shore before it was dark and found only two vessels laden with provisions from Bristol to be sent to Londonderry. We advised them follow us which they did all night, but we lost them.' This small incident is illustrative of the fact that the seas on the north and east coasts above Dublin, including all the coastal waters, were entirely dominated by English shipping, and the Irish could do nothing about it.

20

The Enniskillen relief force

THERE WERE STILL HOPES in the city that relief would come from Enniskillen, but there had been no news. The great motivator for the Enniskillen troops was cattle theft rather than the relief of Derry. War had given both the Enniskillen men and the Irish irregulars the excuse to take that which many of them could never have hoped to possess. The country was plundered. Houses were burnt, stores were removed, and livestock slaughtered or driven off. Gangs on horseback ranged across the counties of Sligo, Leitrim, Roscommon, Fermanagh, Cavan and even into Meath. Obscure strong points changed hands or were destroyed. Security lay in quick raids and then getting out before the other side arrived in force. Land once overrun, could never be held, but Enniskillen was becoming more than a mere nuisance, and the Dublin government planned to deal with it.

Rosen was ordered to gather together a force to form a punitive expedition. To his annoyance, while the experienced troops were needed to guard Dublin and Cork, he was to make do with new troops as soon as they were equipped to march. Fumeron, the paymaster, wrote to Louvois on 6 June from Trim ('a nasty place on the route from Dublin to Enniskillen'), where he had been sent to organize the troops who were to be sent off with Rosen. 'We have here two battalions of infantry and five and a half companies of poor quality and badly mounted cavalry.' They were 'lacking everything needed for going to war'. Other troops were to join them, but no one knew where they were. Rosen would have marched off without them, but on inspecting his troops, he found there were not forty working muskets among them. The infantry had no belts or bandoliers and had to carry their swords in their hands. Those swords were 'all old and broken', and their distribution had been so slapdash that the infantry had been given cavalry sabres and the cavalry given infantry swords. The consignment of muskets from France had been so badly packed that most of the moveable parts were missing (even the serpentines, the metal arms that hold the match to fire the matchlock muskets, had come off). The ordnance people ('who are naturally lazy and uncouth') had supplied them with musket balls of the wrong calibre, and had shown 'so little intelligence' that they had sent four cannons with a supply of cannon balls too large to fit in the barrels. Rosen had to send everything back to Dublin to be exchanged. Eventually, after further delay, some, but not enough, bandoliers and belts arrived with two hundred muskets and fresh ammunition. Rosen was determined to march out regardless, with as many equipped and armed soldiers he could gather from the two battalions with him, and some of the cavalry, and to leave the rest to follow on later.[1]

Enniskillen knew nothing of Rosen's expedition, and by early June the Enniskilleners saw their position as having improved. Their strongholds at Enniskillen, Ballyshannon and Donegal were confined to the north by the Irish army outside Londonderry, and the Irish outpost at Omagh. To the west, an Irish force under Sarsfield had established itself in Manorhamilton, but that was twenty-five miles away. Nowhere, it seemed, did the Irish army have the men to do anything more than hold the line.

Gustavus Hamilton, the governor of Enniskillen, was conscious that the town's survival depended on Londonderry's ability to hold out. If the city fell, the Irish forces released from the siege would march straight on Enniskillen. The news that the Londonderry garrison was running out of supplies added urgency to the situation, and Gustavus Hamilton was determined to strike a historic blow. It was a great opportunity for the Enniskillen forces to do something more than steal cattle. They knew the Irish army at Derry was divided by the river. The smaller part was guarding the artillery on the east bank, and if that position was attacked, it would take days for the main army to relieve it. The Enniskilliners could march through Omagh and Newtownstewart, and make their way along the east bank of the Foyle. They could attack and destroy the artillery, get supplies from across the river into the city, and before the main Irish army could march down to Strabane to reach them, they could get away by racing eastwards to Claudy and through the mountains. They would simply disappear.

This was to be the most daring plan of the war, but there needed to be a consensus among the men to for the plan to be approved. Many of them had fled with their families to Enniskillen and saw little attraction in stripping the town of its defenders and marching fifty miles into hostile territory. They had to be satisfied that marching on Derry was not only in the interests of the great cause, but that it was in their interests as well. It took all his powers of persuasion, but Gustavus Hamilton got his way. He could not send others off to take the risk for him, and so agreed to command the raid in person.

Gustavus Hamilton marched out of Enniskillen with fifteen hundred men on 10 June. That night they reached Trillick, and on the following afternoon they marched towards Omagh, the halfway point. The route ahead was cleared by 'freebooters', men who considered themselves unconstrained by Hamilton's orders. They were a great asset. They took the risks of pushing into enemy territory in the hope they would get to any plunder first, and those risks were great. The men in the lead party were ambushed and (in the language of the time) 'knocked on the head', including 'one Mr Rowland Betty, a very honest gentleman, who was shot dead off his horse'.[2] The Enniskillen army pressed on, their numbers boosted by volunteers from all over the county. By the time they reached Omagh the force had doubled in size to over three thousand men. On that second night, they camped a mile outside Omagh and prepared for a morning attack.

The Irish garrison at Omagh was formed of two companies of dragoons, about a hundred men, who, on the appearance of the rebel force, burned down most of the town. The Irish posted themselves in a sturdy house belonging to Henry Mervyn at the far end of the main street, where they were surrounded by a wall. On the morning of 12 June, Gustavus Hamilton marched into Omagh and drew up his rebel army. Their advance guards crept up under the cover of the burnt-out houses and gardens with the Irish 'firing out very thick both at them and the body of foot that stood in view of them'. Gustavus Hamilton sent a trumpeter with a demand that they surrender.

> They sent back an answer in writing that they knew no authority we had either to bear arms or summon them, therefore they would defend that place unless they see an order from King James to the contrary, and withal told the trumpeter to come no more with messages, else they would welcome him with their firelocks.[3]

As the Irish dragoons were both surrounded and outnumbered by somewhere in the region of thirty to one, it was a brave reply. While the shooting was in progress, some of the Enniskilleners scouted along the road on the far side of the town and captured five Irish soldiers from an advanced party marching up from Dungannon. The prisoners said that they 'belonged to Lord Clancarty' and (quite falsely) that behind them were two regiments of foot, a regiment of dragoons and a regiment of cavalry, all of which would be in Omagh at three in the afternoon.

This rather threw the rebels. Gustavus Hamilton called a council of war. To his officers, the two main objections to the expedition came back to the fore. They had brought no provisions with them, either for the relief of Derry or even for themselves, and there was a real fear that as soon as they marched to Omagh, the Irish army at Manorhamilton would hear of it and Sarsfield would attack Enniskillen. Now there was a new fear that Lord Clancarty's Irish army was coming up behind them. The Enniskilleners gave up the idea of relieving Derry, and marched back the way they had come.

> We had marched but eighteen miles, yet we had two and twenty more ere we could come at Derry the nearest way, so we retreated meanly to Enniskillen without doing anything. We might have burnt Omagh, but of the value we had for Captain Mervyn, the worthy gentleman that owned it, although it was a relief to the enemy, we forbore.[4]

That was to be the only attempt to relieve Londonderry from the land. Ironically, Enniskillen was safe for the time being. Rosen's Enniskillen expedition had been cancelled as soon as King James got news of the English ships on Lough Foyle. The fleet was a real threat rather than an irritant, and Rosen was ordered to march with all speed to Derry. Delayed by his attempts to equip his men, Rosen set off late, and the roads through the mountains were, he was told, 'almost impassable', so he took the longer route through Dundalk and Newry in the hope that it would be quicker.[5]

On Sunday, 9 June, the Irish guns outside Derry fell silent for two days to mark both the Sabbath and the feast of St Colmcille, who was, noted Ash, 'held in veneration by the Irish'. After two days of peace, on 11 June, the shelling began again. The two small mortars fired twenty eight bombs, 'one of which killed Dr Lindsay'.[6] The following day, there were 'No bombs or anything else', but they started again on 13 June.

That same day, at '6pm the fleet appeared on our lough'. The feeling inside the walls was that Kirke was just in time. Everyone was weakened by the restricted diet, and disease was raging. 'Every day since the siege began there were buried, one day with another, thirty at least.' Although Kirke's fleet carried only three regiments, it also included provision ships, believed in the city to be crammed with biscuit, meal, beef, brandy 'and strong beer that will make a cat speak'.[7] There was great rejoicing in the city, marked by jubilant firing of all the city's guns.

The fleet needed to be told that the city was desperate and needed immediate relief. It was hoped to get a boat small enough to cross the boom in the night and slip onto the lough and for this purpose, Captain William Crookshanks, one of the gate-shutting apprentice boys, had built a boat designed for eight oars on each side, but, noted Ash, 'the oars [were] placed so close that the men had not room to row'. Nevertheless, they made two attempts to get down the river, but 'were forced to return, it being impossible they could endure the showers of shot that were poured in upon them from each side the River'.

The third attempt to get outside help was made at night on 13 June. Captain Arthur Noble (the bravest character in Walker's *Account* apart from Walker himself) went up the river away from the lough. With him in the boat were probably about thirty armed men.[8] Interestingly, Ash writes: 'they were commanded by [in this order] Capt. Noble, Col. Murray, Capt. Holmes and Capt. Dunbar', which rather suggests that Noble was in charge and the rest were there for the adventure. Also on board was Alex Poke, the gunner, with two small field guns.[9] To neutralize any loose talk, it was put out that the party intended to 'to rob the fish-houses in the isle', meaning, it is to be supposed, at Corkan Island outside Lifford, but the real mission was to drop off two small boys with letters for Enniskillen.

This is illustrative of the divisions in the city. Walker thought the mission 'a design to Rob the Fish-House'. He had been misled. 'It was *given out*', said Mackenzie, 'to rob the fish-houses in the isle, but the real design was to land a messenger'. Whoever was sending the message did not want Walker to know. As one of the governors from whom all correspondence would be expected to come, not only did the message not come from him, he was not even told why the boat went upriver. Others were in the know. Ash knew nothing of fish houses, but knew why the boat had set off.

The Irish were concentrating on stopping relief from the lough, so there were few watchful eyes upriver. Nevertheless, there was something of a shock as the boat set off and was narrowly missed by one of the field guns at Tamneymore, positioned in the wood opposite the trenches at the end of Windmill Hill. The boating party pressed on and got as far as Donnelong Wood about four miles up the Foyle, where it was hoped to drop the boys off on the far bank, but they were being followed by two boats full of Irish soldiers. The terrified boys refused to get out, and the expedition turned back and headed for home. This meant passing the Irish boats, and there was a long exchange of fire on the river. According to Mackenzie, both sides ran out of shot. The men on one of the Irish boats tried to board them but, having fewer men and no cannon on board, they rather bit off more than they could chew. According to Michelburne, 'We gave them a broadside of two pounders.' 'Our men were as quickly in upon them, beat back some of them into the water, and killed three or four others, besides a Lieutenant in the enemy's boat; whereupon the rest threw down their arms and called for quarter', wrote Mackenzie. 'We took thirteen prisoners in this boat. The enemy in the other boat seeing this ill success of their friends, made off with what haste they could.'[10]

Under fire from the far bank, the prisoners and the captured boat were taken back to the quay. 'In all this adventure not one of our men was hurt (except Colonel Murray, who received some shots in his head-piece, that bruised his head, and for a while indisposed him for service), but one of the prisoners that sat among them was wounded by a shot from the shore. So remarkable was the guard of divine providence about us.'[11] Baker was unhappy about bringing in prisoners as they would have to be fed. Michelburne agreed. 'You should have sent them to catch fish, and seen if the Irishmen could swim.'[12]

With two boats they could go where they had never ventured before. There was a whole brigade of the Irish army in Strong's Orchard guarding the mortars, which were active throughout their time on the river. ('Twenty six bombs', wrote Ash, 'which killed seven persons and spoiled many houses'.) Almost immediately opposite the city, but upriver, was a small detachment guarding the field gun in the woods at Tamneymore. Buoyed by their success, they clambered into the two boats and set off again to capture it. But they were too late. 'She was away e'er our men got there.' Nevertheless, they beached the boats and made it into the woods to chase after the gun. The Irish responded by sending a large party from Strong's Orchard to cut them off. Noble and his men raced back to the boats in the nick of time, and pushed off into the river.

This action concerning (as Aickin put it) 'the barge of intelligence' was hailed in the printed accounts as being a great triumph. It showed great and aggressive enterprise by the men defending Londonderry and involved the two great fighting heroes of the siege, Noble and Murray. But it was mentioned nowhere else. None of the French accounts noticed it. It was petty stuff. More curious is the fact that the boats, which together could have carried fifty or more men quickly across the river, were never used again. Nor did William Crookshanks build any more, nor were 'the fish houses on the isle' disturbed.

On 15 June, Captain Leake in the *Dartmouth* frigate came up the lough to take soundings ('17½ feet at most at high'). On the following day, he was joined by much of the fleet on the same business. The sight of over twenty ships off Culmore caused great excitement in the city. 'Our cannon were thrice shot round the walls and from the steeple, which was answered by their cannon', wrote Ash. In the Irish camp, Hamilton panicked. He issued an order that everyone should be ready to leave by nine o'clock in the evening, and that the tents should be struck at ten to break camp. The French were amazed. No one knew what Kirke planned, and whatever he tried, they would be able to block him. Rosen was on the way with reinforcements and Berwick's troops at Castlefinn were covering Hamilton's back. 'Nothing warranted such a speedy retreat', Massé argued. The cavalryman Dominic Sheldon agreed. If Kirke tried to land, he would be beaten. If the people in the city tried to sally out, they would be beaten. And that would happen even if Hamilton was reduced to having 'only his cavalry that had justly earned itself such a good reputation'.

Hamilton was persuaded to stay put, but 'as nothing remains a secret here, the rumour of the breaking up of the camp had spread throughout the camp, and the fear so affected the soldiers' morale that more than 300 men deserted that night'. No one thought to send the counter-order across the river, so the three mortars were sent away and 'the infantry disbanded and ran off to the hills'. Had it not been for the four companies of dragoons who remained, said Massé, the enemy could have quite easily crossed the river and disabled the single cannon that was left. 'You see', he wrote to Louvois, 'the manner in which war is waged in this country'.[13]

21

Rosen arrives

HAVING BEEN ORDERED TO abandon his expedition to Enniskillen, Rosen arrived at Derry, in the pouring rain, on 17 June. He had driven his three battalions of exhausted men along at a great pace, 'three days and three nights without break'. On arrival, he found little to encourage him. Thirty-two ships now sat at anchor on the lough in full view of the camp. Both sides watched the fleet with either hope or dread. The effect on the Irish, especially after Hamilton's initial reaction, was great. 'The troops were deserting at the rate of three or four hundred each night.' Rosen took immediate steps to allay fears by placing himself at Culmore 'within range of the ships' cannons', with two of the regiments he had marched up from Trim, so that the fleet would see that he was ready to oppose any attempts to land.[1]

Rosen was a character to reckon with. He took his unpopularity with King James' chief advisors and senior officers as a compliment, attributing it 'to my excessive exactitude and activity', which in turn made him popular with the troops and his own officers. 'I can say with no vanity that my presence alone has reassured the whole army more than the relief I had brought.' He then spent his first three days inspecting the camp, the approaches, and the positions on both sides of the river. He wrote to Louvois:

> I am unable, Sir, to give you a strong and full enough description of the pitiful state of this siege. M. Hamilton has been in position for nine weeks with what is left of the twelve thousand strong troops that the King has sent at intervals, which now amount to 5,000 men and 1,000 women. However, the garrison of the town is still 3,000 strong, of seasoned men now used to gunfire after several clashes which happened during the siege in which they have almost always had the advantage, having killed the best officers and the most daring of our soldiers.[2]

Rosen's point was blunt. Derry's sturdy walls made it one of the strongest places in the kingdom. It was impossible to siege the place without the numbers and the equipment. The Irish had neither. 'We are generally lacking in everything needed for an attack and the reduction of this place.' Two daring attempts on the Windmill had failed and all they could do now was blockade the city, but that needed time and, with the fleet in the lough, time was not on their side. The 'four or five' heavier cannons they had were too few and were needed to stop the relief ships getting up the river. The boom was in his eyes for show rather than effect, a bluff to deter the ships. The trenches that had been dug by the Irish troops were to protect their camp rather than threaten the city. His arrival sparked a programme of frenetic nocturnal trench digging around the city's defences to confine the garrison, and to put the garrison in fear that a serious attempt was being made to get close to the walls to spring a mine. He had to start from far out because the trenches were being dug within range of the superior guns on the walls, and he did not have the men or the firepower to beat off any sudden sallies from the city. Even if all went well, it would take weeks to get close enough to mine the walls, but not only was there a great shortage of entrenching tools, they did not have the tools to cut wood. The trenches themselves, and the guns, needed fascines and gabions (large cylindrical baskets filled with earth) to protect them. The men had had to improvise with knives and, as all the wood was across the river, they then had to haul it across the water by ropes.

Any attack on the city would be a pointless waste of life that would have the twin effects of depleting the numbers of the troops available, and reducing morale. Hamilton's two attacks, made without the wherewithal to succeed, wrote Rosen, had left the officers and troops so dispirited that there was now great difficulty in getting the men to serve in trenches. The Irish regiments were commanded by 'old lords or gentlemen who have never served', but those officers could not be replaced because the regiments were made up of their servants and tenants, who had also never been in the army. Their only bond was with their officers rather than their regiments. If the officers were replaced, the men would desert.

> A captain in Sir [Neil] O'Neill's regiment of dragoons having died, 25 dragoons of his company deserted together with their horses. Those who remained refused to serve, saying that they were only pledged to serve their captains. We had them draw lots and one of them had his head broken, and in order to carry out this execution the regiment was obliged to borrow arms from the Lord Mayor's regiment.[3]

John Stevens, an Englishman who was in Dublin at the time, but was soon to spend the rest of the war as an officer in the Grand Prior's regiment, saw the problem as being not so much with the colonels as the new and inexperienced officers in the regiments:

> They will follow none but their own leaders, many of them men as rude, as ignorant, and as far from understanding any of the rules of discipline as themselves. This was the utter ruin of the army, none fitter to raise men than he that had been ever bred in the mountains. When raised there was no respect from soldier to officer, they were all fellow mountaineers. The commissioned officer could not punish his sergeant or corporal because he was his cousin or foster-brother, and they durst not correct the soldier lest he should fly in their face or run away. These officers had seen and knew no

> more than their men, and consequently understood as little how to exercise or train them.[4]

The solution, or partial solution, was to attach professional French officers to the regiments, as without them leading from the front, they would get no one to go into the trenches. Nevertheless, the use of French officers had its drawbacks. 'The language difficulties are no small obstacle for successful command, particularly during action, where the whole outcome of an affair depends on a single movement, carried out well or inappropriately.'

The problems, if not insoluble, would need time and expense to rectify. A fortnight after his arrival, Rosen was still bemoaning the poor state of command and low morale. Thousands of men had left. 'The army is diminishing with every passing day, some through illness, and the others through not being paid, and because they are put off by the gun fire and the work. There is, in this, a great deal of negligence on the part of the officers', he wrote to King James. 'You can judge the difficulty and embarrassment I face in tackling this.'

> So you see, Sire, the state of your troops. I let Your Majesty judge if an honest man, guided by honour, can remain calm without feeling uneasy at finding himself at their head, at a time when your enemies have taken particular care in supplying good and fine arms to your rebellious subjects and all those who have risen up against you. I have no doubt that we shall see them marching towards us at first light, their protections in their pockets and their arms in their hands, as has already occurred several times, and happens every day.[5]

Reinforcements were sent up when they were in a fit state to march, but without arms because there were none. They had to march through Omagh, running the great risk of being attacked, and unable to defend themselves should that happen. 'Bagnell's regiment was ordered to escort the [paymaster's] treasure without giving it a single shot to fire.'[6] 'My heart bleeds, Sire, when I reflect on this continuing negligence, as it seems to me that no one is concerned that your affairs are being lost.'

> The troops that Your Majesty has most recently sent have arrived in much the same condition as those sent earlier, having been forced to take what arms they were given, that is, for the most part broken and wrecked, which are effectively arms lost, since you do not have in your army a single armourer to mend them. The arms of those who remained here with M. Hamilton are in an even worse state and the regiments entirely lost and ruined, the strongest battalion not numbering more than two hundred men and more than three quarters of those without swords, belts, nor shoulder straps. The cavalry and the dragoons are no better for being more numerous, the

> strongest company having no more than twelve or fifteen horsemen in a fit state to serve.[7]

When, at the end of June, Richard Butler's newly raised regiment arrived at the camp without muskets, Rosen was furious. He told Melfort he could not run a siege 'using unarmed troops and lacking everything else … Since leaving school I have forgotten how to fight with my fists.'

Stevens also made reference to the lack of arms and training in the Irish army. Their equipment was scarce and, as the officers were also new to the army, training was improvised.

> For want of arms most of the army was taught the little they learnt with sticks, and when they came to handle pike or musket they were to begin again … Many regiments were armed and sent upon service who had never fired a shot, ammunition being kept so choice that they were never taught to fire, and it is hard to guess when these men were upon action whether their own or the enemy's fire was most terrible to them.[8]

The Irish were camped in pitiful conditions, some in tents, but most huddled together in squalid makeshift shelters where conditions were as crowded as in the city. While the Irish were free from the disease that was raging in Derry, they coped, but soon they too began to suffer from 'the fever', and thousands died. As in the city, there were many civilians in the camp. The men began to look shabby, and as their uniforms frayed and wore out, they were dressed in whatever cloth could be found for them. Michelburne noticed that tartan, 'a sort of Scotch pladding', was 'much in use in the Irish camp for breeches'.[9] John Stevens observed with reference to the Irish soldiery in the war, that all things are relative to one's expectations:

> Unless it be the Scotch, no people have more encouragement to be soldiers than these, for they live not at home so well at best, as they do at worst in the army for diet and clothes, and yet none will sooner murmur or complain of hardship than they. It is not through prejudice I give this account, but of love to truth, for few strangers love them better or pity them more than I do. And therefore, to do them justice, I cannot but say it is not to be admired they should be poor having been so long under the heavy yoke of the Oliverian English party, whose study it was always to oppress and, if possible, to extirpate them. Poverty is a source from whence all other worldly miseries proceed, it makes them ignorant, not having wherewithal to apply themselves to studies, it enervates the spirit, and makes them dull and slothful and so from race to race they grow more and more degenerate wanting the improvements of a free and ingenious education, and being still brought up in a sort of slavery and bondage. This may be easily evinced by

> such of their gentry who having been abroad become very accomplished men either in learning warlike affairs or the more soft and winning arts of the court.[A] [10]

Rosen made a point of saying that he had not taken over the running of the siege itself, which he looked upon as Hamilton's affair. He repeatedly reminded King James, Melfort, d'Avaux, Louvois and King Louis, almost as a sort of mantra, that he had advised against a siege in the first place, and so was devoting himself, as the senior officer, to the overall command of the activities of the Irish army in the north-east. Nevertheless, Rosen's influence on the siege was immediate and obvious, and was not confined to trench digging. He camped himself at Culmore with two of the new regiments and, to prevent any attempts from Enniskillen, he had the third new regiment sent across the river to strengthen what he could see was a 'very weak post' on the Waterside. Before Rosen's arrival, Hamilton had brought the dragoons from the Finn into the camp. They consisted, said Rosen, of only three hundred 'poorly equipped and poorly armed' troops, and that was not the way to keep the Enniskilleners at bay. He ordered them back to guard the fords and sent Berwick to command them, which pleased Berwick 'as I did not like the whole business, nor did I like the new general'.[11]

Berwick left the camp on 21 June with the horsemen and set up a new base at Cavan Park, one of Lord Mountjoy's properties a few miles upriver beyond Castlefinn. In his first week there, he set out overnight and made for Donegal town, which he reached early in the morning. The rebel garrison fled into the castle, which Berwick had no means of besieging, and watched the town and all their provisions burn around them. Berwick then withdrew the same day back to Cavan Park with, he wrote 'fifteen hundred oxen, cows and sheep'.[12]

A few days later a company of Enniskilleners was caught in or near Lisnarick on the north side of Lower Lough Erne, some ten miles from Enniskillen. They were not attacked by the Irish army, but by irregulars, and it appears that the Enniskilleners ran out of ammunition when they most needed it. 'These rebels wanted no quarter and defended themselves as long as they had fire-power. Seven were killed and 45 were taken' and led off to Berwick's camp. Such was the state of Fermanagh: a county infested by bands of armed men intent on defending property or cattle, or intent on depriving the owners of either or both. The Irish irregulars, who would have been classed by their enemies as rapparees,[B] formed a substantial body of men, and saw themselves as having a licence to attack rebels, to give quarter and to take prisoners back to the Irish army.[13]

[A] He continued: 'Though the Scotch abroad be not inferior to them, yet at home they are as poor, as ignorant, more brutish and more nasty without any excuse for it, having never been oppressed or kept under as the others by a foreign yoke.'

[B] Until 1689, Irish bandits were known as tories. 'These were afterwards called rapparees', explained Mackenzie, 'a sort of Irish vultures that followed their armies to prey on the spoil'.

The shortage of food in the city worsened each day. Food had to be paid for. There was no community soup kitchen or hospital. Mackenzie wrote of the Presbyterian Sunday assemblies where collections were taken 'for the relief of the poor people, and the sick and wounded soldiers, who had otherwise perished for any care was taken of them'. If you had money, you could buy food privately. The only people to get rations from the garrison's stores were the soldiers, and distribution required careful and strict management. Each company was computed to be made up of sixty men, and the initial system had been to give to each captain or his representative an allowance for his company. Throughout the siege, Walker's distribution was based on there being 117 companies. This simple system allowed the storekeepers to deal only with the company commanders, who took the responsibility of distributing his company's allocation. But the companies were of varying sizes and, as we know, even a month into the siege Michelburne estimated that Baker's companies were no more than twenty-six men strong. It was not until 15 June, a whole month after the fight between Baker and Michelburne over the tobacco allowance, that the system of distribution was changed. The companies were no longer allowed an equal amount of food, and the rations were distributed with reference to how many men were there.

The continued dissatisfaction with Walker's administration of the provisions now boiled over into violence. Walker, wholly unconvincingly, explained this away as being the result of a mistaken rumour. In the second week of May, Captain Thomas Cole had come back into the city after being captured by the enemy following his wild dash to Redcastle to persuade Colonel Cunningham not to leave. Walker, having left much out of his *Account*, devoted a page to Captain Cole who, said Walker, had been taken before Richard Hamilton. Hamilton asked Cole what sort of a man Walker was 'and who he was most intimate with'. On Cole saying that he knew Walker well, 'the Lieutenant General asked, whether he would do Service for K. James, and carry some proposals he had orders to make to Mr. Walker?' Cole agreed, 'hoping by this means … to obtain his liberty', and so was given a pass to return to the city, but was 'so well pleased with his liberty that he forgot his business [and] only casually mentions it to some of the garrison'. Cole's story was then forgotten for the best part of a month, when Walker found himself mocked by people who had heard Cole's story, gathered from it that Hamilton wanted to make proposals directly to Walker, and 'saluted him [Walker] by some great names and titles'.

> Mr. Walker easily saw the danger of this, and finding it was occasioned by discourses of Mr. Cole, he ordered him immediately to be confined; and being examined, he unriddles the mystery, and gave all people satisfaction, so that they remained in no more doubt of their Governor.[14]

In case this made little sense, Walker also provided another version of the incident in order to show his cunning. 'The Governor', he wrote of himself, 'has several intimations given him by a friend in the enemy's camp, that he should look to himself, that some mischief was intended him'. As far as he allows us to know in his *Account*, his only friend in the enemy's camp was Cole. 'Soon after this, he understood some jealousy was entertained among the soldiers, that he had great quantity of provisions hid in his house.' So the crafty Walker, knowing that the enemy were behind this, got one of the soldiers to pretend that he also suspected that Walker was hoarding provisions, and so 'it was contrived that the house was privately searched, and their curiosity being satisfied, they return to the good opinion of their Governor'.

All of this was a fabrication by Walker. Mackenzie's version is very different. Infuriated as much as anything by Walker's repeated description of himself as 'the Governor', Mackenzie confirmed that Cole 'came into town again' after a month's imprisonment in the Irish camp, 'but Governor *Baker* being suspicious of his being an agent for the enemy, ordered him to be confined'. None of this had anything to do with Walker and Cole had not been released by the Irish to carry out a mission. Once Baker was satisfied that Cole 'had secretly made his escape from the enemy', Cole was released. That was the end of the matter.

However, according to Mackenzie, Walker's new crime was trying get £500 ransom for Colonel 'Wicked Will' Talbot, one of their mangled prisoners. By agreement, a surgeon from the Irish camp had been allowed to enter the city to treat Talbot. Talbot's wife offered to pay a ransom for his release. Talbot was dangerously ill, as was Baker (although no one knew just how ill) and an impromptu meeting about the proposed ransom was held in Baker's bed chamber. Baker thought the ransom a bad idea and turned it down. 'But Col. Walker urged it with some violence and threats against those that opposed it', wrote Mackenzie, and ordered that a bier should be made available to carry Talbot away.

When this got out, there was a riot. 'The rabble of our garrison took a vagary', wrote Captain Ash in his diary on 17 June. 'The multitude', says Mackenzie (he did not like the word 'rabble'), 'were so enraged, that Mr. Walker should take so much on him, that they took the bier and made a fire of it in the main guard'. They then stormed round the city looking for Walker, 'who had fled for sanctuary to Baker's chamber in the Bishop's House'. To prevent any ransoming, all those prisoners still able to walk were seized from their various lodgings, together with John Buchanan, the deputy mayor 'suspected for a papist', and marched off to the common gaol.

> They had searched Mr. Walker's own lodging, whence they took the beer, mum,[c] & butter which they found to the store; and being informed that Mr. Walker was in the Bishop's House, they pursued him, some threatening to shoot him, others to send him to the gaol.[15]

Henry Baker appeared from his sick bed to calm them down. He promised them there would be no ransoms, and 'for his sake to pass by what Mr. Walker had

[c] 'Mum' is malt beer.

done, and suffer the prisoners to go to their own lodgings again'. The 'multitude' agreed and melted away. Such is the pleasing image painted by Mackenzie. They obeyed the orders of the man they revered, despite him having at his shoulder the cowering figure of the man they detested. The unspeakable Walker, a man with unmentionable personal vices, had been entrusted with the stores and had built up his own stash of beer and butter. The goodly multitude correctly confiscated Walker's contraband and returned it to the public store for distribution among the deserving.

Mackenzie's description was as fanciful as anything written by Walker. Thomas Ash, not writing for a London publisher, and perhaps unaware of the party politics that so clouded Mackenzie's mind, wrote of the prisoners being bundled into the gaol. After that, he said, the rabble 'went and took meal and whatever they could get without respect of persons or property'. Whatever sparked the riot, it ended up, as riots often do, in widespread looting. Within a day Netterville, Aylmer, Newcomen and the others were released and sent back to their quarters. Wicked Will Talbot died of his wounds four days later. 'And', wrote Walker, 'we lost the benefit of our bargain'.

There was another riot four days later, this time for firewood. The market house, which housed the main guard, had been badly damaged by the shelling. Ash's entry for 18 June ends with this: 'That evening the market house fell, or rather was pulled down by the rabble, and the timber taken away.'

Baker had by then been struck down by 'the fever' and was confined to his bed. His condition deteriorated, and on 21 June, wrote Ash, 'a council of war was held at Col. Michelburne's to choose a governor in place of Gov. Baker, until he should recover of his sickness'. The council sent Colonel Lance and Lieutenant Colonel Fortescue to Baker's sick bed to ask who should stand in for him. 'He named Col. Michelburne, saying he was the fittest person to fill that station'. It was the obvious choice, but not everyone was so sure. What was manifestly clear was that a military commander was needed, and there was no one else who had anything approaching Michelburne's experience. 'The major part of the council consented, and Michelburne was confirmed governor', wrote Ash, 'which proves no malice has burned in Mr Baker's mind against Mr Michelburne, though there had formerly been a difference between them'.

We can accept that is what happened, but Walker and Mackenzie each put a different slant on the change in leadership. 'Col. *Michelburn* is chosen and appointed to assist Governor *Walker*', wrote Walker, 'that when one Commanded in Sallies the other might take care of the Town; and if one should fall the Town might not be left without a Government, and to the hazard of new Elections'. Walker's cheek is quite breathtaking even more than three hundred years after the event. Michelburne was chosen to assist Walker, so that when Walker was leading a sally, Michelburne could look after the town, and so that if Walker should fall in fighting the enemy, Michelburne's appointment as Walker's assistant would prevent the need for an election. That is what Walker wanted the London readership to understand. Mackenzie rather tersely wrote: 'Col. Michelburne was deputed by Baker governor during his sickness.' There was no consultation. It was just a temporary measure for the short duration while Baker was unwell.

22

Kirke

OUT ON THE LOUGH, on 19 June, starting at eight in the morning, Kirke presided over a council of war on the *Swallow* frigate. All the colonels and their lieutenant colonels were there, including William Steuart, the guards captain who had taken over Cunningham's regiment in May; his lieutenant colonel, Thomas St John, an old Tangier hand; Colonel Sir John Hanmer and his lieutenant colonel, William Wolseley, both career soldiers; four French Protestant lieutenant colonels, Isaac de la Melonière, Mainvilliers, de la Barte and de Louvigny; majors Henry Rowe, Zachary Tiffin and William Carville; Jacob Richards, the engineer; and the naval captains Wolfran Cornewall, John Leake, Thomas Gwillam, William Sanderson and Edward Boyce.[1] This was as good a gathering of military and naval minds as could be found anywhere in the British Isles.[A] The only question was whether they should attempt to force their way up the river. They unanimously decided not to.

> That it being manifest that there was a boom made over the river about Brook Hall ... people had reported the sinking of boats laden with stones ... and the town of Londonderry has not sent any message to us of their condition, which in the opinion of the council of was great assurance that they were neither pressed very much by the enemies or by want of victuals or provisions ... the council of war thought it more prudent and for their majesties' service not to run any imminent danger in going up the river, but to continue here in Lough Foyle till more forces join us from England or Scotland with which we might be able to force them by land to raise the siege, or that in the meantime our friends in Derry should have sent us a statement of their condition, which if desperate might make us take measures for their relief.[2]

What weighed on their minds more than anything else, was the fear that a ship would be taken in the narrows. The incident with the *Greyhound* showed that the Irish had the capacity to bring cannon down to the riverside, even as far as Culmore. Should anything go wrong, a ship could be caught on the shore whether

[A] These were loyal, able men, and some went on to great things: William Steuart ended his career as a lieutenant general; Sir John Hanmer and Isaac de la Melonière became major generals; William Wolseley was the following month to be the hero of Newtownbutler; Henry Rowe was promoted to colonel; Zachary Tiffin became a brigadier; and John Leake lived to be one of the greatest admirals of his generation.

through the shifting of the wind, by striking a mud bank, being damaged by gunfire or by striking the boom.

> The loss, though great to his majesty, would be of much more and of greater consequence in the leaving the enemy the possessors of so many great guns with our stores of war and victuals, which if they had they would certainly make a more formal attack upon the town of Londonderry, which to this time they have not attempted, we suppose for no other reason than for the want of artillery enough. Besides the miscarriage would so dishearten the town and encourage the enemy as to be of extreme consequence.[3]

Those were the collected thoughts 'maturely considered', said Richards, of the professionals. They could not risk giving the Irish the means to batter the walls by losing a ship's onboard cannons. Unless the city's plight forced some earlier action, they would wait for substantial reinforcements to allow a land attack. No one argued otherwise. They all signed the declaration and a copy was sent to London. And they waited.[4]

While Kirke and the fleet remained on the lough, they were being watched at all times. The Irish commanders made a point of showing great politeness to Kirke. In mid-June Richards wrote: 'some few troops of horse appeared on the hills. My Lord Dungan and Col. Carroll sent off several times to compliment the Major General and told among other things that he might command any refreshments that were ashore'.[B] These were refreshments for Kirke, not for his fleet generally, but in any event, wrote Richards, they did not have much to offer: no wine, brandy or beer. We do not know what gifts were sent by the Irish, other than that on 1 July, 'My lord Dungan sent the Major-General a very fine and large salmon'. The tedium of sitting on Lough Foyle had its effect on the ships' provisions. Kirke's stock of wine and brandy ran low, and he sent the *James of Derry* ketch to go to Greenock to find some.

The most surprising message from the shore came from Lord George Howard, who asked Kirke 'for a passport' to come on board. Lord George was the youngest brother of the late duke of Norfolk. A major in the Horse Guards just before the revolution, he had fled to France and then had accompanied King James to Ireland, where he commanded a troop of dragoons. He and 'another gentleman' came on board. They 'were very civilly received by the Major-General' and spent a most convivial evening on the ship. 'They commended much their entertainment, saying they had not such a meal's meat the Lord knows when.' We do not know what intelligence, if any, Lord George gleaned of Kirke's intentions during this meeting, but Richards recorded that 'they complained much of the French

[B] Lord Walter Dungan, then in his twenties, was the only son of the earl of Limerick and his Spanish wife. He died at the Boyne. Francis Carroll was the lieutenant colonel of Dungan's regiment of dragoons.

officers' insolencies, and were almost weary of being under their command'.[C] [5] Rosen, they said, commanded at Derry rather than Hamilton. After dinner, Lord George returned to the shore.[D]

We can now only imagine the dinner party thrown for Lord George that evening, with the raucous voices of Kirke and his guests carrying through the night across the still waters of the lough to the ears of the hundreds of seamen and soldiers in the ships anchored around them. When Samuel Pepys stayed in Tangier six years before, he was disgusted by Kirke's drinking, his fast and violent temper, his bawdy table talk, his boasts of his sexual conquests, his 'damns and curses', and his flagrant corruption.[6] Kirke, now an overweight 40-year-old 'of monstrous bulk',[7] had been in the army since his teens, and was, said Pepys, 'a very brute'. James Caldwell (of whom more below) wanted to know 'Whether Lord Howard and other public enemies' were feasted while 'the garrison of Londonderry starved and perished for want … Whether a general or army influenced or led by a person of such principles can be thought to be attended with blessings or success? … Whether professed atheism and debauchery are fit weapons to beat down popery?'[8]

There was anger and puzzlement at Kirke's delay in both Londonderry and in England. On 19 June, while Kirke's council of war was taking place, Londonderry was being debated in Westminster in the House of Commons. 'It has been some wonder to me', said the member for Chichester, 'that the relief of *Ireland* has been so slow'. The veteran member of parliament for Weobly in Herefordshire, John Birch, vented the country's frustration:

> 'Tis pity these brave Fellows in *Ireland* should be deserted; we are likely to lose those 10,000 brave men, to our shame all the World over. It is said there is a boom cross the River to *Londonderry*; a new fashioned thing! … I wonder, notwithstanding this boom, we land nowhere else. Let them waft over, and cut this boom in pieces … if you do not land men, never think to regain *Ireland*.[9]

Sir John Edgeworth, of Co. Longford, who was then in Lancashire, volunteered to do it himself:

> I propose that, if his Majesty will give me the command of the *worst* ship now at Liverpool, or in Major-General Kirke's fleet, I will, in six days from

[C] There are many references to the friction between the Irish and the French, as lampooned in the dramatic farce *The royal flight* (1690), which has Tyrconnell saying 'By St Patrick, y'are a proud Frenchman', and d'Avaux replying: 'By St Denis, y'are a beggarly Teague'. Walker has it that the Irish 'express'd great prejudice and hatred of the French, Cursing those Damn'd Fellows that walked in Trunks, (meaning their Jack-Boots) that had all Preferments in the Army that fell, and took the Bread out of their Mouths, and they believ'd wou'd have all the Kingdom to themselves at last.'

[D] Howard lasted in the Irish army for another year. He surrendered after the battle of the Boyne, was allowed back to England in 1691 and was pardoned in 1692.

> the date of my orders, wind and weather serving, find my way into Derry or perish. If the King will grant me this post of honour, I will take it for the greatest favour he could confer.[10]

The decision not to force a passage up the river left Kirke with other problems. As well as the sailors, he had on board three regiments who needed to be put down safely on dry ground. He decided to investigate the Isle of Inch,[E] which, although only about eight miles overland from Culmore, by sea is over seventy around Malin Head. Within a day of the council of war, he sent the *Bonadventure, Greyhound* and *Kingfisher* back to sea to go into Lough Swilly to inspect Inch. If it proved suitable, he could occupy the island and use it as a foothold. The three ships weighed anchor on 22 June and got there two days later.

Inch was ideal. It is about five square miles in size, is protected from the open sea by its position well into Lough Swilly, and it had a population of several hundred Protestants. Although a proper island, close enough to the shore to be joined in the nineteenth century by two causeways, it was fordable at low tide, and the ford was narrow enough to be defended. On the far side of Lough Swilly, across the main channel, was the only village of any size, Rathmullan.

Once the ships came into Swilly, people rowed out to welcome them. Captain Hopson on the *Bonadventure* was told by people from Inch that 'one of the enemy's quartermasters was there, gathering up provisions for all the Irish army, this being a very fertile isle and abounding in all sorts of grain'. A lieutenant was sent ashore and succeeded in capturing the quartermaster, taking all his papers and £5 in cash, but let him go. It was clear from the seized papers that the Irish camp and their horses were 'near starved', and that they depended on supplies from Inch. 'By which it is evident', wrote Richards, 'that if we can keep them out of this island, it will be of great consequence', and 'several hundreds of Protestants will fly to us and take up arms'.

Kirke's provision ships and the *Swallow* lay off Culmore, where they could keep a close check on the enemy without inviting cannon fire from the fort. There was little to be learnt through their telescopes, although Richards spotted that the Irish were attempting a timber construction on the Otter Bank, which at low tide becomes a mud island halfway between Culmore Fort and the boom. The lack of news from the city was not only thoroughly frustrating to Kirke, it prevented him from making any decisions. He needed to know whether he should risk everything in an urgent attempt to break in, whether it would be safe to approach nearer, whether he should land troops on the far bank or whether he should prepare the ground by drawing off the Irish forces by making a landing elsewhere. He needed to know how long the city could hold out without him.

[E] So called because the Irish word for an island is *inis* ('inish'). An early cartographer must have asked an Irishman what that piece of land was called, and wrote down a phonetic approximation of the answer.

In the absence of any messages from the city, Kirke determined to find out what the situation was by sending his own messenger. On one of the provision ships from Glasgow was a local man, James Cromie. He knew that the safest way to the city would be on the east bank of the Foyle where there were fewer Irish troops, and they were mostly concerned with guarding the battery in Strong's Orchard. At night, he could take a great circuitous route around the artillery camp and get to the river through the woods just above the ferry. The problem was that Cromie could not swim and his plan involved getting a man to go with him, slip into the water and swim the short distance to the city to get a boat. Kirke called for a volunteer to go with Cromie and swim the river. James Roche, a 39-year-old Irish seaman, stepped forward.

At ten at night on 25 June, Cromie and Roche were rowed ashore in the *Swallow*'s longboat to the fish house on the opposite bank from Culmore Fort and disappeared into the darkness. They made their way through the night for perhaps ten miles or more to give the Irish sentries and camps on the riverbank a wide berth. In the early hours of the morning, before daybreak, they reached Tamneymore Woods. Cromie hid with Roche's clothes and Roche waded into the river and swam across, emerging from the river below the ferry. 'He told us', Ash noted, 'that there were thirty ships below Culmore and they expected the remainder very soon'. To let the fleet know that he had arrived, Roche asked that the city give the prearranged signal, which was the discharge of four guns on the steeple at noon.

Michelburne took a very dim view of Roche. The plan had been for him to swim across the river, alert the governor, and have a boat row across to pick up Cromie. Roche, wet and cold, instead insisted on a fire, and so was taken to 'the *Sun-Tavern* in *Ship-Key-Street*'. When he was eventually brought to Michelburne, he said he knew nothing because Cromie 'has all the business'. Michelburne exploded: 'Why did you not hold your tongue, and not tell from whence you came till you came to me? And now the poor gentleman [Cromie] will be hang'd by your countrymen for your coming to warm you by the fire.' 'What shall I do with this ignorant fellow?' asked one of the officers. 'This fellow', roared Michelburne, 'has spoiled all. I admire that in the whole fleet none but an Irishman should be picked out'.[11]

James Roche was a man wholly incapable of telling the truth. Years later (long after the deaths of Percy Kirke and King William) he wrote dramatic descriptions of his mission to the city. His version of events is that Kirke, 'considering it was a dangerous enterprise, offered a reward of 3,000 guineas to any person that could carry his orders into the city'. But no one volunteered. At last, and after some time, Roche put his hand up. He did so 'out of zeal he had for the late King (of glorious memory), and for the Protestant Religion, and interest in Ireland'. The reward offered by Kirke (according to Roche and Roche alone) was the equivalent of a sum that now would be counted in millions. It was a fantastic amount. The rest of Roche's account was also fantastic. 'He passed through the enemy's camps and guards, which extended eight miles; and when he was got beyond them, he swam down the lough for three miles.'

The important thing was that the city now had news of 'the Ships, Men, Provision and Arms in them for our relief', wrote Walker, and 'the great concern of the Major General for us, and his care and desire to get with his Ships up to the Town'. This good news was spread around the city. What they then needed was for Roche to complete the second and more important part of his mission by reporting back to Kirke. The governors needed to make sure that Kirke knew how desperate they were. Walker wrote a letter for Roche to take back with him that evening, as the longboat would be returning to pick him up with Cromie by the fish house.

At sunset, Roche, naked, he said, except for a letter that was 'tied in a bladder in his hair', slipped into the water again to swim across the river to meet Cromie. In his account of his return journey, he reverted to fiction. He had to swim three miles back to where he had left his clothes, but got there to find they had been stolen. He then had to flee naked cross country for three miles, he was spotted by the enemy, escaped by streaking through a wood where the horse could not catch him, was badly torn by brambles, got to the lough, was attacked by Irish dragoons, had his jaw broken by a halberd, but made it into the water and as he swam off was wounded in his arm, breast and shoulder by musket shots. 'After all these difficulties, by God's providence, he got back to London-Derry'.[12]

Or, to put it another way, as Ash did, 'At night Roche attempted to go back and swim over the lough, but seeing the enemy on the shore opposite to him, he desisted, and returned to us, where he yet continues.'[F] During the day, Cromie had been captured and Roche had no intention, even if he thought himself able to do so, of trying to get back without a guide. No one in the city, it seems, volunteered to show Roche the way. 'This extremely troubled us', wrote Mackenzie, 'that no messenger could get down to give the Major-General an account of our distressed condition'.[13]

That same night, Wednesday, 26 June, having seen Roche's signal from the steeple, the fleet knew that at least one of the messengers had got through, and so made preparations to pick them up at the place they had been put ashore. Richards wrote of what happened in the dark by the edge of the lough.

> The boat being come within pistol shot of the shore, laid still upon their oars, and in a small space of time somebody hailed the boat ashore. The lieutenant in the boat asked the word, and they or he said he had forgot it. Then the lieutenant asked the name of the ship, which he also said he had forgot, and desired the boat would come nigher in; but being asked where the other man was, he said he had not seen him since he went into Derry. The lieutenant told him if he would wade off, they would take him in, otherwise not, at which the man that spoke retired, and immediately several muskets were discharged upon the boat, but did hurt nobody. Upon this the

[F] Ash always used the word 'lough' when referring to the river.

> boat returned on board and gave us this account. By which I judge either one or both of the men are taken in their return to us.[14]

Roche's written accounts of his adventure are all of a solitary mission that no other man would dare attempt, but before Roche could make up a better story, Ash recorded what he said at the time: 'Mr James Cromie came with him from the fleet to show him the way.' Cromie was picked up by the Irish and held in the camp in Strong's Orchard.

23

Trenches

HAMILTON KNEW THAT THE city was in a desperate state. The time was approaching, he thought, when the rebels would be begging for terms, and he wanted them to know that notwithstanding the horrors of the past few weeks, he was willing to offer the same conditions. On 26 June, he sent a trumpeter, and a parley was arranged by the gallows. Colonel Gordon O'Neill appeared for Hamilton, and Colonel Thomas Lance and Lieutenant Colonel William Campbell were sent to talk to him. If the town surrendered, everyone could go home or even abroad if they wished, and would be compensated for any damage to their properties. Lance and Campbell took the proposals away and agreed to let O'Neill know the answer that evening.

On that same day, a brave man named MacGimpsy presented himself to Adam Murray and offered to swim down to the fleet. Promising him a reward, Murray informed Michelburne, who told Walker, and consequently MacGimpsy ended up carrying three letters. The shortest letter was written by Walker alone. He told Kirke that Hamilton's latest proclamation had been received by the garrison that very day. 'If we would surrender the town … we should have a free pardon' and liberty to leave and reprisals of goods. Although they had 'absolutely refused' the conditions, unless they got 'a speedy supply, and that in a few days, not exceeding six, we must, we fear, accept terms worse that now is offered'.[1]

The second, longer letter, was signed by both Walker and, from his sick bed, Baker, as well as Michelburne, Chichester Fortescue, James Morrison, James Strong and Edward Davys. It a plea from what might be termed the conformist establishment in the city. It set out, at some length, an account of all that they had achieved against the besieging army, the names of the important captives they had taken, and their desperate need for supplies. 'Our poor soldiers having lived upon horse flesh for the most part of the last week' and they now only had food left for eight or ten days. 'Take pity on our condition, and please to send us up a small vessel or two laden with provisions of any kind, of which let a good part be biscuit, cheese and butter, for we have no firing [firewood or coal] left to dress meat.' Importantly, they also said that 'there is but one small field piece and a few little drunken dicks[A] at Culmore, for all the rest of the guns were removed hither, the ships may come up to our quay (we hope) without any hazard … we understand that the boom is certainly broke so that you may come up with ease'.

The third, and the most telling, letter was written by those who saw themselves as representatives of the Presbyterian soldiery, and was signed by Adam Murray,

[A] The term 'drunken dicks' referred to the gunners rather than their equipment.

John Cairnes and James Gledstanes.[2] MacGimpsy was *their* man, and they needed him to take their message. 'We beseech and obtest you honoured sir, in the bowels of our Lord Jesus Christ, that ye fail not to hasten to our relief.' They were weakened by famine. 'Our men have eaten horse flesh this while past', and were further dispirited 'through some treacherous men daily running to the enemy with their arms, and others treating and tampering with them [the enemy] clandestinely, and these none of the meanest station here … We know not what sad effects their so doing may have on the poor honest man that desires to defend this place and oppose popery with the hazard of all that is dear to them in this world.' The gentry, the officers and the governors were not to be trusted.

At ten at night, MacGimpsy made his way out of the city to the Shipquay and slipped into the river. The letters were 'close tied in a little bladder in which were put two musket balls, that if the enemy should take him, he might break the little string wherewith it was tied about his neck and so let it sink in the water'.[3] All the letters were dated 26 June, and the letter from the governors included instructions to Kirke to 'hang up your flag on the maintop and fire some guns at the hour of eleven in the morning which may be a signal of his [MacGimpsy's] arrival with you'.

There was no such signal. 'We have fished this morning a drowned man, who floated on the river with bladders about his arms', wrote Rosen the following day. 'When he was taken up, we discovered, that he had come out of Derry to swim to the fleet. We found, in another bladder fastened to his neck, the three letters enclosed.'[4] No one in the city knew how poor MacGimpsy had met his end, but it was feared that he 'was killed by running himself against the boom … Within a day or two, they hung up a man on a gallows in the view of the city on the other side the water, and called over to us to acquaint us it was our messenger.'[5]

Later that day, 27 June, O'Neill was back for another parley with Colonels Lance and Campbell. O'Neill presented a set of written proposals from Hamilton, based in part on the conversation they had had the day before. It set out in fuller terms the proposed heads of an agreement

> All such as have a desire to live in Town, shall have Protection, and free Liberty of Goods and Religion … [and those who] have a mind to return to their Homes, shall have a necessary Guard with them to their respective Habitations, and Victuals to supply them; where they shall be restored to all they possessed formerly, not only by the Sheriffs and Justices of the Peace, but also by Governors and Officers of the Army, who from time to time will do them right, and give them Reprisals of Cattle from such as have taken them to the Mountains.[6]

It was an extraordinary document not just because it offered so much but because, following the previous day's talks, Hamilton felt obliged to insert the words 'That General Rosen has no power from the king to intermeddle with what the

Lieutenant General does with the siege … All conditions and parleys are left to the said Lieutenant General Hamilton.' The defenders could perhaps deal with a gentleman like Hamilton, but not with the French. Lance and Campbell agreed to take the proposals back to the city, but their answer 'it seems, was not agreeable', wrote Ash, 'for that night ten bombs flew into the city. One fell on Joseph Gallagher's house in Bishop's Street, where two barrels of powder were lodged. There were fourteen killed by it, viz: six grenadiers belonging to our regiment, four horsemen and four women. Another fell upon the lanthorn in my quarters, knocked down the dormant, then fell into the street; it did not other harm, thank God!'[B] [7]

In his *Account*, Walker claimed that he had replied with distain to Hamilton's terms in this way:

> Our Answer to the Lieutenant General was, that we much wondered he should expect we could place any confidence in him, that had so unworthily broke Faith with our King; That he was once generously trusted, though an Enemy, yet betrayed his Trust, and we could not believe that he had learned more sincerity in an Irish Camp.[C]

This was fictional bravado reserved for the London readership. Walker sent no such message. We know that because the Irish were still waiting for an answer a fortnight later. Nor in any correspondence with Hamilton did Walker use the term 'our King' to mean William rather than James. The city was now in deep trouble. Kirke showed no sign of taking action and there was no way of getting a message to him. People were starving, disease was rife, and women and children were dropping dead in scores each day. It was not the time to start cheeking the enemy when fortune may deliver you into their hands any day soon.

After Cromie had been captured on 26 June, he was handed over to Sir Edward Vaudrey 'to frighten and interrogate him strictly'. Vaudrey was then a 35-year-old Englishman who had been plucked from the army to be the duke of Berwick's tutor. He had taken the then 15-year-old Berwick to witness his first campaign at the siege of Buda, after which Vaudrey was knighted and made the lieutenant colonel of a cavalry regiment. He was surprised to find that Cromie could speak French fluently, was of a good family and had estates in Ireland worth five hundred guineas a year. All that Vaudrey got out of him was a pack of lies.

Cromie told Vaudrey that he had recently joined the fleet from Scotland and so was able to give an account of what was going on there, and that Kirke had two

[B] A lanthorn (lantern) is a structure on the roof to let in light; a dormant (dormer), a window standing proud of the sloping roof.

[C] Which translates as: 'Since Hamilton breached King William's trust when he was released to treat with Tyrconnell, we are surprised that Hamilton expects us to trust him now, as we do not suppose that he could have become any more trustworthy after living with Irishmen.'

regiments on board, as well as great quantities of arms, ammunition and provisions. That was the background, his cover story, and was at least broadly correct, but Cromie then changed tack. Kirke, he said, was only holding back for the arrival of a further two thousand men commanded by Count Charles Schomberg. This new expedition would be the biggest yet and included two regiments of cavalry. Look out for the *Henrietta* yacht, Cromie said. It sailed from Lough Foyle eight days ago to meet the English fleet, 'so that return of the yacht to the lake will be a sure sign of the arrival of the fleet'.

It was all false. Charles de Schomberg was in Germany with the emperor's troops, sieging Kaiserwerth outside Dusseldorf.[8] There was no plan to send him to Ireland. There was no discrete Londonderry relief force, and nor was Kirke expecting one. Kirke was expecting, as was everyone on both sides, the arrival in Ireland of a great army led by Charles Schomberg's father, the duke of Schomberg, not a paltry two thousand men set aside to help relieve Derry. But it all sounded so plausible, and everything Cromie said was believed. A few days later, Rosen wrote to King James:

> Kirke is still at his same post while waiting for the three cavalry and two infantry regiments which are to join him under the orders of Count Charles de Schomberg. There is no doubt that this wait has prevented him from attempting to get supplies into Londonderry, which it would be easy for him to accomplish just by risking a few ships.[9]

There was now great need for speed. The senior officers in the Irish camp mulled over what they should do next. The only idea that presented itself was to cajole or threaten Cromie into delivering a different message. In simple terms, he was 'to give the besieged a discouraging account' of what supplies were on the lough and what Kirke was planning, and not to mention anything about Count Schomberg being on the high seas. As Roche had already got into the city, this proposed play-acting had little prospect of success, but there was nothing to lose.

On 28 June, a white flag was hung out for a fresh parley, this time on the other side of the river. A boat was sent for two officers from the garrison. Two of the lieutenant colonels, Chichester Fortescue and Thomas Blair, were chosen. They were met by Sir Neil O'Neill and Lord Louth,[10] who had with them the prisoner Cromie. So as to give the impression that the Irish had not had time for him to make anything up, Cromie said that he had lain in the woods until Thursday, and then gave his revised report on the pitiful state of the fleet. Blair asked him how it was that his version was so different from the uplifting account given by James Roche. 'He replied, he was in the enemy's camp, Roche within the walls of Derry.' He did not need to wink.

Cromie was removed. Blair and Fortescue asked that they be allowed to take Cromie with them. It was not an unreasonable request, since they already had Roche, but both sides knew Roche was no more than the courier's guide. The Irish

1 George Walker, governor of Londonderry and author of *A true account of the siege*, engraved by Peter Vanderbank from the now-lost portrait by Sir Godfrey Kneller commissioned by King William in 1689. (National Portrait Gallery)

2 Eastwood Cook's model of Londonderry in the first half of the eighteenth century, largely unchanged sinc before the siege, but with the rebuilt market house. (Derry Guildhall Museum)

3 The Royal Bastion, Double Bastion, Bishop's Gate and Church Bastion. (Photographs by Tony Boyle, Derry Guildhall Museum)

4 Londonderry in 1685, by the military surveyor Thomas Phillips. (British Library)

5 Contemporary map of the Foyle showing **a**, the city to the Otter Bank (with the boom stretching from Charles Fort); and **b**, from Otter Bank to Culmore and the lough. (British Library)

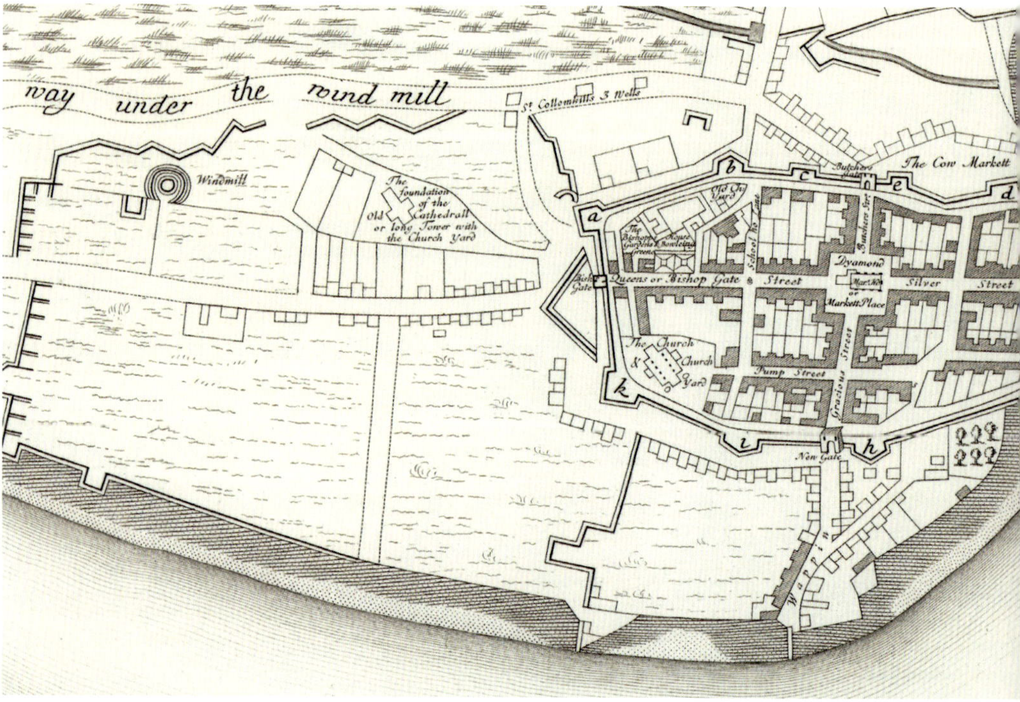

6 Francis Nevill's map (as engraved for the Ordnance Survey Office, 1837) showing the defences on Windmill Hill. The Double Bastion is marked at **a**, the Royal Bastion at **b**, and the Half Bastion at **c**.

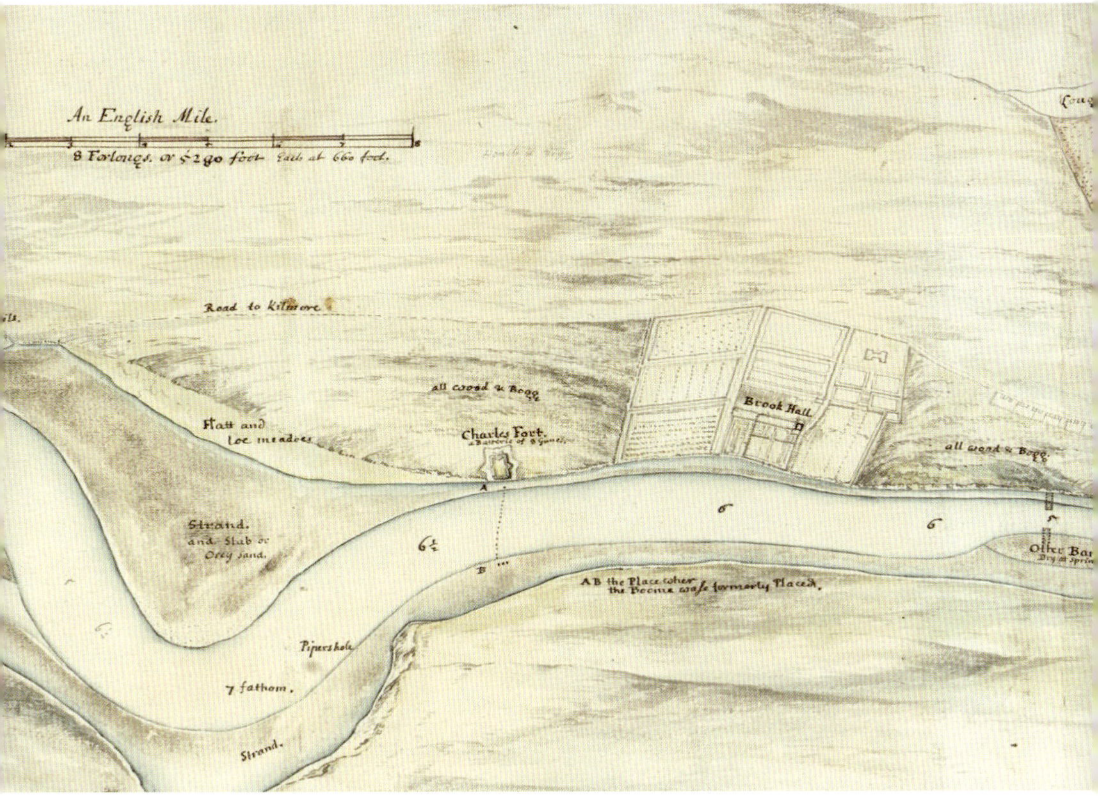
An English Mile.
8 Forlongs, or 5280 foot Each at 660 foot.
Road to Kilmore
all wood & Bogg
Flatt and
Lee meadoes
Charles Fort.
Brook Hall
all wood & Bogg
Strand.
and Slub or
Ozey sand.
6½
6
6
B
AB the Place where
the Boome was formerly Placed.
Pipershole
7 fathom.
Strand.

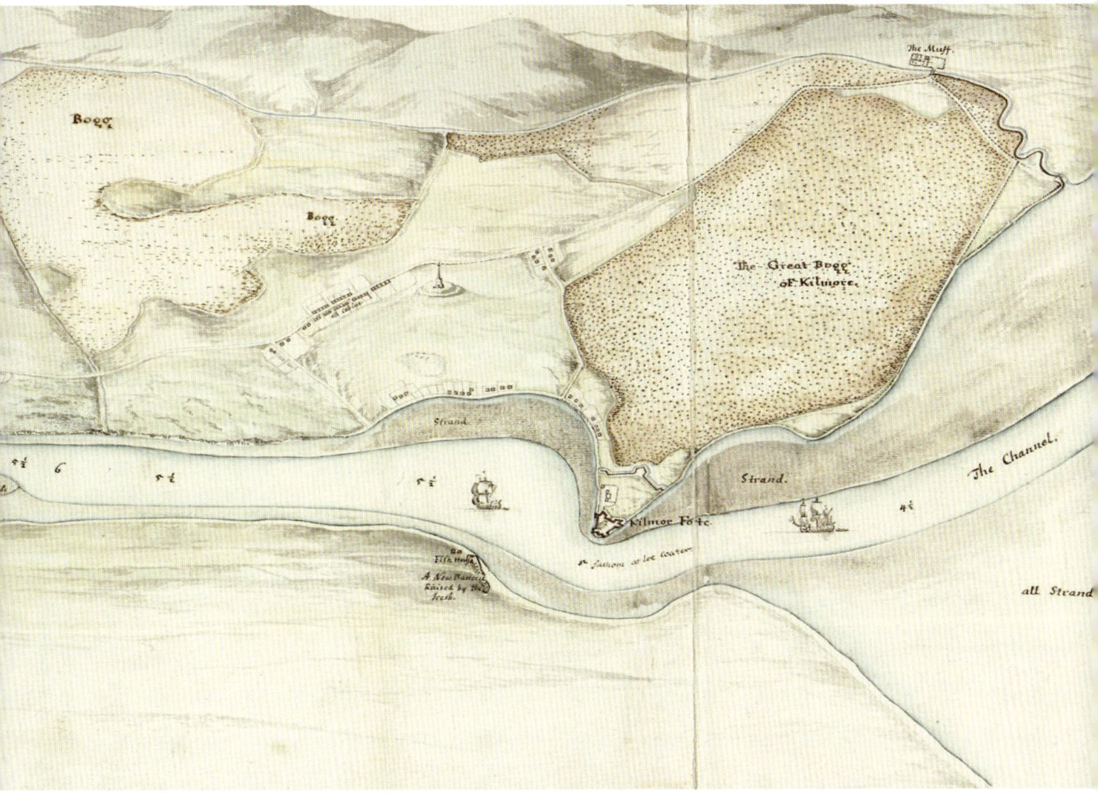
Bogg
Bogg
The Muff.
The Great Bogg
of Kilmore.
Strand
Strand.
The Channel.
6
Kilmor Forte
all Strand

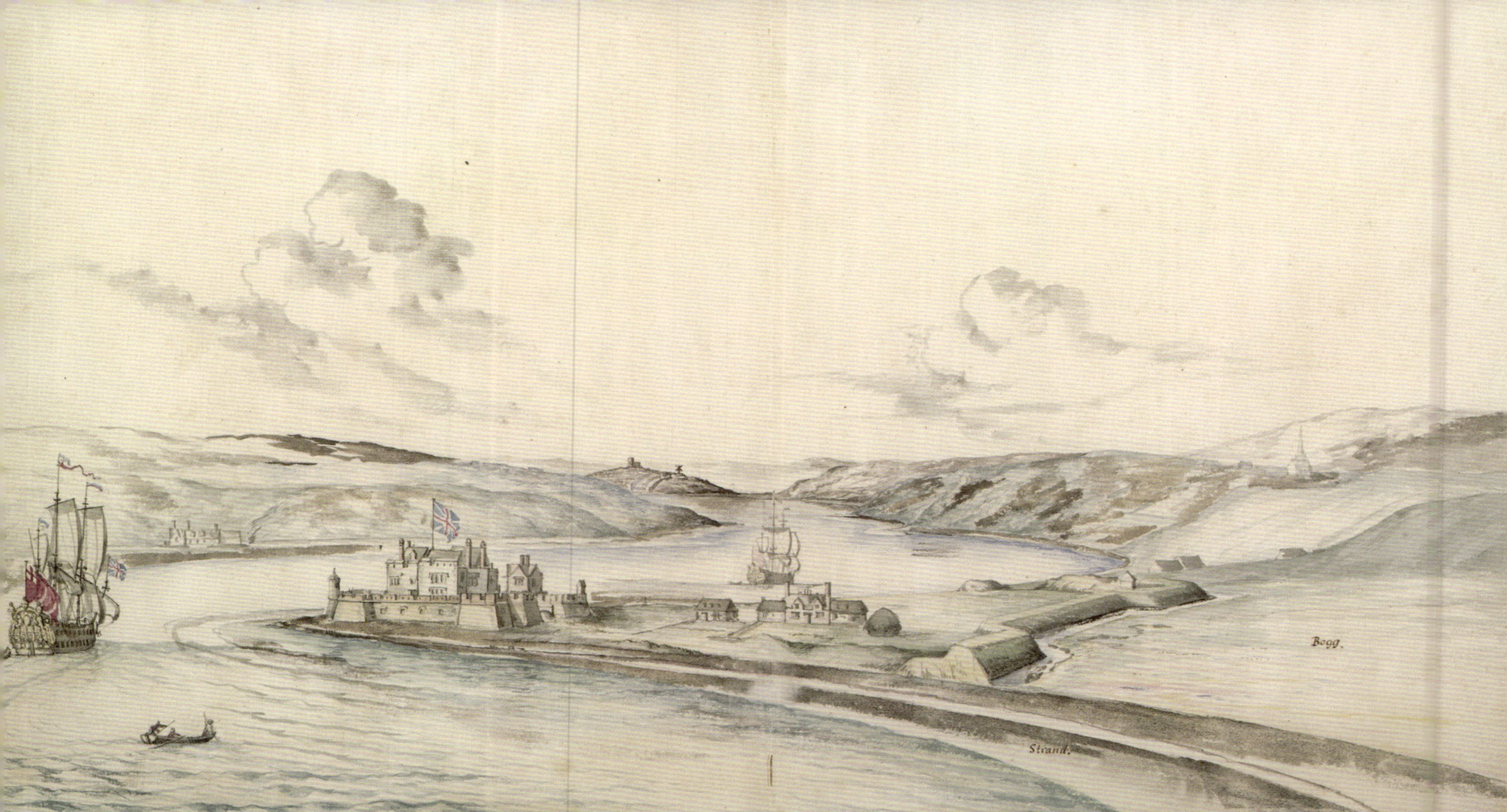

7 Thomas Phillips' watercolour of Culmore Fort (to which a union flag has been added) before its destruction 1689, with Londonderry in the background. (British Library)

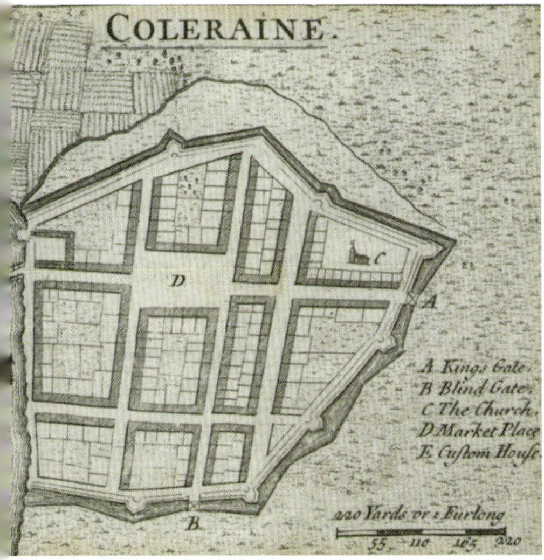

ontemporary plan of Coleraine. (British Library)

9 The ruins of Pennyburn Mill from S. C. Hall, *Ireland, its scenery* (1841). The mill was dismantled in 1860.

10 The windmill today, in the grounds of Lumen Christi College.

11 Sir William Stewart, Lord Mountjoy.
(National Trust)

12 David Cairnes, from H.C. Lawlor, *History of the family of Cairnes* (1906)

13 John Michelburne, the military governor, from the portrait he commissioned for his dramatic account of the siege, *Ireland preserv'd* (1705).

14 Major General (later Lieutenant General) Percy Kirke. (Courtesy of the Trustees of the PWRR and Queen's Regiment Museum)

15 John Leake, captain of the *Dartmouth* frigate. (Alamy)

16 Jean-Bernard-Louis de Saint-Jean, baron de Pointis, the architect of the boom. (Alamy)

17 King James II. (Alamy)

18 Marshal Conrad de Rosen. (Alamy)

19 James FitzJames, duke of Berwick. (Alamy)

20 The walls today from the Double Bastion (*right*) to the Royal Bastion (*left*), on which stand the remains of Walker's monument.

21 The view up the slope from St Colmcille's Wells to the Royal Bastion.

22 Two of the city's surviving demi-culverin cannons on the Double Bastion.

23 French gun emplacement at Londonderry, by Romeyn de Hooghe, 1689. (Rijksmuseum, Amsterdam)

24 Mortars in action, by Romeyn de Hooghe, 1689. (Rijksmuseum, Amsterdam)

25 Infantrymen firing by rank at Londonderry, by Romeyn de Hooghe (1689). (Rijksmuseum, Amsterdam)

26 A view from the Long Causey over the Swilly Burn, across what was once bog but is now land criss-crossed with ditches and dykes, to Lundie's rendezvous on Binnion Hill.

27 The Isle of Inch from Greenan Mountain, now joined to the mainland by two causeways. The old ford crosses at the narrowest point in the bottom right side of the photograph.

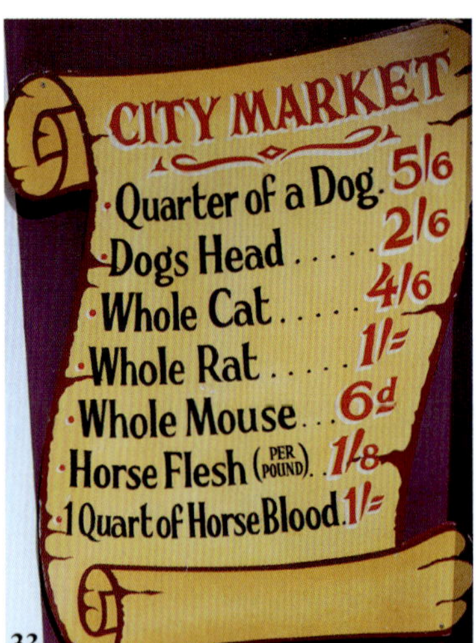

28 Walker in clergyman's bands and armour (see note on p. 242) (National Portrait Gallery); **29** Roche the swimmer (*Look & Learn*, 1968); **30** Lundy the Traitor, condemned to his annual burning (Tower Museum, Derry); **31** a uniformed David Cairnes defending the city (Tower Museum); **32** Walker's price list (Siege Museum, Derry); and **33** James Gordon, forever saint-like, over the nineteenth-century Ferrykey Gate.

were asked if Cromie could be exchanged for any one of the prisoners held in the city. This got a simple refusal from Louth and O'Neill, the meeting came to an end and Fortescue and Blair were rowed back.

This parley across the water also generated one of Walker's flights of whimsy.

> When they hung out a White Flag to invite us to a Treaty, Mr. Walker ventured out to come within hearing of my Lord Louth and Colonel O'Neill, and in his passage had an hundred Shot fired at him; he got the shelter of a House, and upbraiding them with this Treachery, bid them order their Men to be quiet or he would order all the Guns on the Walls to fire at them; They denied they knew anything of it: And this was all the satisfaction to be expected from persons of such a Principle.

This may have sounded quite plausible when it was written in London later in the year. Mackenzie answered with sarcasm.

> I have heard some incredulous people say that the smoke of the 100 shot was as invisible as the flying of bullets; and they could not imagine whereabouts the house stood (all without the gates, next the Irish camp, being pulled down) that so happily yielded the doctor a safe shelter till he could call to the men on the walls to fire the guns at theses treacherous villains.[11]

Ash recorded no shooting, other than:

> That day and night, twenty bombs were sent to us, which killed one man, two women and a child, and afterwards Alex Poke's wife, her mother and brother.

During the negotiations, the usual day-to-day business of the siege continued. Trenches were dug and widened for troop movement. In the days after Rosen joined the camp, Ash noted overnight on the 19–20 June, the Irish dug 'a strong ditch above the meadows against the windmill in order to prevent our men from relieving their guards in that line next the meadows, and made two other trenches next where the tiled house stood over the bog. They are come close to our skirts now, so that none without great hazard dare go to Columb-Kill's well for water.' A day later, he noted 'the mortars were removed to this side the water over the bog … two of our men were killed near the line next the meadows, from their new trench they made opposite the windmill. Our people are frequently killed going to or coming from Columb-Kill's well.' On the following day, 'our neighbours were running a ditch through Col. Campsie's orchard, towards the sea. Many shots were fired at them from the wall.' A new trench was opened facing Butcher's Gate, the purpose, wrote Rosen, was 'as much to demonstrate to those in the town and in the fleet our resolve and firmness in this matter, so as to approach the place and take it in the accepted manner, if our enemy gives us the time, which is unlikely to happen'.[12]

The conditions for trench digging were appalling. The rain did not stop, and everything had to be done by workmen under fire. On the 28 June, the work came to a halt because the tide had flooded the trenches and repeated efforts to drain the water away by digging ditches were not working, and there was not enough equipment to go round. At the same time, on the drier ground above them, the rebels were also digging an entrenchment to 'counter-line' them, and throwing up a breastwork using old casks filled with earth.[13]

> The Enemy work every Night to bring their Trenches near the Walls for Mining. Our Men were diligent to counter-line them, being incited to it every Night by Governour *Mitchelburn* ... Hereby the Enemy were kept from getting to the near side of the Bogg, without which they could Draw no Mines: There was besides a *Blind* rais'd by the Persons forementioned before the *Butchers-gate,* to defend it from the Enemies battering Guns, which had already done some hurt to it.[14]

Butcher's Gate was the only gate in the city that the Irish could fire at. They needed to remove that 'blind' made of posts, timbers and earth filled casks to allow the cannon a clear shot. The task of removal was given to a company of grenadiers from the newly arrived Clancarty's regiment. As they were new men who had not been on active service before, they would be led by French officers.

The 28 June was a dark, miserable, wet night and the grenadiers filed into the forward trenches to await the signal. At or shortly before midnight, they began their advance, got as close as they could to the rebel entrenchments, and then rushed them. The defenders on the outworks ran off to find shelter behind the ravelin outside the Bishop's Gate. Once the Irish had been seen, after that initial shock of them sprinting out of the night, nothing else could be done by surprise. The sentries, safe high up on the walls, opened fire. The alarm was sounded. The defenders rushed to their posts to shoot or hurl rocks at the Irish below them. The Irish began tearing down the blind by smashing the casks and ripping up the timbers and posts from the wet mud. The Irish cannon and mortars started firing. All along the walls and the entrenchments on the Windmill, the defenders started firing into the night to beat off an imagined general assault. Those in the raiding party not directly involved in destroying the blind carried out a rather one-sided duel with the men above them on the ramparts. Some of them, to take shelter while they reloaded, ran under the walls where the defenders could not get at them without exposing themselves to those firing back.

It is uncertain how long this went on for but, once it was clear that there was no general attack, orders were issued, perhaps by Baker himself, for a counter-attack. A large party, led by three captains, came storming out of the ravelin. 'The drums beat alarum and we got a party together and sallied out at another gate', wrote Captain Holmes, 'fell upon them and put them to the rout and recovered our own ground again, [we] came so near them that we might have taken them alive, but we gave them old quarter'. The Irish raiders ran back into the night, now lit by explosions and gunfire, into view of the gunners on the bastions who fired at them with case shot ('that's musquett bulletts', explained Holmes). 'I never heard so many shots in so short a time', said Ash. Out on the lough, the fleet could see and hear 'Great volleys of small shot from Derry and on Windmill Hill'.[15]

The new defences were too well constructed to be destroyed in the short time the grenadiers had, but it was by any standard a very bold action. Mackenzie thought otherwise: the Irish 'were forced to quit our Works, and run to their own Lines, to their great dishonour as well as loss'. According to Ash, twenty-five or thirty Irish soldiers were killed. Mackenzie reported the higher of those figures. Both say that three captains were killed, and Mackenzie adds a French lieutenant colonel and says that a Captain MacCarthy was captured. These figures were probably not far out. The French reported (and it was their operation) that 'two officers were killed, one of whom was French called Paget, as were about fifteen soldiers. Thirty officers and soldiers were wounded.'[16]

The French were impressed with the daring way in which the raid had been conducted. The marquis d'Anglure, a former guards officer who had come to Ireland as a volunteer, was especially commended by Fumeron. D'Anglure 'commanded at the head of this detachment and led it right up to the city gates, accompanied by several French officers here, who expose themselves greatly and at every opportunity are always the first so as to set a good example to the Irish officers who in this respect do not in any way do their duty'. D'Anglure was wounded in the arm, but so impressed Rosen that he made him a brigadier. Rosen also singled out the grenadier captain the sieur de Penhouët, who 'achieved marvels during the last attack, having marched at the head of a detachment of grenadiers in order to destroy an entrenchment made by the enemy, and advanced to the very gates of Derry, sword in hand'.[17]

When Walker came to write this up several months later, the bare facts of the raid on the outworks appeared rather tame after all his descriptions of great victories. In his *Account*, he elevated it into something far more important. The Irish were not concerned with knocking down the blind outside the walls, they were trying to undermine the walls themselves. We know this false rumour had spread around the city because Ash heard that the Irish intended to spring a mine. In case any London readers were puzzling over how this could be done, Walker went one further and invented a cellar under the wall which the Irish miners had broken into. From there, he knew he need not spell it out, they could blow up the entire wall and capture the city. As if that were not enough to catch the reader's imagination, the Irish were led not by an anonymous officer, let alone a French one, but by Lord Clancarty. He wrote:

> My Lord Clancarty at the Head of a Regiment, and with some Detachments, possesses himself of our Line, and enters some Miners in a low Cellar under the half Bastion. Capt. Noble, Capt. Dunbar and several other Gentlemen sally by Order at the Bishops-Gate, and creep along the Wall till they came very near the Enemies Guards; our Men receive their Firing quietly, till they got to a right distance, and then thundered upon them. Our Case-Shot from the Bastion and small Shot off the Walls second the Salliers Firing so effectually, that his Lordship was forced to quit his Post, and hasten to the main Body of the Enemy, and to leave his Miners and an hundred of his best Men dead upon the place; besides, several Officers and Soldiers were wounded and died of their Wounds some days after this Action, as we were informed. We were often told, that some great thing was to be performed by this Lord; and they had a Prophecy among them, That a Clancarty should knock at the Gates of Derry; the credulity and superstition of his Country, with the vanity of so brave an Attempt, and some good Liquor, easily warmed him to this bold Undertaking; But we see how little value is to be put on Irish Prophesies, or Courage so supported.[18]

Walker's embellishments of miners and the cellar and Clancarty were all untrue. There was no cellar and at no time did the Irish have the means to undermine anything. Nor were any explosives or mining apparatus recovered. Londonderry's defences were not a medieval construction. The walls had not been weathered and rebuilt over centuries. There were no buildings erected against the walls under which any cellars had been excavated. At the beginning of the century, the Corporation of London had approved the plans of a new town laid out in a grid pattern, with a central square and marketplace. The houses were built inside the wall, but at no point were the houses or their gardens or yards against the wall. The wall was fronted by a ditch, and at its back was an open lane so that everywhere on the wall could be reached at a time of emergency by reinforcements. Nowhere could there have been 'a low cellar' under the wall, let alone under a bastion. And there was nowhere that anyone could have dug a mine under the wall without being seen by the troops on the bastions and the walls. No one else can or has suggested otherwise and, yet like so many of Walker's preposterous inventions, this mining fantasy has over the centuries gone unchallenged. The worst rebuke it met with is Mackenzie passing it by in embarrassment.

To correct Walker's version of events, Mackenzie simply wrote that the enemy 'attacked our out-works at the Butcher's Gate', but in his last pamphlet, he was emphatic: 'Neither they nor we ever drew a mine.'[19] Nor did he repeat Walker's estimate of the Irish losses being a hundred dead (which is more than the whole company of grenadiers involved).[20]

This was not Walker's only fantasy about miners creeping about the city's cellars. After he wrote his *Account*, and before Mackenzie's *Narrative* was published, Walker wrote a pre-emptive blast, his *Vindication,* in which he apologized for having missed several things out of his *Account*. He modestly explained that 'Mr. Walker will not say but that there may be other as considerable things omitted, but they may too nearly concern Mr. Walker himself and it would not become him to sound his own praises.' He then gave, by way of an example of such an omission, another mining story:

> A Bomb from the enemy broke into a cellar near Butcher's Gate. Some had the curiosity to examine what mischief it had done, and there they saw seven men lying dead, that had been working at a mine unknown to us, that, if it had not been for so miraculous a counter-mine, might have gone on in their work and have ruined us.[21]

There is no mention of this miracle or of miners anywhere else. Had there been the slightest chance of there being any truth in this fiction, it would have been the talk of the city. The bomb would have been (in Mackenzie's terminology) 'guided by an Unerring Hand'. He would have seized on the story, even if he had to qualify it with his 'as was reported' caveat. There certainly was a fear of being mined and that fear without doubt preyed on the minds of those defending. It would have been the frequent talk of Michelburne and his senior officers. This fear was exactly why Michelburne was having trenches dug outside Butcher's Gate and along the western wall as a 'counter-line' to keep the Irish trenches back. But these were early stages, as the Irish trenches were still several hundred yards away and were on the other side of the bog. If there was any immediate fear, it was not that the Irish army would undermine the walls from the outside, but that the walls might be undermined by disaffected people on the inside. Mackenzie was quite clear on this (my emphasis):

> About the same time, Governor Baker (*fearing lest enemies within the town should work in cellars near the walls*,) took with him Mr. William Mackie, one of the citizens that was very active and industrious for defence of the town: and they two searched all cellars near the walls, under pretence of examining the provisions, but found nothing of what they feared.[22]

This was written after Mackenzie had read both Walker's references to miners. Walker knew so little about the practical measures being employed by the soldiers in the defence of the city that he concocted his two mining yarns after getting the wrong end of the stick.[D] There were no Irish miners tunnelling their way in and, on inspection, there were no traitors tunnelling their way out. There were no miners.

Donough MacCarthy, the earl of Clancarty, was a teenager when the war broke out, and was still only twenty during the siege. At the age of eight, he had

[D] Note that Mackenzie refers twice to Baker and Mackie checking cellars 'near' rather than 'under' the walls.

inherited one of the largest estates in Ireland, but was described variously as being 'debauched and dissolute', and a 'young fool'.[23] In early 1689, he had been made the colonel of an infantry regiment commanded by Lieutenant Colonel James Skelton. The observation made by d'Avaux has already been quoted above: 'Most of the colonels have not even seen their regiments.' As he was underage, Clancarty sat by special dispensation in King James' parliament in Dublin, which was in session from May 1689 until late July. Clancarty's regiment had recently marched up from Trim with Rosen.[24] There is no contemporary suggestion from the French or Irish that Clancarty had either absented himself from the Dublin parliament or that he ever joined his regiment, nor is it likely that he ever spent a day of his life in or around Derry. The fiction of Clancarty's presence in the Irish camp was adopted by Mackenzie (but not in the attack, which he wrongly deduced was led by Colonel Skelton).[25] The fanciful prophecy was also of Walker's invention and was at all times improbable as Clancarty's people, the MacCarthys, were a Munster family and had never had anything to do with Derry or Ulster generally.

Mackenzie also added another detail, which clearly was the talk of the walls. He wrote that 'one on horseback comes close to the gate and called for fire to burn it'. George Holmes recalled 'one of them knocked at our gate and called for faggots to burn it with'. All sorts of things may have been said to frighten the defenders, but the Irish had not brought any means of starting a blaze. Surprised though Penhouët and his men may have been to actually get to the gates, it had not been part of the plan. Any supply of faggots (and especially of faggots not soaked through with the rain) would have been, in the circumstances, an impossibly long way off. Even though it did not happen, the attempt on the gates became a moral tale used to caution those guarding the city at night: 'We were in some danger', wrote Holmes. Men dozing on sentry duty could cost the city dear.

Captain Francis Nevill had left the city at the very beginning of the siege. Five years later, long after the publication of both Walker's *Account* and Mackenzie's *Narrative*, he prepared a detailed map of the city, which he published in Dublin in 1694. In providing a key to the points of interest, he recorded some of what were by then folk legends of the siege. In his entry for Butcher's Gate, he wrote: 'The Lord Clancarty led his regiment at ten of the clock at night … it's said he set his back to the gate and called for fire to burn it.'[26] The story had developed. There was no more talk of miners, nor was there an anonymous horseman calling for fire. It was Clancarty himself.

Although it seemed that he had got over the worst of his fever, Governor Baker was still unwell. He was awoken from his sick bed by the enormous discharge of musketry and cannon fire. Fearing a general attack, he went to the walls 'thinking his presence there absolutely necessary to encourage the men, and to give such necessary orders as should be convenient'.[27] He stayed out in the wet throughout the night, and only went back to his lodgings in the morning. He relapsed. The fever came back, and he died two days later on 30 June.

'He was a great loss to the garrison', wrote Ash, 'greatly beloved and very well qualified for the government, being endued with great patience and moderation; free from envy or malice'. Baker had been a remarkable success. He had lived through a crisis where his personal qualities had proved to be of great importance. Facing mutiny and violence from those around him, he had established and maintained his authority, and no one had anything bad to say of him. Walker wrote: 'his death was a sensible loss to us, and generally lamented, being a Valiant person; in all his Actions among us show'd the greatest Honour, Courage and Conduct'. Mackenzie agreed. Baker was 'justly lamented by the Garrison, in whose affections his prudent and resolute Conduct had given him a great Interest'. He was buried in a vault in the cathedral. 'The pall was borne by the governors Walker and Michelburne, Cols. Lance and Campsie, Lieut. Col Campbell and Col Munroe. His funeral sermon was preached by Mr White.'[28]

The unhappy failure of MacGimpsy, illustrated by his body dangling on the gibbet on the other side of the river, weighed heavily on the minds of the garrison. If only Kirke knew how bad things were, he would be forced to make an effort. Luckily, they still had Roche, and he was a navy man and knew about naval signals. They asked him to signal the fleet for them to let them know of their distress. He was very willing. Before he left the ship, he said, Kirke had personally given him a set of signals which he had committed to memory. As he let parliament know years later, he made himself very useful to the garrison by giving 'the general notice from time to time from the steeple of Derry, how long the town could hold out'. The city could at least be satisfied that Kirke knew what was going on.

It was all blarney. Roche had absolutely no idea, but he was enjoying his important role too much to admit his ignorance. He instead impressed the garrison by getting them to perform signals of his own devising. Richards was with the fleet. On 29 June he wrote:

> This morning we saw flying on Derry steeple a much larger flag than was wont, hoisted upon a very large flag staff, which they lowered and hoisted four times, and fired two guns. The sign we understood not. Some are of the opinion that it is a flag taken last night from the enemies, when we supposed them to sally out. Others think it is only a bravado-ing their enemies, and some mark of their last success against them.[E29]

[E] Roche certainly fooled Mackenzie, who complained bitterly about Kirke making no attempt to relieve the city 'notwithstanding the frequent signs we made to them of our Distressed Condition'.

24

Rosen the barbarian

WALKER ESTIMATED THAT THERE were thirty thousand people in the city at the time Lundie left. No one has challenged that figure, but in the days and weeks that followed, people began to leave. According to Walker, a third of them, ten thousand people, left the city and took the king's protection.[A] [1] After that initial exodus, there was a continuous outward flow. In the early days, Hamilton had been told, no doubt by the French, that he was not to let anyone out. The rebels were to be made to surrender together, not individually. Nevertheless, d'Avaux reported in mid-May that Hamilton was still allowing 'fifty or a hundred people to leave Londonderry every day against the express orders he has been given'. In early June, Massé complained that 'every day, the surplus mouths are allowed to leave'.[2]

This was one of the two principal reasons for the failure of the siege.[3] Mackenzie conceded as much: 'Those many Protestants that at the beginning of the Siege left the City, and took protection, and even the great numbers that died the last six weeks of the Siege, made those Provisions last the longer.' Anyone from the city could go to the Irish lines, promise to behave, and ask for a protection. The king needed to demonstrate he was not hostile to the Protestants, nor even hostile to those who had rebelled, just so long as they stopped rebelling. The rebels would see their error, and live peaceably or even join his army. The policy had generally been a success in that, rather than rebel, most Protestants in the northern counties felt it wiser to stand back with the king's protection. The same policy was extended to Derry. As if to alleviate the misery of those who chose to stay inside the walls, Hamilton was allowing out anyone who had had enough. If people became sick or hungry or frightened, they would receive the king's protection, leaving more food for those who remained. Lundie's calculations had not anticipated Hamilton's generosity.

Each day, permission was given for people to leave. In addition, 'every day', wrote Walker, 'some or other deserted the garrison'. All it took was a white flag or handkerchief to be waved at the Irish positions, a request for protection, and the Irish allowed the person or persons to go on their way. At the end of May, Captain Ash recorded escorting his sister from the city 'to beyond the orchard' after Baker had given her 'a pass to go to her husband'.[4] Mackenzie gave two examples of men

[A] Mackenzie did not adopt the thirty thousand figure. He wrote: 'What the number of Men, Women, and Children, in the Town might be is uncertain', but did not think it so inaccurate as to offer an alternative figure. He also did not accept that ten thousand left: 'Some of the aged people, Women and Children, with some few others, to the number of near a thousand, left us.'

who 'at about this time' left the city. Captain William Beatty, who had spent the last ten weeks trying to kill as many of the Irish as he could, became unwell:

> Captain Beatty also went away, and took protection, and lived at Moneymore; but the reason of it was because he had a violent flux, which rendered him useless to the garrison, and he went to try if he could recover his health, for he had been at all the encounters and skirmishes with the enemy before and ever behaved himself with great integrity and valour.[5]

If the Irish did not let a man leave, it was his own fault. 'Mr. Andrew Robinson left us, but the enemy stripped and sent him back, because of some imprudent expressions.' Had Robinson resisted the temptation to answer back, he could have walked off.

This was a great frustration to the French, who hoped to run a close siege. After the first peaceful overtures had been made in April, everyone had made a choice. They chose either to leave or to stay in rebellion. That choice, from the French point of view, should have been enforced. No one should have been allowed out until the city surrendered. Especially not 'the pregnant and the young, the women and the old men past their prime, a swarm no use in war, but prompt to eat remaining rations'. Allowing people to leave, d'Avaux felt, prevented the growth of opposition 'against the most obstinate'. People who did not want their families to starve would make their feelings known within the walls. By mid-June, perhaps earlier, the Irish stopped the exodus. Those inside the walls were kept inside.[6]

In the Irish camp, Rosen had had enough. The siege was hopeless. Everything was sodden. There was continual rain and the forward trenches flooded with every tide. They had neither the means nor the men to storm the walls, and the garrison was mocking them by delaying their answers to Hamilton's ludicrously generous terms. The city's only weakness was that it was starving, and would have starved itself into submission long ago had not Hamilton allowed anyone who felt a bit peckish to leave and go home with a protection.

As he watched the rain from his tent, Rosen came up with a plan, or as he put it, 'my project'. The more he thought of it, the more he felt it bound to succeed. He drafted a new proclamation to be sent to the city. They were to surrender within twenty-four hours, or he would carry out his project. He wrote to Louvois, King Louis' minister of war: 'I have taken the decision to exterminate this race.'[B] [7] And by race, he meant race. He would exterminate the British. There was no meaningful distinction between the Protestants and the rebels. Extermination was the solution, and he would arrange it so that they would exterminate themselves. They would starve. He would correct the mistaken policies of the past. He would round up the rebels from all over Ulster and put them in the city. Every person who had been allowed

[B] 'J'ay pris ma resolution d'exterminer cette race.'

to leave with a protection, would be brought back. Every Protestant associated with those in the city, whether he or she had been in the city, would be rounded up. They would be marched to the walls and left there. If they tried to get out again, they would be shot. Those inside the city could feed them or watch them starve. They could shelter them, or watch them perish in the rain. Either way, the time would come when they would all die. Their only hope would be to surrender the city, and the king could then decide what to do with them. No doubt the king would agree something ridiculously indulgent, but Rosen's job would be completed. Should however, his project be rejected, and should the English land an army, he wanted approval for the second part of the project, which was to lay waste the whole area.

He needed permission to do this, and in the same inspirational frenzy he wrote to King James. He did so in different terms. 'My zeal and attachment for your Majesty's service, and for preserving your army, have induced me to-day to determine to exterminate all the *rebels* throughout this area.'[c] [8]

> These rebels … are totally unworthy of your Majesty's clemency, and deserve to be starved to death. Besides, when the country is plundered and burnt, the English troops who may make a descent, finding neither subsistence nor shelter, must perish in a miserable manner; and we shall be in a better condition to maintain our superiority in the other parts of the kingdom. I am to begin instantly, Sire, to put my project in execution, and I shall continue the same plan, unless your Majesty forbids me expressly.[9]

This was a bold way to write to a king. He dated the letters 30 June. Looking out on the grim spectacle before him of the rain splattered city, he decided there was no point in waiting. It was such a good plan that he may as well get on with it straight away. On that very same day, in the morning, he had his proclamation copied and sent to 'The Commanders, Officers, Soldiers, and Inhabitants of the City of Londonderry.' He gave them until six in the afternoon of 1 July to surrender on Hamilton's conditions, failing which

> He will forthwith issue out his Orders … for the gathering together of those of their Faction, whether Protected, or Not, and cause them immediately to be brought to the Walls of Londonderry where it shall be lawful for those that are in the Town (in case they have any pity for them) to open the Gates, and receive them into the Town; otherwise they will be forced to see their Friends and nearest Relations all starved for want of Food.

Should an English army land, 'he will forthwith cause all the said country to be immediately destroyed'. He would burn the houses and mills 'not only of those

[c] 'J'ay…. m'a fait prendre aujourd'huy la resolution d'exterminer les rebelles qui sont dans l'estandue de ce pays-ci.'

that are in actual Rebellion, but also of their Friends and Adherents'. He would 'cause all the Men, Women and Children, who are any ways related to those in Londonderry, or anywhere else in open Rebellion, to be forthwith brought to this Place' and would send out orders for them to be brought in from 'Coleraine, Antrim, Carrickfergus, Belfast, Dungannon, Charlemont, Belturbet, Sligo' and by his flying columns around Ballyshannon, Enniskillen and on the Finn. If his deadline was not met by the sending of hostages, there would be no further offer of terms. His army would continue the siege and 'shall have Orders to give no Quarter, or spare either Age or Sex'. They would be exterminated.

There was no written response to Rosen's proclamation. Walker and Michelburne instead responded the next day to Hamilton's first demand. They had given the conditions careful consideration, which had been 'much hindered by the death of one of our governors and by the disturbance given us by the camp'. They had, they said, since received Rosen's proclamation, which they then repeated in full as if they felt unsure that Hamilton knew how disgraceful its contents were.

> It gave great offence to the people here; and caused many of them believe, that no articles or capitulation, that should be made with us, should ever be performed or kept; when they find and believe, that the said marshal hath, or pretends to have, a power of command, in the army, above the said lieutenant general.

The point was well made. Hamilton had told them he had the king's authority to make terms, but his commission to treat with them was dated 1 May. Since the sitting of the Dublin Parliament and following Rosen's proclamation, it seemed Hamilton no longer had that authority. Rosen was now threatening to rescind all the protections issued by Hamilton in the king's name. They did not know who they were dealing with. The letter from Walker and Michelburne read:

> Though we expect favour from his Majesty and the said lieutenant general, and others with them; yet we expect no mercy, nor favour, or keeping of conditions with us, from the said marshal or his countrymen with him … We, therefore, desire the said lieutenant general to procure from His Majesty a new fuller commission to treat with us: and that His Majesty may assure us, that we shall have performances of what articles we make with the said lieutenant general; so that it may not be in the power of the said marshal, or the said Frenchmen with him, or any other, to break what articles shall be made for our advantage.

To Rosen, it was another mockery. They were simply playing for time, but they were not going to get it. He had already allowed them an extra day after the six o'clock deadline on the Monday. On the Tuesday evening, 2 July, the first batch of Protestants, those who lived in the Laggan, Inishowen and the immediate area, were led to the city at gunpoint. 'They drove them in a herd like beasts to the wall.'[10]

There was great fury in Londonderry. But it was impotent fury that could only be revenged upon the handful of Irish prisoners held in the city. The gentlemen prisoners, who had been allowed to live in private lodgings in the city, were seized and locked up in the gaol, and told that they were all going to be hanged in the morning. After their initial rage, the governors then had second thoughts. A letter was drafted for the prisoners to sign, and four of them did so.[11] It was addressed not to Rosen, but to Hamilton 'knowing you are a person that does not delight in shedding innocent blood'. It pointed out that the garrison had 'used and treated us with all civility imaginable', but that Rosen's decision to round up the Protestants had 'so incensed the governors and others of this garrison, that we are all condemned by court-martial to die to-morrow unless these poor people be withdrawn'. Their blood would be on Rosen's hands, not on those of the garrison. 'The lives of twenty prisoners lie at stake, and therefore require your diligence and care. We are all willing to die (with our swords in our hands) for his Majesty, but to suffer like malefactors is hard.'

On the next day, the Irish army brought the next batch of Protestants to the city. This time it was a thousand 'of all ages and sexes'. The reality of the round-up was brutal. They 'drove in all the Protestants for near ten miles round, protected as well as unprotected, men, women, and children. Many tender people, and some women with child, died by the rude and barbarous usage they met with on the road (being most stripped, and guarded in dirty pounds and rotten houses, &c.)'.[12]

When they arrived at Derry, it was to find that the governors had issued orders not to let them in or to give them any food. Notwithstanding that, Ash noticed, 'many of the garrison took in their friends privately and fed them'. Feelings in the city may have been running high, but Rosen's plan was the most dangerous of threats. If he persisted, the end was very near. Michelburne and Walker knew, or at least feared, that they would no more be able to keep out the starving masses than Lundie had been.

They tried signaling the fleet again, and got James Roche to go up the steeple to let Kirke know that things were really desperate. 'In the evening, James Roche, by the governors' orders, struck the flag on the church three times, and as often hoisted it up, then made a wave which was done to let the fleet see our great distress.' This was, Roche assured them, 'a signal frequent made at sea'.[13] Out on the lough, the fleet was baffled.

Having not hanged the prisoners for the second day running, Michelburne had a gallows erected on the double bastion. It was a display of hopeless rage, and whatever he may have said or written afterwards, Michelburne cannot have expected it to have any effect. In formulating his project, Rosen would naturally have asked himself what the rebels could do in retaliation. The only thing they could do was execute the prisoners. And more fool them if they did, because they would get the same. Both sides claimed to be civilized people, and the whole civilized world would be outraged if Michelburne hanged prisoners simply because he did not like the idea of his coreligionists being put into his care.

Rosen was unmoved by the gallows. It was all bravado on the rebels' part, and Rosen did not care who they hanged. The Irish army generally was unlikely to be moved either. All that had happened, in their eyes, was that enemy sympathizers had been made to join the enemy rather than remain at liberty to get up to every sort of mischief. This was war. Everyone was aware, especially after the break of Killyleagh two months before, that hundreds of men with protections in their pockets had taken up arms to fight the Irish. No one was interested in the legal niceties of whether or when a protection may be withdrawn. Hamilton replied to the letter from the prisoners. 'Gentlemen, in answer to yours, what these poor people [the rounded-up Protestants] are like to suffer, they may thank themselves for, being their own fault, which they in town may prevent by accepting the conditions that have been offered them; and if you suffer in this, it cannot be helped, but shall be revenged on many thousand of these people (as well innocent as others), within or without the city.' Rosen had no intention of giving in, and Hamilton, whether he liked the project or not, was in no position to stand up to him. The only way that Rosen could be stopped, was by him being overruled.

Rosen was overruled. King James was furious. Rosen's letter and copy declaration reached him by 2 July, on the same day that the first batch of civilians arrived at the city walls. James had been doing all that he could in Ireland to demonstrate his adherence to the rule of law and his policy of no religious discrimination among his subjects. He needed a clean image if he was to get England and Scotland back, and now his senior French officer in Ireland was rounding up all the Protestants, however harmless, classing them as rebels and putting them at immediate risk of starvation and the violence of the army's cannonade. Not only that, but they had been given royal protection. Rosen was overruling the king.

On the very day that the news reached Dublin, the king was approached by Lord Granard, one of the few Protestants sitting in the House of Lords, who asked him about Rosen's round-up. 'None but a barbarous *Moscovite*' said the king, 'could have thought of so cruel a contrivance'.[14] Later in July, James instructed Lord Dover to get King Louis to replace Rosen: 'We must show our dislike of his procedure by having him recalled.'[15] Writing from Dublin, d'Avaux told Louvois that Rosen's declaration 'has caused a big stir here'.

> The King of England appears outraged, particularly because he [Rosen] made it without consulting him and it is against His Britannic Majesty's declaration, and against the protections promised to the Protestants … Lord Melfort said that the King's honour, and the execution of his word, had to take preference over the keeping of all of his kingdoms, and if M. Rosen had been a subject of the King of England, he would be hanged.

> I found this language rather strong, but I did not want to respond, as the King was already very angry.[16]

Nevertheless, d'Avaux spoke up for Rosen. In these exceptional circumstances, he argued, Rosen could not be expected to wait for instructions and (this must have been untrue) 'both I and M. Rosen were in ignorance of the declaration made by His Britannic Majesty to the Protestants, because we were never told of this'. His point was that as Rosen and d'Avaux had not been told directly by the king, they did not know that protections were being issued. D'Avaux recognized the weakness of this defence and did not want to say any more. 'I wanted to avoid any sort of specific points', he wrote. James of course knew that d'Avaux and Rosen knew, but diplomatically accepted the explanation that Rosen had acted in ignorance. But he was adamant that Rosen should be stopped. The king wrote back through Melfort to Rosen on the 3 July from Dublin Castle:

> We have received your project, and we wished we had seen it before you had issued any orders to put it in execution. We are thoroughly persuaded that you have seen none of the declarations, in which we have promised our protection, not only to those who choose to submit to us and live peaceably at home, but also to all those who choose to return to their habitations and behave as good subjects for the future; as we are convinced that, had you known, you would not have issued orders so contrary to our intentions and promises. It is positively our will, that you do not put your project in execution.[17]

He was content that the second part of Rosen's project, to lay waste to the whole neighbourhood should the siege be raised, as being 'necessary for the success of our arms before Londonderry'. In the meantime, Rosen was to stay where he was and await further orders.

The dispatches to Rosen were sent back at great speed, carried by relays of horses. A system of post stations had been settled in Ireland during Commonwealth times along the main routes. Although there may have been wartime changes, the 180-mile route to Derry followed the relatively good road from Dublin through the eastern counties and then through Coleraine. The system involved a series of 'standing posts', often inns, where the post master was to have a supply of horses and guides available at all hours.[18]

The speed at which a document travelled depended on the stamina of the rider. Distances varied between each post station, but they were generally about twenty miles apart. The horse would be changed at each post, but the courier would continue his journey with a fresh horse until he reached the next post station, and would then change again. At each post station he would be given a mounted guide who would ride with him, and then return with the horses while the courier went on with a fresh guide and horse to the next station. In the crudest of terms, a horse would be doing well to cover about twenty miles in an hour. Between Dublin and Londonderry, the rider would change horses some nine or more times, and would spend over ten hours in the saddle. He would need to be fed and to catch some rest on the way, and would expect the occasional holdups at post stations, but during the summer months he would aim and expect to be at his destination well within two days.

The display of royal anger described by d'Avaux happened on the 2 July after the king received Rosen's letter of 30 June setting out his project. D'Avaux wrote to Louvois, 'I thought, Sir, that I should inform M. Rosen of all these things.' It was imperative that Rosen stopped whatever he was doing before he received the king's dispatch. Anything else would cause a diplomatic storm. D'Avaux needed to know how much time he had to warn Rosen. 'I asked Lord Melfort when he intended sending the courier; he told me it would not be until the following morning.' Melfort also told him 'he would send the courier to me in order to pick up my letters'. D'Avaux did not trust Melfort, and it would not suit his purposes to have his own warning reach Rosen at the same time as the king's order. D'Avaux worked quickly, and sent a courier to Rosen in the evening of 2 July. Melfort, he later discovered, somewhat sneakily had sent his letter at two in the morning on 3 July. Knowing he was playing a difficult hand, d'Avaux carefully worded his report to Louvois. 'I sent another [courier] myself to M. Rosen', but did not tell Louvois that he had sent his first.[19]

On 4 July, Rosen received the dispatch from d'Avaux and was forced to release the civilians, and to do so speedily. He did so that very afternoon. The Irish, noted Ash, 'gave them provisions and money, which was distributed among them on the strand beyond the gallows in the evening', a gesture which Leslie attributed to Hamilton 'who was much against that Driving'.[20]

On the day after he released the Protestants, Rosen sent two letters to the king. We know the first of these was written at least a day beforehand because he was still begging for the king's approval of his project, but he dated the letter 5 July to conceal the fact that he had already acted. The letter ended with a request for a reply to the letter in which he set out his project: 'I hope, that the return of this express will bring me your Majesty's ultimate orders; and I wish they may arrive in time enough for me to put them properly in execution.'[21]

He then wrote a second letter once he had reflected on both d'Avaux's despatch and the wholly unwelcome order from Melfort. He also dated this letter 5 July, and acknowledged the unequivocal order from the king. The king was not to worry because Rosen had not done what he said he would do, but had only conducted a test. The test failed because the cruel rebels fired at 'the small number of accomplices' he had rounded up to see what impression it would make, and so he had sent them home. The king's letter was too late to stop him from doing that which he had already stopped doing on an experimental basis.[22]

It was a lie. Rosen's project was very much underway at the time he was stopped. He had rounded up and delivered the first twelve hundred civilians, and for all that is known, there were already several thousand others being driven along the road to Derry. Rosen's false reason for not pressing ahead was now to be the official line. D'Avaux and Fumeron dutifully passed on Rosen's version of events to Paris.[23] Significantly, d'Avaux's report to Louvois was also dated 5 July, so the French in Dublin knew on that date what Rosen was writing on that same day to inform King James. James would not know what had happened until a day or more later. The French collectively kept the king in the dark. With d'Avaux's help, Rosen was covering his own back. He had done no wrong and there was nothing for the king to be angry about. It was time to change the subject and move on.[24]

There had been gunfire on 2 July when the crowd appeared. There was, said Ash, a single cannon shot from the walls. There had been no general firing and there was no repeat. None of the civilians was hurt, although (and this is unbelievable) the happy rumour got around the city that the cannon ball was (said Mackenzie) 'directed by an Unerring Hand [and] touched none of our friends, but as we afterwards heard, killed some of those merciless soldiers that were pushing them on'. It was, wrote Ash, 'an instance of the wonderful providence of God in favour of the poor Protestants!'[25] The second group of a thousand civilians who were herded to the defences on the next day were not shot at. None of the civilians were chased away or threatened by the garrison. When the time came for them to be released, some of them were let in to join the garrison. And some of the townspeople joined the large group of twelve hundred or so, and tried to get themselves away in the crowd. According to Ash:

> Many of our sick men and women thought to have taken the advantage and gone with their friends in the country, but the enemy, with Argus eyes, soon observed by their faces and legs to what place they belonged and would not let them go, though some got away unknown, and some of those who had been driven by the enemy staid with us, so that I think our number is much the same.[26]

The Irish were well aware of the attempt to smuggle out the weak.

> Of those who came out and mixt with the people that were driven to the walls by Mons. de Rosen, several were known by their wan and lean countenances, and nauseous smell, that made every one think they had the plague, and others fell down dead on the strand, for these being weak and sick people had been starved in the town, where the strongest fellows seized on the meal and other provisions and let the others starve.[27]

This about-turn was not well received in the Irish army. The Protestants were rebels, and Rosen was right. Letting them go suggested a lack of resolution.[28] In the city, there was great relief and a sense that firm action had saved the day. A victory had been won. No one knew anything of King James' orders or his disgust at

Rosen's project. All they knew was that the Irish had lost their nerve. The 'Lofty Gallows', as formal an emblem of defiance as the bloody flag, 'obliged the Foe to let the Affrighted People Retreat from Danger'.[29] Once the civilians were released, Michelburne had the prisoners returned to their quarters and ordered the gallows to be taken down.[30]

The siege settled back into its daily routine of small skirmishes and shooting, but things were now much quieter. Work stopped on the trench on 1 July. The next phase would have been to extend it closer to the walls, but there were not enough tools and, with Kirke so close on the lough, there was unlikely to be enough time. 'There are barely twenty musket shots fired from either side each day', wrote Fumeron. 'We only throw a few bombs into the place, but not to any great effect.'[31] The worst of the bombing came to an end on 6 July. The grand mortar, says Plunkett, 'cracked', and was not fired again. For the rest of the siege the city was subjected to bombing by the two smaller mortars, which, although still terrifying, caused far less damage. Ash recorded only two deaths from mortar fire for the rest of the siege.

25

Inch

WITH MOST OF HIS WARSHIPS on Lough Swilly, Kirke waited on Lough Foyle. On 28 June, Captain Hopson and the *Bonadventure* returned with the encouraging news about Inch. Kirke mulled this over, but also needed to know what state Enniskillen was in. On the following day, he sent the *Bonadventure* off on a second mission, this time along the coast to Killybegs, where a letter was sent inland promising both aid and the imminent arrival of an English army. Enniskillen rejoiced with bonfires, firing of volleys and drinking the health of King William and Queen Mary.[1] Hopson offloaded 'thirty barrels of gunpowder and some firelocks' at Killybegs, and took on board two delegates from Enniskillen, John Rider and the Reverend Andrew Hamilton.

While the *Bonadventure* was still at sea, Sir James Caldwell arrived on Lough Foyle from Donegal town, 'forty leagues round a most dangerous coast, all in the enemy's hands, in a small open boat'. Caldwell was a Belleek landowner and was, he said, 'the only person of my fortune and quality that stayed behind in Ireland, and that took up arms for the present government', raising 'a regiment of foot and two troops of horse for my two sons'. He told Kirke that 'if he could not relieve the city of Derry by sea, and would send a ship with arms for 1500 men, the forces we had would do it by land within ten days, or I would forfeit my life'.[2]

Greatly encouraged, Kirke held another council of war on 2 July and ordered a regiment to be sent to Inch 'to cause a diversion to the enemies'. The next day, in revenge for Rosen's round-up, he ordered a raid on the shore. Two boatloads of men landed to look for Irish dragoons, but instead plundered 'the parson's house above Whitecastle', and 'brought off about forty poor people' who were later sent to Scotland. 'This alarmed the enemy very much', wrote Richards, 'thinking we had landed a much greater force, so that before night I perceived three battalions of foot march from this side of Culmore'.[3]

The next day, one of those unfortunates who had been driven to Derry and then released was brought to Kirke. He relayed the news that 'all the young lusty fellows' included in Rosen's round-up had been taken into the garrison. Importantly, he told Kirke that the city had told the Irish that 'they had provisions for one month more, before which they were well assured to be delivered; if not they would live on dogs and cats sooner than ever trust to their faithless offers and promises'. This was an important piece of intelligence. It confirmed what the council of war believed. There was no urgency requiring Kirke to take any desperate risks.

By the evening of 9 July, the *Dartmouth* and the *Portland* had made Lough Swilly with the transports and were off Rathmullan. The following morning,

Colonel Thomas St John landed two hundred men on the mainland below Inch and went inland to reconnoitre. Richards, escorted by an ensign and twenty redcoats, landed on the island itself. He made for the ford to the mainland, staked out a position to build a redoubt, and sent a messenger to Colonel Steuart for field guns, more men and tools. While he waited, 'several poor Protestants with a few cattle forded over to us'. Inevitably, they were spotted by mounted Irish scouts. Richards sent an urgent request to the *Greyhound* to Major Henry Collier for reinforcements. By the time Collier arrived with thirty men, there were some forty Irish dragoons watching them from across the ford. There was no retreat because, as far Richards could see, the island had 'no defiladed and enclosed grounds' where they could take cover. 'The enemy's dragoons were making over to the island. We went with 30 men and met them on the middle of the strand, but after the first discharge they retired.'[4]

There were no casualties on either side, but this was a missed opportunity for the Irish. In one swoop, they could have taken Richards and scuppered Kirke's plans for Inch. Richards supposed the Irish suspected an ambush, because 'I could not conceive why forty so good horse should retire from us, on whom they had so much advantage', but the reason for the Irish retreat soon became clear. Behind them, they had spotted St John's men racing downhill towards them.[5]

At four in the afternoon, Colonel Steuart arrived from the *Deptford* with four field guns and the tools. Richards showed him the plans for the redoubt, which would take three or four days to construct. Steuart was not sure about this. His instructions from Kirke were not to land unless 'he could with safety make an immediate defence'. In the meantime, some hundreds of Protestants had come from all around with their cattle, and if Steuart and his troops were to leave, the Irish would be down amongst them in no time.

It was decided to stay, but then the arguments started over Richards' plans. Both St John, 'who pretends to be an engineer', and Steuart thought the redoubt too big. They at last agreed that two redoubts should be built for the field guns, and Richards set 'about 109' men to work, as he had no more tools for the rest. Using two of the field guns he 'fired over into the enemies' flying camp to let them know we were prepared for them'. The work carried on until midnight. Richards wanted to labour on throughout the night, 'but it being nobody's opinion but mine to continue', the troops were ordered back to the other side of the island three miles away, where they could camp safely protected by the warships. The field guns were wheeled away to shelter under the guns of the *Greyhound,* which sat alone off the south end of the island, half a mile from the ford. Richards spent the night on board. 'We left no sentinels or small guard', he wrote, 'to hinder anyone going over to the strand to advise the enemy what boy's play we were at'. There were several false alarms during the night 'caused by the fearfulness of the islanders who imagined the enemies were entered [onto] the island'.

At first light on 11 July, Steuart and St John returned with their men and started building the second redoubt. Richards got the four field pieces into a battery and again had them fire at the horsemen across the ford. Despite his protests, the work stopped when the tide went out. The two colonels ordered the men back across the island, and the field guns were again taken back under the *Greyhound*'s guns. Disheartened and undefended, the Protestant civilians 'fled to the hills and did not spare to say that we did not dare to face the enemy, but would let them come in and cut all their throats.' But once the tide came in, work resumed from six in the evening until one in the morning 'at which time it rained pretty hard'. The troops were marched off to safety, the guns were removed, and Richards went to the *Greyhound* for another fretful night.

Richards was up early next morning on 12 July and went back to the works, but found no one there. He gathered together about forty of the country people and set them to work on the second redoubt but, as the tide ran out, he had them stop because there was no one to guard them. In the afternoon two troops of horsemen came down to the water and rode 'up and down, and from side to side to see, I suppose, if they could discover anybody lying in ambush'. Although the Irish did not try to cross the ford, Richards got Captain Gwillam to let him have twenty-four seamen to drag two of the field guns to the redoubt. Richards' enthusiasm was infectious. Gwillam and Collier came with him. 'Never were two guns by men drawn so soon away, for had we horse I do not believe it would have sooner been performed'. The Irish horsemen were 'within a large musket shot of us, and at our appearance halted'.

> We kept before our guns that they might not see them till they laid to pat, and so fired two round shot in among them, at which they made *volte face*, but before they got much further, we gave them two more, and forced them quite off the strand. We could not perceive to have killed any of them, though we have great reason to believe we have hurt some of them by their so soon retreat.[6]

They were still vulnerable, but were soon joined by Colonel Steuart with three hundred infantrymen. He and Richards agreed that if the Irish horsemen did get onto Inch, it would be difficult to drive them out, and more would follow. Rather than abandon the position every time the tide turned, they marched all the men from the ships to the new defences. Richards ordered all four guns to be brought over the island and placed between the two redoubts, and then set about making a battery with embrasures for eight guns. The rest of the soldiers arrived, together with some five or six hundred Protestant volunteers, 'commanded by gentlemen of this country', who had been brought across the lough from Rathmullan with some hundreds of cattle. By midnight, said Richards, 'it was tenable', and they were in a position to make a stand. In the early hours, for the first time at low tide, 'all stood to their arms to be ready to receive our threatening enemies'.

The next day was spent finishing the batteries, but Richards fell out with the infantry officers. He wanted two lines of communication dug between the redoubts, but 'others pretending to be better engineers than I, were against it and ordered otherwise, though contrary to my opinion and made their men work according to their fancies contrary to all rule and method of defence'. Richards was furious. 'I absolutely declared against them and troubled myself no further with the works, of which I am sure anyone that pretends to be an engineer ought to be ashamed.' He had another two guns brought from the ships, and when the tide went out they formed up again 'in battalia as the day before, and with the new raised companies we levied here we made the greatest show we could'.[7]

Back in the city, there were no attacks, just bombs: fourteen on 4 July, 'which killed a boy and wounded a woman'; nine on 5 July, 'which did harm to houses and raised the dead out of their graves'; fifteen on 6 July; and eighteen on Sunday 7 July, which came as a surprise because 'until this day none were fired on Sunday since the siege began … One of them killed a man and hurt many others.' On the next day, 8 July, there were fourteen bombs, 'one of them broke an ensign's leg in Butcher's Street, of which he died'.

The Irish completed their new battery facing Butcher's Gate, from where they began firing their two larger guns.[A] 'One of the balls, which weigh near fourteen pounds, came through the gate and killed a man in the street.' At night, Michelburne had large timbers placed on the outside of the gates to shield them. On the following day, the cannon started again on Butcher's Gate 'and shattered it much', but the gunners were erratic. 'Some of the balls flew over the town and fell into the lough', wrote Ash. 'I wish they had all done so.' At night, more timbers were ordered 'and all the officers who were there, desirous to have the work firm, put to their hands and carried sods from Ferry Gate'.

The shelling had another serious effect, of causing a shortage of drinking water. Usually drawn from wells within the walls, the bombing combined with the complete lack of sanitation had polluted the water with mud and worse. The only place to get clean, fresh water was then from St Colmcille's Wells, just outside the walls below the Double Bastion, but they were in easy musket shot of the forward Irish trenches. 'The besieged found … great difficulty to come to the wells for water, which they often fought for, and cost some of them their blood', wrote Walker. 'Many were shot', wrote Nevill, 'some falling into the wells dead'.[8]

And now supplies were dwindling.

> This day a pound of tallow [suet], otherwise called French butter, was allowed to every soldier in garrison. They got as much last Friday: this they mixed with meal, ginger, pepper and aniseeds, and made most excellent pancakes – charming meat! This fortnight past, horse's flesh was eaten: now dog's flesh is reckoned good meat! Every day all the parks and fields in the island are full of people gathering herbs and weeds for food.[9]

[A] The battery was placed near what is now the William Street roundabout outside St Eugene's cathedral.

Michelburne described preparing a dog with 'decayed claret', a dish 'we call in French *ragout de chien*, in English, a ragou of the haunch of my dog, Towser. It does not eat so well boiled as roasted, it is something strong but it eats best when baked.' Ash wrote of 'one man who owed some money to another. The poor fellow had killed a dog and was dressing it to eat. The other came in and insisted on having his money or his dog. Money, he had not, and therefore with languishing eye and rueful stomach, he was obliged to part with his dog.'[10]

26

Negotiations

THE SUDDEN NIGHT ATTACK by Clancarty's grenadiers on the outworks had shaken the city. No one had seen the enemy coming, and the Irish had got to the walls before anyone knew what was happening. Next time, the gates could be blown in by a petard. Michelburne took over. His first act was to impose a new discipline learned from his Tangier days. 'The officers were appointed to meet in four several places in the city and remain there all night … They are to go the rounds by turns, and the soldiers of each company are to stay at their quarters except such as are on out-guards, with their clothes and arms, standing in rank … The officers aforesaid are to have candles, tobacco, pipes and Adam's ale every night ... At four o'clock every morning, two great guns are to be shot against the enemy, at which time the officers and those who were up all night are to go to rest, and the volunteers and inhabitants of the city who are not listed in companies, are to come to the walls and stay until seven o'clock.'[1]

Since the Creggan disaster two months before, the only attack made by the rebels had been their unsuccessful attempt on the Irish trenches at the end of May, but since then the Irish had concentrated around the new battery facing Butcher's Gate. Michelburne saw this as an opportunity to make another attempt on the trenches. He was not going to risk another disorganized attack led by Murray or any other untrained volunteer. Unlike Baker, he intended to lead from the front. If there was to be an expedition, it would be done in a proper military fashion.

On 11 July, taking five or six men from each company, Michelburne formed a body of six hundred or more on the Windmill. He then led them with colours flying over the defences towards the old gallows. Brigadier Buchan ordered the Irish army to arms. The Irish camp sprang to life and lined their trenches in readiness. Two companies of infantry marched down to reinforce the Irish lines, and a small body of cavalry formed up on the Strand. It was a quick response. Seeing the Irish were ready for him, Michelburne ordered his men back to the Windmill.

At the same time, some of the Irish rushed forward to within easy musket range and opened fire. Michelburne's men, with their backs to the Irish, quickened their pace. 'Immediately you might have seen all the men running over the ditches as if the Devil drove them.' The panic was widespread. They ran beyond the trenches in a great unordered body, past the Windmill and back past Lundie's ravelin, where they 'stood thrusting and thronging each other at the gate'. Michelburne was doubtless at his best: 'You dogs! Damn'd rogues! Sons of whores!' But he could not get any of them to go back to form a defensive line inside the trenches to face down the Irish, and, not wanting the Irish to get too good a look at this scene, ordered the gate be opened to let them in.[2]

Only Ash records this in detail, suggesting that he was present and was shocked by what he saw. Mackenzie's description was rather different: 'It growing dark, our men, by mistaking the word of command, came within our own lines again in some confusion. Colonel Barker [of the Irish army] received a shot in his hand, which put him into a high fever, whereof he was reported to have died.' It was all an unfortunate error. The men ran because perhaps they thought they had been told to run, and the day's action ended on a high note. Notwithstanding any confusion, we mortally wounded Colonel Barker. It was a success. Except, there is no record of Colonel Barker being wounded, and he certainly did not die from any wound received that day.[3]

Michelburne's parade demonstrated the state of morale in mid-July. The garrison was stuck to its walls, with all its hopes relying on something that might never come. Hamilton reasoned that Kirke's plan was to raise what volunteers he could in Lough Swilly or beyond, and then to join up with the rebels in Enniskillen. Londonderry was doomed. The rebels were no longer a threat to the Irish army, and they were dying in great numbers. They needed to surrender and he needed to encourage them to do so by giving them an honourable way out. The only barrier to that in Hamilton's mind was Rosen. He wrote to the king about it. Hamilton must be the ultimate power in any negotiations and Rosen was not to interfere. King James obliged and wrote to Rosen. He was to leave everything to Hamilton.[A] [4]

King James also sent Hamilton two letters on 5 July. One carried his instructions, and the other was to show to the rebels to let them know that Hamilton had full powers to treat with them. 'Whereas we have through the whole course of our reign endeavoured to reduce our subjects to their duty by clemency rather than force, we are at this time resolved to give an additional instance thereof in regard to our subjects of the Protestant religion now in arms against us.' Hamilton was told: 'You shall let them know that, if they do not now yield to such propositions as you shall offer to them, we will hereafter exclude them from ever partaking of our royal mercy. You are to give them as little as possibly can be.'[5]

On 10 July, Hamilton had a hollow bomb fired into the city. In the bomb was a set of his proposals. He wanted to ensure that his generous terms were known to the ordinary citizens and not hidden from them by a cabal of fanatics.[B] Addressed 'To the Soldiers and Inhabitants of Derry', the message read:

> The conditions offered by Lieut. Gen. Hamilton are sincere. The power he hath of the King is real. Be no longer imposed upon by such as tell you

[A] Rosen replied somewhat irritably after the negotiations had finished to say that the king need not have written as he had no intention of getting involved in any treaty.

[B] The hollow shell is on permanent display in St Columb's Cathedral.

> to the contrary, you cannot be ignorant of the King's clemency towards his subjects. Such of you as chose to serve the King shall be entertained without distinction in point of religion. If any chose to leave the kingdom they shall have passes. You shall be restored to your estates and livings, and have free liberty of religion whatsoever it be. If you doubt the powers given to Gen. Hamilton by the King, twenty of you may come and see it with freedom, under the King's hand and seal. Be not obstinate against your natural Prince. Expose yourselves no longer to the miseries you undergo, which will grow worse and worse if you continue to be opinionate, for it will be too late to accept of the offer now made you when your condition is so low that you cannot resist the King's forces longer. July 10th 1689.

On the next day, the day of Michelburne's parade and a week after the release of the Protestant civilians, Hamilton sent a trumpeter to the town to ask for a reply to the proposals that had been given to colonels Lance and Campbell by Gordon O'Neill on 26 June. This time there was a response. Never mind the attitude Walker attributed to the garrison a few days before: 'They will not entertain the least thought of Surrendering, and it would cost a man's Life to speak of it.' Times had changed. A message was sent back to Hamilton that evening. 'We considered that most of the ships were gone, we knew not whither; provisions grew extremely scarce; and therefore to gain time, it was thought advisable to agree to it'.[6]

The Irish suggested there be six commissioners on each side, and that the garrison should send them the names of the city's commissioners together with what terms were wanted above those in the proclamation. This generated a dispute, wrote Mackenzie, between the governors, the council of fourteen and 'the colonels and other officers'. What Mackenzie meant was that the governors were conformists, the council of fourteen were mostly conformists, whereas 'the colonels and other officers' combined were not.

There was a mistrust among at least some of the Presbyterians of what the conformists might do. An important theme for Mackenzie was that only Baker had been elected (and Mackenzie was not happy with how that had been done). Baker had without anyone's say-so (as Mackenzie saw it) appointed Walker as his deputy. It was a personal appointment. When Baker fell ill, he made another personal appointment by nominating Michelburne to stand in for him. It followed that all authority lapsed on Bakers' death, and there should be an election for a new governor. Mackenzie wanted Walker dismissed and all power vested in a Presbyterian-dominated council free to choose a new governor, who would be, perhaps, an educated churchman not disadvantaged by being a conformist, such as John Mackenzie.

The last thing the garrison needed was the division that an election would certainly bring, and if the commission was not sent in the name of the governors, Mackenzie was told, the enemy would think they were 'a confused multitude without any government'. A compromise was reached (but 'not without great opposition' says Mackenzie) whereby the commission was to represent 'the governors, commanders, officers, soldiers, and citizens'.[7]

The terms proposed by the garrison were described by Ash as being 'too tedious to mention', but in brief they were these: provided the city was surrendered by 26 July, everyone in Ulster and Connaught would receive a full pardon for all crimes committed since 7 December last (the day the gates were shut on Antrim's regiment). Everyone would have liberty to go with their goods and chattels to England, Scotland or anywhere in Ireland. Those men, women, and children not able to travel home would be fed and given bedding.

In addition, the garrison would be allowed to go to Culmore to be shipped away with their arms, colours flying, drums beating, lighted matches and a suitable quantity of ammunition. Those officers, gentlemen, citizens and townsmen who elected to stay in the country could keep and wear pistols and swords, and keep their muskets, and everyone else could keep and wear their swords. Clergymen would be allowed to practise their religion as before, no one would be forced to take any oath; no one would be molested in the event of an English invasion; all taxes owed would be cancelled; the 'half-pike men, and rabble of the mere Irish' were to be disarmed, 'and not suffered to cottier and wander in the country, or use reproachful language to the Protestants'.[c] Hostages would be exchanged, and all the articles would be confirmed by an act of parliament.[8]

Everything was conditional on the city being allowed to hold out until 26 July. If there was no relief by then, they would all be starving and would be unable to defend themselves in any event. They would not surrender before that date. Kirke had two weeks to break his way in.

Mackenzie, although a Presbyterian outsider from Cookstown, was by then a big enough name in the city to insist that he be one of the commissioners. Ash, who was a Londonderry man, clearly did not know him and recorded him as 'Mr M'Kenny'. But Mackenzie was a sensible choice in that, like Walker, he was a clergyman with a university degree (in his case from Edinburgh). The other commissioners were Colonel Hugh Hamill, the Lifford landowner; Colonel Thomas Lance, from Dunboe outside Coleraine; Major Robert White, the Englishman who presided over the courts martial in town; Matthew Cocken of Londonderry, formerly one of the city sheriffs; and William Dobbin from Moneyglass, Co. Antrim. Their names were taken back by Hamilton's messenger, and as a sign of goodwill, Hamilton called a ceasefire on 12 July, which greatly annoyed the French, as it allowed the townspeople to flood out to the wells and take in a large supply of fresh drinking water.[9]

The written commission sent to Hamilton set out what was to be negotiated by the commissioners: 'the rendering up of the said city and garrison to the said Lieutenant-General, for his Majesty's use, with all the stores, ammunition, artillery, arms, implements, and habiliments of war … to conclude on such articles,

[c] A cottier was a wage-less farm labourer allowed the use of a cabin and a plot of land.

matters, and things, for the delivering up of the said city … and for the giving and receiving of hostages.' It described the six commissioners as 'appointed, and authorised' to 'treat with the Right Honourable Lieutenant-General Richard Hamilton, now encamped against Londonderry, with an army of his Majesty's, King James the Second'.[10]

The commission was signed by Walker and Michelburne and thirty-four others, including Richard Crofton, Adam Murray, Henry Monroe, and William Campbell; and a string of captains including Arthur Noble, Thomas Ash and George Holmes. Although all manner of documents and tables were annexed to his *Account*, Walker excluded all mention of the commission, even though he had authorized it. Londoners would not like to read that a surrender had been seriously considered, and especially would not like to read that Walker had signed a document recognizing the king as being James rather than William.

The proposals and the list of commissioners were sent to the Irish camp. On the following day, partly as a gesture of goodwill, and partly because feeding them was too much of a burden, the prisoners taken in the boat on the river on 13 June were released and sent back to the Irish lines.

The guns remained silent on Saturday 13 July, the day of the treaty negotiations. The Irish commissioners were colonels Dominic Sheldon, Gordon O'Neill and Sir Neil O'Neill; Sir Edward Vaudrey and Lieutenant Colonel Skelton; and the obscure Captain Francis Marow or Murraugh, who no one knew and who Ash described simply as 'another captain'.[11] The commissioners from the city were led towards the Irish camp on Ballougry Hill and were shown into a large tent especially erected for the occasion. There 'they dined and were well entertained'.

Having seen the proposals on the day before, the Irish commissioners were able to agree all the city's proposals except three: they were content for the garrison to march to Culmore to be put on Kirke's ships, but not that they should march fully armed. It was enough, they said, that the officers should be armed, but not the men. This was a negotiating ploy to be conceded if need be, as the Irish commissioners had firm instructions from King James 'not to delay bringing the town into our possession upon that account, but positively to grant that to them that they may go on board the rebels' ships with their baggage and arms'. Nor did the Irish agree to the Irish hostages being put on Kirke's ships, but this was also a minor matter.

The only real sticking point was the date. The Irish could not agree to the clause that gave the garrison until 26 July to comply. They insisted that the garrison should only have until noon on Monday 15 July. The Irish wanted two days, not two weeks. 'With great difficulty', Mackenzie wrote, the commissioners from the city 'obtained time till next day at twelve o'clock to return an answer'. The negotiations broke for the night, and the city's commissioners were escorted back to take instructions.

While they were in the tent, the city commissioners had no idea of what was happening on Inch. As they negotiated a surrender, Richards was preparing redoubts. On the day before the ceasefire, three messengers had been sent from Inch to make their way to the city. At least two of them managed to get through and were brought to Walker. One of the messengers was an 11-year-old boy, William Irwin, the son of Alexander Irwin, one of those who had shut the gates on Antrim's redshanks.[12] Concealed in his garter was a letter to Walker from Lieutenant David Mitchell, who had been in the garrison until 10 May when he got away, probably with Walker's permission, left the country and then returned on Kirke's fleet. The letter contained the joyous news that Kirke's men had landed on Inch. As the commissioners were still out, Walker wrote a reply in duplicate. He was surprised Kirke had not yet tried to relieve the city, 'their provisions were now very short and they could not hold out longer than fourteen days more, [and] that the enemy had offered them very honourable terms'. The two messengers were sent back each with a copy of the letter. The boy made it back to Inch, but without Walker's letter. The city lacked the ingenuity of the navy tailor, and Walker's letter had been hidden in the folding of his breeches. Irwin was caught by the Irish, and 'for fear of a discovery he swallowed the letter, and after some short confinement and endeavour to extort something from him, he made his escape'. Walker's second letter did get through on the following day, the first communication from the city to be received by Kirke in a month of waiting.[13]

Walker took Mitchell's letter and transcribed it. He did so because, no doubt, it was very small in order to fit into a garter and, having been in a tightly folded state, was probably almost illegible. But, says Mackenzie, in doing so, Walker altered it. Mitchell had said quite accurately that Kirke had sent 'some' troops to encamp on the Isle of Inch. Walker wrote out the whole letter for circulation but improved it by replacing the word 'some' and with the words 'four thousand horse and nine thousand foot'.

Putting aside the sheer improbability of Kirke having thirteen thousand soldiers and four thousand horses, none of this would have mattered, but it fed into Mackenzie's general narrative that Walker was a dishonest man. When the commissioners returned in the evening, a council meeting was called. The commissioners reported on the progress of the negotiations and set out what the sticking points were. Walker showed everyone his transcription of Mitchell's letter. According to Mackenzie, and only to Mackenzie, Walker argued that the city should not insist on the 26 July, but should agree an earlier date. 'He earnestly urged a compliance with the enemy's demands for surrendering the town the next day.' The obvious point was made: if Kirke had landed such an unexpectedly large force on Inch, only about six miles from where they were sitting, and four thousand of them were mounted, why on earth should they surrender at all? Walker's 'indiscretion', wrote Mackenzie, 'joined with his ill advice, had like to have proved of as dangerous consequence to himself, as … to the garrison'.

We may part company with Mackenzie on his analysis. All that had happened was that there was a debate as to what should be done. The options were considered and caution was voiced by some, one of whom may have been Walker. If Walker added false figures to the letter, there can only be one explanation. He wanted to use it to galvanize the garrison, but did not want to fool the council. He was open about his intention to spread a report with enhanced figures of Kirke's army. There were those who did not trust Walker, but most did. Neither Ash nor Holmes say anything hostile about him. They were both among the signatories who agreed to send the commission and the proposed terms to the Irish camp. Ash was not on the council and so was not present when Walker confessed to making up figures. Ash's account of this is important. He refers to the boy coming to Walker 'with a letter from one Mitchel in the fleet'. The letter gave an account 'whether true or false I know not, that 12,000 are landed at Lough Swilly, and that 2,000 horse are gone round to land there also'. The troops clearly got Walker's version of the news. They were to hold out because a mighty army was on its way.[14]

Whatever position Walker took in the debate, now knowing that Kirke had made a landing of however many men on Inch, the council agreed to surrender only if they were not relieved by 26 July. The Irish would know more about the Inch landings than they did, and if the landing of twelve or more thousand men was true, the Irish would never accept that date. If it was false, the Irish may well agree to a fortnight's extension. The Irish reaction would establish the truth. The council also insisted on the Irish hostages, who would be the Irish commissioners, being placed on Kirke's ships. The Irish would, they reasoned, simply have to comply with any terms agreed so long as Gordon and Sir Neil O'Neill, and Shelton and Skelton were safely held by Kirke. The third point of disagreement, the army marching out to Culmore with its arms, was not something they were going to insist upon. It would be 'left to the commissioners to debate'.

The commissioners went back to the tent at noon, with instructions, said Ash 'not to abate one hour of the time specified'. They let the Irish know their answer. 'The enemy refusing absolutely to grant these terms, the treaty was ended.' It had been a close call. Had the Irish agreed, there would have been an immediate ceasefire until 26 July, and that would have been the end of the siege. As Mackenzie put it: 'So evidently did that gracious God … infatuate the counsels and harden the hearts of our enemies. Had they accepted the proposals, the city had been unavoidably surrendered, and we could not have held out three or four days longer than the time we desired.'[15]

The Irish were disappointed. They could not afford to play this waiting game whereby a brittle treaty could be shattered at a moment's notice by Kirke's reappearance. They were 'so incensed with us', wrote Ash, 'that scarce had the commissioners got within our lines, they began to vent their malice in playing bombs and great guns against the city, which blessed be God, did little mischief'.[16]

On 12 July, out on the lough on the day before the negotiations began, the frigate *Bonadventure* returned from Killybegs with the Enniskillen delegates. As Caldwell had done, they painted for Kirke an enthusiastic picture and were eager to get Kirke to approve their plan to relieve Derry from the land. They had the men to form an army of eight thousand foot and twelve hundred horsemen and could march up from Enniskillen, but they needed arms and ammunition, commissions for their officers, and an experienced English officer to lead the expedition.[17]

The Irish were also taking an interest in Enniskillen. On 13 July, Berwick arrived with his flying column to reconnoitre its defences. Gustavus Hamilton pulled all his men behind the town's defences and sent out a hundred foot soldiers to guard the approach. This detachment was 'cut to pieces' by the Irish horsemen, and only a handful escaped death or capture. Berwick did not have the numbers to attack the town, but he rode away knowing it was vulnerable.[18]

27

Nearing the end

King James needed the siege to end. If negotiations failed, he needed the city to be taken, and quickly. He began to regret that he had relied on Hamilton for so long when he had the vigorous, angry Rosen on hand. 'The long continuance of the siege of Derry has been of so ill consequence to our affairs', he wrote to Hamilton on 12 July. 'We believe that you have done what you thought best for our service, yet we do think fit hereby to will and require you that if the city of Londonderry shall not yield on the conditions we have offered, you may in your station be assisting to the Marquis de Rosen in the pressing of it with all the vigour imaginable that no time may be lost in bringing it into our power.' Hamilton, perhaps three months too late, was being sacked.[1]

The king ordered Rosen to take over the siege, but not to interfere with Hamilton's negotiations. As soon as he got the letter, Rosen wrote back on 15 July. He refused. 'I am in despair, Sire, as my health, which gets worse daily, prevents me from executing this order. M. Hamilton, who Your Majesty has until now charged with the direction of the siege, is perfectly capable of bringing this affair to a close in a satisfactory manner.' Rosen was so fed up, he let the king know the rest. His poor health was in part due to the fact that, ever since he arrived, his advice had not been taken. He had allowed Hamilton to strip away his men for the siege and was now left every evening alone with a single battalion to face the fleet and guard the boom. 'I beg Your Majesty very humbly to allow me to leave and recover either at Charlemont or at Coleraine, so as to be in a better condition to show evidence of my zeal.' Hamilton was back in charge.[2]

That same day, 15 July, the bombing continued. In the evening, two thousand Irish troops 'marched down from their camp in order towards the works on the Wind-Mill'.[3] Fearing an all-out attack following the breakdown of the negotiations, Michelburne ordered the men out to line the defences. The Irish gun in the wood at Tamneymore started firing 'which killed but one of Capt. Gordon's men'. The Irish 'came to the middle of the hill stopped, and wheeled about, and marched back again', wrote Mackenzie. 'Our men raised an huzza from one end of the line to the other, waving their hats to them to come down.' It was the same exercise Michelburne had conducted four days earlier. If the response had been poor, Hamilton may have been tempted to plan a third attack on the Windmill. The response was energetic, and so he did not.

On Tuesday, 16 July the last of the ships disappeared from the Lough. Walker's exaggerated account of troop landings on Inch had put everyone's mind at rest. It was clearly all part of Kirke's relief plan, as Ash calmly noted in his journal: 'All the fleet left Culmore and went to Inch.' The garrison busied itself in building new defences outside the Royal Bastion in the form of 'a small fort' made of casks filled with mud. As there was no immediate danger of a relief attempt by sea, Hamilton moved his two large cannons from the boom and by the next day they were in the battery straddling the road four hundred yards outside Butcher's Gate.

With the battery in position, the Irish carried out another raid on the trenches to destroy the blind so that the heavy cannon could get a clear shot at Butcher's Gate. It was a repeat of the night assault by Clancarty's men. The trenches and blind were within a few feet of the walls, in easy musket range and within rock throwing distance. At ten in the morning, twenty men dashed forward to smash or roll away the earth-filled casks. The trenches, records Mackenzie, were empty at the time, but the Irish could not hold them under a hail of stones. It was another almost suicidal action and, again, we do not know if they had any success in carrying out their limited objective. 'Some few were killed, and one taken prisoner'. Ash heard that six were killed 'and most of the remainder wounded'.

Later that day was a second incident that has elicited much comment since. It was a failed attack on the Irish by Arthur Noble and Adam Murray, described by Ash and Mackenzie. Captain Noble went out, says Ash, 'beyond the gallows to attack the enemy trenches' which were on the high ground beyond the bog. The Irish had built a new earthwork there, 'the new fort'. Noble's plan was to get alongside or above the fort and then rush it. At the same time, to distract the Irish, Adam Murray led a frontal attack on the fort. Noble was 'beat back' before he got into position. One of his men was killed and three were wounded. Murray fared even worse. His cousin, James Murray, 'was killed as he was throwing stones into their trenches', Sergeant Lynn was killed 'and as the colonel was coming off himself, he was shot in the thigh, notwithstanding his armour, dangerously near the bottom of the belly'.

Mackenzie wrote a less detailed description, which minimalized the incident and made no reference to Captain Noble's party. Murray had only 'about twelve' men with him and retreated when his ammunition was spent. He was then 'shot through both the thighs up near his body', a wound 'so dangerous to him that he did not fully recover of it till near November'. There is a degree of improbability in Mackenzie's reference to 'about twelve' men. This was a daylight attack on the same trenches on which thousands of men had made three failed attempts on 30 May, and which Michelburne had to pull away from with six hundred or more men.[4]

It has been argued that Walker mentioned neither the incident nor Murray's wound because Murray was a Presbyterian, but the explanation for Mackenzie's deliberately misleading lack of detail and Walker's silence is simply that the raid was a failure. It showed what was obvious to those in the city. The raids from the city were dangerous and the besieged had a sense of caution that was impossible to admit in the published accounts. Walker's blanket assertion for the London reader that in these raids the besieged 'always came off with great Execution on the Enemy' was a nonsense. These brave, forward men sometimes came off in dispiriting defeat. And sometimes simply never came back.

Ash ended his diary for 17 July:

> In the morning we had six bombs, and about midnight, eight. The first of the eight killed Mr Henry Thompson, an old inhabitant of the city. It fell upon him as he lay in bed, and broke him all to pieces'

On the Isle of Inch, Richards was still working on the defences. By 14 July, he had eight pieces of ordnance in the battery, six 3-pounders and two 6-pounders, but he needed more. Every day fresh rumours came in: the boom is broken, the Enniskilleners had defeated Berwick, there was a French fleet off Carrickfergus with twenty thousand men on board, a sally at Londonderry had killed five hundred of the enemy.

Kirke's men were safe on Inch, but not on the mainland. Rathmullan was occupied and barricaded by Captain Echlin and perhaps only two companies of men. James' son Berwick, whose camp at Cavan Park was only ten miles away, sent a force to attack the village on the night of 17 July. 'Twenty of Clancarty's men, and the major, had attempted to lodge themselves in a house, within twenty yards of our advance; but in vain, the major having been wounded in the arm, and about twelve of the soldiers killed or wounded.' Echlin reported beating them off and killing a hundred and fifty, and in London the figure grew to two hundred and forty. 'Of ours none were killed but Captain Cunningham. His ensign wounded in the head.' All the casualty figures are suspect, and it was another victory after which the victors had to abandon their position immediately. Rathmullan was too exposed and was left to the Irish. Echlin and his men were rowed across to Inch.[5]

Even now, well into the close siege, there were people going in and out of the city on various errands. Some were to do with the prisoners, some were authorized to take messages and, for all one knows, tobacco and brandy pedlars were still plying their trade on both sides of the lines, as described by Michelburne. 'Each day people from the town are allowed to come and go without being overly checked', complained the French engineer, d'Astier, and spies were warning the city of the Irish plans: 'They entrench themselves before us as we advance.' The defenders also thought themselves betrayed by informers. John Buchanan's 'son or daughter' brought intelligence to the Irish every day, wrote Michelburne. 'Twas plain', Aickin wrote, 'the Irish had Intelligence'. When the defenders planned to make a raid on a Monday morning, the Irish troops would shout over to them on the Sunday: 'Are you not ready for your great Sally?'[6]

The newly positioned heavy guns were all in range of the cannon on the bastions, and manning them was dangerous work. Nevertheless, by the next day, 18 July, the Irish cannons had smashed down the breastwork that screened the gate.

During the dark hours, the defenders rebuilt it with barrels and sods and, when daylight came, most of that was smashed down as well. At about nine o'clock in the morning of 19 July, disaster struck. The French engineer, Massé, went to the battery with John Wauchope to check the guns to see what effect the cannon were having on the gates. As he looked, a cannon in the city fired a cannister shot at his battery. 'Mr. Massé was killed; one Captain Bourke had his left hand shot off, and wounded by splinters through the shoulders; a gunner and two soldiers hurt; all by one shot … Colonel Wauchope had escaped narrowly … within a moment thereafter, two soldiers had been killed by a second shot; whereof the wind had so burned Major Geoghegan's face, that he was in danger of losing his left eye.'[7]

King James was disappointed by Rosen's reply. He wanted the city attacked. He wrote to Hamilton: 'It is the utmost importance in the world to us that Derry should be taken before any relief can come to it … more men will be saved by attacking this town briskly though we should lose men in the doing of it, than by prolonging the matter … you are to press it with all the vigour and application imaginable.' The rebels had been willing to surrender by 26 July, and that was now less than a week away. However, the king recognized that Hamilton was the man on the spot, and left him with an alternative: 'If you and our other general officers find that it is not to be taken by force then … you are to continue the blockade … every day being of importance for it is probable that they have not much provision after the 26th of the month'.[8]

On 20 July, Hamilton called a council of war with all his senior officers: Thomas Buchan, Sir Charles Cairney, John Wauchope, Léry-Girardin, Dominic Sheldon and Berwick, who was ordered up from Castlefinn. Rosen did not attend, but stayed in his tent, sick and sulking. Hamilton was of the view that the city could not be taken by storm. They all agreed. Their only prospect of success was to continue the blockade and let famine do its work. Hamilton got each of the senior officers to write and sign a short note. Greatly relieved that he had been given the option, he wrote back to the king to that effect, enclosing the brief opinions of his six senior officers in support.

There were differing views on the relative strengths of their own forces and those of the rebels. Hamilton estimated that, when 'the trench was opened' and the siege proper began in mid-June, the Irish 'had fourteen battalions, consisting, at most, in six thousand men'. The besieged had then about, he thought, five thousand men, but 'sickness and mortality' had taken their toll. His own forces for the same reasons (as well as desertions) 'did not, by a great deal, amount to the number of five thousand men'. Two of his Scots officers thought both numbers even smaller. Wauchope wrote that 'our army is reduced by sickness and fatigues and desertion, not to the number of three thousand men able for service', but that the numbers in the city 'are far inferior to our number'. Cairney thought the enemy had 'at least two thousand'. Nevertheless, everyone came to the same conclusion: further attacks would be a waste of lives. Now that it was clear Kirke intended to land elsewhere, they needed to save their forces in order to stop him linking up with the rebels in Enniskillen.

On the day of the conference, the French paymaster Fumeron wrote not only of the army's dwindling numbers, but of their low morale. The men knew that they were too few to take the city, and their condition was miserable. Almost all of them were ill. Sickness and desertion had reduced the Irish regiments, each of which should have had eight hundred men, to an average of two hundred, 'Of the 15 battalions which are here no more than 3,000 men are in a fit state to carry arms. The same is true of the cavalry as instead of a thousand horse, which should be there, one cannot count on more than 300.' Disease was now the great enemy. There were only nine surgeons for the six hundred to seven hundred sick or wounded in the hospital in Strabane. 'There is a fever in the camp which is passed on like a sort of plague ... everybody has caught it, and far too many have died of it; M. Rosen had it very badly as did M.de Léry, and they are not yet free of it.'[9]

Disease was raging inside the city, and food was on everyone's mind. There were now regular desertions. Those who did leave were bitter about what was happening within the walls. Fumeron wrote: 'We learn that these rebels are at the end, lacking food; the governor and a minister in there distribute what little there is with great economy only to those who can bear arms, leaving the rest, the women and children, to die of hunger.'[10]

Captain Ash wrote in his diary for 20 July: 'No bombs, nor anything of consequence, but a new kind of subsistence for the men, viz. starch otherwise called Dutch flour, made into pancakes with the same ingredients which were in those of tallow' (which was, said Walker, 'an Infallible Cure of the Looseness'). On 21 July, 'We had 28 bombs.' On 22 July, the 'two battering pieces played above forty shots against the walls and houses. One of them shot a ball of nineteen pound weight and another of fourteen pound, which killed and maimed some who lay in garrets.'

By 22 July, James had received Hamilton's message. Accepting 'It is impossible to take the town of Derry, but by famine', he gave his consent to end the siege. 'Our will and pleasure is, that, so soon as you receive this, you prepare for raising the siege, and then actually raise it, unless you be of opinion, that, in continuing the blockade, the town will be forced to surrender for want of provision.' When they withdrew, they were to blow up Culmore Fort 'that it may not stand in our way another time'. Rosen was ordered to implement his plan to lay waste to the whole area.

At night on 18 July, little William Irwin got back into the city. It had taken him two days to get there from Inch. Hidden in a cloth button on his breeches was a letter from Kirke outlining his plans in hopeful terms. He had sent officers to Enniskillen to lead their army straight up to Londonderry to join with his forces. They would beat the Irish away and relieve the city from the land. In short: 'It gives us an account that he will with God's assistance relieve us very soon.

Governor Michelburne knows his hand, for he was promoted by him in the army at Tangier.'[11] That next day, Walker and Michelburne replied with the most important and effective letter of the siege.

> Sir
>
> Yours of the 16th we received and in short must tell you to our grief this garrison hath lived upon cats, dogs and horse flesh this three days, and now there remains no victuals of any kind in the garrison to live upon than three pound of salt hides, one pound of tallow, and one pint of meal a man which we compute will not keep us alive any longer than next Wednesday. Above 5,000 of our men are dead already for want of meat and those that survive are so weak that they can scarce creep to the walls where many of them die every night at their post.
>
> We are afraid we shall lose our outworks every minute and then we shall be all cut off. Their miners are coming with their lines close to our walls. But hitherto their sinking underground is prevented. We are offered very honourable terms from the enemy which we still rejected in hopes of relief, and now no expectation of aid during the time of our victuals. God knows what will become of us, for they vow not to spare age nor sex. A great many admire that such a fleet as yours should lie so long before us and send us no victuals whereas the wind presented fair many times. Trust none of the enemy's deserters for we have been often deceived by such people. There came two battering guns here last night which plies us day all day and broke our curtains and shattered our gates.
>
> The enemy's guns are brought up from Culmore and that boom which is cross the river is broke so that a small ship with provisions might easily pass up here without hazard. The enemy's regiment of fusiliers are marched up to Dublin and 'tis certain their regiment of guards marches in a day or two. The rest of their army consists most part of rabble.
>
> We are, sir
>
> Your very humble servants,
>
> Geo Walker, Jno Michelburne
>
> Londonderry July 19th 1689[12]

Much of the letter was untrue. The curtain walls (the walls between the bastions) were not 'broke', nor was the boom and the miners were not coming, but the wording of the letter was necessary, and it was written in terms that brought about exactly the result Walker and Michelburne wanted.

William Irwin carried the letter back. The first message from the fleet had been 'with great ingenuity' sewed into his garter, and the second was hidden in a cloth button. As he had been forced to swallow the last letter he tried to smuggle out, a new method of concealment was needed. The letter was 'made up within a piece of a bladder, in the shape of a suppositor, and the same way applied to the boy'. It was, said Michelburne, put up the boy's 'fundament'.[13]

Kirke reached Lough Swilly on 19 July, and the next day came ashore at Inch. He was impressed at what had been done, and ordered all the remaining troops to disembark. Inch was going to be a fortress. The men set up a camp and spent the day unloading ammunition and provisions into the newly built magazine. For the Enniskilleners, two ships were sent off to Ballyshannon with sixteen hundred muskets with ammunition and match, twenty barrels of gunpowder, eight small cannons and a supply of hand grenades. Kirke also issued commissions for five regiments to be made up of over four thousand men. To prevent another Omagh fiasco, he sent William Wolseley to command the Enniskillen forces. Zachary Tiffin was promoted to colonel and sent along as well. The Enniskillen commissioner, Andrew Hamilton, sung Kirke's praises: 'No man could have shown more zeal than he did for their majesties' service, and the preservation of the Protestants.'

William Irwin arrived on Inch in the late afternoon and produced the letter from Londonderry. The effect on Kirke was electric. Here was the first positive assertion that the boom was broken. Even if it was untrue, the fact that it was now in writing covered him. If he succeeded, all well and good. If the ships were blocked by the boom, the blame would lie with Michelburne and Walker. Either he made a relief attempt now or else the city would fall without any attempt having been made. There would be no second chance and so loss of cannons or provisions to the enemy no longer mattered.

'Immediately', wrote Richards, 'with a great deal of privacy', Kirke 'ordered three ships laden with provisions with forty musketeers in each' to go up the lough.[14] Kirke accompanied them in the *Swallow*. 'I thought it no time to delay', he wrote, and sent an urgent dispatch to Captain Rooke of the *Deptford*, demanding a frigate to accompany the victuallers so that an attempt could be made at the first opportunity. Rooke ordered Captain Leake to take the *Dartmouth* to follow Kirke to Lough Foyle. Kirke also sent a messenger back to Derry, choosing for this last mission the 16-year-old who had been sent to Scotland in May by Baker.[15] As the boy was known to Walker, there was no written message. He just had to deliver the news. Kirke was coming.

28

Back on Lough Foyle

Michelburne and Walker were not the only people trying to get through to Kirke. The duke of Schomberg, half-German, half-English, with a wealth of military experience, having commanded French, English and Portuguese armies, had been given the command of the English invasion of Ireland. Schomberg was mightily frustrated at both Kirke's inaction and the lack of news from him. If Kirke had done as he had been told, all would be well. In the preceding weeks, Schomberg had sent two copies of his orders to Kirke ordering urgent action, but neither had arrived. One copy was sent by a packet boat from Chester, and the other in the hands of the lawyer, David Cairnes, who was to travel through Scotland.[1]

Feelings in Scotland ran high. The Protestants of Ulster were mostly Scots rather than English, and thousands had fled to Scottish ports. The privy council of Scotland urgently needed to do something other than watch and wait for London for act. Warrants were issued to those who wanted to attack Irish shipping, rescue Protestants, take supplies to Londonderry or simply to go to Ireland to fight for the cause. In May a warrant was issued to release eight hundred bolls of meal[A] for the relief of Protestants in and around Londonderry.[2]

This was all piecemeal. What Scotland needed was a navy, not just for Ireland but to stop supplies and men joining King James' forces in the Highlands. In March that year, urgent measures had been taken to create one by hiring two large Glasgow merchant ships, the *Pelican* and the *Janet*, which were then, on 13 April, put under the command of two experienced officers, William Hamilton and John Brown. They were told to get what ordnance they could and were allocated a company of redcoats. They were also given somewhat ambitious orders to search out and destroy Irish and French shipping from Cornwall to the Isle of Skye, but in particular they were to seek and destroy birlinns[B] in the creeks between Mull and Kintyre.

David Cairnes had spent the summer in London, where he appeared before the House of Commons Committee on Irish Affairs. He was given orders to travel to Scotland and then on to Londonderry to take Schomberg's urgent orders to Kirke. By 4 July, he was in Edinburgh, where he was given a warrant to travel to Ireland.[3] Two days later, he sailed from Greenock for Lough Foyle, but faced

[A] A Scottish boll was a measurement of forty-eight gallons. Eight hundred bolls is the equivalent of 38,400 gallons (174,570 litres) of meal.

[B] Birlinns were the large rowing boats favoured by the highlanders, usually with six or eight oars, which ploughed across the sea to Ireland and back.

contrary winds, and by 10 July had got no further than the Mull of Kintyre. He was overhauled by the two ships of the Scots navy escorting the *James of Derry* ketch, which had been collecting Kirke's urgent supplies, 'two hogsheads of wine and some brandy'. While Cairnes was talking to Captain Hamilton, three larger ships appeared on the horizon. Hamilton suggested that Cairnes transfer into the *James of Derry*, while he took the *Pelican* and *Janet* to investigate.

It was the worst of moves. The three ships were the French men-of-war lent to King James by King Louis. They had just left Carrickfergus to transport an Irish regiment to Scotland to join Lord Dundee's army. Also on board were thirty-five of King James' Scottish officers, including Colonel Alexander Cannan, a veteran of King William's Scots brigade; and Melfort's brother in law, Sir William Wallace of Craigie, who was to command King James' horse in Scotland. The French ships hoisted English colours to get in close and, once their prey could not escape, they attacked. While *La Lutine* engaged the *Pelican*, *La Jolie* and *La Tempête* caught the *Janet*. The *Janet* had only twelve guns, and each of the French ships had over thirty. The *Janet* was pulverized. Captain Brown was killed in the cannonade, as were most of his men. By the time the French boarded her, of the eighty men on board there were only fourteen survivors, half of whom were wounded. The French then turned their undivided attention to the eighteen-gun *Pelican*. Before her capture, Captain Hamilton and ninety out of the hundred and twenty men on board were killed. So ended the last action of the Scots navy.[4]

From 'a pretty distance' the fighting was seen by those on the *James of Derry*. They made a run for it, but were chased and, rather than risk capture, the *James* was beached at the north end of the Mull of Kintyre. Abandoning Kirke's wine and brandy, everyone ran off into the hills, and Schomberg's orders to Kirke got no further than Campbeltown, from where Cairnes wrote a report to the duke of Argyll.[5]

The French ships took their passengers to Mull in time for them to take part in the battle of Killiecrankie on 27 July. It was a costly disaster for both sides. While winning a famous victory, the Jacobite commander, Lord Dundee, exposed himself to the enemy musketry and was killed, as were over a third of his men. The two Scots prizes were sailed down to Dublin and taken into the harbour. On their way, the French flotilla captured the Chester packet boat that was carrying the second set of Schomberg's orders to Kirke. Without knowing it, the French had managed to prevent the delivery of both copies. Schomberg's letter ended up instead in Dublin. The effect was to alert King James of the advanced preparations for an invasion, and his own plans to invade Scotland fell away. He needed to concentrate on beating off the coming invasion, and Derry faded into insignificance.

Accompanied by the three victuallers, the *Mountjoy*, *Jerusalem* and *Phoenix*, Kirke arrived back at the mouth of Lough Foyle in the *Swallow* on the Sunday 21 July. Only the *Portland* was there to meet them, because Captain Rooke had taken the other ships to chase the French frigates that had just wiped out the Scots navy.

The next day, 22 July, Kirke moved up the lough, and sent the victuallers to wait off Culmore.

Late that same night, the (otherwise unidentified) 16-year-old messenger arrived in the city from Inch. Officers had been sent to Enniskillen, he said, 'and they are to be down in four days to join the English forces and, with God's assistance, to raise the siege'. Kirke was now definitely on his way and relief was at hand within a week. The youth also brought some pleasing gossip. Both Lundie and Colonel Cunningham were in London and had been 'confined in the Tower'.[6]

The Irish were now carrying out Rosen's scorched-earth policy. Farms and villages were put to the torch all over the Inishowen and Fanad peninsulas. On the 22 July, wrote Richards from Inch, 'about twelve at night we heard much firing from the N W part of the island … a little time after we saw a great light from Rathmullan caused by the Irish setting fire to that place, to hinder which one of our ships that lay thereabouts fired several cannon at them'. Rosen wrote to King James: 'The environs of Derry and Inishowen are completely ruined by the length of the blockade and the siege. Rathmullan, guarded by 300 men, was razed by fire … in view of Kirke and his fleet, by a cornet called Carroll, whose action deserves reward, and as we retreat we will endeavour to do as much damage as possible.' Kirke was told: 'Our retreating (and with reason) from Rathmullan, has given room to the Irish to lay that place in ashes and have most barbarously murdered some few Protestants that were left therein.'[7] To the troops on Inch, it was a far from pleasing sight, but the villages going up in flames was in one sense encouraging. It meant the Irish army was moving out.

The next day, 23 July, the *Dartmouth* and the *Deptford* arrived in Lough Foyle. Kirke ordered the *Dartmouth* to go up to the victuallers 'till the first opportunity of wind should permit to carry them up the river'. The *Dartmouth* was to cover the first two victuallers by engaging the fort at Culmore. To avoid the risk of blocking the river, the *Jerusalem* was ordered 'not to weigh till a signal given by the *Dartmouth,* who was not to give the sign till one of the other ships had passed the boom'. Accompanying the ships was the thirty-foot longboat from the *Swallow.* It carried ten men, five to row on one side and four on the other, under the command of John Shelley, the boatswain's mate. Heavy boards were nailed up over the sides to protect the oarsmen from musketry. It was, in the terms of the time, 'well barricado'd', and was to be used to tow the ships if the need arose and, should there be a boom, to attack it if the ships could not break through.

Kirke now had other ideas for Inch. The relief attempt was highly risky, and if it failed it could not be repeated, especially if the passage was blocked by damaged vessels. Failure could result in the city surrendering, and Rosen's army, suddenly released from the siege, would descend in a great body on Inch. Kirke wanted his men safely offshore before that happened, and ready to sail to join the Enniskilleners. On 25 July, Colonel Steuart received detailed orders to re-embark the men. 'I should be very loath to be beat out of it [Inch] in confusion', wrote

Kirke, 'therefore I think the best way is to be in readiness to make a handsome retreat in case we are pushed'.

The order was wholly unwelcome, and Steuart refused to obey. He instead called a council of war, and got his officers to agree that he write back to Kirke to ask him to reconsider. All the men were now dry in huts, the provisions were good, the enemy had no guns and, even if they did, they could not do much harm from the far bank. Also, they could not desert the twelve thousand Protestant civilians on Inch 'who can expect no mercy at so cruel an enemy's hands'.[8]

As Kirke's reply would take three or more days to get to him, Steuart ordered eight more guns to be unshipped and added to the defences by the ford. 'Some women that came over to the island this day say that they saw three ships at Derry quay which, if true, that place is relieved by the major-general.' For the next two days, Richards had the troops working hard. A new line of communication was dug to his orders and all the carpenters were busy on the new gun platforms. Two of the smaller ships were ordered to lie dry on the strand with 'forty musketeers in each with some hand grenades, and three guns in each, so that now we have twenty two cannon to play on the strand besides the *George*'s guns, the *Fisher* ketch and *Greyhound*, which lay at some greater distance afloat'.[9] Inch was secure.

29

Hunger

BEHIND THE CITY WALLS, there was danger from without and from within. On 23 July, 'the battering pieces killed two brothers lying in a garret in Bishop's Street, and injured many houses'. To keep order in the city, a court martial of thirteen officers was convened daily. One of the officers sitting on the court martial was Captain David Ross. A complaint was received that some of Sir Arthur Rawdon's saddles had been stolen, and Captain Ross was ordered to search for them. He enquired in, or attempted to search, the rooms occupied by the wounded Adam Murray. Also in the room was Samuel Lindsay, one of Murray's troopers. They argued, Ross drew his sword, and Lindsay shot him dead with a carbine.[1]

Many thought they were about to die, and there was a sizeable body in the city who saw surrender as their only chance of survival. A plot by 'some turbulent persons to raise a mutiny in the garrison' was discovered. Confident 'that they should have assistance enough to make terms for themselves and to give up the garrison', the plotters intended 'to secure the gunners in the first place, and to nail up the guns, then to beat drums' to arrange a parley with the enemy.[2]

Thomas Ash lived through the siege and also made a note of the extraordinary prices being paid. He referred three times to food in the final ten days:

> 20TH July: At the commencement of the siege, meal was sold at fourpence a peck,[A] it is now six shillings. All provisions are excessively dear: milk at 3 pence ha'penny a pint: I paid so much for it, and 2s 6d for six ounces of butter.
>
> 24TH July: That day 6s was offered for a dog to eat! Dogs and cats are frequently eaten!
>
> 27TH July: this day the cows and horses, sixteen of the first and twelve of the last were slaughtered. The blood of the cows was sold at four pence per quart, and that of the horses at two pence. The soldiers got one pound of meal mixed with Dutch flour, and next morning one pound and a half of horse beef per man. There is not a dog to be seen, they are all killed and eaten.

In Ash's entry for 20 July quoted above, he describes an inflationary increase in the price of meal of 1,700 per cent. The purchasing power of a penny piece in 1689

[A] A peck is a dry measure equivalent to two gallons (eight quarts) or 9.09 litres.

is illustrated by *Ireland's lamentation,* a London pamphlet published in May that year, which set out a list to show how cheap food then was in the west and north of Ireland: 'Forty-five eggs for one penny. A fat goose for three pence. A fat turkey for six pence. A fat hen for three half-pence. A fat Lamb, or Kid, for a Groat [four pence].'[3]

George Holmes, the other man who wrote a private account, albeit one to impress his wealthy reader in Cumberland with the trials he had been through, made these remarks: 'Our provision grew scant and our allowance small, 1 lb. of oatmeal, and 1 lb. of tallow served a man a week, sometimes salt hides ... I saw 2s. a quarter given for a little dog, horse blood at 4d. per pint, all the starch was eaten, the greaves of tallow,[B] horse flesh was a rarity.'[4]

Walker printed in his *Account* his famous price list, which over the centuries has been reproduced in school books as a shocking record of the hardships suffered in the siege. By 30 June, Walker claimed, the garrison had been brought to the point of extreme necessity that they were forced to 'feed upon Horse flesh, Dogs, Cats, Rats and Mice, Greaves of a year-old, Tallow, and Starch, of which they had good quantities as also salted and dried Hides, &c.'. He then set out a list of prices for the foodstuffs available:

> Horse flesh sold for 1s. 8d; A quarter of a dog, 5s. 6d; A dog's head, 2s. 6d per pound fattened by eating the bodies of the slain Irish; A cat, 4s. 6d; A rat, 1s.; A mouse, 6d; A small fluke [a flat fish] taken in the river not to be bought for money or purchased under the rate for a quantity of meal; A pound of greaves, 1s; A pound of tallow, 4s; A pound of salted hides 1s; A quart of horse blood, 1s; A horse pudding, 6d; An handful of sea wrack, 2d; Or chick weed, 1d; A quart of meal when found, 1s.[5]

Walker's price list was a fiction. He drew it up, probably sniggering with a collaborator in a Fleet Street ale house, as they added one more outrageously silly item after the other. People died of hunger and we need not doubt that some ate everything and anything. Dogs and cats were certainly eaten, but there was no market in vermin, and no one except Walker suggests that there was. When Mackenzie came to 'To Rectifie the Mistakes' in Walker's *Account*, having replicated many of the lists printed by Walker, he rectified this particular misrepresentation by neither mentioning nor including it in his *Narrative*, nor by dignifying it with a correction. It was not worthy of comment. He wrote instead: 'the Garrison was furnished with Bread (though the allowance was little) till the end of the Siege'.[6]

Walker's list illustrated the hardships that people suffered in the siege, but did so by caricature. Immediately after his list, he inserted, by way of an authorial

[B] Greaves are a by-product of candle making, 'the fibrous matter or skin found in animal fat, which forms a sediment on melting and is pressed into cakes to serve as meat for dogs or hogs, fish-bait, etc.; the refuse of tallow'. *Oxford English dictionary.*

wink, this anecdote: 'We were under so great Necessity, that we had nothing left unless we could prey upon one another: A certain Fat Gentleman conceived himself in the greatest danger, and fancying several of the Garrison lookt on him with a greedy Eye, thought fit to hide himself for three days.'[7]

There were people who had surplus food to sell to those who could pay for it, and it must be that those who had surplus food profited greatly while the siege lasted, and those who had money did not starve. But overwhelmingly those who had fled to the city had no money when they left home, and after three months of siege all but a few were in desperate plight. A private soldier on the walls, John Hunter, wrote:

> I could not get a drink of clean water, and suffered heavily from thirst, and was so distressed by hunger, that I could have eaten any vermin, but could not get it. Yea, there was nothing that was any kind of flesh or food, that I would not have eaten if I had it. May the good Lord, if it be his pleasure, never let poor woman's son meet with such hardships as I met with at that great siege.[8]

The court martial sat on 24 July and ordered that all the cattle in town 'which have been kept in houses this month or six weeks should be slaughtered for the use of the garrison'. There was not going to be enough to go round. From the walls, as if to taunt them, they could see cattle grazing on the pasture between the Irish trenches and the Irish tents. If they could overrun the trenches, they could race up the hill, make a brief show in front of the Irish as if they intended to attack, get beyond the cattle, and drive them straight back under the guns.

Later that day, a council of war was called, 'and all sworn to secrecy'. The plan was to involve three simultaneous sallies out of three of the gates at three in the morning. Two hundred men were to sally out of Shipquay Gate, another two hundred out of Butcher's Gate, and eleven hundred should be ready within the Ravelin for a Reserve. The reason for the large reserve away from the intended action was, said Ash, because they dreaded an attack on the Windmill. The first two parties were each commanded by three captains and were to attack the trench that ran through the orchard from both ends. Ash was one of those captains. The word, he said, was 'Orange'.

Although motivated by the prospect of getting some booty, especially of foodstuffs, they must have known that the chances of seizing the herd of cattle, or any of them, was remote. Their target trench was the section closest to the river on the north side of the city. It was occupied by men from Sir John Fitzgerald's regiment, which, with Clancarty's, was one of the two new regiments that had arrived with Rosen to be posted to Culmore. Less than a fortnight before, Rosen had noted that only a quarter of them had arms fit for use. How many had working muskets as they filed into the trenches that night, we do not know.

In the early hours of 25 July, from Shipquay and Butcher's gates, the men 'ran with great celerity upon their trenches, which the enemy seeing fled in confusion.

They were absolutely surprised, for most of their matches were out, quite unprepared for an attack.' Captain George Holmes, wrote: 'I led the forlorn hope which was about 100 men of the best we had, with which I ran full tilt into their trenches.' As the Irish scrambled out and away, the guns on the walls opened fire. Walker gives the detail that one regiment drew 'in good order, but had only three of their matches lighted'. That figure, three, was used by a Protestant who had fled the city, when he told Richards that the 'Derry people killed 2,000 of them' and that 'they most basely murdered them when they had not three matches lighted in the trenches'. They were caught asleep, said Holmes.

'The execution had been much greater, but many of our men being much weakened with hunger were not able to pursue them, some falling with their own blows.' Francis Nevill was told: 'It was observed when our men came to club musket and made their stroke, they could not recover their arms again.' Nor could they hold the trenches. Having seen the attack, wrote Ash, 'the enemy on the hill came down in haste. Our men, weak from want of sustenance, could not cope with them, but drew off within their trenches at Bishop's gate.' Holmes wrote that 'we durst not stay long, not above half an hour'. It was an untidy flight. 'There were but few of our men slain and those by their own carelessness for, seizing the knapsacks of the enemy which they prized more than gold, they fell heartily to eat so forgetting to return with the whole body of their party. They were killed whilst the meat was in their mouths.'[9]

Richard Hamilton reported the incident to the king as a triumph: 'Fitzgerald's and Dick Butler's regiments were in the trenches', he wrote, and although Fitzgerald's regiment was beaten out, Butler's kept their post. Jack Hamilton rushed down with whatever reserves he could get ready, 'and so beat back the enemy', which showed 'that the town's men cannot stand before the King's men in the field'.[10] The French took a different view and were furious. Never mind the final flight of the sally party and the shooting of stragglers. 'Not only was the trench's defence carried out very negligently, the officers and soldiers were leaving it or sleeping there whenever they felt like it, I was told that a short while before this sortie an order was given to snuff out some of the matches on the pretext of saving them, which makes one suspect treachery in the command of this siege, which greatly troubles the troops.'[11]

'They could hardly suppose that a poor hungry starved people would come out upon them in that manner', wrote Ash. Walker says improbably (as ever in these matters) that three hundred Irish soldiers were killed, 'besides officers'. Mackenzie could not bring himself to adopt that figure, and simply wrote 'a considerable number'. Nevill was told 'a great number' had been killed. Of those in the thick of it, Holmes wrote that his men in the advance party were responsible for all the deaths, 'before our body came up, we had slain 80 men', and Ash (who was also there) wrote that 'there were of the enemy sixty men killed, and undoubtedly, as many wounded'.[12]

It was the Irish who recovered the bodies when they reoccupied the trenches. According to Fumeron, 'we had about fifteen men killed and over twenty wounded;

Fitzgerald's lieutenant colonel was killed there, along with a few other officers'. Such had been the surprise and the silent sprint to the trenches, the besieged lost very few. 'We lost but three', wrote Ash, 'viz. Lieut. Fisher, and two privates'. Fumeron also put the figure at three. The only Irish account was that given by Richard Hamilton. He accepted there were 'near thirty killed', but said that 'nine of theirs were left behind'. On searching their pockets they 'found starch in them, as a sign of their great wants; and that a dying man of their number declared, that he had fed on nothing else for five days [but] that they expected provision every moment'.[13]

They did not get near the cattle. 'As soon as we sallied out', said Ash, they 'drove them over the hill'. The only booty was what they could snatch during their brief time in the trench: some oatcake bannocks, some beef and mutton, and a 'good store of arms and knapsacks, also several tools as spades, shovels, pickaxes &c.'. And they got the clothes and their contents of the men they stripped as well as four prisoners, including Captain Nugent. Ash described the bickering when they got in:

> Capt. Nugent had about him £26 in gold and silver, as he said, but none was found, though strict examination was made concerning it, except four louis d'ors and a guinea, which were given to those who took him, and one Mr Burrel who brought him in. The English sergeant got his sword, and his scarlet coat was given back to him, which had on it large plate buttons.

An old French major, the sieur de la Panouse, who had been left behind by his men when the trench was overrun, was clubbed unconscious with musket butts, stripped and left for dead. He came round to find that he had lost fifty louis d'ors and his clothes.[14]

Apart from Captain Nugent, Ash wrote of three prisoners having been taken, Ensign Cartie and two privates. The last three were taken to the main guard, which was in the town house. They or their guards were allowed to smoke.

> A spark fell out of the pipe on the floor where some grains had been scattered, which took fire, and ran along to where half a barrel [of gunpowder] stood and blew it up. It much disfigured the three prisoners and three men of the garrison. It broke down the floor of the guard house where the court martial usually sat. One of our men died the next day.

When the council met on the day after, they released Cartie and the other two, 'who were much hurt with the powder and incapable of doing us much hurt this campaign'.

During the day, 25 July, having been hauled by his anchors up the lough, Captain Leake in the *Dartmouth* was in position off Culmore with the three provision ships. Eager to enter the river, but held back by a southerly breeze, they waited.

'Since the siege commenced', wrote Ash, 'searchers were appointed to bring provisions into the store from those who were well supplied, in order to divide with those who had come afar off and stood in need'. Much had been stashed away. The gunners, 'who for the most part liv'd in Town', were ordered to search for provisions. They dug up cellars and 'got much Provision under the ground'. Mackenzie put the discovery of some of the hidden supplies down to chance. Mortar shells, 'by tearing open the Ground, discovered some concealed Provisions, which put us on searching for more with good success'. Michelburne described the searchers as being 'all white' with meal, and using long metal rods to poke through sacking. On 26 July 'an oath is imposed that everyone shall give a true account of what provisions they have, and a week's competency is allowed them according to their families, and the remainder is taken to the store house'.[15] That same day, 'an experiment was tried' with a cow. The Irish had returned their cattle to graze in the orchards, and to entice them closer a cow was tethered outside Shipquay Gate, and 'smeared with tar, and tow stuck to it, which was set on fire to make her roar'. The bellowing cow broke loose and had to be shot before she could reach the others.[16]

The troops were using their last reserves of strength simply to man the defences. John Hunter left us with a description of his own condition:

> I, myself, was so weak from hunger that I fell under my musket one morning as I was going to the walls, yet God gave me strength to continue all night at my post there, and enabled me to act the part of a soldier, as if I had been as strong as ever I was, yet my face was blackened with hunger ... I am sure it was the Lord that kept that city and none else, for there were many of us that could hardly stand on our feet.[17]

On Saturday 27 July, Ash recorded that 'two of our men were killed at Butcher's Gate from the orchard'. That day the remaining sixteen cows in the city were slaughtered along with twelve horses. The soldiers were each issued with a ration of a pound of meal mixed with starch, and a pound and a half of meat. There was no more, but now everyone was expecting the ships to make an attempt. Everything now turned on this final throw of the dice.

> This morning, we heard the great guns at or near Inch. The wind is S.W. which I suppose hinders our ships from coming up to us. And, God knows, we never stood in so much need of a supply, for now there is not one week's provisions in the garrison. Of necessity we must surrender the city and make the best terms we can for ourselves. Next Wednesday is the last, if relief does not arrive before it.[18]

30

Fever

THE SUFFERING WITHIN THE CITY cannot be exaggerated. By the end of July, half the people within the walls had died from disease and hunger.[A] There is no way of checking the figures because there were no records kept of burials or of who was in the city. Walker asserted that at the beginning of the siege there were 30,000 people in the city. Mackenzie is vague ('the number … is uncertain') and the other sources are silent. Walker calculated that over 10,000 left following General Hamilton's offer of protection (although Mackenzie put the figure at 'near a thousand') and that another 7,000 died of disease and famine, which would have left 13,000 to be relieved at the end of July.

No one has accepted the lower figure of 7,000 dead given by Walker, nor the higher figure of 15,000 estimated by Holmes.[1] Mackenzie, after reviewing Walker's figures, wrote this: 'it is thought that no less than ten thousand died during the siege, besides those that died soon after'. On hearing the evidence of those who were later pursuing back pay for the troops, the House of Commons in 1705 adopted the figure of 12,000 people having perished 'by sword and famine' during the siege.[2] But comparatively few men, under a thousand on each side, had died violent deaths, whereas disease killed thousands both in the city and in the Irish camp.[3]

The number of men defending the city was given by Walker and adopted by Mackenzie. At the beginning of the siege, there were 7,361 officers and men. By 27 July there were 4,708 left. Overall, from the beginning of the siege to the end, Walker's figures suggest that 2,653 men died, over 36 per cent of the original garrison.[B] That figure of 36 per cent cannot be applied across all the people packed inside the walls. The distribution of foodstuffs, of which Walker was in charge, was calculated not for each person in the city, but for each man defending the city. Those not on the muster rolls, the old, the young, and the women, were not included.

[A] It may be that more than half died. According to Gilbert Burnet, hunger 'destroyed near two thirds of their number'.

[B] Walker's figures should be taken only as broad estimates and are confusing in that he variously gives figures for 'men', 'officers' and 'the army'. We arrive at the figure of 4,708 by adding together 4,456 men and 252 officers. If Walker's 'garrison' of '4,456 Men' on 27 July was intended to include officers, it represents a reduction of just under 40 per cent, or 2,905 dead. The officers, according to Walker, declined by 29 per cent from 351 to 252, but promotions during the siege may have boosted that last number. Kirke's reorganisation was for four regiments, suggesting no more than 3,380 men and officers were fit for service after the siege (i.e., only 46 per cent of Walker's original 7,361).

The Irish described the pitiful state of those who had been pushed out of the city to be taken away after Rosen's round-up three weeks earlier. Conditions were dire. There was no sanitation in the city. Human waste was collected on dunghills or thrown over the walls. Twenty thousand people were crammed into a city with fewer than two hundred houses. Had everyone been housed, there would have been on average a hundred people in every house. Many were in makeshift shelters on any patch of ground they could find. Margaret Maurice described how in the siege two of her sons, seven other relations and their servants starved to death 'in one room'.[4] Captain Holmes painted the grimmest of pictures:

> I believe there died 15,000 men, women, and children, many of which died for meat. But we had a great fever amongst us, and all the children died, almost whole families [had] not one left alive.

'All the children died.' Mary Piggott, the widow of a captain of dragoons in the city, wrote that of the two thousand children in Londonderry, her child was one of only six 'left alive and preserved from starving in the said siege'.[5] Weakened by hunger and lack of cover at night, there was little resistance to the 'great fever' that was raging in the city.

'It is a great happiness that the country produces no venomous creature', wrote John Stevens, an English officer in the Irish army, in the following year, 'but it were much happier in my opinion did it produce no vermin. Whether nastiness or the air be the cause of it, I know not, but all the kingdom, especially the north, is infected with the perpetual plague of the itch'.[6] The itch, now known as scabies, is an unpleasant skin condition caused by the mite *sarcoptes scabiei* which burrows under the skin.[c] Scabies mites are easily passed on in unhygienic conditions by direct contact with an infected person, or that person's clothing or bedding. Vermin were a fact of life among the poor of the seventeenth century, and the siege population was for the most part made up of agricultural tenants and workers and their families. Many brought vermin with them, and conditions in the city made it difficult to avoid scabies or lice. As early as June, a London pamphlet (based on accounts from Dublin) described the defenders as being 'so crowded, that they are very noisome and full of vermin, for that several who have been taken and killed, are found to be so'.[7]

Scabies does not kill, but what did kill thousands of people huddled inside the walls was epidemic typhus, often referred to in the eighteenth century as 'gaol fever'. Parasites thrived in the overcrowded city, and among those parasites was the body louse. Lice do not live on the human body, but on clothing

[c] No one in the British Isles then knew what caused the itch. Its cause was first identified in 1687 following research in Florence by Giovanni Cosimo Bonomo, whose findings were not published in English until 1704.

and bedding. Their eggs, the nits, are laid in clothing next to the wearer's skin. Lice populations spread in cramped, unhygienic conditions. Where people are unable to wash themselves or wash or change their clothing and bedding, typhus occurs simultaneously in epidemics. Typhus is caused by the bacterium *Rickettsia prowazekii* carried by lice. When a louse bite is scratched, the louse's faeces are rubbed into the wound. If the louse is infected, its faeces carry the bacteria.

In the seventeenth century, Londoners particularly associated the Scots with lice: 'They pretend to be descended from one Madam Scota, daughter to King Pharaoh; but the best proof they give of it, is their bringing two of the plagues of Egypt along with them, viz. lice and the itch, which they have entailed upon their posterity ever since.' English slang of the time referred to Scotland as 'Louse-land'; a comb was jocularly called a 'Scotch louse-trap'; and 'Scotch fiddle' was a term used for the itch.[8] Although lice were common, typhus was not, and no one then knew what caused 'the fever'.[D]

Although the often disgusting diet resulted in all sorts of gastric problems, and there are several references to 'flux', the references to the pestilence in Derry were consistently to the 'fever'. Michelburne wrote of 'spotted fevers and malignant distempers'. After an incubation period of one to two weeks, the typhus sufferer is incapacitated by a high temperature, intense headaches and rapid breathing. When not fatal, these symptoms last about a fortnight and are usually accompanied by muscle pain, vomiting, coughing and a body rash (which, incidentally, spares the face, palms and soles). Without modern antibiotic treatment and supportive care, fatalities can reach 60 per cent among untreated patients.

Those in Derry during the siege, and those who died, were overwhelmingly people who had fled there. With no established place to live in the city, they were huddled together with thousands of other fugitives. A pamphlet printed just after the siege remarked 'that several of the most ancient Persons in Londonderry have survived the miseries of War and Famine', including John Mogridge, Alderman Gervais Squire, Robert Sherrard 'and others', but that 'some of the younger and more likely Persons are Dead'. Those older citizens had their own houses in which to live. Although not immune, within the comparative safety of their own families, they had better protection from continual intimate contact with lice-infested clothing.[9]

No class of person was safe. Although a population weakened by famine was more susceptible to the effects of the disease, even the comparatively well-fed died. Those who ate well, and the families they fed, died of typhus. Those with money, and those at the top of the administration ate well to the end, yet even

[D] The connection between lice and typhus was only made in 1909 by the French bacteriologist Charles Nicolle following his observation that typhus patients who are bathed and given clean clothing cease to be infectious. He was awarded the Nobel prize for medicine in 1928.

Michelburne 'had the irreparable misfortune of losing his dear lady, and children, with all his family, by the rage of pestilence, and deadly famine'. He was the only one of the governors to have his family with him, and he wrote of losing both his small children, a girl and then his four-year-old son, 'the only comfort of my heart'.[10]

Reference has been made above to Hamilton's decision to allow some ten thousand or so people to leave the city. That in itself was one of the two principal reasons for the failure of the siege. The second principal reason was that so many people died of typhus. When the siege ended, the city was down to its last two or three days of provisions. By that time the original population of perhaps thirty thousand (as seen by Lundie) had been reduced to about ten thousand. As Mackenzie put it: 'Those many Protestants that at the beginning of the Siege left the City, and took protection, and even the great numbers that died the last six weeks of the Siege, made those Provisions last the longer, which had they failed sooner, necessity would have forced us to submit to an enraged Enemy.'[11]

The arrests of the 'turbulent persons', five days before the end of the siege, had not put an end to the plotting. On the last full day of the siege, an informant got out from the city with a letter to Brigadier Buchan with the news that 'the rebels had killed all their dogs, horses, and cows; and that it was the last provision they expected; and all their hopes were in the four ships that were before Culmore'. The letter was signed by 'the sergeants and soldiers of Derry' and contained an offer to surrender the place on the next day 'if they could but obtain some favourable conditions for themselves'. D'Astier heard of the plot from Hamilton's lips. 'Twenty officers, and as many sergeants and corporals had promised him to deliver it [the city] and the governor to him without fail.' One way or the other, the siege was going to end before the end of July.[12]

Desperate thoughts and plans were not confined to the lower ranks. 'We must come at last', wrote Michelburne, 'to eat one another'. The prisoners and those caught hoarding provisions should be eaten first. 'They'll be a fortnight's provision. The surgeons must be sure to bleed them well, tho' we'll eat their flesh, we'll have nothing to do with human blood.' One miscreant, he wrote, 'has good plump buttocks to boil, the rest of him will make good pork pies'.

The idea was as fanciful as Michelburne's plan for a breakout to the bogs beyond the Finn where the Irish cavalry could not follow. 'All the women and children must take to the church', he wrote. The Irish would be too busy plundering the undefended city to give pursuit. And if they did, he would scatter behind him several bushels of 'crow's feet', four-pointed iron spikes made in such a manner, that however they are thrown, they always land with one of the spikes pointing upwards. 'They are good against horse and foot, especially these Irishmen who wear altogether brogues.'[13]

As the garrison faced the end, it must have been that all options were debated, including cannibalism or escape, but the reality was that no one was going to be eaten, and there could have been no breakout. The men were so weakened that, even if they did manage to slip past the Irish, they would not have made it halfway to the Finn. There were only two possible outcomes. Either Kirke relieved the city, or the city surrendered.

31

Breaking the boom

On Sunday 28 July 1689, at six o'clock in the evening, 'there sprung up a moderate gale at north-north-west'. The relief expedition weighed anchor and made for the river led by the 28-gun *Dartmouth*.[1] Gun ports closed and his men under cover, Captain Leake sailed past the fort under heavy fire from both musketry and cannon, which 'plied him very hard'. Once beyond the fort, but in musket shot of it, he ordered the sails to be taken in. The anchor was dropped, and the battering of the fort began. It was an unequal contest, as had been the duel involving the *Greyhound* (before it grounded) seven weeks before. The fourteen guns facing the fort pounded the walls, returning fire at the rate of 'five or six to one'. In the engagement, which lasted until eight in the next morning, Kirke noted that the *Dartmouth* 'received little or no damage, only one soldier killed, one wounded and Mr Lee his purser has a contusion in his cods'.[2] The *Mountjoy*, distinguished by the mythical sea horse painted on her stern, entered the river behind him, followed by the *Phoenix*. Under cover of the *Dartmouth*'s cannonade, they made their way slowly towards the boom with the *Swallow*'s longboat keeping pace between them. The wind slackened, and the pace slowed. By the time they approached the boom, there was a dead calm, and the ships were carried up on the tide at half a knot.[3]

The sound of gunfire at Culmore alerted the garrison as to what was happening. 'They were the ships Major General Kirke had sent us, according to his promise', wrote Walker, depicting himself as having just finished a sermon in the cathedral to the effect 'that God would not (after so long and miraculous a preservation) suffer them to be a prey to their enemies … and that they need not doubt, but that God would at last deliver them from the difficulties they were under'. On reading this, Mackenzie could not help himself. 'Mr. Walker', he wrote, 'about this time had preached a discouraging Sermon'.[4]

All along the river, Hamilton's men formed up to shoot at the ships. Cannon were fired, and dragged up river to fire again. As they neared the batteries at the boom, the cannon fire intensified. But the ships came on.

Over the years, there has been confusion as to what happened next. There is only one written eyewitness account, and it was written by a man whose business it was to observe and, if possible, to prevent the ships getting up the river. Paul-François de Lozières d'Astier was one of the two French engineers left outside Londonderry. He wrote:

> The two other ships continued on their way, having only a feeble wind, and to get anywhere the large ship had to be towed by an armed and

> fortified cutter. We made heavy fire from both banks of the river, which were entrenched, but this in no way inconvenienced them as they made no manoeuvres nor came out from under cover, allowing themselves simply to be carried by the tide and their cutter. When they were within close range of the cannon of the battery positioned at the boom, where there were cannons of one 12, one 18 and one 24 [pounder], we fired several shots without touching them although they were getting ever nearer. Arriving at the boom, one would have thought that it would offer some resistance, but it broke with no more resistance than if it had been just glass.[5]

That was the end of Pointis' famed boom, just one kiss from a merchant ship and it snapped. That is what had kept the provision ships away for nearly two months. In the Irish camp, in hindsight, the overall plan and the defects of the boom were clear. The river 'was not either choked by sinking some vessels in it or secured by a strong boom'. The boom was 'tied at both ends on the shores with some old ropes, which being rotted by the weather or not sound before, gave way to the first small vessel that attempted the passage'.[6] D'Astier described what followed:

> The cannon continued to fire, and although they were no more than 30 toises[A] away from us, we only managed one hit on the small ship after they had passed the boom. The pull of the tide bore the large ship about 15 toises near to the bank, where it remained for a good quarter of an hour without moving. At first we thought that it had run aground or that it wished to surrender, but it was neither one nor the other, as it began to manoeuvre away from the bank firing thirty or so musket-shots and two cannon-shots, and continued on its way towards the town without us being able to inconvenience them in any way, the river being 300 toises wide after the boom.

The uncertainty and the tension were described by Mackenzie:

> The smoke of the shot both from the land and from the ships clouded her from our sight and she was (as we afterwards learned) unhappily run aground. And when the enemy who gathered in swarms to the waterside raised a loud huzza along the shore, telling us our ships were taken and we perceived them both firing their guns at them and preparing their boats to board them, this struck such a sudden terror into our hearts as appeared in the very blackness of our countenances. Our spirits sunk and our hopes were expiring.[7]

Those not on the riverbank could see little through the gun smoke, and wrote accounts based on the sailors' yarns that spread afterwards. Those who heard from

[A] Toise, the old French measurement of 1.949 metres.

the crew of the *Mountjoy* had the cannons blazing and the soldiers from behind their wooden and canvas screens firing back continuously. The lead ship, *the Mountjoy*, ploughed into the centre of the boom, which it pushed upstream until it flexed, but held, and catapulted the ship, in slow motion, backwards. The angle was such that the ship was forced off the channel, struck the soft bottom, and stuck. Irish cavalrymen were ordered to race into the shallows to seize her. 'The ship let the horse come up within a pike's length of her side and then shot three cannons at them loaded with partridge shot which lay several of them on the ground and the others fled away.'[8]

Other mariners gave a different account. Racing ahead as fast as her oarsmen could pull, the *Swallow*'s longboat had surged forward, all of its men save Shelley blind to what was happening either side of them, their wooden screens splintering and cracked under the hail of musket balls. They struck the boom, and Shelley broke cover, hatchet in hand. The garbled report that reached Richards on Inch was that 'a boat with a house upon it' reached the boom first and 'of a sudden a man (a witch they say) struck three strokes with a hatchet upon the boom and cut it asunder'. The Admiralty preferred to believe that the boom was broken by Shelley's axe and rewarded the crew of the longboat accordingly. King William told Lord Halifax that 'he would remember Shelly who cut the chain at Londonderry'.[9]

With the remains of the boom floating uselessly astern, the *Mountjoy* was afloat and moving with the same agonizingly slow progress. At some point, the deck was raked with musket shot. Many of the crew were wounded, and six were shot dead, including Captain Michael Browning, the Londonderry man who had been given the honour of leading the city's relief.[10] There were casualties on the *Phoenix* too: the pilot, John Smith, was mortally wounded, and his son was crippled by splinters.[11]

The Irish kept firing, but it was all to no effect. Fumeron blamed it on bad gunnery: 'our cannon did not perform well; being navy officers and gunners completely unable to adjust their guns to fire on land'. Plunkett attributed the failure of the gunners to their being drunk with brandy.[12] Neither was to the point. Wooden seafaring ships needed to be sturdy, as the seven-hour battering of the *Greyhound* had demonstrated. Nothing was going to stop the tide, which simply carried the two ships higher and higher towards the city. 'The ships went up with so little wind that the longboat towed the *Mountjoy* all the way to the town.'[B] [13]

As they got closer to the city, the ships fell under the protection of the guns on the walls, and were met by those boats from the city which had lain idle for six

[B] The nine seamen in the *Swallow*'s longboat were awarded £10 each, roughly the equivalent of seven months' pay. At the end of the year, another payment of £90 was made by King William to the surviving crew of the *Mountjoy*, of which James Gordon, 'Capt. Browning's second in the ship', was given £10, and the rest received £5 each. Browning's widow, Jane, was not forgotten. Thomas Ash (whose nephew married her granddaughter) tells us that 'King William did her the honour of tying a diamond chain around her neck, and settled on her a pension' of £60 a year.

weeks. Together with the longboat, they pulled the two ships to the quayside 'to the inexpressible joy of our garrison'. The *Phoenix*, with her eight hundred bolls of meal from Stirling Castle, being the smaller of the two vessels and so the more attractive to pull, was brought to the quay first, at high tide at just after midnight. The *Mountjoy* was next with over a hundred tons of 'beef, peas, flour and biscuits all of the best kind'. A barrier of old casks filled with mud was made to protect the unloading. The days of starvation were over.

Watching everything, was the engineer, d'Astier:

> I was with M. Hamilton throughout as he gave orders all along the river, until he stopped at the boom before the ships passed, and once they had passed it, he told me that it was very unfortunate and that without the arrival of this aid we would have entered the place the following day.[14]

D'Astier set out his frustration (not for the first time) in his letter to Louvois. 'In my last letter', he wrote, he pointed out that the boom was 'not able to resist the weight of the smallest ship'. The wooden beams were linked together with 'very small and very badly made iron rings', and as it was so long, the rings often became detached by the tide and had to be repaired. It could have been strengthened, 'but all the proposals that I put forward to M.Hamilton and others came to nothing. He found everything impossible, although all he had to do was give the orders.' Nor was there any need to rely solely on that one slender boom.[15]

> I also suggested to him that we should arm the sloops in order to try and capture or burn the ships which attempted to enter. He told that would be no use. However, I dare to assure you, sir, in truth, that if we had just had two, we would have taken or burnt those two ships with the greatest ease in the world, and without losing even ten men, as there were no more than 40 armed men in the big ship and 10 in the small one which were otherwise full of foodstuffs. It would not have been at all difficult to arm the sloops, as we had six of them.[16]

Even after the boom was broken, he felt, the rebels were vulnerable. It would have been easy to attack them as they anchored off the quay only sixty yards from the trenches. 'When the tide was low, one could walk there on dry land on level ground, and without risking the loss of even 20 men, and maybe take the town, as the gate was left open in order to bring in the provisions off-loaded from the ship.' Hamilton did not like that plan either. There had been enough bloodshed, and they were leaving.

The feeling in the Irish camp was predictable. 'I think', wrote Brigadier Thomas Buchan, 'I can do the King more service in Scotland than here.'[17]

32

Retreat

THE RELIEF WAS NOT THE END of the siege, but it rendered the blockade pointless. Hamilton had failed over three months to bring about a surrender, and his only realistic hope had been to starve the defenders into submission. Now that the city was not going to starve, the already agreed plan of withdrawal needed speedy implementation. On the evening of the relief, Hamilton announced his decision to raise the siege.

Too jubilant and too weakened to do anything to the Irish, the city's collective mind focused on the new supplies. All Ash had to say of the 29 July was that 'some men were appointed out of each company to bring the provisions on shore and to carry them to the store houses'. On 30 July, he wrote, 'nothing worth note'. The Irish manned their trenches and continued to fire their muskets when targets presented themselves, but the large cannons were not brought back from the riverside. 'We have started to burn all the houses', wrote d'Astier. 'We are taking with us all the cattle from this province towards Dublin, and the Catholics were abandoning all their homes in order to go and establish themselves in places where they will be safer.'

Apart perhaps from Mackenzie, Kirke's most bitter critic in Ireland was Sir James Caldwell, who in the following year produced a document demanding that 'diligent enquiry' be made into thirty complaints about Kirke's behaviour in Ireland in 1689. The first is this accusatory question: 'Why Londonderry was no sooner relieved which might have saved the lives of thousands which perished by that delay?'[1] His simple point, which has been taken up by many since, was that if ships could get up the river at the end of July, they could have done so when Kirke first arrived on 12 June. All that had changed between then and late July was that the Irish had time to build up their riverside defences. Powley places this argument on Kirke's lips:

> I might so have earlier acted had not the seamen advised against it. Failure of such an attempt, with a ship sunken and blocking the channel would probably have produced the immediate surrender of the city which pictured relief only by its waterway. I avoided the risk and worked at an alternative until no other course lay before me. I acted. I relieved Londonderry.[2]

Although thwarted in taking the city, the feeling in the Irish army was not that they had been defeated by the defenders. There was nothing to be ashamed of in their performance. Their own numbers were inadequate for the task asked of them, and the walls of the city were too strong for their limited artillery.

> We sat down before it [Derry] with not the fourth part of the number that was within, and, though supplies were continually marching down, the strength of the besiegers was not much increased, the numbers being so small they only made up for those that daily deserted. That for battery there were but two or three pieces which played only upon great days, and that with much moderation, ammunition being scarce and the charge of carrying it so far great.[3]

The French thought the withdrawal a shambles. 'The soldiers are leaving in bands as they please', wrote d'Astier. 'If we were to levy troops in the least civilized place in the world, they could not behave as badly as these here.' The officers were to blame: 'It is impossible to conceive the level of their nonchalance and laziness.' Fumeron was sent to remove the hospital at Strabane and evacuate the sick and wounded. There were almost three thousand men unable to make their own way back, and he estimated he would need more than a thousand carts to get them out. 'It is likely that half, or at least a good third will perish', he wrote. 'I have ordered that all those able to drag themselves away should leave and attempt get themselves out of danger as best they can.' With no transport, many had not made it to the hospital but had been left in the camp. Hospital supplies were divided between the soldiers to take on to Charlemont. Fumeron was outraged at the wastage. The grain that could not be carried was sold to local merchants, arms and equipment were left in the camp 'all broken and covered with soil. Some had been discarded in heaps and completely unusable, which I loaded onto artillery wagons as I had no other transport.' Nor was there any money to pay the troops, who would have to wait until they got to Charlemont. 'We have to think about completely rebuilding the corps that served for the siege; the men, the arms and almost all necessary things having been ruined.'

After dark on 31 July, the Irish army pulled out. 'We perceived them firing several parts of the Country about. In the Night they burnt all the Tents and Huts of their Camp round the City, and before the daylight had gone off towards Lifford and Strabane, keeping a strong rear-guard of Horse. We had no Horse left to pursue them, and our Foot were in no condition to make such an Attempt.'[4] It was a day of great triumph in the city. The army that had kept the rebels hemmed in for three months had given up, and it was shattered. As Walker put it for the London public:

> Thus after 105 days, being close besieged by near 20,000 Men constantly supplied from Dublin, God Almighty was pleased in our greatest Extremity to send Relief, to the Admiration and Joy of all good People … The Enemy lost between eight or nine thousand Men before our Walls, and a hundred

> of their best Officers, according to the best Computation we could make of both, by the Information of the Prisoners we took, most of these fell by the Sword, the rest of Fevers and Flux, and the French Pox, which was very remarkable on the Bodies of several of their dead Officers and Soldiers.[A] [5]

The relief ships sent to Enniskillen had set out on 20 July from Lough Swilly, but were forced back into the lough by the south-westerly wind that took Kirke and the provision ships out to sea to head for Lough Foyle. The result was that William Wolseley did not reach Enniskillen until 28 July. Even then, it was without all the ammunition and supplies, which ended up being three or four days behind him. But when he did arrive, it was to great celebration: 'Nothing was heard but loud acclamations welcoming those gentlemen and praising God that their English friends had not quite forgot them, but that there was some sign of relief come at last.'[6]

Events overtook Wolseley. On the day after his arrival, the news reached him that an Irish army led by Justin MacCarthy, Lord Mountcashell, had attacked Crom Castle, less than twenty miles away. He took immediate control (Gustavus Hamilton was in bed with fever), gathered all the troops he could, and marched out. MacCarthy was indeed marching on Enniskillen with a new army overwhelmingly of recruits. He had hoped to join with the forces under Sarsfield and Berwick, but Berwick was recalled by Rosen to cover the retreat. Nor was there any coordination with Sarsfield, who only needed to divide the Enniskillen forces by advancing on Ballyshannon. Everything went wrong. MacCarthy lost control of his men when he attacked Crom Castle, which he had no means of taking in any event, his cavalry vanguard went on ahead and into an ambush, and in the half-hour battle that followed at Newtownbutler on 31 July, his army ceased to exist, the survivors scattered and the fugitives were slaughtered in the bogs. MacCarthy led a desperate counter-attack with a handful of his officers, had his horse shot from under him and he was dangerously wounded. It was a total defeat. As MacCarthy was led away into captivity, he told his captors that he was unwilling to outlive that day and was sorry to have survived.

Reports reached the Irish that Marshal Schomberg, 'with an army of twenty thousand men', was expected in Ireland within ten or twelve days. Rosen took over. He saw no point in holding onto country that could not be defended. The fort at Culmore was mined by d'Astier and blown up. 'The countryside is completely ruined and spoiled, and unavailable for the subsistence of the troops', and any forces left to occupy it 'would perish or desert'. The only prudent option was to abandon western Ulster and pull back to the other side of the Blackwater at Charlemont, the best part of sixty miles away. There was nothing of military value in between, and Rosen was not going to stretch himself by supporting operations against Enniskillen. With Berwick's mounted troops covering his

[A] Walker's reference to the 'French pox', or syphilis, was met with silence from Mackenzie.

withdrawal, he ordered the wholesale destruction of everything his troops could burn.

On 3 August, while the army was leaving Strabane, the news came through of the disaster at Newtownbutler. The messy retreat became untidier amid wild fears that Wolseley's triumphant army would jointly attack with Kirke. 'This so alarmed them', wrote Mackenzie, 'that for haste they burst some of their big guns, threw waggons of arms into the river and left many of their army that were sick behind them'.[7]

In the city, all was quiet. The stores were unloaded. People were fed. 'We are now under some Impatience', wrote Walker, 'to see Major-General Kirk, under God and the King, our Deliverer'. On the day after the Irish left, Ash left to inspect his farm on the Waterside. 'The roof of my house was smoking on the floor, and the doors falling off the hinges.' On the next morning, Captain White led a small delegation to Inch to let Kirke know that the Irish had gone. They arrived, noted Richards, with 'both horse and foot', and were forced to spend the night there 'by reason of extraordinary windy and rainy weather'. In the city, others had the same urge to get out and on 2 August 'a great number of black cattle were brought from the country for the use of the garrison'. Colonel Crofton went to Inch to get leave to take two or three hundred men out into the country to protect Protestant property 'and to bring in a vast quantity of cattle'. Kirke refused permission. On 3 August, Ash wrote, 'The cows that were taken yesterday were restored to their owners.'

On the morning of 4 August, Kirke rode in triumph to Londonderry followed by three companies of his English troops, who were to camp on the Windmill. At about 11 o'clock, he entered the city with a group of his officers. 'All the soldiers were drawn up in the high streets, the cannon all round the walls discharging, great acclamations of joy were heard from every part of town.' Kirke processed through the city flanked by 'the governors Michelburne and Walker with him, one of each hand'. The civic sword and mace were borne before them, and a crowd led by the aldermen processed behind them. Kirke was treated to a very good dinner 'considering the times', with 'small sour beer' and milk and water, 'with some little quantity of brandy'. Afterwards, accompanied by the officers, Kirke rode on Michelburne's white mare ('which he had saved all the siege'[B] [8]) to inspect the Windmill, where he ordered Richards to stake out the ground to encamp the soldiers from Inch. In the evening, Kirke rode back to Inch, from where he wrote to the duke of Hamilton:

> I was at Derry yesterday to order a place to camp: since I was born, I never saw a town of so little strength to rout an army with so many generals in it

[B] Michelburne's preservation of 'two Excellent *Horses* in a Seller under Ground' raised speculation that tho' the Besieged were Reduc'd to the greatest Extremity; Yet their diet was not so extreamly Bad (as has been reported)'.

> … the houses are generally broke down by the bombs, there having been five hundred and ninety one shot into the town. The walls and outworks are not touched.[9]

The next day Michelburne and Walker rode to Inch and dined with Kirke. Walker wrote that he offered his regiment to Kirke, because 'after doing the King all the Service in his power, he might return to his own Profession'. Kirke would not accept the kind offer, and so Walker 'gave it to Captain White, as a mark of his Respect, and the Gentleman's known Merit'. These were the happiest of days. 'Upon this', wrote Walker, 'we call a council at Derry, the Governor is prevailed on to go to the King, and to carry an address from the garrison'. This was Walker's masterstroke and, predictably, it infuriated his enemies. 'Col. Walker was appointed by the Major General to go', wrote Mackenzie. Walker had not been prevailed upon to do anything, he had not been ordered to go, and the council had not chosen him. He had begged to go and Kirke had chosen him as Kirke's ambassador.

'A Humble Address' was drawn up 'of the Governors, Officers, Clergy, and other Gentlemen, in the City and Garrison of Londonderry' to send to King William and Queen Mary with the city's 'due acknowledgments to Almighty God, and to Your Sacred Majesty, and, under you, to the indefatigable Care of Major-General *Kirk*, for our unexpected Relief by Sea'. It promised 'our unfeigned loyalty' and 'to lay ourselves entirely at Your Royal feet, and do most heartily and resolvedly offer and engage our lives and fortunes to Your Service'.[10]

The Humble Address was subscribed (we only have the copy published by Walker) with a hundred and forty-five signatures, with Walker's name prominently (in his version) at the top and in capitals. His name was followed in the printed version by those of Michelburne, the colonels and aldermen, although many of those are carelessly misspelt, often to the extent of being unrecognizable. Even the names of the senior officers were mangled in transcription. Colonels Murray, Lance and Monroe are represented as Adam Morrow, Thomas Lane and Henry Monry. The address was not for everyone to sign, it was by invitation only, and limited to 'the officers, clergy and gentlemen'.

Listed among the names of those captains recognized as being among the most active during the fighting (Arthur Noble, Alexander Sanderson, Philip Dunbar and James Gledstanes) was one Thomas White, who, given the many lazy errors of transcription, could only have been Thomas Whitney, who had been locked up throughout the siege. The prisoner Lieutenant Thomas Newcomen, who had been captured on the Windmill, also signed, as did John Buchanan, the city's black sheep and formerly Cormack O'Neill's deputy mayor. Of the eleven surviving Church of Ireland clergymen only six signed (including Walker), but none of the Presbyterian ministers. There were some surprising omissions, such as John Mogridge and Robert White, the court martial chairman and now one of the new colonels. It was, wrote James Caldwell, the work of Kirke 'and his creatures' for the purpose of 'imparting that he had relieved Londonderry to the best advantage'.[11]

To Walker, it was his passport to wealth and fame. Those who did not want Walker to have either were less than enthusiastic. 'Many of those that signed it', wrote Mackenzie, 'neither knew of the bearer, nor were well pleased with the great complement passed on the major general in it, but were not willing at that time to make any disturbance by any public opposition to it'.[12]

On 7 August, Kirke marched from Inch at the head of his three English regiments. Michelburne drew up the city's forces to welcome them with 'three huzzas' and a salute of musket and cannon fire. After another mid-day dinner, the field officers were called to a council of war. Something needed to be done about the state of the city and the regiments in it. Both could do with improvement, and it was going to be a major operation. Kirke declared the next day, 8 August, as a day of thanksgiving. 'Beef is now sold at three half pence a pound, and butter three pence', wrote Ash, 'a great alteration in a short space of time'. The day was spent 'with a great deal of joy and merry making by the treble discharge of all our cannon and small arms. With the whole garrison being posted around the walls'.[13]

On the following day, Friday 9 August, Walker set off with his humble address to the king and queen. 'After assurance from the Major-General, of his Care and Favour to his Men, and particularly to his own Regiment, he took leave of them and embarked for England.' With that, Walker waved goodbye to Londonderry for the last time.

As Walker sailed down the lough, Kirke issued a proclamation that 'everyone who expected pay for the good service they did in defending the garrison, should appear in their arms on Monday next at 10 o'clock'. The day of the great Londonderry parade was Monday 12 August. The whole garrison was marched out and formed up by regiment for Kirke's inspection. 'The soldiers went out the more cheerfully', wrote Mackenzie, 'because it was reported the Major General would that day distribute £2,000 amongst them'. They were to be disappointed. The partially uniformed array of undernourished men, unequally armed, in companies and regiments of irregular sizes, with varying numbers of officers, and those of very differing abilities, was not what Kirke wanted. He had the regiments disbanded and amalgamated. Michelburne's and Crofton's regiments were broken and joined together, with Michelburne as colonel. Poor Crofton was reduced in rank to captain. Walker's and Hamill's regiments were amalgamated under a new colonel, Robert White; Monroe's and Lance's regiments were joined under Colonel Lance; and Baker's and Murray's regiments were merged under Colonel St John.

To prevent any trouble, the announcements were left until after the three English regiments had arrived. 'All of Colonel Murray's (except a very few) refused', wrote Mackenzie, 'and went off into the country with their carbines and pistols'. Kirke had their saddles seized (and probably Arthur Rawdon's saddles as well), and also (says Mackenzie) seized Murray's own horse, which he had 'preserved with great care during all the siege'. New captains, many from the fleet, were appointed 'to most' of the companies, and those new captains chose their own lieutenants and ensigns, turning out those who had served in the siege. 'This was', wrote Mackenzie, 'ill resented in the Garrison'.[14] Kirke responded as Lundie had done. He ordered a gallows to be erected to be used on anyone who objected to his reforms. He meant it, and they knew he meant it.

Notwithstanding their service in the siege, the Londonderry regiments were not highly rated. By the following January, only two survived to be taken on the establishment (Michelburne's and St John's) and only about a fifth of the siege officers were given positions in the new regiments. As Schomberg later remarked (descriptively rather than insultingly), they were 'mostly peasants', and the number of men did not warrant so many officers. Rather than being given their own commands, 214 of them were placed in the ranks of the reformed regiments as 'supernumerary officers' to fill the gaps as and when needed. Of the 156 officers required for Kirke's four new regiments (three officers for each of the thirteen companies in a regiment), up to a half were officers appointed by Kirke from outside the garrison.[15]

Nor was Kirke allowing undisciplined armed troops loose on the countryside. He ordered the sentries to seize the arms of anyone leaving the city. He also wanted the town cleared. It was still at least five times more populous than it had been before the rebellion, and everyone who did not live there was to go home. He gave them a week. If they wanted to take any possessions with them, they would have to apply for an order. He was not going to allow the city to be plundered. 'Hereby', wrote Mackenzie, 'the bedding of many was detained from them … The weak and sick soldiers had nothing allowed them to subsist on out of the stores, whereby they were forced to travel, and beg their bread in the country, which being extremely depopulated, many of them perished for want.'[16] A proclamation was issued forbidding any burials within the walls. The city was going to be left fit for a new garrison and those who lived there. The old garrison was turned out, and Richards was ordered 'to mark out a camp for the town soldiers, for here in garrison we find it a hard matter to make them rendezvous and do duty'.

Many were content with what Kirke did. Captain Thomas Ash had been in Monroe's regiment, which was disbanded, and so joined Lance's regiment as a captain, and eventually, in the following March, joined Michelburne's. Whereas Mackenzie complained about the poor rates of pay, Ash did not. He took his two shillings a day and stayed in the army. Overwhelmingly, the rest did the same, even the private soldiers on two pennies a day. There was a war to be fought. Some prospered under the new arrangements. George Holmes, the Cumberland man, who had arrived at Londonderry before the siege with nothing, did very well out of it. He had been in the thick of the fighting. 'I was shot in the skirt of my coat and both the hinder skirls of it taken off with a cannon bullet, and I was not hurt, I praise God. I was in the head of my company and the pike that was in my hand was cut in two with a cannon bullet and I not hurt: musket bullets has light [have alighted] about me like crabs off a tree, and still God protected me.' He was one of the ones that Kirke wanted: 'I had a good character given of me to Major General Kirke for my service, for which he made me Major to a Regiment.'

Most of those who had survived the siege were not primarily concerned with the soldiers' pay and conditions. Thousands who had fled to the city for safety from the Irish had perished. The city was one great charnel house.

> They then began to clean and repair their city: every cellar was a grave, where many dead carcasses lay piled upon another, in stench and rottenness, without shroud or coffin to cover them; where they saw without a figure, that corruption is our father, and the worms our mothers and sisters; mothers saw their children, husbands their wives, and the wives their husbands, in the manifold and foul embraces of loads of vermin that gorged and wantoned upon them without control. So that there was scarce one thing that is grievous, horrid or shocking to human nature which these poor people were not in this case so fully acquainted with, that the dead of 'em may justly be said to have had by much the better of the living.[17]

No efforts were made to harass the Irish army. Everything could wait until Schomberg's army arrived. 'Some small parties of Irish that stayed behind' burnt Newtown Limavady and several houses, but they were not the only pest to infest the county. 'Great Droves of the Country People's Cattle were brought near the Town, upon pretence of their belonging to the Enemy, and so few could recover their own again, that many Families were deprived thereby of the only considerable means of their subsistence. Col. Michelburne was made Governor by the Major General, in whose hands the Cattle were left, who sold them according to the Major General's Orders for good Rates to the Butchers and others.'[18]

Eighteen months after the siege, Bishop King arrived in Londonderry. He gave this description of the countryside:

> I found the land almost desolate, country houses and dwellings burnt: on an inquiry being made I ascertained that there were in the diocese of Derry, before the troubles, about 250,000 head of cattle, there were left after the siege was raised, about 300; out of 460,000 horses, two remained, lame and wounded, with seven sheep, and two pigs, but no fowl, whence the miserable state of that province was sufficiently manifest.[19]

33

Aftermath

On 13 August, the day after the great Londonderry parade, Marshal Schomberg arrived off Bangor. He brought with him some six thousand men. There was no one to oppose him. He marched through Belfast, and on 20 August reached Carrickfergus. After a week's siege, the Irish garrison was allowed to march out.[1] Within a month, the Irish army had abandoned Ulster save for their stronghold at Charlemont. There was no civil administration, and the province was a shambles. 'There has been a rising amongst the peasantry in the neighbourhood of Coleraine and Carrickfergus, with whom are mingled some Scotch people', Schomberg wrote to King William from Carrickfergus. 'Those of Londonderry have also risen and, under the pretence of robbing the Roman Catholics, rob also those of their own religion.'[2]

Schomberg occupied Dundalk, but his further advance was blocked by the Irish army twelve miles away at Ardee. Schomberg estimated the enemy as being 'at least double the number of ours, of which a part is disciplined, and pretty well armed, and better nourished with bread, meat, and beer than ours'. This later became: 'the enemy are not only strong in number, but also well disciplined, and the situation of their camps as well chosen as the ablest generals could contrive'. The armies faced each other for two months during which time Schomberg's army rotted away before his eyes. His complaints to King William were strikingly similar to those that had been made by Rosen to King Louis in the previous months. He had an army of newly raised troops led by the worst of officers: 'If I broke all the officers who deserved to be broken, there would be few left.' Some of his regiments were down to only three hundred out of eight hundred men and there were no recruits to fill the gaps because of rumours in England that there was plague in Ireland. The equipment and provisions were inadequate. The rain had rotted the tents, the soldiers needed clothing and shoes, and disease was rife.[3]

Of the reformed Londonderry regiments, only Michelburne's was sent to the camp at Dundalk. 'I cannot but think', wrote George Story, 'that the fever was partly brought to our camp by some of those people that came from Derry, for it was observable that after some of them came amongst us, it was presently spread over the whole army, yet I did not find many of themselves died of it.'[4] Men curled up and died in their thousands of the cold, the damp, typhus and dysentery.[5]

In early November, Schomberg ordered his army to withdraw for winter quarters. The weather was bitter, and the hills covered in snow. The need to get out of Dundalk became urgent.[6] The withdrawal turned into a hurried retreat with the army's rear harassed by Irish cavalry. Stores and equipment that could not be easily removed were set on fire. When the Irish occupied Dundalk, it was deserted other than by the sick and dying troops the English had left behind.[7]

Schomberg's army at Dundalk had been some fourteen thousand strong. Over half of them died or were permanently invalided out. Wherever the army went, it took typhus with it and, as in the siege, civilians were often the most vulnerable, more so in the towns used as winter garrisons. 'The fever was very violent at this time all the North of Ireland over, in so much that it was impossible to come into any house but some were sick or dead, especially at Belfast where the hospital was.' The Irish army fared little better. 'The enemy did not at first die so fast as we did, because they were born in the country and were used to bad lying and feeding', was Story's assessment, 'but before they decamped they were nigh as ill as we, and abundance died after they got to quarters'.[8]

The year 1689 ended miserably for both sides, and the war lasted for more than two years after the relief of Derry. Focus moved on to the battles and sieges that followed: King William's victory at the Boyne, Marlborough's capture of Cork, King William's defeat at Limerick, Ginckel's victories at Athlone and Aughrim, and finally to the treaty of Limerick where Sarsfield was allowed to take the Irish army to France to prepare for an invasion of England that never happened.

It has been argued that had there been no siege of Derry, or had the city surrendered in the first months, there would have been troops to spare for an invasion of Scotland. As Mackenzie put it:

> K. *James* might have poured so considerable a Force into *Scotland,* as would not only have embroiled that Kingdom, (for that was done by a few) but in all human probability either overrun it, or at least turned it into a Field of Blood.[9]

This conjecture relies on two factors: whether 'so considerable a force' could ever be spared, and whether that force could be got over to Scotland. Neither was likely. So widespread was the northern rebellion, so great was the fear of a Protestant uprising in Dublin and so inevitable was an English invasion that King James could never have afforded to leave Ireland undefended. Even if a considerable force could have been spared, the wholesale transfer of troops would have been almost impossible while the English navy was the only power on the seas. Throughout the whole of 1689, King James managed to get four hundred troops to Scotland in three borrowed frigates, which then raced back to the safety of Dublin harbour. King James saw his great misfortune as not the siege, but the French navy's failure to capitalize on their victory at Bantry Bay on 1 May. Had the French fleet stayed in Irish waters, 'they might at least have prevented the sending [of] forces from England, till his Majesty had recruited his Shattered troops'.[10]

The successful defence of Londonderry undoubtedly made a great difference to the next stages of the war. Rosen's army was devastated by exhaustion, desertion and disease. The siege had, in King James' own words 'destroyed the Army, so that no service could be expected from it of a considerable time'.[11] When Schomberg's army arrived in Ireland, the Irish did not have the numbers to attack it, and Schomberg was allowed to wait for reinforcements in the spring. That was the real strategic effect of the siege. No one can now guess the outcome had Schomberg been forced to do battle against a triumphant Irish army in the autumn of 1689.

None of the above alters the fact that, had there been no siege of Londonderry in 1689, or had the city surrendered, the English would have invaded. England could never have afforded the risk of a client French state on the other side of the Irish Sea. Hindsight allows us to make that statement with confidence. The great tragedy of Ireland at the end of the seventeenth century is that King James, and Tyrconnell, had raised a false hope founded on the romantic idea that the two British kingdoms would rally around their true king, and the French would guarantee victory. Neither of these things happened.

The 1690s was a difficult decade for Ulster. Londonderry had been 'reduced to a poor and ruinous Condition'. Murray and Michelburne petitioned for back pay for their men (and themselves) for their service during the siege. Both spent time in the debtors' prison in London. Hugh Hamill also pursued his men's back pay and, finally exhausted by failure, handed the task over to his brother, William Hamill, who by 1710 had spent some £4,000 in pursuing his case, and in 1722, at the age of seventy-five, was himself in a debtors' prison.[A] [12]

Regiments on the establishment were entitled to be paid, but those not on the establishment were treated as volunteers. None of the defenders got satisfactory pay for their actions, and only a handful got special bounties for their actions. Walker did well (as did his son, who got Walker's pension), Anne Baker received a pension of £300 a year, Mary Murray £90 a year and Jane Browning an annual pension of £60. Smaller sums were paid to those who managed to get to London to plead their cases in person.[13]

George Walker's heroic status in London was established long before his arrival. Newsletters spoke of his bravery and tactical genius, and enterprising printers had even published bogus sermons in his name.[14] In September he published his *Account* and, distracted by the pamphlet war with Mackenzie and his supporters, published his *Vindication* two months later. In November 1689, he presented a petition to the House of Commons on behalf of the two thousand widows and orphans in Londonderry, and was invited to the bar of the house to be praised for the 'extraordinary service you have done to their Majesties and to England and

[A] The process was hindered, said Captain Robert Gregory, by the Hamill brothers insisting on a one-sixth commission and then inflating the claim to three times what was owed.

Ireland'. Walker's self-effacing manner was much admired. He told the House of Commons: 'As for the service I have done, it is very little, and does not deserve this favour you have done me.'[15]

The king commissioned Godfrey Kneller, then the highest-paid portrait painter in the country, to paint Walker's portrait,[B] and expressed his desire that Walker should be made the bishop of Derry. The incumbent bishop, Ezekiel Hopkins, agreed to vacate the diocese and move to Cashel and, leaving these manoeuvrings behind him, Walker returned to Ireland. On his way back there, on 26 February 1690, he received his doctorate from the University of Oxford, and, not to be outdone, Cambridge bestowed a doctorate in his absence. He was henceforth 'Doctor Walker'.[16]

When King William arrived at Carrickfergus in June, Walker was there to welcome him and, without any official position, he stayed with the army and was present at the battle of the Boyne on 1 July 1690. The initial Williamite attack was severely mauled, and in the ensuing mêlée, Schomberg was killed while caught in the open by Irish cavalry. 'Doctor Walker going as some say, to look after the duke, was shot a little beyond the river'. He 'received a wound in the belly, of which he survived but a few minutes'. His corpse was 'stripped immediately, for the Scottish Irish that followed our camp were got through already and took off most of the plunder'.[17]

When King William heard of Walker's death, 'he is reported to have said, "Fool that he was, what had he to do there?"' It may or may not have been said, but it was the obvious question to ask. William had high plans for Walker and he had been killed in the thick of the action after crossing the river. It is a remark that anyone may make of a dear friend who had invited danger and suffered for it. The question remains unanswered. It is difficult to see why Walker, a non-combatant, was riding in the thick of the battle, other than that he was unable to resist an almost pathological need to push himself into the limelight.[18]

Thirteen years after the battle, a man approached Walker's widow claiming to know where Walker had been buried. She paid him to collect his remains, and he returned with a collection of random bones. (On inspection in 1838, it was found that 'there were two thigh bones for either the right or left side, both bones for the same leg'.)[19] She had them reinterred in Walker's old parish at Castlecaulfield, and erected a monument to his memory inscribed in Latin with the words: 'His fame shall be more durable than rock.'[20] In 1826 a 9-foot statue

[B] The painting held by the National Portrait Gallery (copies of which hang in the Chapter House at St Columb's and the Boyne Visitor Centre) is not of George Walker, but of a much younger man in armour and what appear to be clerical bands, and holding a marshal's baton. Either it is a fanciful portrait painted long after Walker's death, or else it is of someone else and a practical joker or fraudster has painted the legend 'Revd George Walker Governor of Derry' in the bottom left-hand corner. The painting was donated to the nation by Lady Ardilaun in 1924, with the information that it had formed part of the collection at Macroom Castle in Co. Cork since 'certainly before 1800'. It in no way resembles the engraving of the Kneller portrait, and should be seen for what it is. A fake.

of Walker on an 81-foot stone column was erected by public subscription on the walls of Londonderry.[c]

Poor John Mackenzie's position after the siege was very different from Walker's. Almost two months after the publication of Walker's *Account* in London, a delegation of Irish ministers urged a meeting of the Antrim Presbytery to finance a new history of the siege. Money was raised, but it took too long, and Mackenzie, in hard financial straits, took himself to London 'as a private sufferer'. There he laboured on his *Narrative*, supported by other veterans of the siege and by those who had left before it (Sir Arthur Rawdon clearly approved of him). After Walker's death, Mackenzie returned to his living in Cookstown, never published again and led a life of such obscurity that no one knows anything of his final years or even when he died. His successor at Cookstown was appointed in 1701.[21]

Richard Hamilton fought with remarkable bravery at the battle of the Boyne in the year after the siege, and launched the cavalry charge that caused such confusion in King William's army (and which resulted in the death of both Schomberg and Walker). It was perhaps his finest hour. He was wounded and captured, and eventually locked up in the Tower of London. Hamilton returned to France after being exchanged for Mountjoy in April 1692, and was given the somewhat empty title of lieutenant general of King James' forces in England. He kept both his rank and position in the royal household after James' death, under James Stuart, the 'Old 'Pretender', who he accompanied in the invasion fleet for the abortive attempt on Scotland in March 1708. In 1713, his career ended in disgrace after plotting to take over as secretary of state of the Jacobite court in St Germain. Forbidden to move from St Germain without royal permission, and kept out of the royal presence, in the last year of his life, he found himself in such poverty that he went to live with his niece, the abbess of a French convent. He adopted a life of piety and died there in his late sixties, a bachelor, in December 1717.

Mountjoy had a similar end to Walker. He was kept a prisoner in France until he was exchanged for Richard Hamilton, and like Walker, wanted to make something of his fame and sufferings. Having no position in the army, he followed King William's army to Flanders in 1692 to press his suit and demonstrate his loyalty. He was present at the battle of Steenkirke, although, unlike Walker, he was not in the thick of the fighting. He watched the action from far enough away to be out of musket range, but not out of cannon shot, and was killed, a distant spectator.

Conrad de Rosen left Ireland with d'Avaux in April 1690 and returned to France to command the light cavalry. He played a significant and successful part in the war over the next decade, although never again in overall command. He took part in the battles of Leuze and Landen, and the sieges of Mons, Namur, Charleroi, Brussels, Ath and Nijmegen, in the last of which, at the age of seventy-four, he led a cavalry action in which 'the allies lost twelve hundred men', and Rosen came away with

[c] The column was destroyed by a bomb in 1973. The statue's head is now on display in the Siege Museum.

'an immense booty'. Promoted to marshal of France in 1703, and knighted in 1705, he died at his château, Bolweiller in Alsace, in 1715, at the age of eighty-seven.[D] [22]

As sole governor of Londonderry, Michelburne's war was spent guarding the frontier between Ulster and Connaught. In the summer of 1691, he was sent with a small army to take Sligo, an expedition that ended badly because, wrote Michelburne, of the indiscipline of his own troops, who were mostly militiamen, 'whole droves of idle People, especially the Lagganeers; and for one honest Man twenty Thieves, and not a man of the Militia but had two or three attenders, to run away with what Horses or Cattle they could Rapparee or Scamper, as they call'd it.'[23] He was forced to retreat, and was heavily, perhaps unfairly, criticized.[24] He made another expedition to Sligo in September 1691, but this time under the command of Lord Granard, and when Sligo surrendered, Granard got the credit.[25]

After the war, Michelburne spent much of the rest of his life in Derry, travelling occasionally to London to petition for his and his regiment's arrears of pay. The criticism he faced for his handling of the first Sligo expedition spurred him to write *An account of the transactions in the north of Ireland*, his authorship disguised by the initials 'J.H.' to suggest it was written by John Hamilton, his major.[26] He also developed a sense of resentment that his part in the siege had not been recognized. 'For who can doubt, but that if he had come for England with Dr. Walker, he had been at least as well intituled to a Reward for his Services as the Doctor.'[27]

He was a Londonderry alderman until he published two leaflets in London in 1699, in one of which he wrote that the 'Inhabitants, and the Neighbours of the Town made one single Company, who were called the Company of Gunners: Those were all the Inhabitants, who acted in the Defence of that City: The other Defendants were Persons from other Parts of the Country, who voluntarily came in.' The suggestion that the men of Londonderry had played so small a part in the defence caused uproar in the council chamber, and when he refused to disown the remarks, he was voted off the corporation.[28]

In the 1690s, hoping to get proper recognition for his services, Michelburne tried his hand at writing a dramatic version of the siege, *The siege of Londonderry*, which he eventually worked into a play entitled *Ireland preserv'd* and had printed for private circulation in 1705. Nearly two decades after his death, an enterprising Dublin bookseller, Samuel Dalton, published a slimmer, stripped-down edition of *Ireland preserv'd*, 'written by a gentleman who was in the town during the whole siege'. This edited version of the play proved very popular and by 1839 had run to a twenty-fourth edition.[29]

In later life, Michelburne became something of a grand old man in the city, and in 1718 persuaded the bishop of Derry to fly the siege flag over the cathedral. He remarried twice, and died in 1721. He was buried in Glendermot churchyard

[D] There is a suggestion that among his descendants was the German General von Rosen; see Richard Freiherr von Rosen, *Panzer ace: the memoirs of an Iron Cross Panzer commander from Barbarossa to Normandy.* (2018).

alongside Adam Murray and both of them had stone memorials erected by the Irish Society in the 1830s. His will included a bequest of £50 'for maintaining the flag in the steeple of Derry'.[30]

Adam Murray was found a place in the militia for the rest of the war, but not a commission in the army proper. After the war, his father got into a dispute over grazing rights on the bishop's lands, which resulted in two of his brothers being shot dead by soldiers from the Londonderry garrison. Murray unsuccessfully petitioned the Lord deputy to bring the killers to justice, and after this tragedy was commissioned in 1694 as the lieutenant colonel to Lord Charlemont's regiment, which was raised in England for service in Ireland. The regiment was disbanded in 1698 at the end of the Nine Years War. Murray campaigned for the payment of the arrears, expenses and losses suffered by the Londonderry garrison during the siege, and lived for the rest of his life on half-pay of six shillings a day until his death in February 1706. His widow was granted a pension of five shillings a day to provide for his four children.[31]

Lundie was kept a prisoner in the Tower for almost a year. It was difficult to know what to do with him. His failures had to be balanced, as the months went by, with Schomberg's greater failure to beat the Irish away from Dundalk. In August 1689, Lundie was examined twice by the House of Commons committee. 'They could find nothing against me', he wrote, 'for indeed I was not accused but by an ungovernable rabble'. The committee instead recommended 'that Colonel *Lundie* be sent over to *Londonderry*, to be tried there for the Treasons that are laid to his Charge'. There was then no civil administration in the northern part of Ireland, and the lord chief justice's opinion was that it was 'very doubtful' that he could be tried by martial law. Walker's view was 'that 'tis not fit to send Lundy into Ireland as yet (and much less to London-Derry where he has a faction for him) for the most material witnesses against him are dispersed. So that he [Walker] concludes if Lundy should go now he would certainly escape [conviction].' No trial took place, and Lundie was released in 1690. He applied for positions, preferably in foreign service, but with no success for over a decade.[32]

In 1704, after King William's death, Lundie was commissioned in Queen Anne's pay as adjutant general to the king of Portugal's army and was shipped to Lisbon. On his arrival, he was ordered to Gibraltar, then under attack and in great need of experienced officers. Lundie arrived there on 14 December 1704 and served throughout the siege until it was raised in April 1705 (uncomfortably, perhaps, as the chief military engineer at Gibraltar was then Lieutenant Colonel Joseph Bennett, who had given such hostile evidence against him before the House of Commons). On the way back to Lisbon, his ship was captured by the French and he was taken to France as a prisoner and four years later was exchanged for twenty French prisoners. He received back pay for the time he was a prisoner of war, and kept his adjutant general's position up to 1712. He died before 1717.[33]

Kirke served the rest of the war in Ireland. He was very active at the Boyne, captured Waterford and Duncannon, and was wounded in the siege of Limerick.

In September 1690, he led a relief force to Birr, where he had most of the town pulled down for firewood and ordered that all houses between Birr and Banagher be burnt. He was withdrawn from Ireland in April 1691, promoted to lieutenant general, and posted to Flanders, where he fell ill and died in Brussels on 31 October 1691. His successor as colonel of his regiment petitioned the Treasury for £1,000 because Kirke 'had received the pay of the regiment and applied it to his own use'.

After the siege, William Irwin, the 11-year-old messenger, was brought over to London. Walker had him smartly dressed for presentation to the king, and arranged for him to be sent to school in Chester. After Walker's death, King William required the master of Charterhouse 'to admit William Irwin, who carried letters for the King's service into Londonderry, into the first scholar's place in the Charter House, which is in the King's nomination'. But he never went there, and what became of William Irwin, the juvenile saviour of Londonderry, remains a mystery.[34]

James Roche, 'Roche the swimmer', did very well out of the war. He got to London where, with Walker's approval, he was given £20 and then a pension of £40 a year.[35] He unsuccessfully applied for the command of a frigate and, after Kirke died in 1691 and was not there to contradict his fantastic lies, Roche petitioned for the money he claimed Kirke had promised him for swimming to Londonderry. He succeeded in getting a grant for an estate in Co. Waterford, a pension of £200 a year and, after a private act of parliament, a further £1,148 9*s.* ¾*d.*[36]

He was successful not only in being granted land and money, but in creating an imaginative backstory, reinventing himself as the kinsman of the late Lord Fermoy. He also claimed that his father had been exiled with Charles II, that he had been offered great inducements by Tyrconnell to serve King James, and that he was a colonel at the time he swam up the river for Kirke.[37] He then styled himself 'Colonel Roch' for the rest of his life and, as a senior military man, a war hero and living in a county where no one knew anything of his past except that which he chose to tell them, he was made the high sheriff of Co. Waterford in 1714.[E] He died in 1722.

[E] Although his appointment as high sheriff could be yet more blarney, as it appears that the only source for this is Burke's *Landed gentry*, and Burke's information came from the Roche family.

Note on sources

THE FIRST MODERN HISTORY of the siege is Cecil Davies Milligan's *History of the siege of Londonderry 1689* (1951). He also wrote the *The walls of Derry* (part 1, 1948 and part 2, 1950; published as one volume in 1996). All subsequent histories of the siege (including this one) owe much to Milligan's extensive research. Since his death in 1956, there have been four full-length books on the siege: Tony Gray, *No surrender! The siege of Londonderry* (1975); Sir Patrick Macrory, *The siege of Derry* (1980); Carlo Gébler, *The siege of Derry* (2005); and Richard Doherty, *The siege of Derry 1689: the military history* (2008).

A number of shorter works have also been produced in this time: J.G. Simms, *The siege of Derry* (1966); Peter Robinson, *Their cry was 'No surrender': an account of the siege of Londonderry 1688–1689* (1988); Derek Miller, *Still under siege* (1989); and Michael Sheane, *The great siege: the siege of Londonderry in 1689* (2002). The siege has also been covered, sometimes in great detail, in J.G. Simms, *Jacobite Ireland, 1685–1691* (1969); Edward Powley, *The naval side of King William's war* (1972); Brian Lacey, *Siege city: the story of Derry and Londonderry* (1990); John Childs, *The Williamite wars in Ireland, 1688–91* (2007); and B.G. Scott, R.R. Brown, A.G. Leacock and C.J. Salter, *The great guns like thunder: the cannon from the city of Derry* (2008).

The French correspondence relevant to the siege is to be found in James Hogan (ed.), *Négociations de M. le comte d'Avaux en Irlande, 1689–90* (1934); James Hogan (ed.), *Négociations de M. le comte d'Avaux en Irlande, 1689–90: supplementary volume with indexes* (1958); Lilian Tate (ed.), 'Franco Irish Correspondence, December 1688–August 1691', *Analecta Hibernica*, 21 (1959); Sheila Mulloy (ed.), *Franco-Irish correspondence, December 1688–February 1692*, vol. 1 (1983); vol. 2 (1984); vol. 3 (with index) (1984).

The manuscript writings of Lundie on the siege are to be found in 'Ane Acounte of Coll: Robt Lundies Proceedings in Irland since the 13 day of December 1688', National Records of Scotland, GD26/7/37/2 and GD 26/7/37/1 (4). Michelburne's early manuscript versions of his play are to be found in the British Library, Stowe MS 977, 'The siege of Londonderry: a prose drama'; and Egerton MS 3380, 'A prose play on the siege of Londonderry, 1689, by John Michelburne'.

There are several very good short summaries of the lead up to the war: James McGuire, 'Richard Talbot earl of Tyrconnell and the Catholic counter revolution' in Ciaran Brady (ed.), *Worsted in the game: losers in Irish history* (1989); John Miller, 'The earl of Tyrconnel and James II's Irish policy, 1685–1688', *Historical Journal*

(1977), pp 803–23; Sheila Mulloy's preface in the first volume of *Franco-Irish correspondence*; and the first three chapters of J.G. Simms, *Jacobite Ireland* (1969). For a longer, but highly readable account, see Tim Harris, *Revolution: the great crisis of British monarchy, 1685–1720* (2006). The best (by far) biography of Tyrconnell, is *The last cavalier: Richard Talbot (1631–1691)* by Pádraig Lenihan (2014).

ABBREVIATIONS USED IN NOTES:

AH, FIC	*Analecta Hibernica*, 'Franco Irish Correspondence'; see Tate above
Ash	'A circumstantial journal of the siege of Londonderry by Captain Thomas Ash', Thomas Witherow (ed.), *Two diaries of Derry in 1689* (1888)
d'Avaux	James Hogan (ed.), *Négociations de M. le comte d'Avaux en Ireland, 1689–90* (1934).
Bennett	[Joseph Bennett], *A true and impartial account of the most material passages in Ireland since December 1688 with a particular relation of the forces of Londonderry* (1689)
Berwick	*Mémoires du maréchal du Berwick, écrits par lui-même* (1778)
Clark	Ruth Clark, *Anthony Hamilton, his life and works and his family* (1921)
CSPD	E.K. Timings (ed.), *Calendar of State Papers Domestic series, James II, June 1687–Feb. 1689*, vol. 3 (1972); W.J. Hardy (ed.), *Calendar of State Papers Domestic series, William and Mary, Feb 1689–April 1690*, vol. 1 (1895); *May 1690–Oct. 1691*, vol. 2 (1898); *Nov 1691–end of 1692*, vol. 3 (1900)
CTB	William A. Shaw (ed.), *Calendar of Treasury Books, 1702*, vol. 17. (1939); *1706–7*, vol. 21 (1952); *1709*, vol. 23 (1949)
CTP	Joseph Redington (ed.), *Calendar of Treasury Papers*, vols 1–6 (1868–89)
Dalton	Charles Dalton, *English army lists and commission registers*, vols 1–6 (1892–1904)
DIB	James McGuire and James Quinn (eds), *Cambridge dictionary of Irish biography*
DNB	H.C.G. Matthew (ed.), *Oxford dictionary of national biography*

Dwyer	Philip Dwyer, *The siege of Londonderry in 1689* (1893, 1971)
False libel	*Mr John Mackenzyes narrative of the siege of London-Derry a false libel: in defence of Dr George Walker, written by his friend in his absence* (1690)
FIC	*Franco-Irish correspondence*, vol. 3 (1984) (see Mulloy above)
Hamilton	Andrew Hamilton, *A true relation of the actions of the Inniskilling men* (1690)
Harris	Walter Harris, *History of the life and reign of William Henry, prince of Nassau and Orange* (1749)
Hempton	John Hempton, *The siege and history of Londonderry* (1861)
HMC	Historical Manuscripts Commission publications: Duke of Hamilton (1887); House of Lords, 1689–90 (1889); Le Fleming (1890); Marquess of Ormonde, new series, vol. 6 (1911), vol. 8 (1920); Finch, vol. 2 (1922), vol. 3 (1957)
HoC Journal	*Journal of the House of Commons*, x: *1688–1693* (1802)
Invisible champion	*Dr Walker's invisible champion foyl'd: or an appendix to the narrative of the siege of Derry: wherein all the arguments offered in a late pamphlet to prove it a false libel are examin'd and refuted, by John Mackenzie, publisher of the Narrative* (1690)
Ireland preserv'd	John Michelburne, *Ireland preserv'd, the first part: the troubles in the North*; *Ireland preserv'd, the second part: the siege of Londonderry* (1705);
James II	Rev. J.S. Clarke (ed.), *The life of King James the Second, king of England, etc., collected out of the memoirs writ of his own hand* (1816), vol. 2.
Kerr	W.S. Kerr; *Walker of Derry* (1938)
King	William King, *The state of the Protestants of Ireland* (1691)
Leslie	Charles Leslie, *An answer to a book intituled the state of the Protestants of Ireland* (1692)
Londerias	Joseph Aickin, *Londerias or a narrative of the siege of London-Dery* (1699)
Lundie	'Ane Acounte of Coll: Robt Lundies Proceedings in Irland' (see above)
Luttrell	Narcissus Luttrell, *A brief historical relation of state affairs (1857)*

McCarmick	William McCarmick, A *farther impartial account of the actions of the Inniskilling men* (1691)
Mackenzie	John Mackenzie, *A narrative of the siege of London-Derry: or, the late memorable transactions of that city, faithfully represented, to rectifie the mistakes, and supply the omissions of Mr Walker's account* (1690)
MacPherson	James MacPherson, *Original papers containing the secret history of Great Britain* (1775), vol. 1.
Montgomery	George Hill (ed.), *The Montgomery manuscripts* (1869)
Plunkett	[Nicholas Plunkett] John Gilbert (ed.), *A Jacobite narrative of the war in Ireland* (1892, 1971)
Poema	[Thomas Nugent, Lord Riverston] Pádraig Lenihan & Keith Sidwell (ed.), *Poema de Hibernia, a Jacobite Latin epic on the Williamite wars* (2018)
Powley	Edward Powley, *The naval side of King William's war* (1972)
Rawdon	Edward Berwick (ed.), *The Rawdon Papers* (1819)
Richards	'The diary of the fleet [by Jacob Richards]', Thomas Witherow (ed.), *Two diaries of Derry in 1689* (1888)
Simms	J.G. Simms, *Jacobite Ireland 1685–91* (1969).
Stevens	Robert H. Murray (ed.), *The journal of John Stevens, containing a brief account of the war in Ireland, 1689–1691* (1912)
Story	George Story, *A continuation of the impartial history of the wars of Ireland* (1693)
Stowe	British Library, Stowe MS 977
Walker	George Walker, *A true account of the siege of London-Derry by the Reverend Mr George Walker* (1689)

Notes

FOREWORD

1 *Londonderry Sentinel*, 22 Sept. 1956.

1. INTRODUCTION

1 W.E.H. Lecky, *History of Ireland in the eighteenth century* (1892). 2 Joshua Gillespie, *A narrative of the most remarkable events in the life of William the Third* (1823), p. 224; Kevin McKenny, *The Laggan army in Ireland, 1640–1685* (2005). 3 McKenny, *The Laggan army*, p. 157

2. THE COMBER LETTER

1 C.D. Milligan, *The walls of Derry* (1966). 2 Robert Simpson, *Annals of Derry* (1847), p. 7. 3 Bennett, pp 27–8. 4 Laurence Eachard, *An exact description of Ireland* (1691); Edward Maclysaght, *Irish life in the seventeenth century* (1979 edition), pp 183, 189; L.M. Cullen, *Anglo-Irish trade, 1660–1800* (1968), ch. 2; Patrick Melvin, 'Sir Paul Rycaut's Memoranda', *Analecta Hibernica*, 27 (1972), p. 152; Milligan, *Walls of Derry*, pp 80–4; Richard Cox, *Hibernica Anglicana* (1689), p. 16. 5 King, p. 327. Also set out in Harris, app. xiv; George Douglas, *Derriana* (1794), p. 193; Simpson, *Annals of Derry*, p. 203; C.D. Milligan, *History of the siege of Londonderry 1689* (1951), p. 12; Plunkett, p. 212. 6 Eileen Black, *Kings in conflict* (1990), pp 289–91; J.G. Simms, *Williamite confiscation* (1956). 7 *A faithful history of the northern affairs of Ireland* (1689). 8 *A faithful history*; King, p. 102; HMC, Ormonde, vol. 8, p. 356; *Montgomery*, p. 285.

3. THE APPRENTICE BOYS

1 Mackenzie, p. 48. 2 Edward Boyle, 'Records of the Town of Limavady', *Journal of the Royal Society of the Antiquities of Ireland* (June 1911). 3 George Mackenzie, *Laws & customs of Scotland* (1678), p. 163. 4 John Malcolm Bulloch, *The strange adventures of the Reverend James Gordon: sensualist, spy, strategist (?) and soothsayer* (1911). 5 King, p. 131. 6 Mackenzie, p. 4; G.H. Harvey, *The Harvey families of Inishowen* (1927); *Reflections upon a paper pretending to be an apology for the failures charged upon Mr. Walker's account of the siege of Londonderry* (1689), p. 11; *CTP*, 15 Aug. 1712 (1879); 'William Jephson's secret service account', *CTB*, vol. 17 (1939); Ash, p. 61. 7 Mackenzie, p. 48; *Observations upon Mr Walker's account* (1689); *An apology for the failures charg'd (1689)*. In the *Observations*, Irwin was described as 'a young Presbyterian Scot', but the register of Derry Cathedral and his later employment by the crown (and perhaps his closeness to Walker in London) suggest otherwise. 8 *Rawdon*, p. 94; Mackenzie, p. 4. 9 Mackenzie, p. 48. 10 Mackenzie, p. 6. 11 *Rawdon*, p. 294. 12 Mackenzie, p. 5; *Rawdon*, p. 295. 13 Between 1681 and 1684, *Ordnance survey of the county of Londonderry* (1837).

4. REBELLION

1 Hempton, p. 236. 2 Mackenzie, p. 7. 3 Hamilton, p. 2. 4 Dalton, vol. 2, p. 413; Bernard Burke, *Genealogical and heraldic history of the landed gentry of Ireland* (1912). 5 Bennett, p. 6; HMC, Ormonde, vol. 8, pp 10, 357. 6 HMC, Ormonde, vol. 6, pp 544–5. 7 *CSPD*, July 1688. 8 The articles are printed in full in Mackenzie, pp 50–1; HMC, Ormonde, vol. 8, p. 20. A version was sent to England without the embarrassing declaration: British Library, Add. MS 34773, ff 2, 3. 9 McCarmick, p. 11. 10 King, pp 346–7. 11 *A faithful history*, p. 23. 12 HMC, House of Lords, pp 141, 189; Patrick Melvin & Lord Longford, 'Letters of Lord Longford and others on Irish affairs, 1689–1702', *Analecta Hibernica*, 32 (1985), pp 58–9.

5. ON THE BRINK

1 All the quotations from Lundie (unless otherwise specified) come from his 'Acounte'. 2 *Montgomery*, p. 276; *Analecta Hibernica*, 32 (1985), p. 51; Leslie, p. 89; *The present dangerous condition of the Protestants in Ireland* (1689). 3 *A faithful history*, p. 23. 4 *The case of John Michelburne* (1699), BL Egerton MS 3348, f. 43; *Faithful history*, p. 26; Leslie, pp 86–8, *Ireland preserv'd*, pt 1, pp 72–9. 5 Mackenzie, p. 14. 6 *A faithful history*, pp 29–31; Mackenzie, pp 11–12. 7 *A faithful history*, p. 32. 8 *Rawdon*, pp 299–300; HMC, House of Lords, p. 144. 9 Melvin & Longford, 'Letters', pp 51–2, 58; P. Wauchope, 'Colonel John Michelburne', *Irish Sword*, 80 (1996), p. 138; HMC, Ormonde, vol. 8, p. 358; British Library, Add. MS f. 170. 10 Lundie.

6. UPRISING

1 HMC, House of Lords, pp 137, 139, 160. Dalton, vol. 3, p. 103. 2 McCarmick, pp 26–8. 3 James Boyce, *A vindication of the reverend Mr Alexander Osborn* (1689); Mackenzie, p. 13; N.N., *Some remarks on Mr Bois book* (1689); McCarmick, p. 26; Walker, p. 21. 4 HMC, House of Lords, p. 180 5 *A faithful history*, p. 37. 6 D'Avaux, *Supplementary correspondence* (1958), pp 7–8. 7 *Montgomery*, p. 281 8 Bennett, p. 14; *A faithful history*, p. 37; d'Avaux reported the rebel dead as numbering '60 or 80 … and on the king's side not a man killed'. 9 *Montgomery*, p. 281. 10 *A faithful history*, p. 18. 11 Mackenzie, p. 15; Bennett, pp 14–15; Hamilton, p. 35; Samuel Lewis, *A topographical dictionary of Ireland* (1840), vol. 1, p. 464. 12 Harris, p. 217; Bennett, p. 15.

7. KING JAMES

1 François Alexandre Aubert de la Chesnaye-Desbois, *Dictionnaire de la noblesse* (2nd ed., 1770–86), vol. 12, p. 320. 2 François-Joseph-Guillaume Pinard, *Chronologie historique-militaire* (1761), vol. 3, p. 131. 3 Pinard, *Chronologie*, vol. 3, pp 131–4; de la Hode (Yves Joseph la Motte), *Histoire de la vie et du regne de Louis XIV* (1742), pp 333–7. 4 Walker was born in 1644 or 1645 (according to the *DNB*) or between 1643 and 1648 (according to the *DIB*), most probably in Wighill in Yorkshire, where his sister's baptism was recorded in 1650. Kerr gives the 'most likely date' for his birth as being 1646. Throughout the nineteenth century Walker's date of birth was given as 1618, an error which originated with John Graham in his *History of Ireland* (1839) (at p. 362), who asserted that Walker was 'then, according to credible tradition, 71 years of age'. Graham improved on this two years later in his *Ireland preserved* (1841) where he wrote that 'the renowned governor of Derry was born in 1618' (p. 381). 5 Robert Clavel in his introduction to George Walker, *A vindication of the true account of the siege of Derry in Ireland* (1689) speaks of Walker's 'affection to the Scottish Nation where he had his Education'. Dwyer, p. 68. 6 Dalton, vol. 2, p. 174; *CPSD*, Sept. 1688. 7 *HoC Journal*, 12 Aug. 1689; Mackenzie, p. 14. 8 Petition of Margaret Maurice, *CTP*, Dec. 1694 (1868). 9 Walker, p. 14; Mackenzie, p. 22; *HoC Journal*, 12 Aug. 1689. 10 Petition of Margaret Maurice, *CTP*, Dec.

1694 (1868). **11** HMC, House of Lords, pp 229–34, 243; *CPSD*, Jan. 1691, 1692; *An account of the transactions in the north of Ireland* (1691). **12** Lundie; Mackenzie, p. 19; HMC, House of Lords, pp 143, 163–4. **13** Walker, p. 42. **14** Mackenzie, p. 19. **15** McCarmick, p. 33; Mackenzie, p. 17.

8. COLERAINE

1 Mackenzie, p. 19; Bennett, p. 16. **2** Mackenzie, p. 26, Bennett, p. 17. **3** D'Avaux, p. 76 **4** *An account of the present miserable state of affairs in Ireland* (1689). See also: *Journal of Rowland Davies*, p. 7; Melvin & Longford, 'Letters', p. 64; British Library, Add. MS 28,876, f. 198. **5** *An account of the great engagement* (1689). **6** Richard Dobbs, 'A briefe description of the County of Antrim, begun the 3rd of May 1683' in George Hill, *An Historical Account of the Macdonnells of Antrim* (1873). **7** G. Boate, *Ireland's natural history* (1652), vol. 8, p. 64. **8** Sir Archibald Edmonstone, Bt., *Genealogical account of the family of Edmonstone of Duntreath* (1875). **9** Mackenzie, p. 20. **10** *FIC*, 1781. **11** Plunkett, p. 45. **12** Mackenzie, p. 27. **13** *Poema*, p. 246 (and for a discussion of its authorship, xxxi *et seq.*); Bennett, p. 48. **14** Bennett, p. 18. Nugent was killed in the new year defending Cavan. **15** D'Avaux, pp 93–6. **16** Lundie; Plunkett, p. 45; Mackenzie, pp 20–1; Bennett, p. 18. **17** *Ireland preserv'd*, pt 1, p. 123. **18** HMC, House of Lords, pp 141–2.

9. PREPARATIONS

1 Stowe, f. 9. **2** Melvin & Longford, 'Letters', pp 64–6; British Library, Add. MS 28,876, ff 198, 200. **3** Samuel Weller Singer (ed.), *The correspondence of Henry Hyde, the earl of Clarendon with his brother Laurence Hyde, the earl of Rochester* (1829), vol. 1, pp 476–7; *An account of the most remarkable occurrences relating to London-Derry* (1689). **4** Mackenzie, p. 27. **5** Ibid., p. 21; Edmonstone, *Genealogical account*. **6** Mackenzie, p. 22. **7** Edward Martin (ed.), *The Ash MSS, written in the year 1735 by Lieut.-Col. Thomas Ash* (1890), pp 20–2. **8** Ash, p. 62. **9** Stowe, f. 5 **10** Hempton, p. 394 **11** Public Record Office of Northern Ireland, *Corporation of Londonderry minute book* (1688–1704), vol. 2, p. 3. **12** John Dunton, *The popish champion* (1689). **13** Stowe, f. 8. **14** Wauchope, 'Colonel John Michelburne', pp 137–8. **15** Stowe, ff 4–10. **16** D'Avaux, pp 96–101 **17** D'Avaux, p. 99.

10. THE BRIDGE AT CLADY

1 Stowe, f. 14. **2** Stowe, f. 12. **3** Bennett, p. 19. **4** Lundie. **5** 'un peu téméraire'. *AH*, FIC, 186. **6** *HoC Journal*, 12 Aug. 1689. **7** *AH*, FIC, 186. **8** Plunkett, p. 46. **9** *FIC*, 1785. **10** Walker, p. 16. **11** Stowe, f. 15; Charles Dalton, *Irish army lists of King Charles II* (1907), p. 115, n. 15. **12** Stowe, ff 5–19. **13** *A true account of the present state of Ireland* (1689). Bennett, p. 19; *HoC Journal*, 12 Aug. 1689 **14** Mackenzie, p. 24 **15** Walker, pp 40–1; *HoC Journal*, 12 Aug. 1689. **16** Mackenzie, p. 17; McCarmick, p. 35; J.G. Simms, 'Sligo in the Jacobite War', *Irish Sword*, 7:27 (1965), p. 124; Melvin & Longford, 'Letters', p. 66. **17** *HoC Journal*, 12 Aug. 168. **18** Mackenzie, p. 18.

11. RELIEF

1 HMC, House of Lords, p. 196. **2** *HoC Journal*, 12 Aug. 1689. **3** Mackenzie, p. 25. **4** Ibid., p. 25. **5** Walker, p. 17; Mackenzie, p. 25. **6** *HoC Journal*, 12 Aug. 1689 **7** *HoC Journal*, reproduced in Hempton, p. 396; William Hamill, *A memorial* (1714). **8** *HoC Journal*, 12 Aug. 1689. **9** Mackenzie, preface. **10** Bennett, p. 20.

12. ANARCHY

1 Stowe, f. 20. 2 *HoC Journal*; Mackenzie, p. 27. 3 Mackenzie, p. 27; Bennett, p. 20; *CSPD*, 24 May 1689. 4 *HoC Journal*, 12 Aug. 1689, Mackenzie, pp 26–7. 5 Milligan, *Siege*, pp 134–5; HMC, Finch, vol. 3, pp 434–6; *CTB*, vol. 17, pp 590–611. 6 *HoC Journal*, 12 Aug. 1689. 7 D'Avaux, pp 96–104 8 Mackenzie, p. 18. 9 Lundie. 10 Bennett, p. 20. 11 *Berwick*, p. 51. 12 MacPherson, p. 186. 13 Ibid., p. 187. 14 Ibid., p. 187; Plunkett, p. 62; Charles O'Kelly, *The Jacobite War in Ireland* (*Macariæ excidium*)(1894), p. 5; *CSPD*, Oct. 1688; Marquis de Ruvigny, *Jacobite peerage* (1904), p. 239. 15 Mackenzie, p. 19; *The state of Colonel Adam Murray's case to the honourable the House of Commons assembled at parliament* (n.d.). 16 Mackenzie, p. 29; Lundie. 17 Mackenzie, p. 28. 18 Ibid., p. 28. 19 Ibid., p. 187. 20 MacPherson, p. 187. 21 Stowe, f. 29.

13. MUTINY

1 Stowe, f. 29; *Ireland preserv'd*, pt 2, p. 42. 2 N.N., *Some remarks*. 3 Mackenzie, p. 30. 4 *An account of the transactions in the north*. 5 Hamill, *Memorial*, p. 38. 6 Mackenzie, p. 30. 7 Walker, p. 20; Mackenzie, pp 30, 33. Walker also missed the independent company and the companies of gunners and pioneers; *Journal of the* [Irish] *House of Commons* (1753), vol. 3, p. 495. 8 Michelburne, 'A prose play', BL Egerton MS 3380, f. 22. 9 Walker, p. 20; Bennett, p. 21; Mackenzie, pp 30–1; Stowe, f. 29. 10 Walker, p. 23; Mackenzie, p. 31; Stowe, f. 29. 11 Ash, pp 62–3; Mackenzie, p. 31. 12 Scottish History Society, ser. 3, vol. 46(1), *An account of the proceedings of the estates in Scotland, 1689–90* (1954). 13 HMC, Finch, vol. 2, p. 204.

14. CULMORE AND PENNYBURN

1 James II, p. 334 2 *Berwick*, p. 52, *AH*, FIC, 190. 3 *AH*, FIC, 190. 4 *AH*, FIC, 189, *Berwick*, p. 53. 5 Bennett, p. 24. 6 *Berwick*, pp 53–4; *AH*, FIC, 189; Walker, p. 23; Mackenzie, p. 31; Bennett (who got into a terrible muddle by confusing this with the action four days later), p. 24; MacPherson, p. 188. 7 *Berwick*, p. 53; Bennett, p. 24; Walker, p. 23. 8 According to Pusignan, Maumont was killed by two shots. The myth of him being killed by Murray's sword first appeared in print later that year in *Apology for Mr Walker fully vindicated*, and was then repeated by Mackenzie. Murray made no such claim, attributing the story to 'common fame, and … what the Irish army commonly said, that he kill'd the French general Mammoo'. *The state of Colonel Adam Murray's case*. 9 *Berwick*, p. 53. 10 *AH*, FIC, 189. 11 Charles François Iberville, *Correspondence 1689–90* (2003), vol. 1, p. 112. 12 *AH*, FIC, 190. 13 Walker, p. 24; *Invisible champion*, p. 8. 14 HMC, Le Fleming, p. 264; Mackenzie (p. 31) also has 'nine or ten' dead, but adds 'several wounded'. 15 *Berwick*, p. 54; *AH*, FIC, 190; Mackenzie, p. 31; Walker, p. 23; Bennett, p. 25; Samuel Hobson, *A grand plat of Londonderry* (1693); *Londerias*, III.4. 16 Egerton MSS, p. 35. 17 Clark, p. 286. 18 James II, p. 335. 19 Ash, p. 84. *Register of the privy council of Scotland*, vol. 13, pp 555, 589; *CPSD*, Oct. 1689, pp 282–311; *Irish Sword*, 64 (1986), p. 211; *Poema*, p. 212. 20 *A full relation of the surrendering of Kulmore near LONDON-DERRY* (1689), published by Richard Baldwin, the famously anti-French and anti-Catholic London publisher, who later published Mackenzie's *Narrative*. 21 King, p. 176; Leslie, p. 161. 22 *AH*, FIC, 190. 23 Mackenzie, p. 32; Walker, p. 24. 24 *A full relation of the surrendering of Kulmore*. 25 Walker, p. 24; Mackenzie, p. 32. 26 Bennett, p. 27. 27 D'Avaux, pp 136, 155, 161. 28 Mackenzie, p. 32. 29 Ibid., p. 32. 30 *Berwick*, p. 55. 31 Ibid., p. 55. 32 Bennett, p. 25. Bennett conflated the two Pennyburn actions (as later, did Plunkett). 33 Mackenzie, p. 32. 34 National Library of Ireland MS37/64. 35 D'Avaux, p. 155. 36 Plunkett, p. 68; *FIC*, 1804.

15. SETTLING IN

1 Walker, p. 23; *Register of the privy council of Scotland*, vol. 8, p. lvii; *A true and impartial account of the most material passages in Ireland since December 1688* (1689). **2** *Berwick*, p. 55; *AH*, FIC, 190. **3** Walker, p. 10; Bennett, p. 28; B.G. Scott, R.R. Brown, A.G. Leacock & C.J. Salter, *The great guns like thunder: the cannon from the city of Derry* (2008), p. 85. **4** Walker, p. 20; Bennett, p. 25. **5** *CPSD*, 30 Sept. 1689. **6** Ash, p. 64. **7** Mackenzie, p. 27. Mackenzie confusedly saw the release of Twynyhoe and Blacker as a ground of discontent against Lundie, helping to explain why the soldiers shot Captain Bell, but Captain Bell was shot before the Irish army arrived at a time when there could not have been any correspondence with Hamilton. The men were released by Baker and Walker. *False libel*, p. 6. **8** Story, p. 57; Harold O'Sullivan, 'The Jacobite Ascendancy and Williamite Revolution and Confiscations in County Louth 1684–1701', *Journal of the County Louth Archaeological and Historical Society*, 22:4 (1992). **9** *Rules and Articles for the better government of His Majesties Army in this Kingdom* (Dublin, 1685). **10** Mackenzie, p. 33. **11** Dalton, vol. 3, p. 392. **12** Hugh Mackay, *Memoirs of the war carried on in Scotland and Ireland* (1833). **13** Mackenzie, p. 32; *Londerias*, III.5. **14** N.N., *Some remarks on Mr Bois Book*. **15** W.D. Killen, *Mackenzie's memorials* (1876), p. 113; Thomas Witherow, *Derry and Enniskillen* (1879) p. 300. **16** Dwyer, p. 74. **17** Dwyer, p. 83.

16. ATTACK ON THE WINDMILL

1 Bennett, p. 24. **2** Stowe, f. 42. **3** Walker, p. 25. **4** *Berwick*, p. 56; Stowe, f. 47. **5** Stowe, f. 44. **6** Stowe, f. 43. **7** Ash, p. 66; HMC, Le Fleming, p. 264. **8** Ash, p. 66. **9** Walker, p. 25; *Invisible champion*, p. 8. **10** Stowe, f. 44, Ash, p. 66. **11** *Poema*, p. 226. **12** Walker, p. 25; Mackenzie, p. 42; HMC, Le Fleming, p. 264; *Londerias*, III.10; *An account of the most remarkable occurrences*. **13** D'Avaux, p. 158, qualified with the words 'I have not yet had the time to clarify this'; *Berwick*, p. 56; FIC, 1844; Ash, p. 65; d'Avaux, p. 186. **14** MacPherson, p. 197. **15** Stowe, f. 45. **16** Ash, pp 65–6. The only Jacobite source to make any reference to the rebel casualties was Plunkett, who wrote 'very few killed, not worth observation', but then it appears that his only source was Mackenzie. **17** Stowe, f. 47. **18** Mackenzie, p. 42 **19** D'Avaux, p. 186. **20** *Their majesties declaration against the French king, 7 May 1689* (1689).

17. COUNTER-ATTACK

1 T. Dunbar Ingram *Two chapters of Irish history* (1888), p. 77; Simms, *Jacobite Ireland*, p. 85. **2** *Stevens*, pp 69–70. **3** *AH*, FIC, 197 (20 May, New Style). **4** D'Avaux, p. 306 **5** *AH*, FIC, 197 **6** d'Avaux, p. 209; *AH*, FIC, 212 (quoted in Simms, *Siege of Derry*, p. 14.) **7** *FIC*, 1810. **8** *AH*, FIC, 206. **9** Walker, p. 26. **10** *Londerias*, III.11. **11** Stowe, ff 55–9. **12** Walker, p. 26; Ash, p. 68; Mackenzie, p. 35, *Londerias*, III.11. **13** Witherow, *Derry*, p. 123; HMC, Le Fleming, p. 264. **14** Francis Nevill added the detail to his 1694 map that many of the Irish were killed. He was not present in the siege and his claim that 'many' of the Irish were killed is not made by any other source. **15** *Londerias*, III.11. **16** *AH*, FIC, 205. **17** Mackenzie, preface; Boyce, *A vindication*, p. 24. **18** Mackenzie, p. 37. **19** Stowe, f. 79. **20** Mackenzie, p. 37. Mackenzie named Colonels Hamill, Murray, Crofton, and Monroe, Lieutenant Colonel Fortescue, and Captains Noble and Dunbar. Whether the list was accurate is unclear: in the *False libel* pamphlet, (pp 3–4) Hamill and Crofton disapproved of Mackenzie's *Narrative*, as did several other officers. **21** *Londerias*, III.9. **22** *Poema*, p. 218. **23** Ash, p. 31. **24** *Londerias*, III.12. **25** *CSPD*, 13 June 1689, p. 147 **26** MacPherson, p. 200

18. BUCHAN'S ATTACK

1 Louis-Gabriel Michaud, *Biographie universelle ancienne et moderne,* 2nd ed. (1843–65), pp 579–80. **2** Rosen, *FIC,* 1890; Girardin, *FIC,* 1896; d'Avaux, pp 26, 135 **3** *CSPD, 13 June 1689,* p. 147. **4** Paul Hopkins, 'Thomas Buchan', *DNB.* **5** Harman Murtagh, 'Jacobite Artillery' *Irish Sword* (2003), p. 392. **6** William Hamill, *A view of the danger and folly of being publick spirited* (1721), p. 10. **7** Stowe, ff 67–8; British Library, Add. MS 32,499, f. 47. **8** *Ireland preserv'd*, pt 2, p. 83. **9** *Ireland preserv'd*, pt 2, p. 83; Milligan, *Walls of Derry*, p. 122; *An account of the transactions in the north*; Stowe, f. 86. **10** Ash, p. 7. **11** Mackenzie, p. 35. **12** Plunkett, p. 77. **13** Ash, p. 74 **14** Plunkett, p. 76. **15** British Library, Add. MS 32,499, f. 47. Walker, pp 27--8. **16** Plunkett, p. 77. **17** Add. MS 32,499, f. 47. Ash, p. 75. **18** Charles Townsend Wilson, *King James and the duke of Berwick* (1876), p. 170. **19** Mackenzie, pp 35–6. **20** *An abridgment of the English military discipline printed by special command for the use of his majesties forces* (Dublin, 1685), p. 61. **21** Plunkett, pp 76–7; Ash, pp 73–5; Walker, pp 27–8; Mackenzie, pp 35–6; HMC, Le Fleming, p. 264; British Library, Add. MS 32,499, f. 47; Aickin put the Irish losses at 2,000. **22** Clark, p. 288.

19. CULMORE RECONNAISSANCE

1 Bennett, p. 23; Richards, p. 17 **2** Mackenzie, p. 37 **3** Brian Scott, 'The deployment of mortars in Ireland', *Ulster Journal of Archaeology*, 73 (2015–16). **4** Plunkett, p. 64. **5** *CSPD, 22 June 1689,* p. 161 **6** Richards, p. 12. **7** *AH*, FIC, 242. **8** d'Avaux, pp 308, 399, 445.

20. THE ENNISKILLEN RELIEF FORCE

1 *AH*, FIC, 225. **2** McCarmick, p. 46. **3** Ibid., p. 46. **4** Ibid., p. 47. **5** *AH*, FIC, 251. **6** *CTP*, 1556–1696, 21 Mar. 1696 (1868). **7** Stowe, f. 60. **8** Noble and twenty men (Walker, p. 31.); six officers and 'about' twenty men (Mackenzie, p. 39); Ash, p. 77; Murray and Dunbar, with 165 men in two boats (Stowe, f. 64). **9** Ash, p. 77; Stowe, f. 64; *Londerias*, IV.4. **10** Stowe, f. 64; Mackenzie, p. 39. **11** Mackenzie, p. 39. **12** Stowe, f. 64. **13** *FIC,* 1844.

21. ROSEN ARRIVES

1 *AH*, FIC, 229; *AH*, FIC, 256. **2** *AH*, FIC, 229, Rosen to Louvois, 27 June/7 July. **3** *AH*, FIC, 271. **4** *Stevens*, p. 64. **5** *AH*, FIC, 271. **6** *AH*, FIC, 267, Rosen to King James 25 June/5 July. **7** Ibid. **8** *Stevens*, p. 64. **9** Stowe, f. 93. **10** *Stevens*, p. 140. **11** *Berwick*, p. 58. **12** Ibid., p. 58; William Bagshawe, *The Bagshawes of Ford, a biographical pedigree* (1886), p. 369. **13** The prisoners were exchanged in early August (McCarmick, p. 65). Fumeron described the Irish at Lisnarick not as soldiers but as '*les habitans du pays*'. *AH*, FIC, 234. **14** Walker, p. 37. **15** Mackenzie, p. 38.

22. KIRKE

1 Powley, pp 226–9: 'Isaac de Dompiere, Mainvilliers, La Barthelhomas and Londigny'; Richards names them as 'Dompiere, De la Barte, Mainvilliers and Sundini'. The *Calendar of Treasury Books* for 8 Aug. 1689 records payments to Monsieur Dompiere, Mainollier, de la Baute and Fauchiamber 'being four French officers sent by order of the Duke of Schomberg to Londonderry'. The English efforts at spelling French names are so varied, we can only identify with any confidence de la Melonière, Mainvilliers and de Louvigny (who died at the end of the year in winter quarters). See David Agnew, *Protestant exiles from France* (1886). **2** Richards, pp 15–16. **3** HMC, Lennoxlove, and Powley,

p. 227. **4** Narcissus Luttrell, *A brief historical relation of state affairs* (1857), 4 July 1689, vol. 1, p. 556. **5** Walker, p. 38. **6** Edwin Chappell (ed.) *The Tangier papers of Samuel Pepys (1935)*, p. 73. **7** *Poema*, p. 284. **8** John Cunningham & Margaret Whalley, 'Queries against General Kirke', *Irish Sword*, 62 (1986), pp 210–16. **9** Grey, Anchitell (ed.), *Debates of the House of Commons* (1769), vol. 9. **10** *CSPD*, 8 June 1689, 1 W & M, c. 67. **11** Walker, p. 29; *Ireland Preserv'd*, pt 2, pp 94–5. **12** *The case of Captain James Roch* (1704); Gillespie, *A narrative*, pp 169–71; 'Proceedings and papers', *Journal Historical and Archaeological Association of Ireland*, 1:1 (1868), pp 150–1. Roche dropped the final letter of his surname, as if to appear less Irish, but he is named as 'James Roche' on his memorial in Ballintemple Church in Waterford. **13** Ash, p. 80; Mackenzie, p. 40. **14** Richards, pp 19–20.

23. TRENCHES

1 Dwyer, p. 89 (and MacPherson, p. 201 for a mangled version of the text). **2** A monument in St Macartan's Cathedral in Clogher records Gledstanes' death as 9 Dec. 1689 aged 57. The cathedral graveyard, wrote William Carleton, contained 'the bodies of mostly every individual in the parish, no matter of what sect or creed'. John Cairnes ('of Claremore, Co. Tyrone') was David Cairnes' nephew. William Carleton, *Autobiography* (1968), p. 16; H.C. Lawlor, *History of the family of Cairnes* (1906), p. 168. **3** Mackenzie. p. 40. **4** MacPherson, p. 204 **5** Mackenzie, p. 40 **6** It must be that Hamilton at least sent word of the declaration on or before on or 26 June (because that is when Walker sent his letter to Kirke referring to the declaration). It was put into writing, perhaps for a second time, on 27 June as that is the date both Walker and Mackenzie quote in their printed versions. When Walker eventually replied to Hamilton, he referred to the declaration as being dated 29 June, so it seems a different letter including clarification of the earlier version(s) was delivered by Gordon O'Neill each time. **7** Ash, p. 81. **8** *CSPD*, 17 Apr., 17 June 1689. **9** *AH*, FIC, 267, Rosen to King James, 7 July. **10** Ash, p. 81. **11** Walker, p. 27; *Invisible champion*, p. 8. **12** *AH*, FIC, 229. **13** HMC, Le Fleming, p. 264; Ash, p. 81. **14** Mackenzie, p. 40. **15** HMC, Le Fleming, p. 264, Ash, p. 82; Richards, p. 20. **16** Mackenzie, p. 41; *AH*, FIC, 227. **17** *AH*, FIC, 227; *FIC*, 1809, 1829. **18** Walker, p. 33. **19** *Invisible champion*, p. 8; Milligan, *Walls of Derry*. Milligan with great care set out all that could then be known about the construction of the walls and the lay-out of the city from its foundation. He also wrote *Londonderry half a century after the siege with a map of the holdings within the walls in 1738* (1947). He took particular care to research 'encroachments' on the walls, all of which were post-siege. **20** Mackenzie, p. 41. Aickin put the Irish losses at a thousand. **21** Dwyer, p. 78. **22** Mackenzie, p. 33. **23** John Evelyn, *Diary*, 3 Nov. 1690 (1907); d'Avaux, p. 518. See also *DNB* and *DIB*. **24** *AH*, FIC, 255, 259. **25** Decades later the story was taken up by Plunkett (at p. 68) who got this information, along with so much else, from the accounts printed in London. Taking Walker's lead, Michelburne made a brief reference to Clancarty and the prophecy. Stowe, f. 120. **26** Milligan, *Walls of Derry*, p. 123. **27** *The case of John Baker (a minor)* (*c.*1695). **28** Ash, p. 83. There is confusion here: by 'Campsie' and 'White', Ash surely meant Crofton and Whittle. **29** *The case of Captain James Roch*; Richards, p. 21; Mackenzie, preface.

24. ROSEN THE BARBARIAN

1 Walker, p. 21; Mackenzie, p. 30. **2** D'Avaux, p. 158; *FIC*, 1810. **3** Mackenzie, preface. **4** Ash, p. 69. **5** Mackenzie, p. 43. **6** *Poema*, p. 228; d'Avaux, p. 158. **7** *AH*, FIC, 231. **8** *AH*, FIC, 232. **9** This English translation is taken from MacPherson. The original and complete French text is to be found in *AH*, FIC, 232; and see Fumeron, *AH*, FIC, 227. **10** Hamill, *Danger and folly*, p. 11. **11** Mackenzie, p. 43. **12** Mackenzie, p. 42. **13** Ash, p. 86. **14** Leslie, p. 62. **15** MacPherson, p. 312. **16** d'Avaux, p. 310. **17** MacPherson, p. 210. **18** See generally:

Mark Brayshay, *Land travel and communications in Tudor and Stuart England* (2014), which includes a map of the Irish stages settled in 1655. **19** D'Avaux, p. 309. It is clear that the copy correspondence we have is incomplete and does not include the letter from d'Avaux to Rosen. **20** Leslie, p. 138. **21** *AH*, FIC, 267. **22** Both letters appear in translation in MacPherson, pp 209–11. **23** D'Avaux, p. 309, *AH*, FIC, 234. The French dispatches are dated in the New Style calendar which was then ten days in advance, so 5 July (Old Style as used by the English) is rendered as 15 July (New Style, as used by the French). **24** D'Avaux, p. 309; *FIC*, 1838. **25** Mackenzie, p. 42; Ash, p. 85. **26** Ash, p. 86. **27** MacPherson, pp 207–9. **28** *Stevens*, pp 71–2. **29** *An account of the transactions in the north*, preface. **30** Ash, p. 86. **31** *AH*, FIC, 234.

25. INCH

1 McCarmick, p. 51. **2** Bagshawe, *The Bagshawes*, pp 368–71; *CTP*, 7 Dec. 1695 (1868). **3** Richards, p. 24. **4** *An abstract of what passed at the isle of Inch*, published in the *London Gazette*, 8 Aug. 1689. **5** Richards, pp 26–8 *et passim*. **6** Ibid., pp 30–1. **7** Ibid., pp 32–4. **8** Walker, p. 27; Milligan, *Walls of Derry*, p. 123. **9** Ash, p. 88. **10** Stowe, f. 108; Ash, 20 July, p. 93.

26. NEGOTIATIONS

1 Ash, pp 86–7. **2** Ash, p. 89. **3** Mackenzie, p. 43. **4** *AH*, FIC, 276. **5** Clark, p. 289. **6** Mackenzie, p. 43. **7** Ibid., pp 44, 59. **8** Ibid., pp 59–61. **9** d'Avaux, p. 320. **10** Mackenzie, pp 61–2. **11** Ibid., p. 61, Stowe, f. 108; Ash, p. 90. **12** . William Irwin was baptised in Derry Cathedral on 3 Sept. 1677. **13** Richards, p. 32. **14** Ash, p. 90. **15** Mackenzie, p. 44. **16** Ash, p. 91. **17** Hamilton, p. 31. **18** McCarmick, p. 55, *Berwick*, p. 59.

27. NEARING THE END

1 Clark, p. 291. **2** *AH*, FIC, 276. **3** Mackenzie, p. 44: he dates this 16 July. **4** Ibid., p. 45, where he places Murray's raid as being on the trenches facing Butcher's Gate. **5** MacPherson, p. 215; Richards, pp 36–7; *An abstract of what passed at the isle of Inch*, published in the *London Gazette*, 8 Aug. 1689; HMC, Le Fleming, pp 256–8 and John Dalton, *George the First's Army Lists* (1910), p. 73. **6** *FIC*, 1851; Stowe, f. 49; *Londerias*, IV.2. **7** MacPherson, p. 216; *FIC*, 1851. **8** Clark, p. 291. **9** *AH*, FIC, 239, 234. **10** *AH*, FIC, 239. **11** Ash, p. 92. **12** Powley. p. 239; from HMC, Duke of Hamilton, p. 185. **13** Walker, p. 30; Stowe, f. 128. **14** Richards, p. 38; *An abstract of what passed at the isle of Inch*; HMC, Finch, vol. 2, p. 233. **15** Ash, p. 94; *Register of the privy council of Scotland*, vol. 13, pp 419–20; W.L. Melville, *Leven and Melville papers* (1843), pp 51, 249.

28. BACK ON LOUGH FOYLE

1 *CSPD*, 27 July 1689. **2** See generally, *Register of the privy council of Scotland*, vol. 13. **3** Ibid., vol. 13, pp 487, 488. **4** James Grant, *The old Scots navy from 1690–1710* (1914); Powley, pp 240–3; HMC, Duke of Hamilton, p. 182. **5** Aickin claimed (not a claim ever made by Cairnes himself) that Cairnes delivered Schomberg's orders to Kirke. *Londerias*, IV.11; Lawlor, *A history of the family of Cairnes*, p. 163; Powley, p. 252. Also wrong, was the claim that Kirke was spurred to action only by James Gordon, the erstwhile minister of Glendermot, who offered to show Kirke how to get up the river. Killen, *Mackenzie's memorials*, pp 54–5. The tale was first published by Wodrow who claimed to have heard the story as early as 1708 (Robert Wodrow's, *Analecta* (1842), pp 124–5). Lord Macaulay rightly dismissed it as 'the gossip of a country parish in Dunbartonshire'. **6** Ash, p.

94. 7 Richards, pp 44–5. 8 Ibid., p. 44. 9 Ibid., p. 47. There was then no *George* (or anything similar) in the navy so, if Richards is right about the name, she would have been a merchant ship.

29. HUNGER

1 Mackenzie, p. 45. 2 Ash, p. 94. 3 *Ireland's lamentation* (1689). 4 HMC, Le Fleming, p. 265. 5 Walker p. 39. 6 Mackenzie, p. 39. Not even Aickin, who had a facility for exaggeration, could bring himself to repeat Walker's claim that 'rats and mice' were sold, but he entered into the spirit of Walker's *Account* by making an improbable reference to a swallow costing 'eighteen pence and more'. *Londerias*, IV.6. 7 Walker, pp 39–40. 8 Quoted in Graham, *Ireland preserved*, pp 365–6. Hunter came from Maghera. 9 Francis Nevill, quoted in full in Milligan, *Walls of Derry*, p. 126. 10 MacPherson, p. 219. 11 Fumeron, *AH*, FIC, 242. 12 Ash, p. 97. Ash was cheered by a rumour that Rosen was dead: 'As I was afterwards informed … one of our cannon struck him dead off his horse.' 13 MacPherson, p. 219. 14 *AH*, FIC, 242; d'Avaux, p. 677. 15 Mackenzie, preface; Stowe, f. 104. 16 Ash, p. 98. 17 Graham, *Ireland preserved*, p. 366. 18 Ash.

30. FEVER

1 *Bishop Burnet's history of his own times* (1734), vol. 2, p. 19. 2 Hamill, *A memorial*, and Hamill, *A view of the danger and folly*. 3 'Any sensible analysis' of course excludes the exuberant figures given by Aickin, who estimated the Irish losses in battle as being over ten thousand. 4 *CTP*, 26 June and Dec. 1694 (1868). 5 *CTP*, Aug. 1698 (1871). 6 *Stevens*, p. 140. 7 *A true account of the present state of Ireland*. 8 E.B., *Scotland Characteriz'd*. (1701); E.B., *A new dictionary of the terms ancient and modern of the canting crew* (1699); *A new canting dictionary* (1725). 9 *Ireland preserv'd*, p. 136; J.F., *A particular and full account* (1689). 10 *An account of the transactions in the north*; *Ireland preserv'd*, pt 2, p. 136; Stowe, f. 120; although no source is given, in *Pedigrees of the families in the county of Sussex* (1830), William Berry has it that Michelburne lost seven children in the siege. 11 Mackenzie, preface. 12 Ash, p. 94; MacPherson, p. 220; *FIC*, 1853. 13 *Ireland preserv'd*, pt 2, pp 147–9.

31. BREAKING THE BOOM

1 Powley, p. 274. 2 Ibid., p. 248. 3 *Poema*, p. 236; Powley, pp 249, 274. 4 Walker, p. 40; Mackenzie, p. 45. 5 *FIC*, 1853. A similar version was given by Sir Robert Rich. Grey (ed.), *Debates of the House of Commons* (1769), ix, 48. 6 *Stevens*, p. 71; *FIC*, 1851; *AH*, FIC, 242. 7 Mackenzie. 8 Ash, p. 50. Walker imagined the three cannons fired a broadside which 'loosened her so that she got clear'. 9 HMC, Le Fleming, p. 255. 10 MacPherson, p. 220. 11 *CTP*, 12 Mar. 1717 (1883). 12 Fumeron, *AH*, FIC, 242, Plunkett, p. 84. 13 HMC, Le Fleming, p. 255; 'William Jephson's secret service account', *CTB*, vol. 17 (1939); HMC, House of Lords, 1693–5, p. 21; Ash, p. 100. 14 *FIC*, 1853. 15 *FIC*, 1851; *AH*, *FIC*, 242. 16 *FIC*, 1853. 17 MacPherson, p. 220.

32. RETREAT

1 Cunningham & Whalley, 'Queries against Major General Kirke', pp 208–16; John Cunningham, *Castle Caldwell and its families* (1980), p. 33. 2 Powley, p. 266. 3 *Stevens*, p. 71. 4 Mackenzie, p. 46. 5 Walker, p. 42. 6 Hamilton, p. 34. 7 Mackenzie, p. 46. 8 Ash, pp 101–2; J.F, *A particular and full Account of several Great Matters relating to Ireland* (Aug. 1689). 9 *Major General Kirk's letter to his grace the duke of Hamilton dated from the Isle of Inch, August the 5. 1689*

(1689). **10** Walker, p. 43. It was curiously backdated to 29 July 1689. **11** Queries, *Irish Sword*, 16:64 (1986), pp 213. **12** Mackenzie, p. 46. **13** Ash, pp 102–3. **14** Mackenzie, p. 47. **15** *CTB*, vol. 7, 1702 (1939), p. 1083. **16** Mackenzie, pp 46–7. **17** Hamill, *A view of the danger and folly*, pp 13–14. **18** Mackenzie, p. 46. **19** J.C. Beckett, 'William King's administration of the diocese of Derry 1691–1703', *IHS* (Sept. 1944), p. 166.

33. AFTERMATH

1 Story, p. 10; Leslie, p. 161. **2** *CSPD*, 26 Nov. 1689 **3** This and the above is taken from Sir John Dalrymple's *Memoirs of Great Britain and Ireland* (1773), vol. 1, pt II, book IV, p. 86. **4** Story, p. 39. Michelburne remained in Londonderry as governor. **5** *CSPD*, 10 Feb. 1690. **6** Story, p. 35. **7** Ibid., pp 36, 39. **8** *CSPD*, Dec. 1691–2, p. 44; Story, pp 39, 50; *Stevens*, p. 87. **9** Mackenzie, preface. **10** James II, p. 371 **11** Ibid., p. 371. **12** *The case of the city of Londonderry in Ireland* (1695?); *CTP*, 1708–14, 24 Jan. 1710 (1974); Hamill, *A view of the danger and folly*; *Northern Whig*, 7 Feb 1906; *CTP*, 1702–7, 3 Mar. 1703 (1874); *The humble petition of Captain Robert Gregory, one of the officers that served in the late siege of Londonderry* (1715). **13** 'William Jephson's secret service account', *CTB*, vol. 17 (1939). **14** Dwyer, p. 97 et seq. **15** *DNB;* Luttrell, *A brief historical relation*, vol. 1, pp 575, 583; *False libel*, p. 12; Dwyer, pp 245–6. **16** HMC, Finch, vol. 2, p. 268; Anthony Wood, *Athenae Oxoniensis* (1692), vol. 2, p. 903; *False libel*, p. 12. **17** Harris, pp 265, 269; Story, p. 82; HMC, Finch, vol. 2, p. 329. **18** Dalrymple, *Memoirs of Great Britain and Ireland* (1773), vol. 1, p. 379. **19** Abraham Dawson, 'Biographical notice of George Walker', *Ulster Journal of Archaeology*, 2 (1854), p. 275. **20** '*Saxo Autem Erit Fama Perennior…*'. Kerr, p. 35. **21** Kerr, pp 37–40; According to the *DIB*, Mackenzie was buried in Cookstown in 1696 or 1697. **22** Pinard, *Chronologie historique-militaire*, vol. 3, pp 131–6; *Dictionnaire de la noblesse; The Paris relation of the Battel of Landen … publish'd by the French king's authority* (1693). **23** *An account of the transactions in the north of Ireland*, p. 26. **24** *CSPD* 28 Aug., 1 Sept. 1691. **25** Simms, 'Sligo in the Jacobite war 1689–91', pp 124–35. **26** *An account of the transactions in the north.* **27** *The case of Col. John Michelburne, late governor of Londonderry, and the regiment then under his command* (1699). **28** *The case of the governor, officers and soldiers actually concerned in the defence of London-Derry* (1699). **29** Stowe; Egerton MS 3380; *Ireland preserv'd*; *Ireland preserv'd or the siege of Londonderry, a tragi-comedy* (1738); the Rev. John Graham also published a bowdlerised version in 1841, and the 'twenty-sixth Canadian edition' appeared in Milton, Ontario in 1857. **30** Hempton, p. 41. **31** *CSPD, 1693*, pp 386–415; *CSPD*, 1700–2, pp 31–51; *HoC Journal*, vol. 12, 1697–9, pp 295–8; Dalton, vol. 3, p. 392; *The case of Colonel Adam Murray, humbly represented to the Commons in Parliament assembled* (n.d.); *The state of Colonel Adam Murray's case*; *CTP*, 1702–7, pp 446–69; *CTB*, vol. 21, 1706–7, pp 164–75, 433–4 **32** *CSPD*, 7 Oct. 1689; *CTB*, vol. 17, 1702 (1939); HMC, Finch, vol. 2, pp 251–4, 256; Luttrell, *A brief historical relation*, vol. 1, p. 593; Singer (ed.), *Clarendon*, vol. 2, pp 305, 312; *The history and proceedings of the House of Commons, vol. 2, 1680–95* (1742), p. 384; *CTB*, vol. 17, 1702 (1939), pp 757–88. One payment of £50 was even made directly to him while he was a prisoner in the Tower. 'William Jephson's secret service account', *CTB*, vol. 17 (1939), p. 543; British Library, Add. MS 61474, f. 75. **33** *CTP*, 1714–19, vol. 5, pp 372–98; *CTB*, vol. 24, pp 212–24; vol. 26, pp 359–72. **34** *CPSD*, 1690; 'William Jephson's secret service account', *CTB*, vol. 17 (1939), pp 538, 554; *CTB, vol. 17, 1702*. We know from the *Alumni Carthusiani* and the Governors' Assembly Books that he never went to Charterhouse. **35** 'William Jephson's secret service account', *CTB*, vol. 17 (1939), pp 538, 554; *CSPD*, 17 Sept. 1689. **36** Simms, *The Williamite confiscation* (1956), pp 89–90, 115; *CTB*, vol. 23, p. 318; *CSPD*, Nov. 1699. **37** Bernard Burke, *Family romance, or episodes in the domestic annals of the aristocracy* (1854), vol. 1, p. 39; and Burke, *A genealogical and heraldic history*, p. 599.

Index